Political Islam

Revolution, Radicalism, or Reform?

edited by

John L. Esposito

LYNNE
RIENNER
PUBLISHERS

BOULDER
LONDON

#36126422
71569
BP
60
.P64
1997

For Hasib Sabbagh and Basel Aql, whose vision made
the Center for Muslim-Christian Understanding:
History and International Affairs
and our conference possible

Published in the United States of America in 1997 by
Lynne Rienner Publishers, Inc.
1800 30th Street, Boulder, Colorado 80301

and in the United Kingdom by
Lynne Rienner Publishers, Inc.
3 Henrietta Street, Covent Garden, London WC2E 8LU

Library of Congress Cataloging-in-Publication Data
Political Islam : revolution, radicalism, or reform? / edited by John
  L. Esposito.
      p.   cm.
  Includes bibliographical references (p.) and index.
  ISBN 1-55587-262-X (hardcover : alk. paper).
  ISBN 1-55587-168-2 (pbk. : alk. paper)
    1. Islam and politics.   2. Islamic countries—Politics and
government.   I. Esposito, John L.
  BP60.P64   1997
  320.5'5'0917671—dc21   96-38160
                                                                  CIP

British Cataloguing in Publication Data
A Cataloguing in Publication record for this book
is available from the British Library.

Printed and bound in the United States of America

The paper used in this publication meets the requirements
of the American National Standard for Permanence of
Paper for Printed Library Materials Z39.48-1984.

5 4 3 2

Contents

Acknowledgments

Political Islam: Revolution, Radicalism, or Reform? has its origins in the first international conference sponsored by the Center for Muslim-Christian Understanding: History and International Affairs (CMCU), with assistance from the U.S. Institute of Peace. CMCU was established in 1993 in the Edmund A. Walsh School of Foreign Service at Georgetown University. Its mission is to address relations between Islam and Christianity and between the Muslim world and the West, and to examine the impact of those relations on international affairs.

I wish to thank my colleagues who patiently revised and updated their conference papers several times. Thank you also to Patricia Gordon, CMCU's administrative officer, who was invaluable in overseeing all the details involved in planning the conference; Ethel Stewart, our effective "contact person"; and Natana J. DeLong-Bas, my research assistant, who assisted in preparing the manuscript for publication. Special thanks to my colleague, John Voll, and to my wife, Jeanette P. Esposito.

—*J. L. E.*

Introduction

John L. Esposito

Across the Middle East in the late 1990s, Islam takes many shapes and forms: Islamic republics; illegal opposition organizations and groups; and Islamic movements, from Egypt to Pakistan, engaging in social and political activism and participating within state and society.

Internationally, the Islamic republics of Sudan and Iran are accused of training terrorists and exporting revolution; Tunisia, Algeria, the Palestinian authority, and Israel have used the threat of extremism to eradicate their Islamist opposition; Europe and the United States have experienced the wrath of Middle East–based terrorism and considered measures in response, ranging from special legislation on counterterrorism to new immigration policies; and many governments in the Muslim world and the West have charged that veterans from the Afghan war now constitute an international terrorist threat. At the same time, while some Islamic organizations clearly have engaged in violence and terrorism, others have participated within the political and social system, winning elections to parliament and serving in cabinet-level positions, as well as creating effective social service networks.

Governments, policymakers, and experts around the globe debate whether political Islam, or "Islamic fundamentalism," is a multifaceted and diverse phenomenon or a uniformly clear and present danger to be consistently and persistently repressed or eradicated. While some speak of the need to distinguish between moderates and extremists, others declare that there are no moderates. Those who speak of the possibilities of cooperation and coexistence are countered by voices warning of a clash of civilizations, of an Islamist political and demographic threat to regional security and world peace.

This book focuses on both moderate and extremist governments, movements, and organizations, from North Africa to South Asia, and examines the impact of political Islam on current domestic and international politics. The authors explore the nature and agenda of Islamist movements, the effectiveness of government responses, and the causes and export of radicalism and extremism.

The Islamic Resurgence

Since the 1970s, Islam has proven to be a major force in the public life of Muslim societies, confounding the presuppositions of a development theory predicated on the progressive Westernization and secularization of society. In the decades immediately following independence, most Muslim countries turned to their Western allies for development models. The Cold War reinforced the need for a relationship with outside superpowers. Experts talked of the passing of traditional societies and the development of modern (i.e., Western-oriented and more secular) Muslim states; and increasingly, religion tended to be restricted to personal life or administered by the state. Though Saudi Arabia emerged as a self-proclaimed Islamic state, the majority of Muslim countries pursued a modern, Western paradigm moderated by ad hoc measures, such as a requirement that the head of state must be a Muslim, or a declaration that the sharia (Islamic law) was a source of law, regardless of whether this was in fact the case. These states were based on forms of liberal nationalism, linguistic and territorial nationalism, or a variety of pan-Arab nationalisms and socialisms.

In the late 1960s and early 1970s, however, the facade began to crack. The 1967 Arab-Israeli Six Day War witnessed the disastrous defeat of the combined Arab forces and the massive loss of territory (Sinai, the West Bank and Gaza, and Jerusalem, the third holiest city of Islam); in Malaysia, Chinese-Malay riots in 1969 signaled the dominant Malay community's perception of economic threat from its non-Muslim (Chinese and Indian) fellow citizens; the Pakistan-Bangladesh civil war in 1971 made a sham of Muslim nationalism as a source of Islamic unity and identity for the otherwise linguistically and ethnically diverse West and East Pakistan. Lebanon witnessed a devastating civil war in the mid-1970s in which an aggrieved Shii community, behind Imam Musa Sadr and his Movement for the Dispossessed, demanded an equal voice and share in Lebanese society.

Across the Muslim world, many in their disillusionment began to reexamine and question their lot. Why were newly independent Muslim societies and governments impotent, authoritarian, poor, illiterate, and corrupt? Why, despite their Western allies and Western models of development, had so many Muslim countries remained weak and vulnerable? The experience of failure triggered self-criticism and a quest for identity and authenticity, as many decried their loss of not only political power, but also cultural identity. The failures of increasingly discredited secular forms of nationalism—from Arab nationalism to Muslim nationalism—strengthened new voices who appealed to an Islamic alternative, calling for the Islamization or re-Islamization of society.

The Islamic Alternative

For almost two decades, Islam has been reasserted as a source of political development and mobilization. The pervasive belief that nation building required a clear secular orientation has been challenged in diverse ways across the Middle East, as well as in South, Southeast, and Central Asia. The role of Islam as a symbol of political legitimacy and a source of political and social activism and popular mobilization has become global in scope, as governments have appealed to Islam to enhance their legitimacy and authority, buttress nationalism, legitimate policies and programs, and increase popular support.

Nevertheless, a review of contemporary Islamic politics at the state level challenges perceptions of a monolithic "Islamic fundamentalism." State implementation of Islam has varied markedly in terms of its forms of government, domestic programs, and foreign policies. Monarchies, military rulers, presidents, and clergy have ruled governments as diverse as Saudi Arabia's conservative monarchy, Libya's populist socialist state, Iran's clerical republic, and Sudan and Pakistan's military regimes. Within some countries, contending voices and groups have vied for power in the name of Islam. Moreover, the appeal to Islam has also served as a two-edged sword. Those who wield it run the risk of being judged, strongly challenged, or even toppled by that very same Islamic yardstick. The House of Saud's claim to Islamic legitimacy has been challenged domestically in the 1979 seizure of the Grand Mosque in Mecca, by Iran in the 1980s, and by militant critics in the 1990s. Egypt's Hosni Mubarak survived an assassination attempt; his predecessor, Anwar al-Sadat, did not.

Contemporary Islamic Movements

Modern Islamic social movements and organizations have been the driving force behind the dynamic spread of the Islamic resurgence. They have also become a focal point or embodiment of an Islamic threat in the eyes of Western governments as well as many governments in the Muslim world. For some, Islamic movements represent an authentic alternative to corrupt, exhausted, and ineffectual regimes. For many others, they are a destabilizing force—the tool of demagogues who will employ any tactic to gain power. The violence and terrorism perpetrated by groups with names like the Party of God, Holy War, Army of God, and Salvation from Hell conjure up images of irrational, religious fanatics with a thirst for vengeance and a penchant for violence. The assassination of government officials, intellectuals, and journalists in Egypt and Algeria; hostage takings and hijackings; attacks on Coptic Christians and foreign tourists in Egypt by the Gamaa

Islamiyyah; and New York's World Trade Center bombing embody a "Sacred Rage" that has become all too familiar.[1]

Yet the reality is far more complex and diverse than its popular image. Alongside violent radical rejectionists are Islamic organizations that espouse political liberalization and democratization. Since the late 1980s and early 1990s, in particular, Islamic organizations and Islamists have won seats in parliaments, held portfolios in cabinets, and emerged as the leading or a significant opposition in countries as diverse as Tunisia, Algeria, Egypt, Turkey, Lebanon, Jordan, Yemen, Kuwait, and Pakistan.

The varieties of Islamic activist groups and experiences are a testimony to the flexibility of Islam, and of political Islam in particular. They illustrate the extent to which specific contexts, differences of political economy, distinctive personalities and ambitions of individual leaders or ideologues, and Islam's capability of multiple and varied interpretations all shape the ideology and actions of Islamic movements. This diversity underscores the multiple meanings and usages of Islam by Muslim rulers and Islamic organizations and their differing attitudes toward and relationships with the West, as well as the diversity of strategies and tactics employed by mainstream activists versus violent radical revolutionaries. Islamic politics must be viewed within specific country contexts, because, far from a monolithic reality, it manifests a rich diversity of leaders, organizations, strategies, and tactics.

Political Islam as Illegal Opposition

From North Africa to the Gulf, Islamic movements have increasingly clashed with regimes in power. Lisa Anderson, Dirk Vandewalle, and I examine the causes and political dynamics of confrontations between the state and Islamist organizations in the region. In "Fulfilling Prophecies: State Policy and Islamist Radicalism," Anderson explores the determinants of political tactics: What are the conditions that breed political extremism? What does illegality do to political movements? Are the issues religious doctrine or sociopolitical reality, ideology or political economy? Anderson notes that Islam, like other major monotheistic faiths, neither encourages violence nor forbids the resort to violence for religiously sanctioned causes. She places her discussion of the causes and consequences of Islamic opposition movements and their challenge to the political status quo within the context of the political realities of much of the Middle East, characterized by "unmitigated despotism," capricious government policies, fiscal crises, and debt-ridden economies. In such a context, the legal opposition, faced with the tactics of authoritarian regimes, often found itself making common cause with the illegal opposition.

Anderson also reminds us that Islamic movements, despite similarities, are the product of local circumstances and conditions. Drawing on the Tunisian, Algerian, and Moroccan experiences, she demonstrates the extent to which movements have been "reactionary," i.e., developed their policies in reaction to regime policies. Thus, she notes that the failure to provide detailed programs and the tendency to resort to violence are often in reaction to government policies.

Dirk Vandewalle's chapter on Algeria provides a more detailed case study of the impact of state policies on what appeared to be the first example of an Islamist movement coming to power through the electoral process. Algeria provides a singular example: despite its Arab-Islamic culture and the significant role of Islam in its nationalist movement, as well as a particularly long and bloody war of independence, the Algerian government and its elite opted for a secular nationalist state with close ties to France—politically, economically, militarily, and culturally. For several decades, Algeria was governed by a single party, the Front de Libération Nationale (FLN), with support from the Algerian military. But a failing economy with high unemployment, housing shortages, and corruption precipitated a crisis of legitimacy and the growth of Islamic and secular opposition. The result was a political liberalization in the late 1980s that permitted Islamists to form political parties. More remarkably, the Islamists stunned all but perhaps themselves and swept elections.

Algeria's powerful Front Islamique du Salut (FIS) did not set itself in opposition to the country's nationalist past but expressed itself in nationalist terms and adopted the ideals and slogans of Algeria's war of independence and of its postindependence government. As Vandewalle observes, organized opposition rallied "around the government's raison d'être: 'an ideological commitment to equality for all and a moral commitment to uphold the achievements of the 1962 revolution.'" If Algeria's first war of independence was political, its second war is one of identity, a struggle "about an ideological and moral direction for a country coming to terms with its own past." As that war continues, Algeria seems to face two equally authoritarian options—one military and secular, the other religious—with both secular and religious moderates caught in the middle in an increasingly polarized society.

Saudi Arabia and the Gulf states have long been regarded as the heartland of the Arab world. Thus, as I demonstrate in "Political Islam and Gulf Security," one of the great ironies in the 1990s has been the extent to which Islamic movements have challenged, if not threatened, governments such as Saudi Arabia, Kuwait, and Bahrain. In the 1990–1991 Gulf War, many Islamic movements that had long been beneficiaries of Saudi and Kuwaiti support ultimately sided with Saddam Hussein, responding not to the man but to his message: the failures of Arab governments and the excesses and corruption of the oil-rich states, the liberation of Palestine from Israeli control, and freedom from Western intervention and dependency/occupation.

In the post-Gulf period, while countries such as Yemen and Kuwait held parliamentary elections, Saudi Arabia and Bahrain did not. Islamists have participated in electoral politics in Kuwait and Yemen, serving in parliament and in cabinet-level positions, while Saudi Arabia and Bahrain have increasingly witnessed domestic dissent, often expressed in Islamic rhetoric.

I show how the impact of a weakened Saudi economy (due to the cost of the Gulf War), coupled with concerns about substantial U.S. presence, led modernist intellectuals and business leaders, as well as Islamists, to petition the king for political and economic reforms. I also note the rift that emerged within the religious establishment between the majority, who continued to support the government, and a minority of militant younger clerics who challenged the House of Saud. The government cracked down, and by the mid-1990s it had effectively silenced its opposition, coopting some, imprisoning others, and driving still others underground. The explosion of a bomb at the National Guard headquarters in 1995, killing and wounding U.S. military advisers, was seen by many as a reaction to the government crackdown and a warning to Saudi Arabia and other Gulf states about their ties to the West. Measuring the significance of dissent and its potential to destabilize the House of Saud has been a concern of regimes in the region, as well as of Western regimes that depend on access to Saudi and Gulf oil supplies.

In contrast to Saudi Arabia and most of the Middle East, Bahrain is a country where a Shii majority is ruled by a Sunni minority. Much of its history has seen political movements and disturbances divided along Sunni-Shii lines, but in the early 1990s, both Shii and Sunni leaders, representing a cross section of society, called for the restoration of Bahrain's elected National Assembly, which had been disbanded in 1975. The emir's refusal to comply resulted in further petitions for elections, for freedom of expression, and for the involvement of women in the democratic process. The majority of the opposition, reflecting Bahrain's demographics, consists of Shii religious leaders, professionals, and students; and the government's refusal to respond to any demands and its deportation or arrest of some of the opposition leaders led to widespread demonstrations in Shii villages and to violence.

The Bahraini case reveals the skill of the government in exploiting historic Sunni-Shii rivalries to diffuse its Sunni opposition. Its charge that the main cause of unrest is Shiite Iran and that radical Shii success would have a spillover effect to other countries has enabled it to mobilize support from nervous regional rulers and to mute Western criticism of government authoritarianism and human rights violations.

Islam in the Political Process

Contemporary Muslim politics has witnessed the emergence of two self-proclaimed Islamic states: the Islamic Republics of Iran and Sudan. Both have come to epitomize "Islamic radicalism" and the threat of political Islam; both have been declared terrorist states by the United States.

Few events have had a stronger impact on the Muslim world and the West than Iran's Islamic revolution of 1978–1979. All too often, the Ayatollah Khomeini's Iran became the lens through which political Islam was viewed; in the popular mind, it has epitomized Islam in power.

In the 1990s, Iran is regarded by many as not only a terrorist state, but also an authoritarian one. Yet the picture is far more complex. In a climate in which many call for greater democratization in the Middle East, Mohsen Milani's chapter, "Political Participation in Revolutionary Iran," contends that, despite a ban on participation by opponents of the Islamic republic, a higher percentage of the population has participated in the political system than under Mohammad Reza Shah Pahlavi (1941–1979).

Milani traces the origins and development of mass politics in Iran from the Qajars through the Pahlavi dynasty. The early years (1941–1953) of Mohammad Reza Shah's rule—when royal power was weak—saw the creation of popular political parties, newspapers, and professional associations. This culminated in 1953 with the Shah's flight from Iran and subsequent return with U.S. support. Milani demonstrates how, from that moment on, the Shah combined growing autocratic rule, which repressed all independent sources of power, with a single-minded commitment to modernization. The former produced a low level of political participation, a politically passive population, and limited and weak political institutions; the latter resulted in a society dominated by an urban elite.

Nevertheless, the events of the last years of the Shah's rule unleashed a mass political movement in which Islamic symbols, ideology, and political actors played significant roles. And since the establishment of the Islamic Republic of Iran, the nature of governance and political participation in an Islamic government have been central and contentious issues.

Milani explains the development of Iran's "limited popular sovereignty" and the compatibility of that concept with Shii religious doctrine in a clerically dominated state. Khomeini's charisma and masterful manipulation of mass politics enabled his effective suppression of clerical, as well as lay, voices of dissent. In the post-Khomeini period, factionalism has been a divisive negative factor but has also fostered greater political participation and a "primitive pluralism" among governing elites. As a result, parliament is the scene of debate over both domestic and foreign policy; elites have been able to engage in institution building to an extent unknown in prerev-

olutionary Iran; and national elections have taken place uninterrupted for
more than seventeen years.

For many, Sudan is but the most recent example of the dangers of
"Islamic fundamentalism" in power. The role of Islam in Sudan has been
complicated by tribal and regional realities that have threatened national
unity. While northern Sudan was Arabized and Islamized relatively peacefully, the south remained animist and Christian. The tensions between north
and south eventually erupted into civil war in the 1970s and 1980s, continuing into the 1990s.

The history of Islam in Sudan is one of Sufi brotherhoods, which, as
Peter Woodward points out in his chapter, have been not only religious and
socioeconomic societies, but also significant political actors. From the
establishment of an Islamic state by the Mahdist movement in the late nineteenth century, the neo-Mahdists (Mahdiyyah) and Khatmiyyah brotherhoods, or sects, have been rivals for both religious leadership and political
power. As a result, postindependence Sudan has never seen a secular state.
The rivalry of the two Islamic movements, through the neo-Mahdist
Ummah Party and the Khatmiyyah-backed National Unionist Party, dominated Sudanese politics. Whatever the orientation of the government, military or parliamentary, socialist or liberal democracy, "the question of adopting an Islamic constitution was heard increasingly."

Perhaps the most important catalyst for Islamization of modern Sudan
was the creation in the 1960s of Sudan's third major Islamic movement, the
Muslim Brotherhood, and its parliamentary party, the Islamic Charter
Front. Under its articulate, dynamic, and charismatic leader, the London-
and Sorbonne-educated Hasan al-Turabi, the Brotherhood quickly became a
major political force, particularly in Khartoum, attracting many university
graduates and students.

Woodward demonstrates how Hasan al-Turabi and the Muslim
Brotherhood moved from opposition, exile, and prison in the late 1960s and
early 1970s to become a major presence in the governments of Jafar al-
Nimeiri (1977–1985) and General Omer al-Beshir (1989–). The Brotherhood's advocacy of an Islamic alternative to the old order has not been one
simply of symbols and rhetoric, but also of action. Woodward delineates
the ideology, tactics, and goals of the Brotherhood: its demand for the creation of an Islamic state with an Islamic constitution and law (Sharia) has
been accompanied by superior planning and organization. The results of its
strategy are to be seen today in the National Islamic Front–backed military
rule of Sudan.

Woodward also visits the issues of the civil war between north and
south and Sudan's role in implementing the export of its revolutionary
vision, including charges that it is a training ground for international terrorism.

Egypt and Pakistan have provided the soils in which the two leading

Islamic movements were born and developed; from their founding in the 1930s and 1940s, the Muslim Brotherhood (MB) of Egypt and Pakistan's Jamaat-i Islami (JI) have provided the ideological and organizational models for contemporary Islamic movements and organizations.

Egypt reveals the diversity of political Islam even within a single country and also demonstrates the extent to which Islamist responses and tactics, as Anderson has indicated, are often a reaction to government policies. Since the early 1970s, political Islam has become a major social and political force in Egyptian society, spanning the spectrum from violent to nonviolent organizations. In his chapter on centrist Islamic movements in Egypt, Raymond Baker regards the formation of new Egyptian social movements as part of a global phenomenon—the emergence of new forms of cooperative action, i.e., peaceful transnational networks—that seek to limit arbitrary power by mobilizing political participation. Baker sees the presence and role of centrist Islamic groups as a fresh alternative in an Egypt where "neither the corrupt and repressive Arab regimes linked to the U.S. security system (with their betrayed modernist project of development) nor violent Islamic militants (with their atavistic vision of a lost world to restore) are likely to contribute to this postmodern global project."

In the aftermath of the Iranian revolution and the assassination of Sadat, many observers reduced Islamic political activism solely to radicalism and terrorism. In Egypt, however, as in many other parts of the Muslim world, Islamic revivalism has in fact also informed a more centrist social and political activism; normalized and institutionalized, it became part of mainstream society. Islamic schools, clinics, hospitals, and social services, as well as banks and publishing houses, offered an alternative set of social institutions. As such they often constituted a quiet indictment of the government's inability to adequately provide such services.

The Mubarak government, like many governments in the Middle East, has argued that there is no real difference between moderate and extremist Islamists. Baker maintains that the regime has adopted a sweeping policy of repression: "Seizing on the violence of the radicals as justification for a strike against the one force that can effectively challenge its legitimacy, moderate Islam, the regime struck at the Islamic Awakening in all its manifestations." He also calls our attention to the New Islamic trend, a group of diverse, religiously oriented intellectuals, several of whom have mass followings but who often remain unknown in the West.

From its origins in 1947 as a Muslim homeland and an Islamic republic, Pakistan has grappled with the meaning of its Islamic identity. Throughout its short history, successive governments have vacillated between the more military modernist rule of General Ayub Khan and the "Islamic system" of General Zia ul-Haq. All, however, like it or not, have had to remain sensitive to Islamic issues. Vali Nasr analyzes the history and impact of the Jamaat-i Islami in Pakistani politics and places his conclusions within the broader context of relations between states and Islamist organizations.

In contrast to their status in the majority of Middle Eastern countries, religious political parties in Pakistan have been legal and able to function relatively freely in society. With so many questions raised today about whether Islam and democracy are compatible,[2] the example of the Jamaat-i Islami is instructive. In its early years, the Jamaat, led by Mawlana Mawdudi, opposed nationalism and democracy. However, for five decades it has participated as a political party in national, provincial, and municipal elections, and its involvement in Pakistani politics has brought about changes in ideology and strategy. As Nasr points out, the Jamaat has generally been the party of dissent, pressing for constitutional rights and democracy, as well as for the Islamization of politics. Moreover, "since the early 1960s, students, labor, clerical workers, and professional associations, formed by the Jamaat or in cooperation with it, have been instrumental in delineating a space for civil societies and limiting the scope of state authority." Nasr demonstrates the extent to which the Jamaat's ability to function as a legal opposition has determined its ideology and political development.

The International Relations of Political Islam

For several decades, the Arab-Israeli dispute has been a dominant issue in Middle East politics. Both in the lead-up to the Peace Accords of 1993—in particular the intifada, or Palestinian uprising against Israeli occupation of the West Bank and Gaza—and in the aftermath, Islamists have emerged as a significant factor. Islamic organizations (as well as many secular Palestinians) inside and outside Palestine/Israel have generally opposed the Accords.

Within the Palestinian territories, the Movement of Islamic Resistance, HAMAS, has offered an alternative paradigm (Islamic rather than secular) to that of the PLO. Relatively unknown and insignificant ten years ago, it has become a major political force in the West Bank and Gaza, challenging Yasir Arafat's leadership and battling with Israeli authorities. However, a dispute has existed for some time over the real influence, representativeness, agenda, and power of HAMAS. Jean-François Legrain discusses the history and roles of the two major Islamic movements represented in the territories: the Islamic Jihad and HAMAS.

Legrain notes that the Islamic Jihad was a major force during the intifada, challenging not only the Israeli occupation, but also Yasir Arafat and the PLO's failed leadership. However, weakened by factionalism and Israeli repression, it failed to successfully embody a religious nationalism that could attract significant popular support. This, Legrain maintains, was the accomplishment of HAMAS.

Legrain traces the development of HAMAS from the late 1980s, when it emerged as an arm of the Muslim Brotherhood. Combining a network of social welfare activities with political and military action, HAMAS grew stronger and contested PLO leadership in university and professional association elections, as well as in the streets.

Legrain analyzes the extent to which the growth and actions of HAMAS have brought with them internal divisions of ideology, strategy, and factionalism. Its military wing, the Qassim Brigade (Kataib Izz al-Din al-Qassam), has become more daring and violent in its attacks within Israel itself, ignoring the political leadership; this has compromised attempts by the political leadership to transform their movement into a political party and has led to Israel's identification of HAMAS as the key obstacle to peace and its demand that Arafat and the Palestinian National Authority (PNA) control HAMAS terrorists. Yet, despite the polarization between nationalists and Islamists and between the PNA and HAMAS, cooperation has also occurred. Legrain maintains that the more important problem is the division in both the PLO and HAMAS between those who support and those who reject the "self-rule" of the Oslo Peace Accords.

The World Trade Center bombing on 25 February 1993 made the question of international Islamic terrorism a critical domestic issue in the United States. Many of the suspects arrested after the bombing were Arab immigrants who had fought in the war in Afghanistan and were linked to Shaikh Umar Abd al-Rahman, an Egyptian cleric tried and acquitted in the assassination of Anwar Sadat and actively involved in the Afghan war. Some governments, such as those in Egypt and Algeria, charged that these were part of a cadre of CIA-trained fighters who were now using their U.S.-supplied weapons and training to wage jihad against the West and Muslim governments. In "Arab Islamists in Afghanistan," Barnett Rubin examines the history of Afghanistan's links with the Arab world.

Rubin notes that international support for the mujahidin (or Afghan resistance) crossed the political spectrum in the Arab and Islamic worlds, as it did in the United States. Substantial aid to the mujahidin in their resistance to the Soviet invasion of Afghanistan came from the United States, coordinated by the CIA, and from Saudi Arabia and Pakistan, "pillars of U.S. security policy in the Gulf." The mujahidin's primary Islamist links were with Egypt's Muslim Brotherhood and Pakistan's Jamaat-i Islami, both of which enjoyed Saudi support. Moreover, Zia's military regime, which also received substantial support from the United States and Saudi Arabia, officially favored Islamist groups as the representatives of the mujahidin.

While Rubin details the role of Arab Islamists in Afghanistan and acknowledges their potential role in international terrorism, he warns of the danger in the post–Cold War period of replacing the Soviet communist threat with "the undifferentiated image of the 'fundamentalist terrorist.'" Similarly, he notes that "despite the predictable attempts of ineffective, corrupt, or dictatorial governments to find external scapegoats for their problems," outside sources are not the primary cause of domestic problems and opposition.

As noted earlier, Islamist opposition to the Peace Accords has come not only from within Palestine/Israel, but also from many outside Islamic movements. Yvonne Haddad's "Islamists and the Peace Process" explores the range and causes of this opposition, analyzing a spectrum of organizations and their objections and providing a historical context to contemporary political and military responses. Haddad argues that for many in the region, the Accords are not simply misconceived or imperfect, but "a virtual sellout."

Islam is a transnational faith and community of believers (ummah), as reflected in the annual pilgrimage to Mecca, where Muslims from all over the world experience and express a unity and identity of faith that transcends their many nations, tribes, races, and languages. This transnational identity has also been a presence and force in international politics, from the pan-Islamist ideology employed by governments (e.g., Saudi Arabia, Libya, and Iran) to that of Islamic movements.

Muslim history attests to the international linkages of scholars, beliefs and practices, governments, schools, and organizations and movements. If, however, as John Voll warns in his chapter, "one concentrates on the gunrunners, murderers, and military mercenaries, one may, like the French imperial intelligence officers, miss the really important linkages that are, in fact, transforming the contemporary Islamic world."

While terrorist networks obviously exist and cannot be ignored, the rush to equate "fundamentalism" with terrorism and terrorist linkages is, Voll observes, an "assumption comforting to social scientists in the West and the Muslim world who maintain the simple faith that all of the religious revivalism visible in the contemporary world is simply a blip in the long term and ultimate triumph of Western-oriented secularism." More significant in the long run than the small networks of terrorist cells is a transformation of worldview sustained and supported by the interaction of scholar-activists who study and travel internationally, creating a conceptual basis for the exchange and development of ideas. This global Islamic perspective, Voll maintains, though far from monolithic, does enable Islamists to discuss politics, economics, law, and society within a framework that does not depend on the assumptions of Western, secularist, social science discourse.

Concern with the international scope and impact of political Islam and its connection to international terrorism not infrequently focuses on the linkages between Iran and Sudan. The U.S. dual containment policy toward Iraq and Iran has been supplemented by an economic embargo of Iran and an effort to isolate Sudan diplomatically and economically. Voll questions the efficacy of these policies, noting that the importance of Sudanese ties with Iran has increased and that "unless there is a significant change in U.S. policy, the tendency to make the ties even closer will be strengthened."

***

If many once thought that the resurgence of political Islam evidenced in the Iranian revolution was an epiphenomenon, politics in the Muslim world in subsequent years has indicated its far more pervasive global impact.

As this collection of essays demonstrates, political Islam takes many shapes and forms, affecting domestic as well as international affairs. Islamic activists and movements are as diverse as the leadership, governments, and local religious, political, and socioeconomic realities of the Muslim world.

For the foreseeable future, the conditions and issues that have spawned Islamic revivalism and political Islam will continue. The demise of the Soviet Union and the more isolationist attitude in the United States have reduced sources of foreign aid. The political and economic fallout from the Gulf War likewise has severely curtailed economic support from Saudi Arabia and Kuwait. Population growth has increased dangerously, and many governments continue to be plagued by poverty, illiteracy, unemployment, maldistribution of wealth, and corruption. Opposition voices call for greater political participation and accountability at home and charge that Western policy toward democratization is predicated on a double standard. In this climate, understanding the nature, record, and potential impact of political Islam is more critical than ever.

Notes

1. Robin Wright, *Sacred Rage: The Wrath of Militant Islam* (New York: Simon and Schuster, 1985).

2. For alternative viewpoints, see Amos Perlmutter, "Wishful Thinking About Fundamentalism," *Washington Post,* 19 January 1992; Peter W. Rodman, "Don't Look for Moderates in the Islamist Revolution," *International Herald Tribune,* 4 January 1995; Bernard Lewis, "Islam and Liberal Democracy," *The Atlantic* 271:2 (February 1993): 89–98; and Martin Kramer, "Islam vs. Democracy," *Commentary* 95:1 (January 1993): 35–42. For contrasting positions, see Yahya Sadowski, "The New Orientalism and the Democracy Debate," *Middle East Report* 23:4, no. 183 (July-August 1993):14–21; John L. Esposito and James P. Piscatori, "Democratization and Islam," *Middle East Journal* 45:3 (Summer 1993):427–440; John O. Voll and John L. Esposito, "Islam's Democratic Essence," *Middle East Quarterly* 1:3 (September 1994): 3–11, with ripostes 12–19; John O. Voll and John

L. Esposito, "Rejoinder," *Middle East Quarterly* 1:4 (December 1994):71–72; John L. Esposito and John O. Voll, *Islam and Democracy* (New York: Oxford University Press, 1996); Robin Wright, "Islam, Democracy and the West," *Foreign Affairs* 71:3 (Summer 1992):131–145; and Robert H. Pelletreau, Jr., Daniel Pipes, and John L. Esposito, "Political Islam Symposium: Resurgent Islam in the Middle East," *Middle East Policy* 3:2 (1994):1–21.

Part 1
Political Islam as Illegal Opposition

1

Fulfilling Prophecies: State Policy and Islamist Radicalism

Lisa Anderson

Opposition that would be loyal if it were tolerated becomes disloyal because it is not tolerated.

—Robert Dahl

In the United States in recent years, the mention of Islamic political movements often evoked images of wild-eyed fanatics bent on toppling Western allies (like the shah of Iran), assassinating peace-loving political leaders (such as President Sadat of Egypt), or merely wreaking havoc (as in the plot by followers of the Egyptian shaikh Abd al-Rahman to blow up the World Trade Center). Most Americans can easily imagine why the sentiments and organizations associated with Islamist politics might be the object of repression in the Middle East and North Africa. Although few in the United States are well acquainted with the aims or ideologies of any Islamist political movements, many believe Islamist political activists and organizations are exceptionally prone to violent means to further their ends. Is that an accurate perception? What accounts for the resort to violence?

Obviously some political doctrines predispose their adherents to the use of violence; Franz Fanon's famous defense of the psychological benefits of violence in nationalist struggles is a case in point.[1] Whether Islam, or Islamic political theory, is another such case has been widely debated.[2] Since religious traditions are extraordinarily inclusive in encompassing and justifying quite varied human behavior—as the models of devout Christianity provided by both St. Francis of Assisi and the Crusaders suggest—it is unlikely that such a debate about Islam will be quickly resolved. Like other major monotheisms, Islam does not forbid violence on behalf of religiously sanctioned causes, but neither does it encourage it. The substantive dogma of Islam does not tell us when or why its adherents will actually resort to violence to further a quest understood to be Islamic.

Rather than look to the substance of Islam or the content of putatively Islamic political doctrines for a willingness to embrace violent means to desired ends, we might explore a different perspective and examine the political circumstances, or institutional environment, that breeds political radicalism, extremism, or violence independent of the content of the doctrine. As the epigraph of this essay suggests, there may be circumstances that foster radical political strategies and, conceivably, resort to violence, independent of the content of political beliefs, just as there may be conditions that encourage political movements to work within the system, however radical their ideologies.

The question of the relative importance of the institutional environment in providing incentives for cooperation or defection from the system is a long-standing one in politics and political science. Not only is it a venerable issue in the discourse on democracy and democratic politics,[3] but it has been debated intensely in many parts of the Muslim world. In North Africa, where the intellectual elite was particularly influenced by Europe, the debate over whether antisystem parties could be "domesticated" by tolerance evoked twentieth-century European history. The question was whether Islamist political movements, like the Front Islamique du Salut (FIS) in Algeria or al-Nahda in Tunisia, that openly opposed the political status quo should nonetheless be permitted to participate in politics—forming political parties, publishing newspapers, contesting elections, and winning seats in government.

The proponents of political inclusion pointed to the experience of communist parties in Western Europe after World War II. Despite their advocacy of class revolution, and despite their moral and financial ties with foreign powers, the communist parties of France and Italy proved to be responsible electoral competitors, and probably less corrupt than many of their noncommunist counterparts. The advocates of exclusion and repression cite another European precedent, however, recalling that the Nazi Party came to power in Germany in free and fair elections.

Obviously, legality and incorporation may encourage but do not guarantee respect for democratic norms or a willingness to play within the system on the part of political opposition movements. Perhaps, however, we may say something more definitive about the influence of illegality. Legal status and formal inclusion may not be sufficient to guarantee responsible opposition, but they may be necessary.

In exploring this question, we acknowledge that the particular platforms and programs of both governments and their opposition—the substantive preferences or ends each express—reflect a great variety of sources: ideological beliefs, cultural heritages, historical norms, economic interests. Opposition, however, has the unusual characteristic of being defined partly by what it opposes; it develops within and in opposition to an ideological and institutional framework and, as such, reveals a great deal not only about its own adherents but also about the individuals, policies, regimes, and states in authority.[4] This is particularly true of illegal political opposition, since the decision to prohibit the expression of dissident voices is one that can be taken only by those in a position to determine legality: the authorities themselves. Any examination of the nature of illegal political opposition also illuminates the nature of the regimes in power.

Except for institutionalized opposition in established democracies, all political opposition is subject to dramatic and often unpredictable changes in the definition of what is permissible. The less institutionalized the state or political regime, the more capricious and arbitrary the rules governing the expression of political dissent are likely to be. All political opposition in the Islamic Middle East, whatever its ideological stance, exists in ambiguity—sometimes tolerated, even encouraged, as often ruthlessly repressed, but rarely fully confident of its status. One of the principal examples of illegal Islamist opposition in the Middle East and North Africa in the mid-1990s—Algeria's FIS—was not only legal but took the majority of parliament seats in the country's last freely contested elections. Indeed, as the round-up of 10,000 FIS supporters in the aftermath of the military coup that annulled the elections of January 1992 suggested to many observers, formal legality in the absence of stable and legitimate political institutions is not itself necessarily an undiluted good, for insofar as it affords the opportunity for greater exposure to the public, it also entails greater exposure to potentially fickle authorities.

This essay examines the causes and consequences of illegality for the goals and methods of Islamic opposition movements in the Middle East today, in the light of what we know about the nature of political institutions and opposition in general. We begin with the circumstances that brought them to light, if not to official recognition, and then turn to the impact of capricious government polices on their political constituencies and ideological platforms. While the illustrative cases are hardly exhaustive—many of the examples are drawn from the particularly well-documented experiences of the Islamist opposition in North Africa—confirmation of several general political science hypotheses emerges from this brief survey. First, the absence of a reliable, transparent institutional framework for political opposition to work within not only hampers the routinization of opposition of all kinds but magnifies the profile and broadens the constituency of "rejectionist" or "disloyal" parties. Second, the government harassment associated with the process of illegalization of once-tolerated opposition groups fosters more extreme, radical, or violent programs on the part of such parties or movements.

The Political Environment: The Middle East and
North Africa in the Last Quarter of the Twentieth Century

Until the mid-1970s, the Islamic Middle East well deserved its reputation for almost unmitigated despotism. Absolutist monarchies and authoritarian single-party regimes held sway virtually everywhere. Democratic Lebanon seemed an exception for a time, but it collapsed in civil war. Similarly, Turkey enjoyed several stretches of democratic government, but they were almost predictably interrupted by military interventions. Elsewhere, the shah of Iran and the king of Morocco paid lip service to parliaments and political parties but, as the Iranian revolution was to suggest, this was little more than a facade for authoritarian personal rule. None of the other monarchies of the region even bothered with a facade of pluralism, while the single-party regimes had deteriorated into tyrannies of personal rule supported by extensive domestic intelligence services. In this environment, political opposition was virtually always and everywhere illegal and it was often fatal as well.

By the beginning of the 1980s, the international political economy that supported this style of domestic politics—or perhaps better, lack of politics—began to weaken, and international financial support for the regimes of the Islamic Middle East, whether in the form of high oil prices or generous aid policies, started to decline. A glut on the world oil market led to sharply lowered oil prices by the mid-1980s, which in turn reduced aid flows from Arab oil producers. Compounding the problem, the end of the Cold War undermined the rationale for superpower aid, and the demise of the Soviet Union removed one of the region's principal outside aid donors. Soon international creditors tightened the terms for borrowing as the regimes began to run up substantial debt.[5]

The impending and, in some cases, actual fiscal crisis prompted many of the regimes in the Middle East and North Africa to rethink their relations with their citizens. No longer could they afford to simply "buy" acquiescence in their rule; other incentives had to be devised. Among the most obvious of these was to open the political arena and to relax the much-resented restrictions on expression and participation. Starting in the mid-1970s in Egypt and continuing for the next decade and a half in Tunisia, Algeria, Jordan, Yemen, and, to a lesser extent, Morocco and Kuwait, press censorship was lifted, political prisoners released, political parties authorized, and contested elections held.

In none of these instances of political liberalization did regimes intend to actually confront competitors for power. In both intent and content, these reforms were designed not to inaugurate a system of uncertain outcomes—democracy—but to solidify and broaden the base of the elite in power, making possible increased domestic extraction. Indeed, many of the governments seemed reluctant to admit that there were legitimate complaints against their policies or performance. Through much of the previous thirty or forty years, political debate had been discouraged, with press censorship the norm; contested elections had been either nonexistent or transparently manipulated. The unwillingness of regimes to discuss the small-scale discontents and everyday problems of their people magnified and transformed the resentment. Grievances came to be cast not in terms of material demands but in the idiom of moral responsibility and ideological commitment. Having demanded continued sacrifice "for the good of the nation," the governments often found themselves facing a challenge that redefined the boundaries of sacrifice. Islamist movements appeared, rejecting an illfitting "nation" for the far more venerable Islamic ummah and thereby repudiating the governments as well.

Naturally, given the purpose of the liberalizations, the regimes reciprocated this rejectionist stance: from their point of view, acquiescence in the tacit understanding that the regime incumbents were to retain power was the crucial distinction between loyal and disloyal opposition and therefore ultimately between the legal and illegal. In most of these governments, the individuals in power were prepared to sacrifice the regime and its policies well before they relinquished their own personal hold on power. That is to say, whereas in most institutionalized polities the regime type—"democracy," for example, or "socialism"—is considered inviolable, and individual powerholders are sacrificed for its maintenance, in the Middle East, individual interest in retaining power often supersedes fidelity to a particular kind of regime. Thus were the Algerian political elites prepared to forsake single-party socialism when widespread rioting revealed deep popular dissatisfaction and then again to abandon democratic politics when elections threatened to pry power from their grip.

This reversal of conventional political priorities creates a perverse and difficult environment for opposition. As Giovanni Sartori puts it, "Opposition presumes consent on fundamentals, that is, consent at the community and regime level. What the opposition opposes is a government, not the political system as such." Loyal opposition presumes a "system" to which the opposition may be faithful while dissenting from particular politics or arguing with individual officeholders.[6] In the Middle East, personal loyalties often supersede even loyalty to the state or, as the deposed president of Tunisia Habib Bourguiba once candidly observed when asked about the Tunisian political system, "What system? I am the system!"[7]

For both the regimes and the opposition, the risks of creating and entering a "political opening" in these circumstances are considerable. For the regimes, manipulating personal coteries is far easier without the interference of programs, policies, or principles, yet it is precisely such personal and abstract issues that are raised for discussion in uncensored newspapers or contested electoral campaigns. Because the extension of political equality preceded rather than followed the extension of political rights in the

Middle East and North Africa, the capacity of regimes to restrict the arenas of political debate is far more limited than was the case in comparable historical eras in Europe.[8] Not that regimes did not try: as Gehad Auda described Egyptian president Hosni Mubarak's initial strategy, "Democratic politics were to be conducted in parliament rather than the streets."[9]

Opposition groups wishing to contest principles and policies "within the system"—a fairly typical position of liberal political parties, such as Egypt's Wafd or Tunisia's MDS—quickly found that the weakness or absence of formal institutions separable from the personal networks of the incumbent rulers hampered their efforts. Government efforts to co-opt individual members of the opposition with attractive government posts or other favors compromised the integrity and coherence of such opposition.[10] Government disregard of the procedural demands of democratic politics also challenged the liberal opposition; the very high frequency of electoral boycotts on the part of the legal political parties in the Middle East was a good indicator of the magnitude of the dilemmas posed by working within a system that is not itself based on impersonal principles. Although liberal opposition parties have an investment in the continued pursuit of liberal policies, as a matter of both principle and interest, they often found that such positions were honored largely in the breach.

Ultimately, the legal oppositions were often forced to choose between their privileged access and principled positions. At the outset of the liberalization process, many liberals had been received in the freer atmosphere, hopeful that the regimes could be coaxed further—and in any event prepared to cooperate with policies that seemed to promise a substantial amelioration of the political atmosphere. Soon, however, those of the loyal opposition not co-opted into the regime itself found themselves faced with a dilemma: in the liberal challenge to the government—boycotting elections or defending the human rights of members of nonliberal or nondemocratic movements—they made common cause with the illegal opposition by declaring the government was not playing by the rules. This raised the possibility that, as Auda put it, their success in forcing "a more contentious approach to democratization might open the way for the emergence of other opposition forces that would threaten the future of the democratic experiment."[11]

By the end of the 1980s, it was apparent that in many of the ostensibly liberalizing regimes of the Middle East, the major contest was between the regimes and the illegal opposition for the adherence of the legal opposition. Whether by design or default, the regimes had created situations on which "loyal opposition" was viewed by both the regimes and their opponents as a contradiction in terms.[12] The Tunisian and postcoup Algerian governments, for example, borrowed a leaf from their Islamist opponents' book to argue that the battle at hand was not merely a policy dispute but one between Civilization and Barbarism (the Islamists having equated the present godless age with the jahiliyyah, the pre-Islamic era of ignorance). In doing so, they perhaps inadvertently prepared the ground for the growth of the illegal Islamist opposition they would subsequently face.

The Political Constituencies of the Islamist Movements

During the 1970s and 1980s, the Islamic movements in the Middle East and North Africa grew from small groups of like-minded professionals, students, and intellectuals. Much of their original inspiration was found in the works of earlier activists, such as the Egyptian Sayyid Qutb and the Pakistani Abu al-ala Mawdudi, and in the influence of movements like the pan-Islamic group founded in Pakistan, Jamaat al-Tabligh wa al-Dawa.[13] Foreign or pan-Islamist influences were important in providing models to emulate and money to spend. The oil price rises of the 1970s gave an enormous boost to the visibility, prestige, and patronage of the conservative monarchies of the Arabian Peninsula. To counteract the influence of leftist ideologies and movements that had earlier bedeviled them, Gulf monarchies used their new wealth to support what seemed at the time more conservative causes. The Saudi government built mosques and training centers for imams throughout the Islamic world and provided support for Islamic study circles and discussion groups.[14] By the end of the decade, the success of the Iranian revolution gave an enormous boost to the Islamist political cause, seeming to serve as proof of both the righteousness and feasibility of imposing religious standards in politics.

Although the Islamist movements of the Middle East and North Africa shared similar (though not identical) outlooks, adopted similar discourses, and enjoyed many of the same external financial patrons, they were specific products of the circumstances created for them by the policies of each government.[15] This was to be reflected in the relative strength of the movements in Tunisia and Algeria, as opposed to Morocco and Libya, for example, as well as in specific elements of the programs, including the apparent willingness of the Jordanian, Egyptian, Tunisian, and Algerian movements to entertain democratic institutions as a vehicle for political participation—something few Syrian, Moroccan, or Libyan Islamists deemed worth considering.

Although the Islamist movements had widespread appeal in the lower strata of society, the active adherents tended to be university graduates—first-generation members of the white collar salariat, whose fathers had been workers or peasants. François Burgat tells us that in North Africa, the typical militants were schoolteachers, accountants, retailers, artisans; half of a sample of militants surveyed in Tunisia reported that their fathers had been illiterate.[16]

These lower-middle-class Islamists profited from the activities of their movements in both spreading the word and providing concrete benefits. The early conception of Hasan al-Banna and the Egyptian Muslim Brotherhood of the "comprehensiveness of Islam" lent itself both to a broad social project and to a challenge of the social welfare ambitions of the secular postindependence states. As Kepel observed, "In their monopolistic claim on the transcendental order, the Islamists implicitly criticize the established order and devise actions that aim to transform and overturn it."[17] In providing free medicine, distributing school equipment, organizing garbage collection, offering legal and administrative advice, and organizing scouting groups, the Islamists also played roles in social life that governments had once claimed but then abdicated.

Observers argued, for example, that much of the support for the Front Islamique du Salut (FIS) in Algeria was a protest against a single-party regime that by the late 1980s had grown rigid, self-seeking, and out-of-touch; the claim of the Front de Libération Nationale (FLN) to legitimacy as the spearhead of the revolution against France carried little weight among the 75 percent of the population under thirty. For the segments of the population that operated on the margins of the formal economy—and some estimates put half the work force in the "black market" or "informal economy"—economic insecurity was exacerbated by legal ambiguity, and the FIS was quick to understand and exploit this. FIS activists not only provided emergency relief services after floods and earthquakes far more quickly and efficiently than the government, but they also guaranteed law and order where the government could or would not, providing policing, for example, of the illegal but ubiquitous flea markets where contraband imports from Europe were sold.[18]

Thus, although both the FIS and its opponents framed the debate in ideological terms, like its counterparts elsewhere, the FIS represented more than simply an ideological challenge to the status quo. The Islamist movements in both Egypt and Algeria were often better organized, more efficient, and less corrupt than the government administration. As such, they not only effectively discredited the regimes by providing services in their stead but—and this was critical to their capacity to seize the terrain of opposition—they also outperformed the secular political opposition. With the partial exception of ethnically based parties like the predominantly Berber Front des Forces Socialistes in Algeria, the secular legal opposition defined its mandate in narrowly political terms, such as contesting elections or publishing newspapers, and eschewed social and economic activities; as a result it developed little or no grassroots following. By contrast, the popularity of the Egyptian Muslim Brotherhood and of FIS before its prohibition suggested that the support for Islamist movements was increasingly crossing social class. In 1990, a young Algerian explained his support for the FIS in these terms: "You have only four choices: you can remain unemployed and celibate because there are no jobs and no apartments to live in;

you can work in the black market and risk being arrested; you can try to emigrate to France to sweep the streets of Paris or Marseilles; or you can join the FIS and vote for Islam."[19]

The Programs of the Islamist Opposition:
Between Moderation and Militancy

In a survey in Algiers at the end of 1991, only half of those who claimed to support the FIS declared themselves favorable to the installation of an Islamic republic.[20] The widespread support for Islamist movements among individuals who did not adhere to what would seem key elements of their program was both a cause and a consequence of the ambiguity of the program itself. Like political parties and movements out of power elsewhere, Islamists often attempted to win and keep the widest possible sympathy through vague and often emotional appeals to popular sentiment rather than detailed and specific policy proposals that risked alienating elements of their following. Moreover, it is a truism of political science that political parties with no prospect of gaining power often advocate positions they know to be untenable, contesting elections solely to advertise their positions. These general characteristics of political oppositions that have little hope of participation in power make analysis of the "true" ideological positions of Islamist movements difficult.

One element of the Islamist position was fairly consistent across movements, however, and that was rejection of the West and things associated with the West.[21] For some Islamists, as for some Western analysts, this incompatibility was a timeless and essential feature of the relationship between Islam and the West. As King Fahd of Saudi Arabia put it, "The prevailing democratic system in the world is not suitable for us in this region. . . . We have our own Muslim faith which is a complete system and a complete religion. Elections do not fall within the sphere of the Muslim religion."[22] For others, such as Rashid Ghannouchi, leader of the Tunisian Mouvement de la Tendance Islamique (MTI—later known as al-Nahda), it was a historically specific reflection of the modern era:

> Our problem is that we have to deal with the West from both a position of psychological and material weakness. . . . But I maintain that this unequal and perverse relationship with the West is not fatal. Japan piously conserves its traditions and culture, its civilization, and participates nonetheless in the universal development of modernity. . . . To tell the truth, the only way to accede to modernity is by our own path, that which has been traced for us by our religion, our history, and our civilization.[23]

From this historically contingent perspective, the Islamist movements were natural continuations of independence movements that stalled before attaining their final goal. Apparent political independence did not produce free-dom, either for the country in the international system or for the individual at home, nor did it lead to economic prosperity or cultural renewal. Indeed, Western languages, political institutions, economic structures, and cultural influences continued to be strong.

Moreover, to add insult to injury, dependence on and fascination with things Western in the Islamic world was almost completely unrequited. As the behavior of the Western tourists, the structure of the Western oil market, the policies of Western strategic planners all testified, Western interest in the Middle East and North Africa was more a function of its physical than its human or cultural resources. While the governments did not—indeed, could not—acknowledge the psychological dilemma created by this dispar-ity because they could not bite the hands that fed their countries, the Islamists openly expressed the widespread popular resentment of the lack of interest, not to say respect, shown by Westerners for the peoples and cul-tures of the Islamic world.

For a significant number of Islamist leaders, the reciprocal rejection of Western influence was absolute, and notions of popular sovereignty, major-ity rule, and pluralist democracy were equated with exploitation and lack of authenticity. Abd al-Salam Yasin of Morocco advocated a "just imam" to guide the people and called for the banning of political parties.[24] Ali Belhadj, of Algeria's FIS, argued that "the ruler is not qualified to modify the law. . . . That right belongs neither to the ruler nor to the people, but to scholars who know the rules of the Ijtihad at the same time as the temporal conditions existing in the societies to which they belong. . . . Those who followed the Prophet were a very small number, while those who followed idols were a multitude."[25]

Others, even in the same movement at the same time, were more prag-matic, equivocal, or eclectic. Abbassi Madani, for example, who was Belhadj's colleague at the head of the FIS, suggested about elections that "our position will be to accept and respect the will of the people . . . there exist in this country some people who demand Islam and others who do not. As a consequence, to avoid 'Lebanonization,' we understand each other on a minimum, that is to say the will of the people."[26]

As a general rule, the closer the movements were to the prospect of sharing power, the more pragmatic they appeared to be. This may have been duplicitous moderation or genuine political compromise, but Burgat, for example, argued that "sensible corrections" or a moderation of early doctrines was visible in a number of movements. Movements that once por-trayed Islam and the West as two entirely different and incompatible frames of reference moved to reduce the distance. The ideological evolution of the Tunisian MTI between 1975 and 1990, for example, as the prospects for its formal participation in Tunisian politics seemed to be growing, was one of growing moderation, as the movement adopted positions on democracy, the status of women, and minority rights that had earlier been rejected out-right.[27]

Some observers viewed such expressions of moderation as merely Trojan horses and referred to Abdelfatah Mourou, the secretary of the MTI, as "Mr. Valium," for his efforts to be moderate and reassuring (thereby presumably lulling to sleep the otherwise vigilant). Among the fears voiced by FIS opponents in Algeria was the possibility that the willingness of the Islamists, whose attachment to democratic rhetoric and values was never more than qualified, to participate in democratic elections was merely tactical, designed to produce the now notorious outcome: "one man, one vote, one time."

It is impossible to resolve this question definitely, but the Tunisian experience of the early 1980s lends credence to the proposition that the Islamist movements were reactionary not only ideologically but also tactically: they "react" to the strategies adopted to confront them. When the government of Prime Minister Mohammed Mzali challenged the Islamist movement of the day with quasi-legal status and the prospect of participation, much of the original rhetoric of the movement moderated, and although there were divisions, including the breakoff of a number of prominent progressives, there was far more realism. The return to repression after Mzali's demise as prime minister served to radicalize the movement.[28]

Similarly in Egypt during the mid-1980s, Mubarak's willingness to allow the Muslim Brotherhood to participate in nationwide elections, albeit only as allies of other parties, permitted the Brotherhood representation in parliament. This precipitated the defection and marginalization of radical groups and contributed to the "normalization" of the mainstream Muslim Brotherhood. As Kepel put it, under these circumstances, "they must compete, both on the level of actuality and on the level of symbolic values, with other political currents . . . they are much less able to fend off the arguments of their rivals than previously, when the stamp of repression automatically conferred the legitimacy of martyrdom on their discourse."[29] This pattern would seem to argue for a policy of inclusion, rather than the position adopted during the 1990s by virtually all the secular governments of the Middle East and North Africa to exclude and harass the adherents of Islamic political ideologies.

Legality, Constituencies, and Programs: The Making of the Islamist Oppositions in the Middle East

Because, with the brief exception of the FIS in Algeria's doomed experiment and the increasingly grudging toleration of the Muslim Brotherhood in Egypt and Jordan, Islamist movements were excluded from competing for power, they had little incentive to develop detailed practical programs—and ample motive to exaggerate their claims. Therefore, some of the confusion and ambiguity in their platforms must be attributed to the government policy refusing them the opportunity to put programs to the test, at the polls or in power. In the same vein, although Islamist leaders frequently condoned the use of violence—Morocco's Abd al-Salam Yasin, for example, argued that "Islam gives him who spends the night hungry the right to bear arms against him who has deprived him of the bounty of God"[30]—the quick resort to violence for which the Islamists were so often noted was at least partly attributable to the violence visited upon them by their governments.

By and large, the Islamist opposition, both legal and illegal, was equivocal about democratic procedures and institutions—as were the regimes. Indeed, the regimes in most of the Islamic Middle East were ambivalent about both democratic and Islamic injunctions and institutions, paying them lip service when it seemed useful, ignoring them when they were inconvenient. The Islamist opposition mirrored that stance when it came to democracy but, while the regimes often appeared to uphold no principles at all, the Islamist opposition seemed at least to be animated by normative concerns with right and wrong, virtue and vice.

The failure of so many Middle Eastern governments to take democratic institutions seriously resulted in increasing numbers of people who felt themselves disenfranchised, unable to find a patron in governments whose ostensible raison d'être had been the protection and tutelage of their citizens. It is among the socially and politically marginalized—ordinarily the poor but, in socialist Syria, for example, the bourgeoisie as well—that Islamists found their adherents. Disenchanted by their historical experience with institutions alleged to be democratic, few of the disappointed were natural constituents of democratic programs or parties.

Moreover, it is well established that the failure to incorporate significant opposition elements into the system, whether out of principled repugnance or self-interested fear, elicits a predictable response from the excluded. As Sartori observed of European politics,

> An opposition which knows that it may be called to "respond," i.e., which is oriented towards governing and has a reasonable chance to govern, or to have access to governmental responsibility, is likely to behave responsibly, in a restrained and responsible way. On the other hand, a "permanent opposition" which is far removed from governmental turnover and thereby knows that it will *not* be called on to "respond," is likely to take the path of "irresponsible opposition," that is, the path of promising wildly and outbidding.[31]

By the very fact that they are illegal, unrecognized Islamist movements had no motivation to accommodate their opponents and embrace democracy and ample incentive to adopt a "rejectionist" posture.

Principled rejection of "the system" in its entirety may also predispose opposition movements to violence, partly because it is precisely the "forces of order" with whom they are doing battle. Thus did FIS militants who rejected violence during the all too brief democratic experiment in Algeria respond in kind to government violence after the military coup, targeting police and security officials.[32] Similarly, the once-pacific Muslim Brotherhood in Egypt and al-Nahda in Tunisia splintered in the face of government repression, and at least some of the resulting shards advocated the violent overthrow of the regime.

Arbitrary and unpredictable government behavior engenders its own opposition. Politics that gives primacy to personal loyalty over principled programs or established institutions leaves too little room for working within the system, undermining the very notion of "loyal opposition," and making suspect the concept of principled dissent. The goals of opposition in these circumstances cannot be but the overthrow of the system and the establishment of another regime in which the disenfranchised will benefit. The emphasis on persons over principles in regimes is mimicked in the opposition's attribution of problems to corrupt individuals rather than to faulty procedures or imperfect institutions. The often puzzling lack of attention to institutions and procedures among many of the Islamist oppositions movements was hardly more striking than the neglect of institutions and procedures by the regimes themselves.

These dilemmas are not peculiar to Islam or the Islamic world. More than twenty years ago, Robert Dahl observed:

> The hegemonic regime creates a self-fulfilling prophecy. Since all opposition is potentially dangerous, no distinction can be made between acceptable and unacceptable opposition, between loyal and disloyal opposition, between opposition that is protected and opposition that must be repressed. Yet if all oppositions are treated as dangerous and subject to repression, opposition that would be loyal if it were tolerated becomes disloyal because it is not tolerated. Since all opposition is likely to be disloyal, all opposition must be repressed.[33]

This is the cruel paradox the regimes created for themselves in the Middle East and North Africa and within which the opposition worked. The results were apparent in the increasingly desperate resort to violence on the part of the regimes and their opponents alike.

Notes

1. Franz Fanon, *The Wretched of the Earth* (Harmondsworth, England: Penguin Books, 1967).
2. For a recent example of the position that, as he puts it, "Islam has bloody borders," see Samuel P. Huntington, "The Clash of Civilizations?" *Foreign Affairs*

72 (Spring 1993): 22–49; for rejoinders, see the subsequent issue of *Foreign Affairs*. A somewhat more nuanced version of the same debate—and one that speaks to Fanon's legacy as well—is explored in Ahmed Rouadjia, "La Violence et l'Histoire du Mouvement National Algérien," *Peuples Méditerranéens* 70–71 (1995).

3. From John Stuart Mill's work on the technical aspects of electoral systems in *Considerations on Representative Government* to Adam Przeworski's *Democracy and the Market* (New York: Cambridge University Press, 1991).

4. The particular point and several of those that follow appear in an earlier form in Lisa Anderson, "Lawless Government and Illegal Opposition: Reflections on the Middle East," *Journal of International Affairs* 40:1 (Winter/Spring 1987): 219–232; similar arguments are suggested by Jocelyne Cesari, "L'Etat Algérien Protagoniste de la Crise," *Peuples Méditerranéens* 70–71 (1995).

5. On the economic context of the political reform, see Henri Barkey, ed., *The Politics of Economic Reform in the Middle East* (New York: St. Martin's Press, 1992); Ilya Harik and Denis Sullivan, *Privatization and Liberalization in the Middle East* (Bloomington: Indiana University Press, 1992). On the political liberalizations themselves, see Louis Cantori, ed., "Overview: Democratization in the Middle East," *American-Arab Affairs* 36 (Spring 1991): 1–2; Ghassan Salame, ed., *Democracy Without Democrats? The Renewal of Politics in the Muslim World* (London: I. B. Tauris, 1994).

6. Again, as Sartori continues, "opposition is understood as a form of collaboration . . . real opposition has in view the general interest, not merely personal antagonisms." Giovanni Sartori, "Opposition and Control: Problems and Prospects," *Government and Opposition* 1:1 (Winter 1966): 151.

7. Cited in Clement Henry Moore, *Tunisia Since Independence* (Berkeley: University of California Press, 1965).

8. Both Robert Dahl, in *Polyarchy: Participation and Opposition* (New Haven: Yale University Press, 1971), and Samuel Huntington, in *Political Order in Changing Societies* (New Haven: Yale University Press, 1968), argue that the desirable sequencing of liberalization and democratization—as in historical Europe, in that order—is now moot for most of the rest of the world.

9. Gehad Auda, "Egypt's Uneasy Party Politics," *Journal of Democracy* 2:2 (Spring 1991): 72.

10. The practice of awarding ambassadorships to potentially troublesome political figures is by no means limited to the Islamic world, but its effects there are often quite transparent: the Tunisian human rights movement was seriously taxed when President Ben Ali persuaded several of its activists and other sympathetic intellectuals to accept attractive posts abroad after his accession to power in 1987. See Susan Waltz, *Human Rights and Reform: Changing the Face of North African Politics* (Berkeley: University of California Press, 1995), 137 and passim.

11. Auda, 78. Also see Mona Makram-Ebeid, "Political Opposition in Egypt: Democratic Myth or Reality?" *Middle East Journal* 43:3 (Summer 1989): 423–436.

12. Among the victims must be counted disproportionate numbers of human rights activists, such as Yousef Fathallah, president of the Algerian Human Rights League, who was assassinated in June 1994 by unidentified assailants. Although no one claimed responsibility, the *New York Times* noted that he had been "an outspoken critic of both sides in Algeria's unrest," 19 June 1994, 3.

13. On these influences, see Gilles Kepel, *La Revanche de Dieu* (Paris: Editions du Seuil, 1991).

14. Nazih N. Ayubi, *Political Islam: Religion and Politics in the Arab World* (London: Routledge, 1991), 179ff.

15. This point is particularly well made by Sami Zubaida, *Islam, the People and the State* (New York: I. B. Tauris, 1993).

16. François Burgat, *The Islamist Movement in North Africa* (Austin: Center for Middle East Studies, University of Texas, 1993), 99; for similar descriptions of the constituents of Islamist movements elsewhere, see Ayubi, 158–177; Said Arjomand, *The Turban for the Crown: The Islamic Revolution in Iran* (New York: Oxford University Press, 1988); Saad Eddin Ibrahim, "Anatomy of Egypt's Militant Islamic Groups," *International Journal of Middle East Studies* 12:4 (December 1980): 423–453.

17. Gilles Kepel, *Muslim Extremism in Egypt: The Prophet and the Pharaoh* (Berkeley: University of California Press, 1989), 241; Ayubi, 131.

18. Hugh Roberts, "A Trial of Strength: Algerian Islamism," in *Islamic Fundamentalism and the Gulf Crisis,* ed. James Piscatori (Chicago: American Academy of Arts and Sciences, 1991); Arun Kapil, "Les Parties Islamistes en Algérie: Eléments de Présentation," *Maghreb-Machrek* 133 (July-September 1991): 103–111.

19. Quoted in Mark Tessler, "Anger and Governance in the Arab World: Lessons from the Maghrib and Implications for the West," *Jerusalem Journal of International Relations* 13:3 (September 1991): 17.

20. Cited in Burgat, 100.

21. On FIS, see, for example, Abdelasiem El-Difraoui, "La Critique du Système Démocratique par le Front Islamique du Salut," in *Exils et Royaumes: Les Appartenances au Monde Arabo-Musulman Aujourd'hui,* ed. Gilles Kepel and Rémy Leveau (Paris: Presses de la Fondation Nationale des Sciences Politiques, 1994).

22. King Fahd, interview in *al-Siyasah* (Kuwait), 28 March 1992. For examples of Western analysis advocating this same perspective, see Bernard Lewis, "Islam and Liberal Democracy," *Atlantic Monthly* 27:12 (February 1993): 89–98; Martin Kramer, "Islam vs. Democracy," *Commentary* 95:1 (January 1993): 35–42; for critical discussions of these positions, see John L. Esposito, *The Islamic Threat: Myth or Reality?* (New York: Oxford University Press, 1992); Yahya Sadowski, "The New Orientalism and the Democracy Debate," *Middle East Report* 23:4, no. 183 (July-August 1993): 14–21.

23. Quoted in Burgat, 63.

24. Henry Munson, Jr., *Religion and Power in Morocco* (New Haven: Yale University Press, 1993), 169.

25. Cited in Burgat, 125.

26. Ibid., 128.

27. Ibid., 82.

28. Ibid, 224. On the Mzali years, see Lisa Anderson, "Democracy Frustrated: The Mzali Years in Tunisia," in *Middle East and North Africa: Essays in Honor of J. C. Hurewitz,* ed. Reeva Simon (New York: Middle East Institute, Columbia University, 1989).

29. Kepel, *Muslim Extremism in Egypt,* 242; also see Saad Eddin Ibrahim, "Egypt's Islamic Activism in the 1980s," *Third World Quarterly* 10:2 (1988): 632–658.

30. Quoted in Munson, 164.

31. Sartori, 152.

32. See Human Rights Watch/Middle East, *Human Rights Abuses in Algeria: No-One Is Spared* (New York: Human Rights Watch, 1994).

33. Robert A. Dahl, ed., *Regimes and Oppositions* (New Haven: Yale University Press, 1973), 13.

2

Islam in Algeria: Religion, Culture, and Opposition in a Rentier State

Dirk Vandewalle

Across the Middle East and North Africa, secularization and religious revitalization have been two sides of the coin the modern era uses as its coinage: the development of the nation-state and the effort to define a national identity or consensus among its citizens.[1] Among the regimes with secular aspirations in the region, this struggle between the exigencies of the modern state and those of religious affiliation were often summarily settled by the first generation of postindependence political elites. Nowhere in a contemporary setting is this struggle over real and religious/symbolic issues and power more pronounced than in Algeria. The country's single party and its army—the Front de Libération Nationale (FLN) and the Armée de Libération Nationale (ALN)—are confronting both a proliferating number of secular opposition groups and Islamic movements within the setting of a civil war. At least 30,000 people have been killed since 1992, after the government set aside the results of a first round of national elections that promised to bring the country's Islamic party, the Front Islamique du Salut (FIS), to national power.

During the country's war of independence (1954–1962), and since its independence in 1962, the FLN has implicitly acknowledged the moral dimensions and values of Islam—enshrining them within the country's constitution—but has explicitly sought to contain or deny its political energies. Secular opposition was also, until the aftermath of nationwide riots in October 1988, not tolerated. This containment of all opposition, added to by the alienating nature of the country's centralized political and economic systems, and by the gradual decline of a moral vision for the country among its political elites, set the stage for a crisis of national culture.

The irony, in light of Algeria's chosen development path since independence, is that the country's revolution—perceived by its first generation as an inexorable historical force, with strong and clearly articulated state structures that would jettison actors, ideas, and notions of culture in their path—is now the subject of precisely those challenges that were once dismissed as archaic, unscientific, and inappropriate to building the nation. In light of the earlier prevailing mobilization and structural approaches in the discipline, it is not surprising that many earlier observers gave little credence to the importance of cultural discourse, the power of ideas, and the wish for a more equitable and democratic society. They focused instead, much like earlier observers of Iran, on processes of institutionalization and equated institutionalization with consolidation.[2]

The Middle East, the conventional argument of even seasoned observers asserts, simply refuses—for cultural, historical, or religious reasons—to consider political liberalization or moves toward democratization.[3] Although Algeria, Tunisia, Jordan, Yemen, and Egypt have experimented with some forms of opening up the political arena, it is undoubtedly true that the region has been resistant to such change, while other areas of the world seem in the throes of liberal revolutions. I would like to suggest that—applied to Algeria, but generalizable beyond the single case study—a more powerful way of explaining the inability to liberalize may lie in the political economy of the country. Using such an approach, which is focused on the political and economic effects of rentier development—and with a sensitivity toward cultural and ideological elements—can better explain both the persistence of authoritarianism in Algeria and the nature of opposition and of government-opposition relations within the country, while simultaneously providing a finer-grained understanding than the conventional "economic crisis" explanations.[4]

More specifically, rentier and semirentier states like Algeria, with much of their income derived from nonproductive economic activity that accrues directly to state elites, allows both for the seeming strength of authoritarian regimes and for an enfeebled opposition.[5] In rentier states, the bifurcation between institutionalization and consolidation can remain hidden for long periods of time, since there is relatively little demand made on institutions beyond those employed for distributive tasks. Crises can be averted through "soft budget" sleight of hand; potential opposition can be bought off outright or slowed down through economic patronage; extreme patterns of both inclusionary and exclusionary corporatism can be combined to make most individuals clients and to prevent the coalescing of group economic (and subsequent political) interests.

What often looks from the outside like a strong state—with powerful legislative and executive bureaucracies, clearly developed structures, a coherent military, an effective legal system to define property rights, and a visible police presence to enforce announced edicts—in effect turns out to have weak adaptive abilities for social change, or when faced with fiscal crises.[6] The reason is that rentier states develop only certain institutions—primarily distributive ones—at the expense of those—extractive and regulatory ones—that in most productive economies become the true measure of state strength and capacity.[7] When fiscal crises emerge and, as in the Algerian case, a transition toward more market-oriented economic structures is required, the state cannot do so for a closely interrelated set of economic and political imperatives.

Much of the literature on the emergence of Islamic opposition movements and the demand for democratization in the region has attempted to link the growth of opposition to the economic crises most local governments faced—and the growing ungovernability that resulted—without analyzing the growth of economic institutions or their (mis)use over time.[8] The growing "resurgence of civil society" has been interpreted in part as a response to economic adjustment, to the frustration over its accompanying austerity measures, and to declining living standards. The precise nature of the link between economic crisis and opposition in the Middle East, however, remains ambiguous and has not yet been adequately addressed. In Algeria, in particular, the confrontation between Islam and the state is not primarily a struggle over defining new economic arrangements—although it does include an important debate concerning the transformative role of the state in creating wealth as an indispensable ingredient for survival and order—but is intimately linked to radically different versions of what the state should look like, what those transformative functions should be, and what role citizens should assume within this new configuration. Few Algerians, excluding those closely connected to the regime, have much respect or sympathy left for the old state and its representatives, except that it continues to provide, in a fashion, the most basic functions they cannot do without: some (precarious) sense of internal order and territorial integrity that could be swept away if an Islamist government came to power.

Rent and the State as Guarantors of Patronage

The discourse in Algeria between those who claim to represent the state and its opposition is not, surprisingly, about the *role* of the state in economic management, as several observers would have it. A review of a number of recent economic texts, for example, written by a wide range of leftists, liberal economists, and Islamists in Algeria, reveals that even today all tendencies favor a strongly interventionist state.[9] The country's attempt at economic liberalization therefore has met with varying *political* resistance across the ideological spectrum—validating Stephen Krasner's observation that countries in the Third World tend to embrace "principles and norms that . . . legitimate more authoritative [rather than] more market-oriented modes of allocation."[10] This resistance is not necessarily linked to the strategy itself—which several economists view as unavoidable. In rentier states, the resistance to economic reform remains high precisely because it threatens to irrevocably alter, in ways that are both unspecified and cannot be forecast, the economic and political fortunes of the citizens of states that have used their distributive and redistributive economic power for their own purposes since independence; and it introduces markets over which the state has little or no control.[11] Remarkably, however, both "Washington consensus" economists in Algeria and a prominent Islamic economist, Abdelhamid Brahimi, agree that the state must reduce its distributive functions in favor of extractive options that give it more room for monetary and fiscal policy—the former simply refer to "taxation"; Brahimi spends several chapters in his latest book proving how zakat (tithing) can accomplish the same task.

For the Algerian opposition—Islamist or secular—the state continues to be seen as an indispensable guarantor of independence and autonomy. The focus of opposition is against those elites who (badly) govern it, an outrage against elite practice of simply increasing rents at the expense of efficient bureaucratic practice that conserves resources, and against the fact that most of the country's intellectuals and the ALN's officer class are francophone and for decades refused to comment on the corruption within the country's political leadership and institutions. What is at stake is this distrust, expressed in the differing cultural sensibilities embedded between ruler and ruled, within an economy marked in many ways by nonmarket criteria in which citizens simply depend on the state. Finally, and more specifically, it is also about the demand for the creation of a new modus operandi between ruler and ruled—the move toward a "second stage of state-building" that questions the nature and distribution of economic and political power within Algeria's neopatrimonial state—that is at issue.[12]

The catalyst in Algeria of the attempt to recast what were once considered immutable relations between a strong state and a weakened society was a crisis of legitimacy sparked by the material corruption and the moral bankruptcy of the secular-nationalist regime that remains in power and that was unchallenged and seemingly incontestable until the October 1988 riots. If in much of the Middle East and North Africa the discourse between those in power and those in opposition has shifted from nationalist and socialist rhetoric to religious terms, it is ironic that in a country now arguably possessing the best organized Islamist opposition, the confrontation between the state and its Islamic opposition remains fundamentally expressed, on both sides, in explicitly nationalist and developmentalist language.[13]

An "economic crisis" explanation alone, therefore, does not explain the political dynamics of Islamist opposition and its success in Algeria. Rather, its emergence should be seen as the backlash, made possible by the October 1988 riots as catalyst, against a process of economic, political, and ideological/cultural disintegration that started in the wake of the country's independence. This process, I argue, can best be understood against the background of Algeria's development as a hydrocarbon/rentier economy, which created an extreme reliance on rent-yielding exports to the West and made possible a seemingly strong and autonomous neopatrimonial state that dominated local society.

For much of the 1960s and 1970s, the "bonanza" of oil and natural gas, of strategic rents granted by superpowers during the Cold War, and of worker remittances allowed both the inefficiency and the distributive largesse to continue.[14] The rents released the government from excessive reliance on domestic taxes, and the state in return, in its patrimonial fashion, felt itself excused from many of the tasks of domestic accountability: a host of welfare benefits and entitlements, carefully and minutely enshrined in the country's national pacts, made patronage—albeit of a highly asymmetrical nature—a ubiquitous phenomenon throughout Algeria. A host of formal institutions, created or adapted from the French at independence and meant to regulate the economy, either lost their power or, more likely, became personalized instruments through which either the FLN or individuals could keep the patronage system intact. Indeed, in what is virtually a vicious circle, the very structure of the institutions of domestic patronage heighten the relevance and indispensability of the state to the local society and the economy.

Rentier Development,
State Capitalism, and the Politics of Exclusion

Algeria, like most Middle Eastern states in the post–World War II period, has obtained a substantial proportion of its government revenues from economic sources and activities that have added little to its domestic production. In the international division of labor, oil, and natural gas, exporters like Algeria occupy a unique, highly restrictive, and vulnerable niche—a unique place in production for global markets that, as both Hirschman and the world-system theorists have argued, has powerful implications both for each country's politics and for the welfare of its citizens.[15] It allows for rapid accumulation of capital, high profits, and extended benefits to the population. But local development is highly dependent not only on fluctuating revenues and access to markets, but also to the ability to buy large amounts of goods and services on the international market. As Hirschman's analysis suggests, filling this particular niche in the international division of labor was meant to create a "multidimensional conspiracy," promoting the unleashing of entrepreneurial energy as well as of developmental coalitions that sustain development—what the Algerian planners called a strategy of *industries industrialisantes*.[16] In "transitory economies" like Algeria, where oil and gas revenues last only a few decades, the state's role in creating, nurturing, and sustaining both is particularly acute, as local rulers clearly understood. Effective statecraft assumes a critical dimension, to turn an important but very narrow comparative advantage into assets that can sustain growth and development beyond the oil era.

From 1965, under President Boumédienne, Algeria followed an intensive industrialization policy that relied heavily on the income from oil and natural gas. The sociopolitical corollary to this strategy, enshrined in periodically updated "social pacts," was meant specifically to create distributive coalitions that would, in the name of national solidarity, endure a level of personal austerity that would allow for a high level of national savings to be channeled toward industrialization. Second, the pursuit of egalitarianism was meant, at least in official language, to reinforce this element of solidarity among the country's citizens.[17] Finally, an authoritarian one-party system was imposed to direct, rather than to consult, the population. The *mots clés* of that early period were equality, equity, and personal responsibility—slogans that would return to the political discourse in Algeria in the late 1980s, but this time in the tracts and on the cassettes of the Islamists.

In the 1960s, and throughout much of the 1970s, active intervention in the country's economy—based largely on Soviet-style central planning—not only put the state in charge of the traditional commanding heights of the economy, but penetrated the lowest levels of daily economic interaction as well. The state's active economic management, in coordination with FLN priorities, were seen as indispensable to offset the persistent factions and regional differences that marked the country and that had temporarily been suspended during the war against the French. Running through much of Algeria's economic literature of the first two decades of independence was the strong conviction that markets could only bring incremental change, not the wholescale restructuring necessary to turn Algeria into a full-fledged industrial power. The country's planners argued that reliance on the market would not allow Algeria to fine-tune the country's economy—a process for which they thought administrative fiat provided under FLN auspices was indispensable. Those twenty years were the high period of tutelage and intense state capitalism for Algeria. The strategy pursued during the period was made possible in large part by the fact that hydrocarbon revenues accrued directly to the state elite, in effect removing state managers from popular concerns.

Although Algeria managed impressive economic growth for almost two decades, by the end of the 1970s much of the earlier optimism about the ability of the state capitalist experiment to manage and direct economic development was waning. When President Boumédienne died in 1978, it was clear that economic growth had been achieved at a heavy political and economic price, and that the goal of economic and industrial independence—for which so much of the country's resources had been sacrificed—had proven elusive. Rather than an integrated industrial infrastructure providing the largest share of the country's revenues, as its original planners had predicted, the country relied more than ever on oil and natural gas income. The public sector was characterized by extremely low productivity and bureaucratic redundancy. Investment codes presented formidable legal hurdles to the development of a private sector, much of whose energy was channeled toward economic activities at the margins of the inefficient public sector, or toward activities that contributed little to improving the productive capacity of the country. As in virtually all rentier states, the agricultural sector was in shambles: pricing policies and outright neglect had turned a country self-sufficient in food production at independence into an importer of most basic foodstuffs. Virtually all those imports were paid for in hard currency, a commodity originally reserved exclusively for industrialization. Simultaneously, the pressure on official markets was exacerbated by a rapid monetary expansion, which led to excess liquidity and the growth of parallel markets where the real value of the country's currency was a fraction of its official price.[18]

The informal economy—trabendo—long depicted as parasitic and illegal by the state, delivered not only those amenities unavailable to most citizens but eventually provided needed supplies to the official sectors as well. Its growth, interpenetration of the official economy, and range of goods and services were a daily reminder to most Algerians of the failure of the state's promises that had been enshrined in its social pacts. More important, the pervasive influence of trabendo was a constant reminder to Algerians of the inability of state institutions to carry out their basic tasks.[19] This dual economy—with its official "markets," where administered prices and a scarcity of goods prevailed, and the "real" economy of the trabendo—was as much as any other element in Algeria an enduring and visible sign of the bifurcation between the pretensions of a paternalistic state and the growing escape of social and economic activities from that state. The repeated crackdown against the parallel economy, often with army units, only increased popular resentment. Ironically, the state's response to its faltering role in the 1980s would consist of economic liberalization strategies that stressed a return to markets and market-oriented growth. This new strategy, however, pitted the state more openly against an already "liberalized" informal, "real" economy that had traditionally relied upon its market skills to survive—an economy that, by then, as the state correctly but disingenuously argued, had become infiltrated by Islamist entrepreneurs who provided services that had by now proven beyond the regulatory capacity of the state.

Political Contestation and Resurgent Civil Society

By 1979, when Chadli Benjedid took over the country's presidency, Algeria showed clear characteristics of rentier development: fast-growing cities with high levels of unemployment or underemployment, uncontrolled spending, a burgeoning public sector that employed an increasingly large number of citizens for reasons not necessarily linked to economic need or to efficiency, and the maintenance of an increasingly unaffordable social contract for essentially political purposes. By the time Benjedid launched his economic liberalization program in 1980, the FLN's long-standing claim to pursue equity and economic justice for all Algerian citizens had become a source of national ridicule. The growing gap between those who had no access to the patronage of the FLN and an elite of public sector managers, party apparatchiks, and allied ALN officers who controlled the bureaucracies and institutions exposed the true nature of the party. Its claim that it represented an indispensable political intermediary had vanished by the time Benjedid assumed power.

The weakening of the state's ability in the late 1970s and 1980s to use the distribution of rent for essentially political purposes, and the crisis this produced among the country's rent-seeking elites, led to Algeria's attempt to "open up" its economy. This crisis—intimately linked to the loss of rent—as well as the subsequently needed Western financial help to resolve the country's economic problems after years of self-imposed semiautarky, added to the relations between government and opposition in Algeria a dimension few observers have commented on.[20] For the first time, the carefully crafted systems of patronage, as well as the accompanying socialist rhetoric, were under assault.

In this sense, the economic and political outcomes of rentier state development in Algeria and, particularly, its ultimate failure to sustain itself as a developmentalist state necessitated a return to a reliance on the West after an extended period of self-conscious state capitalist development. The unavoidable shift in economic policy—despite a self-imposed austerity plan between 1983 and 1986—provided to the emerging Islamist opposition in Algeria a powerful sense of identity as a refuge from a world hegemonic discourse dominated by Western imperialism, which resonated strongly within the country's political culture, created purposely by those who came to power in 1962. In this process, the seemingly strong state, when faced with a fiscal crisis and with the first signs of sustained opposition, faltered in all except its coercive capabilities.

Old Politics, New Politics:
The Resilience of the Rentier State

The October 1988 riots began ostensibly as a result of widespread unemployment and shortages of essential goods. Algeria's $70 billion income boom, which started after the second oil shock in 1979, had ended by 1985. A year later, the government adopted a new austerity plan aimed in part at reducing the country's $23 billion debt. Although the government could have rescheduled its debt payments, for ideological reasons it refused to do so. The government's self-imposed adjustment plan required draconian measures that most analysts believe were more painful than an IMF plan would have been. At the same time, the state and public companies, which had been told to trim their payrolls for the sake of efficiency, were not able to provide employment to the annual 300,000 university graduates—a promise once made by the state. The 1986 plan had heightened popular dissatisfaction; open dissent and defiance emerged, resulting in riots in Constantine and Sétif that year. In essence, they were a reaction not only to the austerity measures, but also to the hypocrisy of the economically privileged—the official *nomenklatura* and those who had first benefited handsomely from state capitalism and, more recently, from the infitah (economic liberalization) strategy the country had adopted.

Although the background of the rioters cut across social and economic backgrounds, young Islamic militants played a prominent role in the events. For the first time since independence, several hundred Islamists were picked up and brought to trial in 1986 and 1987, while student strikes continued unabated. As many as half of all young Algerians were unemployed at the time of the riots. By September 1988, labor unrest had spread throughout the industrial belt, which stretches around Algiers from Reghaia to Rouiba. At the end of the month, strikes broke out in the public service companies in Algiers. They culminated in the call for a general strike for 5 October. The riots preceded the strike by a few hours. Started by unemployed youth, the riots quickly gained support from Islamists, who used them as an opportunity to gain public exposure after the trials had temporarily put them on the defensive. When army recruits fired point-blank at the demonstrators, leaving at least 200 dead, public opinion openly turned against the government.[21]

Benjedid's response to the riots at the outset appeared bold and imaginative. Within a few months, the country adopted a new constitution that opened the road to multiparty politics and omitted any mention of socialism. The link between the ALN and the FLN was, at least institutionally speaking, severed. High-ranking army officers were no longer seated on the party's central committee. The government adopted a new electoral law in April 1991, and the campaign for national elections started shortly after. More than forty opposition parties, including the legalized Islamist party, the FIS, participated. In retrospect, the reforms came too late and led to a renewal of a *guerre des clans,* which has marked Algerian politics since the war of independence began in 1954. Benjedid wanted to remove the army from the country's political life by replacing the army of the *maquisards* with a new generation "who have chosen the army as a profession."[22] His reforms included creating a general staff, redesigning military regions, reappointing military commanders, and promoting younger, "nonhistoric" officers. But his attempts to limit the political power of what has, for all intents and purposes, been a self-governing institution within the country were stymied.[23]

Benjedid's alternatives after the riots were to move toward a true multiparty system, to sever the link between the party and the Algerian state, or to restructure the party internally to make it more compatible with the realities the country faced after October 1988. To some extent, the Algerian president attempted all three. During the year that followed the riots, he attempted to bring new people, a new structure, and new ideas into the FLN. The institutional structures of the party, from the local cells on up, were redrawn. At the FLN National Congress in November 1989, some new delegates replaced old stalwarts, but the National Assembly retained most of its party apparatchiks, delegates who had been appointed before the 1988 riots. They, in turn, continued to boycott any further political and economic reforms. The country was running out of time.

The search for political pluralism and a greater measure of public liberty in Algeria showed above all the deep scars left by the one-party system and by the systematic evisceration of all potential opposition during the 1960s and 1970s, to the benefit of the FLN/ALN. On the surface, at least, Algeria made remarkable progress in setting the parameters for meaningful reform: it had a myriad of political parties or associations, which until the riots would have been intolerable; human rights organizations were flourishing; and new press codes were announced. The State Security Court, which had once served exclusively to judge dissenters, was abolished. But the January 1992 military intervention, which put a halt to the second round of parliamentary elections that promised to bring the Islamists to power, proved how tenuous those new associations and organizations were, and how dispensable they were judged to be by the real power brokers in Algerian politics. It was ultimately the combination of military, economic, and institutional barriers that gave the political initiatives after October 1988 their contours. And it was the same long-standing combination that slowed down real reform, while an emboldened opposition pressed for rapid change.

The most important result of the riots, however, was the removal of those elites opposed to the infitah in the wake of the disturbances. As a result, the government and its ALN supporters had a much higher stake in the outcome of the privatization effort. Several observers at the time argued that if the strategy showed any sign of failure—for economic or political reasons—the military would have to intervene to ensure its continuation. Not surprisingly, one of the rationales put forward by the military during the January 1992 takeover was precisely this economic argument: the Islamists would make it impossible for the infitah to succeed. Even more ironic is the fact that within a few months after the coup, Abdessalam Belaid—the father of the failed state capitalist experiment of the 1960s and

1970s—was appointed prime minister and promptly announced his commitment to rebuilding the state companies as the cornerstone of his economic strategy. The vacillation not only showed the chaos inside the country, but to most Algerians indicated the cynical nature of the country's political leadership.

Symbols, Culture, and Islamic Politics

Before his forced resignation by the military in spring 1992, Benjedid often spoke of the October 1988 riots as the catalyst of Algeria's second revolution—a "correction" of the first revolution, which had ended in independence in 1962. But his historical reference was wrong. What those few days in October 1988 resembled more than anything else were the events of 11 December 1961, when for the first time during the war of independence Algerians took to the streets. As most French historians agree, that single massive demonstration triggered the Europeans' realization that change was unavoidable. In the same way, the Algerian government's unmistakable fear and hesitancy during the first days of the riots emboldened protesters and led to a turning point in recent Algerian politics.

What the growing and increasingly organized and public contestation in Algeria amply demonstrated at a deeper structural level was the difficulty the state now faces in maintaining both its claim as the sole legitimate representative of the country's political community and its ability to synthesize the country's Arab-Islamic and European cultures. Indeed, the FLN can no longer rely on the symbolic link between ruler and ruled that figured so prominently in Algerian politics after independence. And, because virtually all secular opposition has disappeared, the Algerian military, since January 1994, when it openly assumed the reigns of power, finds itself alone in its struggle against the Islamist movement and an enfeebled secular opposition. In this struggle for legitimacy, both the state's representatives and the Islamists, among others, now brandish the powerful symbols of national identity. The concept of cultural renewal and extension of public liberties has invaded—or, perhaps more accurately, been readopted into—the political vocabulary after a hiatus of almost three decades. And while some of the calls for this renewal have been expressed in secular terms, all clearly carry a religious undertone.

Indeed, if one single element marked the election campaigns in Algeria that led to the canceled 16 January 1992 national elections, it was the claim by virtually all political parties that they are the protectors of Islam in their societies. To most Algerians, this claim, particularly by the FLN, seems fantastic: in its pursuit of socialist development, the FLN was often more aggressive toward the country's cultural symbols and religion than even the colonial power had been. Islam in Algeria, as elsewhere, represents an enduring opposition to the form—and content—of the type of nationalism used earlier by the state. Many of the symbols that are now invoked by the FIS are those the country's rulers skillfully manipulated during and after the war of independence in their own search for legitimacy and national unity.[24] As Algeria's leaders during the war of independence often stressed, the war was as much a struggle for the hearts and minds of Algerians as it was a physical confrontation between the colonized and the colonizers. The confrontation between the Islamists and the FLN/ALN is nothing less.

The current struggle is equally one of persuasion and the manipulation of symbols, ranging far beyond the socioeconomic dislocations that led to the riots. And it is a struggle in which those in power are now at a distinct disadvantage. The question most Algerians ask no longer focuses on whether the state, or the Islamists, have an economic program or a political vision for the country. In the opinion of most Algerians, neither presents an attractive alternative. The Islamic movement in Algeria, as in the Maghreb and the Arab world, now demands greater accountability as the social contract—once carefully maintained through the state's distributive mechanisms—is, willy-nilly, under attack by the government itself.

Ultimately, however, the nature of the Algerian political system and the enormous power and independence of a rentier state elite determined the way opposition to the government's policies formed. Since the regime never relied to any large extent on domestic sources of revenues, it judged—quite appropriately—that opposition was unlikely to be based on economic criteria or that domestic coalitions around the FLN would unravel for economic reasons. But it forgot that, in the absence of protest based on those economic criteria, organized opposition would rally around the government's very raison d'être: an ideological commitment to equality for all and a moral commitment to uphold the achievements of the 1962 revolution. Although the Islamist gains in the first round of the national elections in December 1991 were perhaps a sign of discontent with FLN/ALN pretensions, rather than a direct endorsement of FIS, it is also worth noting that a sizable portion of Algeria's population seemed willing to consider an alteration—if perhaps not quite a full-fledged alternative—to the form of political community in which they lived during the first stage of FLN-guided state building.

Important to note, however, is the more direct involvement of the army in the country's economic and political affairs. The military coup of 1992 still meant to preserve the army's traditional role of "king maker" in Algerian politics. Since then, but particularly in the spring of 1994, the ALN has assumed a much more direct role in ruling the country. As a result, politics in Algeria have become more transparent—but the new political game now also squarely exposes the military to criticisms linked to economic performance. Because the Algerian army has traditionally been involved in so many activities in the country—including, for example, the agrarian revolution—it once was a strong, coherent institution and a powerful vehicle for social mobility and national integration. Those roles now seem increasingly under attack, and it remains to be seen if the army Benjedid desperately tried to reform and adapt to the country's rapidly changing sociopolitical climate can remain immune from the disintegrating challenges other institutions in the country have faced.

The old generation of army generals is now being accused of betraying the essentially anti-Western revolution they once led; the more public role of the ALN will make it likely that it will equally reflect the tension of the society surrounding it. Whether it can do so without losing coherence and the unity it claimed to represent remains at present the most urgent and difficult question to answer regarding Algerian politics. The link to independence traditionally invoked by the army and the FLN has now lost its appeal. Significantly, the confrontations since 1988 have been initiated by a younger generation who shares neither that historical memory nor the ideological references that had been at the heart of the link between their elders and the Algerian state. And it is particularly among the young, especially university students, that the decline of the country's fortunes has been most acutely felt. To this extent, the upheaval in Algeria has the potential for an important intergenerational change that economic improvement and progress alone are unlikely to halt.

Economic Liberalization, the State, and Civil Society

Algerian policymakers, as well as those in Western countries and within international financial institutions, clearly see the success of the ongoing economic liberalization campaign as crucial to muting the Islamist challenge inside the country. Although it is worth repeating that an economic turnaround by itself is unlikely to solve the more profound crises that are fueling the current contestation in Algeria, economic progress and greater equity would undoubtedly reduce some of the pent-up frustration that boiled over during the 1988 riots. Algeria's path away from a command, collectivist economy toward one based on market principles was first promoted after the death of President Boumédienne but failed to take hold until 1986. Even then, obstruction by a combination of FLN/ALN elites and bureaucratic elites linked to the FLN made any real headway impossible until the 1988 riots.[25]

In judging the impact and the efficacy of the liberalization efforts in Algeria, a number of caveats must be noted. The first centers on the fact that the structural reforms the country has begun are unlikely to have an immediate impact on the poorest part of the population, since some of the provisions of the earlier "social contract"— subsidized basic goods and services—are foremost among those targeted for elimination. As a result, it is highly likely that those Algerians who have no stake in their country's economic growth or future will be, at best, indifferent to whatever political and economic experiments the government attempts. This group has little to gain or lose by what is decided between the state and the opposing forces in society. And it is this particular group—the mustadhafeen (d.•inherited)— who already form a ready target for the Islamists.

Second, the move toward economic liberalization in Algeria has not obliterated the heavy-handed economic dirigisme that has marked the country's economic planning since independence. In some instances, it has led to a further and substantial recentralization of power, as government bureaucrats and regional and local party elites impose bureaucratic controls. Indeed, to some extent, it remains unclear even now if the slow pace and restrictive scope of reforming the public sector is not simply an effort to impose a new division of economic tasks that shifts the burden of efficiency toward nonstate actors while leaving the state—primarily the military—ultimately in charge.

In Algeria, this recentralization of power has also paradoxically been linked in part to greater reliance on the international capital needed for local development—making aid a double-edged sword once more and reinforcing the earlier rentier characteristics of the state. Relatively small groups of decisionmakers become allocative agents, using the "power of the purse" to pursue certain economic and political goals. This new power—provided now in part by European capital—has been justified by the wish to reconstruct a state that can confront the centrifugal tendencies of the socioeconomic challenges ahead, a barely veiled restatement of the earlier, now bankrupt strategy. At the same time, neither the liberalization strategies, the institutional restructuring, nor the timid attempt at political pluralism will suffice to allow the state to recapture the loss of energy and confidence it has suffered.

The state in Algeria seems unlikely to succeed in successfully reconstructing itself without recapturing at least one of the two pillars that once sustained its fortunes: that of providing patronage while maintaining, at least partly, its social contract. But that has become impossible. Economic reconstruction in Algeria can be achieved only if the logic of the social contract it subscribed to—a (now admittedly often minimalist) cradle-to-grave welfare system—is abandoned. To break this logic will involve drastic measures that will lead to further confrontations with all levels of society who, during an entire generation of rentier-state development and single-party politics, have known the state only as a provider and arbiter. This turning around of the old logic will perhaps be less dramatic, but also involves a further paradox: if less will be demanded of the state, it will have no choice in the short run but to assume greater power to guarantee that this process can take place in a nonconfrontational fashion. It remains unclear whether state elites in Algeria can take this step in the current climate of lingering contestation without simply solidifying their positions. The 1992 intervention, and the greater involvement of the military in the actual running of the country, confirms the suspicion that the old habits of accumulating power die hard in Algeria. No events since then have changed this fundamental perception.

Third, and despite the attempt at recentralization, the vulnerability of the Algerian government stands in vivid contrast to the power the state enjoyed after independence. Its legitimacy, once based on its alleged ability to act as an arbiter among feuding factions and expressed symbolically in the struggle for independence, and more tangibly in its role as dispenser of economic patronage, has withered away. As a result, Algerian society, after three decades of relative passivity, has started to reassert values and interests that had been handed over to a state that once single-handedly dominated all political, economic, social, and cultural expression in the wake of independence. As in other parts of the world where central management is yielding to a more dispersed kind of decisionmaking, this process in Algeria is chaotic, often undisciplined, and frequently violent. The transition is particularly dramatic because it involves not only a generational turnover in leadership, but also the search for a new consensus and for new economic and political strategies to deal with the unprecedented regional and global circumstances at the end of the twentieth century.

Furthermore, the Islamic-secular confrontation squarely involves lingering problems of political legitimacy and of political exclusion within a society that has now acquired its first real taste of strength and independence. The decades of single-party politics, and the more recent confrontation between the state and the Islamists has, for all practical purposes, squeezed out the secular opposition and turned large numbers of passive bystanders into active opponents to the regime. This is particularly worrisome, since neither the liberalization strategy nor the institutional restructuring of the country's political system will enable the Algerian leadership to recapture its position in the country. Political and economic reforms in Algeria remain, in a manner reminiscent of events after 1962, an elite occupation. But if most Algerians stand on the sidelines politically, the needed economic reforms are constant preoccupations for the country's citizens.

To solve this dilemma, the military can continue to run the country as it did during the Boumédienne period—a strategy it shows all signs of following, despite the few attempts at meeting opposition figures, halfhearted and largely rhetorical attempts at conciliation, and steps toward some form of multiparty politics. But, if the Boumédiennist rentier-state period and the subsequent decade under Benjedid illuminated one aspect of that particular type of development, it is that the relative autonomy of the Algerian state from its domestic constituencies had important political consequences: the government, seemingly strong and impervious, paid little attention to either a growing population of disaffected youth or to the popular impact of the deteriorating economy—until it was too late.

Conclusion

On two occasions, in November 1994 and January 1995, Algeria's opposition parties, in an attempt to break the country's deadlock, met under the auspices of the Community of Sant'Egidio in Rome.[26] The two meetings were meant primarily as confidence-building measures to bring the FIS and the government together, in an attempt at reconciliation that would simultaneously open up the country's political system to the other opposition parties. Sant'Egidio represented an important voice from the country's civil society that had been lost in the country's violence, but it proved insufficient in the end to convince the Algerian regime to participate. The proceedings surrounding the Sant'Egidio initiatives above all made three important issues clear. First, it demonstrated once more how much Algeria's civil war represents a long-festering multidimensional conflict that now pits two sets of adversaries, with diametrically opposed views of the purpose and role of the state, against each other. Second, the conflict between the two sides has effectively left other possible parties to a solution out in the cold. Although the parties that signed the Sant'Egidio agreements represented over 82 percent of Algeria's citizens who voted in the first round of the parliamentary elections in 1991, their voices have in effect been drowned out by the increasingly violent solutions on both sides.[27] It is unlikely that violence can lead to a solution, but for now neither side has the political will or capability to seek other alternatives. Finally, it again made clear that the government was unwilling to participate in any initiative it did not either initiate or control.

What the discourse among the participants in Rome also showed, once more, was how much the debate in Algeria is not only about politics and economics, as local governments and the West have belatedly realized.[28] It is, as well, about an ideological and moral direction for a country coming to terms with its own past. Algerians are no longer moved by the exhortations of local leaders whose legitimacy was once predicated on opposition to the West—but who now demand the reverse as they pursue a more Western-oriented economic strategy under local conditions that increasingly put into question the logic of that decision and that seemingly leave basic inequities unaddressed. That it took so long for this confrontation to emerge so clearly was linked to the rentier nature of the local economy that hid from view the growing economic problems and dislocations, concentrating power among a technocratic elite that showed few concerns for any form of questioning or accountability. In the ongoing struggle, by default, Algeria remains divided between two competing authoritarian solutions that leave secular and religious moderates relegated to the sidelines. Much attention has focused on the secular-religious aspects of the conflict. But what the civil war in Algeria is ultimately about is a more profound debate concerning the nature of the state and about those who represent it: a questioning of the nature of the modern state, of what precisely the state should do for its citizens, and in what fashion. It is, in the end, an intensely nationalistic debate that involves political, economic, and highly symbolic issues and references that have been left unresolved since independence.

Notes

1. In the sense of a new dawlat, a concept repeatedly used *avant la lettre,* by the North African sociologist Ibn Khaldun in his study of the rise and fall of dynasties in empires in the region. See his *Muqaddimah,* translated by Franz Rosenthal (New York: Pantheon, 1958).

2. John Entelis, *Algeria: The Revolution Institutionalized* (Boulder: Westview Press, 1986).

3. Note, for example, Elie Kedourie's remark that democracy "is alien to the mind-set of Islam," in *Democracy and Arab Political Culture* (Washington, D.C.: Washington Institute for Near East Policy, 1992), 2.

4. Although my approach shares insights that can be found in both the rational choice and institutional approaches to political economy, it is not overtly "economistic." While it does privilege characteristics of so-called rentier economic development to explain Algeria's domestic political economy and the role of opposition in it, it also allows for other factors to better explain the complexity of causation in government-opposition relations. I simply argue that these other factors, including culture and religion, contribute, are enhanced, and become legitimized in this process but are not its cause.

5. Although there is now a considerable literature on the so-called rentier state, there remain a number of imprecisions and definitional problems with the term. In general, I prefer to simply use the term *distributive state,* focusing more precisely on what the primary economic function of the state is. For some general works on the rentier state, and on the debates surrounding its definitions and usefulness, see Hossein Mahdavy, "The Patterns and Problems of Economic Development in Rentier States: The Case of Iran," in *Studies in the Economic History of the Middle East from the Rise of Islam to the Present Day,* ed. Miriam A. Cook (Oxford: Oxford University Press, 1970); Giacomo Luciani, "Allocation vs. Production States: A Theoretical Framework," in *The Rentier State,* ed. Hazem Beblawi and Giacomo Luciani (New York: Croom Helm, 1987); Homa Katouzian, "The Aridosolatic Society: A Model of Long-Term Social and Economic Development in Iran," *International Journal of Middle East Studies* 15 (1983): 259–281; Rayed Krimly, *The Political Economy of Rentier States: A Case Study of Saudi Arabia in the Oil Era, 1950–1990* (Ph. D. diss., George Washington University, 1993); Anne Krueger, "The Political Economy of the Rent-seeking Society," *American Economic Review* 64:3 (June 1994): 291–303; and the excellent study by James Buchanan, "Rent Seeking and Profit Seeking," in *Toward a Theory of a Rent-Seeking Society,* ed. James M. Buchanan, Robert D. Tollison, and Gordon Tullock (College Station: Texas A&M University Press, 1980). On Algeria and Libya, see Dirk Vandwalle, "Political Aspects of State Building in Rentier Economies: Algeria and Libya Compared," in Beblawi and Luciani.

6. For a provocative treatment of this distinction between institutionalization and consolidation, consult Eric Selbin, *Modern Latin American Revolutions* (Boulder: Westview Press, 1993). The argument in the text above is in some ways a corollary to the points made by Robert H. Jackson and Carl G. Rosberg in "Why Africa's Weak States Persist: The Empirical and Juridical in Statehood," *World Politics* 35:1 (October 1982): 1–25.

7. I have treated the difficulties rentier states experience in undertaking the transition toward market reform in greater detail in "Qadhafi's Failed Economic Reforms: Markets, Institutions and Development in a Rentier State," in *North Africa: Development and Reform in a Changing Global Economy*, ed. Dirk Vandewalle (New York: St. Martin's Press, 1996); see also Kiren Aziz Chaudhry, "The Price of Wealth: Business and State in Labor Remittance and Oil Economies," *International Organization* 43:1 (Winter 1989): 101–145.

8. See, for example, Azzedine Layachi and Abdel-Kader Haireche, "National Development and Political Protest: Islamists in the Maghreb Countries," *Arab Studies Quarterly* 14:2–3 (Spring/Summer 1992): 69–92.

9. See, among others, Mahfoud Bennoune and Ali el-Kenz, *Le Hasard et l'Histoire: Entretiens avec Belaid Abdesselem*, vols. 1 and 2 (Algiers: ENAG Editions, 1990); Abdelhamid Brahimi, *L'Economie Algérienne: Défis et Enjeux* (Algiers: Dahlab, 1992). In an interesting development, Brahimi's more recent book, *Justice Sociale et Développement en Economie Islamique* (Paris: La Pensée Universelle, 1993) is much more ideologically Third World/Islamic. For a review of the latter, see Arun Kapil, "Islamic Economics: The Surest Path?" *MESA Bulletin* 29:1 (July 1995): 22–24. Kapil's description of Brahimi's notion that "the state should have its hands on all the levers" (22) is somewhat of an exaggeration. For a more nuanced account of Brahimi's ideas about the state and economic reform, see Deborah Harrold, "Economic Discourse in Algeria: Economists Circle the State," in *North Africa*, ed. Vandewalle.

10. Stephen Krasner, *Structural Conflict: The Third World Against Global Liberalism* (Berkeley: University of California Press, 1985), 5.

11. For an insightful analysis of the inability of local Maghrebi regimes to further use distributive mechanisms to regulate both their economies and to "buy off" potential opposition, see Abdelkader Sid Ahmed, "La Crise de l'Etat Redistributeur au Maghreb," paper presented at the conference "Le Maghreb Après la Crise du Golfe: Transformations Politiques et Ordre International" Granada, November 1991.

12. For a deeper analysis of the ongoing attempts at recapturing and redefining this relationship, consult Elbaki Hermassi and Dirk Vandewalle, "The Second Stage of State-Building in North Africa," in *State and Society in North Africa*, ed. I. William Zartman (Boulder: Westview Press, 1992).

13. See, for example, *Preliminary Project of the Political Program of the Front of Islamic Salvation*, a pamphlet published in French and Arabic by the FIS (n.p., n.d.) following the October 1988 riots.

14. For an application to other regions of the world, see David Becker, "Bonanza Development and the New Bourgeoisie: Peru Under Military Rule," in *Postimperialism: International Capitalism and Development*, ed. David Becker, Jeff Frieden, Sayre Schatz, and Richard Sklar (Boulder: Lynne Rienner, 1987); Terry Lynn Karl, "The Political Economy of Petrodollars: Oil and Democracy in Venezuela" (Ph.D. diss., Stanford University, 1982), and her forthcoming *Paradox of Plenty: Oil Booms and Petrostates* (Berkeley: University of California Press); Ian Little, Richard Cooper, et al., *Boom, Crisis, and Adjustment: The Macroeconomic Experience of Developing Countries* (Oxford: Oxford University Press, 1993).

15. Chase-Dunn, 89; Hirschman, 77.

16. Hirschman, 96.

17. The country's official slogan adopted after independence was "From the people, to the people."

18. See Mehdi Dazi, "Informal Economies in Algeria: Path and Pattern," in *Informal Economies in the Middle East and North Africa,* ed. Dirk Vandewalle (forthcoming); Azzedine Layachi, "The Domestic and International Constraints of Economic Adjustment in Algeria," in *North Africa,* ed. Vandewalle.

19. The literature on the informal economy, and its links to the state and to economic reform efforts, remains undeveloped. The classic work, which describes the informal sector in Peru, is Hernando de Soto, *The Other Path: The Invisible Revolution in the Third World* (New York: Harper and Row, 1989). For North Africa in particular, consult Mohamed Salahdine, *Les Petits Métiers Clandestins ou le Business Populaire* (Rabat: EDDIF, 1988), and Mohamed Salahdine, ed., *L'Emploi Invisible au Maghreb: Etudes sur l'Economie Parallèle* (Rabat: Société Marocaine des Editeurs Réunis, 1990).

20. For an exception, see Hartmut Elsenhans, "Algeria: The Contradiction of Rent-Financed Development," *Maghreb Review* 14:3–4 (1989): 226–248.

21. For an excellent recounting of events surrounding the riots, see Ignacio Ramonet, "La Révolte d'une Génération Sacrifiée: L'Algérie sous le Choc," *Le Monde Diplomatique,* November 1988.

22. Mouloud Hamrouche, prime minister of Algeria at the time, quoted in *Le Monde,* 7 June 1991, 4.

23. The abrupt resignation in September 1990 of General Mohamed Betchine, head of the country's information services, and the sudden retirement of Mohamed Attailia, chief inspector of the ALN, hint at the lingering resentment these changes were causing.

24. For a good overview of the Islamist movement in Algeria, consult Ahmed Rouadjia, *Les Frères et la Mosquée: Enquête sur le Mouvement Islamiste en Algérie* (Paris: Karthala, 1990).

25. See Dirk Vandewalle, "Breaking with Socialism: Economic Privatization and Liberalization in Algeria," in *Privatization and Liberalization in the Middle East,* ed. Ilya Harik and Denis Sullivan (Bloomington: Indiana University Press, 1992).

26. For an excellent discussion of the Sant'Egidio proceedings, and of events in Algeria since 1988, see Robert Mortimer, "Islamists, Soldiers, and Democrats: The Second Algerian War," *Middle East Journal* 50 (Winter 1996): 18–39.

27. Figure cited in Mortimer, 38.

28. For a recent publication that aptly summarizes this growing consensus about events in Algeria, and how to respond to them, see Andrew J. Pierre and William B. Quandt, *The Algerian Crisis: Policy Options for the West* (Washington, D.C.: Carnegie Endowment for International Peace, 1996). The publication was the result of a Carnegie Endowment study group on France, Algeria, and the United States.

3

Political Islam and Gulf Security

John L. Esposito

The Gulf states have long been regarded as the heartland of the Arab Muslim world. Utilizing their oil wealth, many of the governments, in particular Saudi Arabia, Kuwait, and the United Arab Emirates, have been major sponsors of Islamic organizations, such as the Muslim Brotherhood and the Jamaat-i Islami, and supporters of Islamic institutions (mosques, schools, hospitals, and banks) and activities (from publishing to preaching). However, one of the great ironies of Islamic politics in the 1990s is the extent to which Islamic movements have increasingly challenged, if not threatened, the security of Gulf states.[1]

From its inception, the promotion and spread of revolutionary Islam was a primary foreign policy objective in Iran. Institutionalization of the Islamic Republic was accompanied by attempts to export the revolution. The Ayatollah Khomeini and the Iranian revolution challenged the legitimacy of regimes, calling for their overthrow. In the Gulf, as elsewhere in the Muslim world, Iran served as a catalyst for an opposition whose primary causes were indigenous factors such as the political and economic grievances of Shii minorities in Saudi Arabia, Iraq, Bahrain, and Kuwait. However, Iranian rhetoric and support for revolution did not result in the overthrow of any regimes in the Muslim world.

The constitution of the Islamic Republic of Iran explicitly proclaimed the Islamic rationale for an activist, aggressive foreign policy whose goal was the unity of the Islamic world and the extension of God's sovereignty throughout the world. No Iranian goal captured as much attention from the media or struck as much fear in the hearts of Western and Muslim governments alike as Iran's goal to export its revolution. So pervasive has this concern been that it has often been difficult to separate fact from fiction. Indeed, both militants and their critics have often been given to hyperbole when discussing Iranian revolutionary activities and results. Reported incidents embrace a vast area: Egypt, Tunisia, Nigeria, Lebanon, Gaza, Saudi

Arabia, Kuwait, Bahrain, Pakistan, Afghanistan, Malaysia, Indonesia, and the Philippines, to name but a few.

The Ayatollah Khomeini espoused a nonsectarian, universalist Islamic revolution aimed at bridging the gap between Sunni and Shii, and liberating not just Shii Muslims but all the oppressed. A goal proclaimed by the constitution of the Islamic Republic was "to perpetuate the revolution both at home and abroad."[2] Broadcasts of Iran's Voice of the Islamic Revolution appealed to Muslims of the Gulf and beyond to rise up against their governments. Yet both the acrimonious rhetoric of Iran and the overreaction of its opponents have made it difficult to distinguish revolutionary rhetoric from political reality and to identify results of efforts abroad.

Shii in the Gulf and Pakistan, who constitute a significant minority living under Sunni rulers, were exhilarated and emboldened to assert their sectarian identity and ritual practices as well as to express their discontent with ruling regimes.[3] Sunni as well as Shii groups, extending from Egypt (the moderate Muslim Brotherhood and radical al-Jihad) to Malaysia (ABIM and the militant PAS), drew inspiration from the example of Iran. Gulf rulers were particularly nervous about the appeal of Iran's revolutionary example and rhetoric. In Iraq, where Shii constitute 60 percent of the population, the Baath socialist government of Saddam Hussein was shaken by eruptions in Karbala, Najaf, and Kufa (June 1979). Khomeini had denounced Saddam Hussein as an atheist and called for the overthrow of his regime. Saddam Hussein countered by denouncing Khomeini and appealing to Iranian Arabs to revolt. At the same time, Ayatollah Muhammad Baqir al-Sadr, one of Iraq's most prominent and influential Shii clerics, had welcomed Iran's revolution and Khomeini's jurist-led Islamic government. The Iraqi government suspected Iranian influence upon and involvement with Iraqi Shii activist groups, in particular, the Islamic Call Society (al-Dawa) and the newly formed (1979) mujahidin.[4] Shii leaders were arrested. Baqir al-Sadr, who had declared the Baathist regime un-Islamic and forbidden any dealings with it, was executed (April 1980), and al-Dawa was outlawed. In an atmosphere in which both governments played upon centuries-long Arab-Persian and Sunni-Shii rivalries and hostility, the situation deteriorated. However, as we shall see, threats of Iran's export of revolution proved exaggerated.[5]

The Iran-Iraq War and Gulf Security

In September 1980, Iraq invaded Iran, initiating a war that would last for eight years and exacerbate relations between Iran and its Gulf neighbors. Khomeini was particularly critical of the Saudi and Gulf governments, both because they were "un-Islamic" monarchies and because of their military and economic ties with the United States, an influence he disdainfully referred to as "American Islam." Audiotapes of Khomeini, leaflets, and daily Arabic broadcasts from Tehran were explicit in their critique and agenda: "The ruling regime in Saudi Arabia wears Muslim clothing, but it actually represents a luxurious, frivolous, shameless way of life, robbing funds from the people and squandering them, and engaging in gambling, drinking parties, and orgies. Would it be surprising if people follow the path of revolution, resort to violence and continue their struggle to regain their rights and resources?"[6]

In November 1979, Saudi Arabia was rocked by two explosive events. On 20 November, as Muslims prepared to usher in the fifteenth century of Islam, the Grand Mosque at Mecca was seized and occupied for two weeks by Saudi-led Sunni militants who denounced the Saudi monarchy.[7] Khomeini's accusation that the United States had been behind the mosque seizure in Mecca led to attacks against U.S. embassies and the burning down of the U.S. Embassy in Islamabad, Pakistan. While still reeling from the seizure of the Grand Mosque, riots broke out on 27 November among 250,000 Shii Muslims in the oil-rich Eastern Province (al-Hasa), where they constitute 35 percent of the population. Pent-up emotions and grievances among Shii, who felt discriminated against by their Sunni rulers and called for a fairer distribution of oil wealth and services, had exploded earlier in the year in response to Iran's revolution and the triumphant return of Khomeini.

Events in the early 1980s did nothing to lessen concern among governments in the Gulf, the wider Muslim world, and the West. Statements by the ruling ayatollahs, which called for an aggressive, expansionist policy, exacerbated the situation. President Khomeini of Iran called upon prayer leaders from forty countries to turn their mosques into "prayer, cultural and military bases [to] . . . prepare the ground for the creation of Islamic governments in all countries."[8]

The Iran-Iraq war, which officially began with Iraq's invasion of Iran on 22 September 1980, inflamed relations between Iran and its neighbors. The Gulf states organized the Gulf Cooperation Council (the GCC) and threw their substantial financial support to Iraq. Khomeini called upon the GCC to "return to the lap of Islam, abandon the Saddam Hussein regime in Baghdad, and stop squandering the wealth of their peoples."[9] The Saudis countered such statements: "Ever since the Iranian and Islamic peoples were afflicted by the Khomeini regime, this regime has failed to render any noteworthy service to Islam, and the Muslims. . . . This regime has tried to create schism among Muslims, not only in their politics but also in their mosques. The Khomeini regime sends its agents everywhere to foment discord."[10]

Iran used the annual pilgrimage (hajj) to Mecca to propagate its revolutionary message. The Ayatollah Khomeini and other senior clerics both rejected the Saudi claim to be the keepers of the holy sites and maintained that the hajj had a rightful political dimension. Iranian pilgrims, displaying posters of Khomeini and chanting slogans against the United States, the Soviet Union, and Israel, clashed with Saudi security in June 1982. Tensions continued during subsequent years and climaxed in 1987, when more than 400 people were killed in a confrontation between Iranian pilgrims and Saudi security forces.

During the same period, the Sunni rulers of Bahrain and Kuwait were threatened by Shii unrest, as these communities, emboldened by Iran's revolution and Khomeini's call for its export, found an outlet for political and economic grievances. In 1981, the government of Bahrain foiled an Iranian-inspired coup by the Islamic Front for the Liberation of Bahrain. Kuwait, 30 percent of whose population is Shii, had been troubled by car bombings of the U.S. and French embassies (1983) and cracked down on Shii unrest in 1987 and 1989. Yet, despite these sporadic disturbances and government fears of massive unrest, Iran's export of its revolution proved to be surprisingly unsuccessful in rallying both Iraqi Shii and the populations of the Gulf states. By and large, most Iraqi Shii, who constituted the majority of the rank and file in the military, chose their nation rather than their coreligionists in Iran. Pockets of Shii militancy in the Gulf states did not translate into significant revolutionary movements, as states used a combination of carrot and stick, addressing socioeconomic grievances while increasing security and prosecution to control dissidents.

The Gulf War of 1990

On 2 August 1990, Saddam Hussein did the unexpected: for the first time in modern history, an Arab nation invaded, seized, and subsequently annexed another Arab country.[11] Saddam cloaked himself in the mantle of Islam and called for a jihad. Just as the events of 1979 (the Iranian revolution) and of 1989 (détente and the triumph of the democratization movement in Eastern Europe) were unforeseen watersheds in world history, so too the Gulf crisis of 1990 altered the map of the Middle East. The Gulf crisis simultaneously presented an apparent united Arab response to a rapacious, expansionist Iraq and, at a deeper level, an Arab and, indeed, Muslim world divided to an unparalleled extent.

In 1980, Saddam had countered the potential threat of an expansionist revolutionary Islam by invading Iran. With the support of moderate Arab states, the United States, and Europe, and heavily financed by the Gulf states, Saddam Hussein had become the defender of Gulf Arabs against an expansionist, fundamentalist Iran. Few denounced this violation of international borders and law; many preferred to see Iraq as an agent of the "civilized world." Thus, Iraq received economic and military support from its allies, who conveniently overlooked Saddam's use of chemical warfare against the Kurds and the Iranians and Iraq's efforts to develop nuclear weapons.

Two years after the Iran-Iraq truce of 1988, the politics of the Gulf and of the Middle East had been reversed. Saddam Hussein did what his Gulf patrons had earlier paid him to prevent. Having turned back the threat to the Gulf from Iranian fundamentalism, he overran Kuwait and confronted his Gulf neighbors in the name of Arab nationalism and Islam. Ironically, he accomplished this with a military machine paid for in large part by the tens of billions of dollars Kuwait and the Gulf states had poured into Iraq and the weapons and technology provided by the Soviet Union, Germany, and France. Even more ironically, Saddam attempted to legitimate his "naked aggression" not only in the name of Iraqi nationalism, but also in the name of Arab nationalism and Islam. Saddam simultaneously sought to appropriate or claim the historic roles of Nebuchadnezzar, Gamal Abd al-Nasser, and Saladin.

While Saddam Hussein failed to win the support of the leadership in the Arab world, he enjoyed a degree of popular support often not fully appreciated in the West, where the tendency was to focus on those governments that supported U.S. initiative and to equate the position of these Arab rulers with that of their people. As a result, little distinction was made between the differing perspectives of Western nations supported by their Arab allies and the views of a significant portion of the populace whose deep-seated grievances and frustrations were given a new voice and champion in Saddam Hussein.

Saddam appealed to many of the same conditions and issues that fed the growth of Islamic revivalism and fueled anti-Western sentiments and acts: the failures of Arab governments and societies (poverty, corruption, and the maldistribution of wealth), the plight of the Palestinians, and foreign intervention leading to Arab dependency. While the support of Arab and Muslim governments for the U.S.-led alliance against Saddam Hussein has often been emphasized, the divisions tended to be downplayed, thus obscuring the gravity of the situation and its long-range implications for Western and Arab/Muslim relations. Rather than speaking of the successful mobilization of the Arab League, some overlooked the fact that only twelve of its twenty-one members supported the anti-Saddam forces. Pro-Saddam and anti-U.S. demonstrations have occurred in many countries: Tunisia, Yemen, Sudan, Algeria.

Arabs and Muslims (secularists, socialists, Islamic activists, intellectuals, and the man in the street) were pulled in two directions. They rallied not so much to Saddam Hussein as to the bipolar nature of the confrontation (the West versus the Arab Muslim world) and the issues that Saddam proclaimed: Arab unity, dignity, self-sufficiency, freedom from foreign intervention, and social justice (resolution of the Palestinian problem and redistribution of wealth). Thus, for many, not to support Iraq was to choose the Western-led alliance and with it the perpetuation of dependence and expanded foreign presence. Talk of a permanent U.S. presence or new security alliance sounded to many like the rationale for new "protectorates."

Islamic movements, like others, found themselves pulled in several directions. Ideologically, they rejected secular nationalism or believed that Arab nationalism or Muslim nationalism must be rooted in Islam. Many rejected the legitimacy of most Muslim governments, regarding them as un-Islamic or anti-Islamic. (This ideological rejection has not precluded a willingness to accept financial support, in particular from the oil shaikhdoms.) Finally, all were anti-imperialist. They rejected the legacy of European colonialism, the result of a policy to subdue and divide and thus to ensure a weak Arab/Muslim world. Saddam's denunciation of Europe's creation of modern Muslim states with artificial boundaries rang true for Islamic activists and Arab nationalists alike. Anti-U.S. neocolonialism struck a common chord as well. Many criticized U.S. policies, ranging from unbalanced support for Israel to the propping up of pro-Western, "puppet" regimes (which the West regards as its moderate allies, such as the shah's Iran, Lebanon, Nimeiri's Sudan, the Gulf states) whose authoritarian governments contradict U.S. ideals of democracy and representative government.

The Gulf crisis witnessed a shift among many Islamic movements from an initial Islamic ideological rejection of Saddam Hussein, the secular persecutor of Islamic movements, and his invasion of Kuwait to a more populist Arab nationalist, anti-imperialist support for Saddam (or more precisely those issues he represented or championed) and the condemnation of foreign intervention and occupation. The key variable or catalyst was the massive Western (especially U.S.) military buildup in the region and its presence near Islam's sacred cities, as well as the threat of military action against an Arab nation and of a permanent Western presence.

Domestic politics and pressure not to respond to popular sentiment, as much as religious conviction, influenced the receptivity of Islamic movements in Algeria, Jordan, and Egypt to Saddam's appeal to Islam and the call for jihad. While initially thousands of Muslim activists in Algeria demonstrated against Iraq's invasion of Kuwait, on a subsequent visit to Baghdad, Abbassi Madani, leader of Algeria's Islamic Salvation Front, declared: "Any aggression against Iraq will be confronted by Muslims everywhere."[12] In Jordan, the Muslim Brotherhood initially condemned the Iraqi invasion. However, after the deployment of U.S. forces, it called for a jihad against "the new crusaders in defense of Iraq and the Islamic world." As one U.S. Muslim observer noted: "People forgot about Saddam's record and concentrated on America. . . . Saddam Hussein might be wrong, but it is not America who should correct him."[13] In Egypt, the Muslim Brotherhood condemned the Iraqi invasion and supported the government's anti-Saddam position, but increasingly, despite Egypt's prominent position in the anti-Saddam alliance, the Brotherhood along with other opposition groups criticized the massive presence of foreign (Western) forces in Saudi Arabia. Islamic activist leaders from the Middle East and Asia, including Algeria's Madani, Sudan's Hasan al-Turabi, and Tunisia's Rashid Ghannouchi, traveled to Iraq and Saudi Arabia in an abortive effort to secure peace in the Gulf crisis.[14]

Even in countries that sent forces to support the anti-Saddam "international alliance," popular sentiment often differed from that of the government. In Syria, Hafez al-Asad, who has a bloody record of suppressing dissent—such as his leveling of much of the city of Hama to crush an uprising by the Muslim Brotherhood, had to contend with pro-Saddam demonstrations. In a poll taken by the Pakistani magazine *Herald,* 86.86 percent of those polled responded negatively to the question: "Should U.S. troops be defending the Muslim holy places in Saudi Arabia?"[15] In Malaysia and Bangladesh where, like in Pakistan, many were critical of Saddam's annexation of Kuwait, popular sentiment reflected an equally strong solidarity with much of the Muslim world's condemnation of the U.S. "double standard." They criticized the United States' excoriation of Saddam for violating international law, the demand for Iraq's unconditional withdrawal, and the West's insistence on a rigorous enforcement of U.N. resolutions when, at the same time, the United States not only had refused to take the very same stand with regard to the enforcement of U.N. resolutions that condemn Israel's annexation and continued occupation of the West Bank and Gaza, but also maintained a close political and military ally in Israel, providing more than $5 billion a year in aid.[16] U.S. reluctance to link the two issues (or more accurately to acknowledge the existence of a linkage) in resolving the Gulf crisis was seen by many in the Muslim world as an attempt to disengage two already interlocked realities.

Security in the Post–Gulf War Period

Saudi Arabia and Kuwait, in particular, had been stunned by what their rulers viewed as the "ingratitude," if not treachery, of most Islamic movements. Their generous dispensation of petrodollars throughout the 1970s and 1980s had made them primary patrons of many movements and Islamic activities. As with PLO support for Saddam, they believed that Islamists had bitten the hand that had fed them. After the war, they determined this would never happen again.

However, the Islamist threat to Gulf security has continued in some Gulf states, fueled from without and in some cases from within. Some experts contend that Iran, despite recent attempts at normalization of relations, remains ready to assert its primacy in the Gulf and challenge the legitimacy of the Saudi government and other GCC states again. Sudan's

Hasan al-Turabi, whose Muslim Brotherhood was once a beneficiary of the largesse of the Gulf states, is now seen as a revolutionary enemy, more of a vocal critic than a military threat.

In the post–Gulf War period, domestic Islamist leaders and organizations have emerged as both moderate and extremist opposition in many states. The electoral power of Islamists in Kuwait and Yemen, working within the political system, has been accompanied by challenges by Islamic militants to the governments in Saudi Arabia and Bahrain in particular.

The Gulf War rallied support from many within Saudi Arabia and Kuwait, but also revealed the fragility and vulnerability of these Gulf states and their inability to ensure their security and survival on their own. Even among those who denounced Saddam Hussein's invasion of Kuwait and threat to Gulf security, many feared the long-term results of Western, particularly U.S., forces, military dependence, and further cultural penetration. These concerns were to be found not only among Islamist movements and others outside the region (from North Africa to Southeast Asia), but also from diverse voices within the Gulf. Some of the strongest warnings came from Saudi Arabia's religious establishment itself, reflecting a growing rift between the majority led by Shaikh Abdul-Aziz bin Baz and a more militant minority.[17] Safar al-Hawali, dean of Islamic Studies at Umm al-Qura in Mecca, and thus a major Wahhabi religious authority, warned: "If Iraq has occupied Kuwait, America has occupied Saudi Arabia. The real enemy is not Iraq. It is the West."[18] Hawali had been critical of Western military presence during the Gulf War in tapes ("the Hawali Tapes") that had circulated widely in and outside the kingdom. The criticisms and implications of statements by Hawali and others was clear. Just as the Wahhabi movement had been an Islamic reformist movement whose war against other Muslims was justified by the contention that reformers were seeking to spread true Islam among those who had strayed from the straight path of Islam, so now militant critics of the regime were challenging the Islamic credentials, legitimacy, and power of the House of Saud.

Pressures for political reforms had swept across much of the Muslim world in the aftermath of the fall of the Soviet Union and the democratization wave that affected many areas of the world. In many quarters, a broad spectrum of society, from secularists to Islamists, called for greater political participation and socioeconomic reform. In Saudi Arabia, women, liberal intellectuals, and Islamists (sometimes called Salafi) were emboldened to challenge the traditional authority of the royal family and call for a broadening of political rights and participation. In November 1990, a group of women demonstrated against the ban on women drivers, drawing a swift and strong reaction from conservative religious forces. In February 1991, some forty-three liberal intellectuals presented a memorandum to the king, calling for democratic reforms. Not to be outdone, in May, more than 500 Islamists, from various sectors of society, submitted their own memorandum, presented by bin Baz, head of the religious establishment, demanding political and economic reforms.

Reformist demands were generally ignored. Confrontation between the government and more militant members of the Islamist movement became more pronounced. The creation of a majles (consultative assembly) did not silence more strident militant Islamists, professionals, and independent ulama and mosque preachers critical of the royal family and its pro-U.S. policies. Many had resented the incursion of large numbers of Western, particularly U.S., military forces during the Gulf War. They objected on religious and political grounds. They believed that non-Muslims should not be in the sacred homeland of Islam and feared that this incursion would provide the pretext for a greater presence and dependence on the United States after the war.

These sentiments were not restricted to militant clergy:

> Many Saudi liberals see the current deployment of American troops in their country as a continuation of America's support for despotic regimes throughout the Middle East and indeed as part of a cultural and racial war against the Arabs. In a letter to me one teacher wrote: They, the Americans, have used the very real tragedy of the Kuwaitis as a way to wage war against the Arab people. They have occupied our country and from it they want to launch an attack that will destroy the people of Saudi Arabia and Iraq.[19]

In response to pressures from domestic critics, as well as encouragement from the United States, in March 1991, King Fahd created the consultative assembly (majles al-shura), originally announced on 8 November 1990. The creation of majles al-shura had been promised on a number of past occasions in times of crisis: in 1962, when Nasser's revolutionary challenge threatened Gulf monarchies, in the aftermath of the 1979 seizure of the Grand Mosque, and again in 1980, when the Ayatollah Khomeini called for the overthrow of the Saudi regime.

In August 1992, 102 scholars and shaikhs petitioned for broad reforms, calling for changes in all aspects of Saudi life.[20] Vocal public criticism continued in January 1992, accompanied by the widespread dissemination of thousands of tapes and faxes circulated within the kingdom. For the first time, university professors dared to publicly criticize the ruling family and religious authorities on issues ranging from the government's close relations with the United States and its support for the Peace Accords to social and educational policies, including its perceived tolerance toward women's groups, "termed 'prostitutes' by the Islamists."[21] The political and religious elites closed ranks and for the first time were forced to respond publicly to Islamist attacks.

The confrontation between the government and militant Islamists continued in 1993. After the Gulf War, in May, a new opposition, the

Committee for the Defense of Legitimate Rights (CDLR), emerged. Its founders represented an alliance of moderates or liberals, more conservative members of the Wahhabi religious establishment, and younger Islamists sometimes referred to as Salafiyyah. The organization claimed to be an independent human rights commission concerned about the decline in Islamic standards after the Gulf War. Many of the younger Islamists were university graduates and professionals, some of whom had been educated in the West, who desired more political participation, more accountability to the people from the royal family, and purification of Islam from the corruption of religion by tribal customs. The CDLR was suppressed quickly. Its spokesman, Muhammad al-Masairi, a professor of physics at King Saud University, was arrested. Shaikh al-Hawali as well as Shaikh al-Audeh, prominent and outspoken Islamic scholars, were fired from their positions and had their passports confiscated.[22] Others employed in the university and government, such as Shaikh Abdullah bin-Suleiman al-Masairi, director of the Office of Complaints (Diwan al-Mathalim), were fired or had licenses to practice law revoked, and their law offices were closed. The CDLR was reinstituted in London in April 1994, where it became a vocal opposition, calling for open representative government, strict application of the sharia, and the removal of the monarchy.[23]

Tensions escalated in September 1994. Thousands of Shaikh al-Audeh's supporters held vigils outside his mosque in Burayda as rumors flew that his arrest was imminent. Although the situation remained calm after his arrest and that of Shaikh al-Hawali, within months, antigovernment activities resumed, with sit-ins at mosques in Riyadh, Jeddah, and Burayda.[24] The government retaliated by sacking or transferring university professors, preachers, and judges suspected of being involved in or sympathetic to government criticism.[25]

In the early 1990s, the king had shored up the royal family's control over and influence on Islamic affairs. The Council of Senior Ulama was reorganized and expanded in 1992; in 1994, the Supreme Council for Islamic Affairs was created and placed under the direction of Prince Sultan; a special committee headed by Prince Salman was established to administer funds for foreign Muslim organizations.

The religious establishment supported the government, albeit at times cautiously. Bin Baz, the most prominent religious authority, joined with King Fahd and senior members of the government in denouncing so-called extremists. Bin Baz issued fatwas, such as those declaring that there were no religious grounds for objection to the government's policy on Palestine or Jerusalem.

As noted previously, prior to the Gulf War of 1991, there had been little organized opposition to the regime other than the Shii minority (15 percent of the population), many of whom worked in the oil-producing Eastern province. The Shii had been the victims of discrimination. Anti-Shii propaganda was readily available in schoolbooks and the Council of Ulama decree, which condemned Shii as apostates. In the aftermath of the Iranian revolution, Shii seemed to heed the ayatollah's call for the overthrow of regimes in the Gulf in a series of disturbances or uprisings that were brutally suppressed. Their voice of opposition found an outlet in *al-Jazirah al-Arabiyyah,* which was published in London. However, after the Gulf War, in the summer of 1993, the Shii opposition struck a deal with the government following a congruence of interests, including mutual concerns over Islamic radicals who denounced both the regime and the Shii. However, the agreement was not accepted by all. Shii opposition to dealing with the government persisted. Indeed, in the crackdown that followed the June 25 Dhahran bombing, scores of members of Saudi Hizbollah, a little-known opposition group, were arrested.

Despite bin Baz and the Wahhabi religious establishment's alliance with the House of Saud and the government's new relationship or policy toward its Shii minority, the uneasy Sunni (Wahhabi)-Shii truce remained fragile. It was again threatened by a fatwa from the office of Shaikh bin Baz, issued by one of his deputies, Abdullah bin Abd al-Rahman, declaring Shii heretics, a position also espoused by many young Islamist extremists.

By 1995, the government policy of containment seemed to have put the lid on its Islamist opposition. As a Human Rights Watch expert noted: "The opposition has been driven totally underground. . . . Mosque sermons, books, leaflets and audiocassettes which once openly criticized corruption and called for more political participation were muted during 1995 as the government enforced its strict ban on public speaking, assembly and association."[26] Hundreds of Islamists were imprisoned, many lost their jobs or were transferred, the free flow of tapes and pamphlets was stopped, and the executions of criminals increased markedly.

On 13 November 1995, a bomb explosion at a training site for the National Guard, which killed and wounded U.S. military trainers and advisers, challenged all assumptions. The act seemed inconceivable and shook the otherwise safe and secure Kingdom of Saudi Arabia as had the seizure of the Grand Mosque in Mecca in 1979, sending ripples throughout the Gulf states. If some thought this an isolated event, nineteen more U.S. personnel were killed, on 25 June, by a truck bomb in front of a U.S. airmen's residence in Dhahran, in eastern Saudi Arabia.

Some were quick to blame external sources, like Iran. Whatever the outside influences, the primary actors were part of a Saudi domestic Islamic underground. Some reports in 1997 indicated that a group called Saudi Hizbollah, with support from Lebanon's Iranian-backed hizbollah, may have been responsible. However, Islamic militant organizations, among them the Movement for Islamic Change in the Arabian Peninsula and the Tigers of the Gulf, claimed responsibility for the bombings. The former called for the withdrawal of all "crusaders" and an end to rule by the House of Saud; the latter warned: "If the Americans don't leave the kingdom as soon as possible, we will continue our actions."[27] Most experts saw the action as a response both to the government's crackdown and suppression and to the U.S. military presence, aimed at undermining the stability of the House of Saud and as a warning to GCC states. The Movement for Islamic Change issued further warnings in April and June, demanding that "Crusader forces" leave Saudi Arabia by 28 June 1995 or risk becoming "legitimate targets."

Little is known about the exact makeup and size of groups like the Movement for Islamic Change. They are part of a radical fringe from among a growing militant Islamist movement. Ironically, many members are believed to be Saudis who were "Afghan Arabs," Muslims who had gone off to Afghanistan to fight against Soviet occupation forces in a jihad, blessed and supported by the Saudi and U.S. governments. Three of the four Saudis who were tried and executed for the November National Guard bombing were from among the estimated 15,000 Saudi veterans of the Afghan conflict. Saudi officials have also claimed that extremists have been influenced and supported by Osama bin Laden. An Afghanistan-based businessman (stripped of his Saudi citizenship), he is opposed to the House of Saud and believed to be funding the training of extremist groups and the export of terrorism internationally, first from the Sudan and subsequently from Afghanistan.[28]

Islamists and the GCC States

The activities of Islamists in other areas of the Gulf have varied from cooperation and participation within the political system to militant opposition. In the post–Gulf War period, Bahrain's government has resisted elections and the restoration of parliament, often clashing with a grassroots opposition that includes a significant Islamist leadership and presence. The governments of Kuwait and Yemen have allowed Islamists to participate in elections and serve in parliament and cabinet positions.

Throughout much of its history, Bahrain has seen political movements and disturbances, often divided along Sunni-Shii lines, demanding political reforms. For example, the beginning of a popular uprising in 1953 was sparked by sectarian clashes. Although a constitution was endorsed by the emir and legislative elections held in 1973, the National Assembly was disbanded from 1975 to 1992 while the emir ruled by decree under the State Security Law. In 1992, 300 intellectuals presented a petition, sponsored by three Sunni and three Shii leaders, to the emir, Shaikh Isa bin Salman al-Khalifa, calling for the reestablishment of parliament. This group of religious and secular liberals, led by Shaikh Abdul Amir al-Jamri, a prominent parliamentarian, represented a cross-section of society, religiously and politically: Sunni (30 percent of the indigenous population) and Shii (70 percent). The emir refused their petition and instead appointed a powerless shura council, which represented Sunni and Shii equally but excluded members of the royal family and Sunni and Shii Islamists.[29] Since the summer of 1994, Bahrain has been shaken by a diverse antigovernment opposition (Sunni and Shii, liberals and leftists, urban professionals and the rural poor, men and women), which has used petitions, civil disobedience, and even violence. The government has countered with crackdowns and repression, using its state security forces and security courts.

In October 1994, a petition signed by an estimated 25,000 people (in a country of approximately 350,000), including Sunni and Shii religious leaders and prominent citizens, was presented to the emir. It called for the restoration of the 1973 constitution (originally proposed by the National Assembly and approved by the emir) and denounced restrictions on freedom of speech and the press, the unemployment situation, and deportation and political exile.[30]

> We are facing crises with dwindling opportunities and exits, the ever-worsening unemployment situation, the mounting inflation, the losses to the business sector, the problems generated by the nationality (citizenship) decrees and the prevention of many of our children from returning to the homeland. In addition, these are laws which were enacted during the absence of the parliament which restrict the freedom of citizens and contradict the Constitution. This was accompanied by lack of freedom of expression and opinion and total subordination of the press to the executive power. These problems, your Highness, have forced us as citizens to demand the restoration of the National Assembly, and the involvement of women in the democratic process. This could be resolved by free elections, if you decide not to recall the dissolved parliament to convene.[31]

Seventy percent of the signatories were Shii and 25 percent were women.[32]

On 5 December 1994, a popular young cleric, Shaikh Ali Salman, and two other prominent Shii clerics and signers of the petition were arrested, sparking widespread demonstrations in Shii villages. The regime's violent crackdown resulted in twenty deaths, hundreds of injuries, and the imprisonment of 3,000 to 5,000 people as the violence continued for six months. On 15 January 1995, Shaikh Salman and Shaikhs Haider al-Setri and Hamza al-Deri were deported. Three months later, in April, Shaikh al-Jamri, the leading opposition figure, was jailed along with 1,000 others, and university campuses were raided by security forces. Amnesty International published a fifty-page report noting:

> Over the past ten months several thousand people were arrested, including women and children, many of whom were held incommunicado without charge or trial. At least 150 detainees have been tried and convicted following proceedings which fell far short of international standards for fair play. The torture and ill-treatment of detainees has been widespread and systematic, with two deaths in custody reported to date. Security forces and riot police repeatedly used live ammunition to quell protestors, resulting in the killing of ten civilians in circumstances suggesting that they have been extrajudicially executed.[33]

Although, on 16 August 1995, a deal was struck between the opposition and the government, which resulted in the subsequent release of opposition leaders and 150 other prisoners, the government failed to deliver on its promise to release all of the uprising's political prisoners by the end of September. Moreover, many teenagers were put on trial. Shaikh al-Jamri and other prodemocracy leaders led a ten-day hunger strike from 23 October to 1 November 1995. Demonstrations in support of the strike occurred across the country and included students, professionals, and religious leaders, including Shaikh Abdul Hussain al-Setri, one of the most senior ulama, and judges of the sharia court. Their demands included political dialogue, the release of political prisoners and cessation of political trials, the return of political exiles, and the restoration of parliament.[34] Mosques and schools continued to be central to the protest movement. Mosques served as centers for mass protests and demonstrations; schools for protests and strikes. Security forces raided schools, arresting busloads of students. Amnesty International noted: "This period has . . . been marked by the brutality with which the authorities sought to quell the protests and demonstrations: the repeated use of live ammunition to disperse crowds and the consequent killing of unarmed civilians and unprovoked attacks on funeral processions."[35] Of particular concern was the use of government-sanctioned torture of women and children and the hostage taking of women and other family members to force suspected "criminals" to surrender.[36] On 5 December 1995, tens of thousands gathered in Manama, the capital, for a mass meeting where opposition leaders called for the restoration of parliamentary government.

The following year saw an increase in violence and the arrest of more than a thousand people. In addition, the government used mass arrests to break up demonstrations, often targeting schools, universities, and mosques where protest meetings were held. In March, Issa Ahmad Qambar was executed, an act that brought not only protests within Bahrain, but also criticism from the international community and human rights organizations, which were concerned because the defendant did not have access to a lawyer until he appeared in court, was denied family visits, and was executed before his family was notified. Throughout 1996, demonstrations erupted into clashes and riots between protestors and Bahraini security forces, while unprovoked police attacks and "collective punishment" continued.

The opposition includes the Islamic Front for the Liberation of Bahrain, the Bahrain Freedom Movement, the National Liberation Movement in Bahrain, and the Popular Front. All claim to be prodemocracy, supporting pluralism and human rights. The Bahrain Freedom Movement maintains that it integrates Islamic values and pluralism.[37] Many of the exiled opposition live in London and Washington; a majority are Islamists.[38]

The government has often played upon Sunni-Shii differences to divide and diffuse its opposition. It has charged that a Shii plot to overthrow the regime exists, assisted by Iran and an underground hizbollah (party of God) organization in Bahrain. On 3 June 1996, the emir announced the discovery of a plot by hizbollah to overthrow the government. However, Sunni and Shii leaders continued to insist that the problems were primarily political and economic, not sectarian.[39] The regime warns its neighbors of a spillover effect and contends that elections with a 70 percent Shii population risk a parliament dominated by Shii fundamentalists, with a pro-Iranian policy. Such charges have enabled the Bahrain government to neutralize some of its Sunni opposition, mobilize support from nervous rulers of other GCC states (in particular, Saudi Arabia), silence calls from the United States and from European governments for democratization and human rights, and in turn convince many in Bahrain that the West supports the regime's authoritarian measures.[40]

Kuwait, like Saudi Arabia and Bahrain, experienced the impact of the Iranian revolution and its effects on its Shii population. Long regarded as the most modern, liberal, and affluent of the Gulf states, political conflict and disturbances shortly after the revolution both threatened the stability of the government and exacerbated tensions between Kuwait's Sunni majority and its Shii minority. However, the government was able to weather the initial storm. The Gulf War strengthened sectarian relations and impelled Kuwait's Islamists to rally behind its government, a position that contributed to their role and credibility in post–Gulf War parliamentary elections in 1992.

The National Assembly had been disbanded in July 1986 during a period of increased repression and censorship. During the elections of 1992, several blocs emerged, among them the Constitutional Islamic Movement (CIM), the Popular Movement, the Nationalists, and smaller Islamic groups. Prior to his leadership of CIM, Ismail Shatti had been a leader of the Society for Social Reform (Jamiyyat al-Islah al-Ijtimai), the Kuwaiti Muslim Brotherhood. Its members tend to come from the upper-middle and upper class: professionals, intellectuals, and bureaucrats. They provide effective social services and publish *al-Mujtama,* which is a, if not *the,* major Islamist magazine in the Gulf and broader Arab world. The Kuwaiti Muslim Brotherhood broke with the World Organization of the Muslim Brotherhood, believing that it had failed to take a strong enough line against Saddam Hussein. The other two major Islamic groups are the Ahl al-Hadith (People of the Hadith, or Traditions, of the Prophet, who led the Popular Islamic Association) and Kuwaiti Shii (National Islamic Coalition), who are Arab and Iranian in origin. It was members of the latter who were appealed to and influenced by Iran after the Iranian revolution; some of their religious leaders were deported by the Kuwaiti government.

Islamists won approximately 25 percent of the vote, holding eight to ten seats in parliament with a total of some eighteen deputies backed by Islamic groups.[41] Despite their differences, all have often found it useful or necessary to couch their political discourse in Islamic terms. Thus, all have supported the full application of the sharia in political, economic, and social life, although what that means for each in reality differs markedly.[42]

Conclusion

At the dawn of the twenty-first century, much of the Muslim world, having attained independence as nation-states, now faces a second revolution or transformation: that of national identity and religious/intellectual reform. Issues of authority, legitimacy, identity, authenticity, political participation, and human rights are prominent. This occurs within a context in which secular forms of liberal nationalism, as well as Arab nationalism and socialism, have either failed or proven insufficient. National resources, histories, and contexts vary, as do their reactions and responses.

Political Islam has proven a formidable force even though Islamic movements or organizations often constitute a minority of the community. It has proven attractive and effective in response to the political and socioeconomic failures of governments and elites: sectarian, tribal, and class grievances; second-class citizenship in terms of access to education and employment; maldistribution of wealth; and official corruption. In societies where opposition is absent, repressed, or muted by governments, Islamists have often proven effective both in mobilizing their own following and, as the only viable outlet or "game in town," in attracting those who wish to register their frustrations or opposition to the prevailing order.

One of the ironies in the Gulf is that, despite the use or manipulation of Islam by many governments as a source of identity and legitimacy and as a high-profile means to promote Islam internationally, Islam also represents a challenge to be reckoned with—a political force with the capability to delegitimate or to support protest and opposition.

Governments in the Gulf remain relatively strong, buttressed by established tribal, socioeconomic, and religious alliances, as well as their security forces. For some, principally Saudi Arabia and Kuwait, the budget deficits caused by the Gulf War are a potential long-term problem, limiting projects, jobs, and those subsidies and services that minimize unrest. Moreover, Saudi Arabia will soon face the problem of succession; both the king, who has been ill, and the crown prince are in their seventies. But in recent years, the House of Saud has taken great care to increase its hold on critical positions in the government and society, to co-opt or silence critics, and to control the funding of Islamist opposition by wealthy businessmen.

Liberal moderate critics have muted their calls for reform, fearful of the rise of militant Islamists.

The tribal states of the Gulf continue to face issues of legitimacy, authority, and national identity. Issues of political participation, official corruption, government accountability, social cleavages, and maldistribution of wealth reflect the political (tribal) and economic (class) struggles in society. Religious symbolism, rhetoric, and activism become an effective vehicle for protest and opposition. In addition, cuts in services and jobs, especially in states like Saudi Arabia, Bahrain, and Kuwait, where petrodollars have become more scarce, make for growing numbers of disaffected youth and young professionals. Increased U.S. military presence in the post–Gulf War period fuels charges of Western military and economic dependence and cultural penetration.

Issues of political participation, democratization, and human rights have increasingly been taken up by a cross section of society. Ulama and Islamists, as well as more liberal sectors of society, have used and will continue to use political participation as a political weapon. Islamist opponents charge that they will use elections to "hijack democracy." At the same time, many governments in the Gulf, as in other parts of the Arab and Muslim world, will be challenged to demonstrate that the options are not simply those of Islamist authoritarianism versus state authoritarianism.

When convenient, Islamists in most states will continue to use domestic issues such as Western military dependence, corruption, political participation, redistribution of wealth and employment, as well as such international issues as the Peace Accords, in their critique. However, it is important to restate that in the post–Gulf War period, Islamist movements, like Islam itself, are not monolithic. Similarly, their relationships to Gulf governments vary significantly, from militant opposition of some in Bahrain and Saudi Arabia to participation and cooperation in Kuwait and Yemen. At the same time, one cannot underestimate or overlook the support the ruling families of Saudi Arabia and other Gulf states have had and continue to enjoy from the religious establishment. However, a common potential source of difficulties is the emergence of a younger generation, educated and more militant. Often their criticisms are directed against not only governments and the official ulama or religious authorities, but also against established Islamist movements like the Muslim Brotherhood.

Finally, while Sunni-Shii differences have been somewhat ameliorated by strategic alliances among the opposition in Bahrain or in support of the Kuwaiti government during the Gulf War, they are rooted in a long history of tension and conflict (political and economic discrimination as well as theological differences) whose memory and impact have not been erased and, in the right circumstances, could erupt once again. However, GCC governments have proven relatively successful in the past in devising policies either to exploit or to co-opt and contain sectarian differences and interests.

There continue to be distinctive differences among and between Islamic organizations and leaders influenced by religious interpretation, personal ambition, national interests, and socioeconomic conditions. Islamist opposition in the Gulf as in other parts of the Muslim world is heavily composed of university students and graduates. Because professional associations are banned in the Gulf, in contrast to many other parts of the Arab and Muslim world, the degree of Islamist presence in the professions is sometimes not as apparent. One of the realities many overlook, especially with regard to Saudi Arabia, is the extent to which Islamist opposition to the government and criticism of excessive dependence on the United States comes from those who have, in fact, had the most exposure to the West.

Years ago, the majority of those who came to the West (the United States and Europe) to study were from wealthy elite families, in many cases Western and secular in their exposure and orientation. In the 1960s and 1970s, the numbers and profiles of students expanded when governments, as part of their development policies, created new schools at home, broadened educational opportunities, and subsidized study abroad. As a result, many from more traditional backgrounds were thrown into situations that precipitated a crisis of identity and a clash of cultures. If some continued to embrace the West, and Western culture in particular, others rejected the West and turned to their Islamic faith and identity. Muslim student organizations and associations sprang up on campuses; many students seeking to reinforce their own identities lived, prayed, and discussed religion and politics together. The result is a cadre of leadership that is well educated, Islamically oriented, and confident of its critical assessment of both government inadequacies and U.S./Western intentions. If some are anti-Western, others are rather critics who oppose dependence on or exploitation by the West but do not necessarily oppose learning from their relations with the West.

Policy Lessons

Islam has increasingly reemerged in Muslim political discourse and politics and has been effective in providing or reinforcing national identity and political legitimacy; it has also been a source of mass mobilization.[43] Governments and opposition movements have appealed to Islamic symbols and slogans. Islamist movements and organizations have proliferated across the Muslim world. However, the appeal to religion is a two-edged sword, as demonstrated by the experience of Saudi Arabia and Bahrain. It can provide or enhance self-legitimation, but it can also be used as a yardstick for judgment by opposition forces and delegitimation.

Regimes with rich resources can co-opt and contain opposition through their patronage, social welfare policies, and strong security. However, closed societies can also breed new forms of radicalism. Suppressing the free exchange of ideas and the airing of differences can contribute to the growth of a militant opposition and to extremism, driving opposition voices underground and to the margins of society.

Many rulers in the Gulf, like those in other parts of the Arab world, increasingly experience Islamists as their most effective opposition and thus regard them as a political challenge or direct threat to be controlled, co-opted, or crushed. Just as Jordan represents the former and Tunisia, Algeria, and (more recently) Egypt the latter, so too Kuwait and Yemen in the Gulf represent an attempt to contain and co-opt, versus Saudi Arabia and Bahrain's more aggressive approaches. Moreover, as the recent example of Egypt demonstrates, more governments are repressing Islamist movements because they represent an effective voice of dissent and opposition and thus a threat, regardless of whether evidence exists that they are violent extremists.[44] As the director of state security in central Egypt observed in an attempt to justify the Mubarak government's crackdown and arrests of 1,000 opposition activists at a time when Mubarak faced a democratic challenge from the Brotherhood in presidential elections, "At present, we admit, the Brotherhood are not engaged in violence. . . . Even though we have no concrete evidence for a court, I have to move. The security of the state is at risk."[45] As a result, the Mubarak government won more than 400 of 440 parliamentary seats.

In many Muslim countries, the distinction between radicals, violent revolutionaries, and moderates or pragmatists (nonviolent opposition who are willing to participate within the system) has become blurred; little or no distinction is made between a political challenge and a direct violent revolutionary threat. It is enough to denounce the opposition as "fundamentalist." The risk is that the "threat of fundamentalism" can become an easy excuse for the failures of governments and ruling elites.[46] As in North Africa or Palestine, Islamic organizations in the Gulf often identify, critique, address, and even exploit real problems and tensions. Failure to address these political, economic, and religiocultural problems will perpetuate the conditions that feed the growth of opposition, religious as well as liberal or secular.

Western governments with a high visibility, military presence, and track record of support for authoritarian and repressive regimes reinforce the image of an imperial West whose primary goal is the presence of its military in the Gulf and access to oil resources, actions that will foster dependence and undermine faith and culture. Muslim allies are seen as increasingly dependent on the West for military protection and for arms purchases that enable them to control their domestic opposition as much as defend themselves against external aggression. Thus, opponents charge that ruling families are compliant puppets of the West, more concerned with preserving power and wealth than with assuring the future of their countries and societies.

The Gulf states, like much of the Muslim world, will continue to experience the impact of political Islam and to contend with Islamic organizations at home and abroad. For most regimes, their relative wealth, size, established alliances, and security forces will continue to ensure stability in the short term. For many years, the ability of GCC states to use petrodollars to support Islamist organizations bought quiescence if not acquiescence. The Gulf War dramatically changed this situation. Saudi Arabia and Kuwait, in particular, have cut off support to erstwhile friends. At the same time, many Islamist movements have been freer with their criticisms of the "un-Islamic" character of monarchies, charging corruption and condemning the lavish and profligate lifestyles of royal families and elites, the weakness and vulnerability of states and their dependence on the West for protection and security, and their support of the Western-brokered Palestinian Peace Accords. The more states choke off the supply of funds, not only from government but also from the private sector, the greater the risk of Islamist opposition.

In contrast to many other states in the Arab world, Gulf rulers have tended to self-consciously use Islam as a source of self-legitimation. Whatever its advantages in the past, in a climate of greater religious awareness or awakening and more limited resources, GCC states today will increasingly be challenged to demonstrate their Islamic credentials, their ability to reinterpret (ijtihad) Islam in a manner that supports development and religious pluralism. In contrast to other areas of the Arab and Muslim world, given the demographics, pluralism in the Gulf will have more to do with Sunni-Shii than with Muslim-Christian relations. Although greater political liberalization will initially appear to be a threat to the traditional authority of established regimes, the strengthening of civil society will prove important to those who wish to lessen the threat of religious (or secular) extremism in a world in which political participation or democratization has increasingly become the litmus test for legitimacy. The alternative is the perpetuation of weak civil societies and a future in which governments and opposition, religious and secular populist movements alike, will resort to and perpetuate authoritarian rule, contributing to long-term instability.

Notes

1. I wish to express my gratitude to my research assistants, Natana J. DeLong-Bas, Elke Kaschl, and Hibba Abugideiri, as well as to the conference respondent, Dr. Khaldoun H. al-Naqeeb of Kuwait University.

2. "Constitution of the Islamic Republic of Iran," *Middle East Journal* 34 (1980): 185.

3. See James A. Bill, "Resurgent Islam in the Persian Gulf," *Foreign Affairs* 63 (Fall 1984): 108–127.

4. See Michael C. Hudson, "The Islamic Factor in Syrian and Iraqi Politics," in *Islam in the Political Process,* ed. James P. Piscatori (Cambridge: Cambridge University Press, 1983).

5. See John L. Esposito, ed., *The Iranian Revolution: Its Global Impact* (Gainesville: University of Florida Press, 1990).

6. Jacob Goldberg, "The Shii Minority in Saudi Arabia," in *Shiism and Social Protest,* ed. Juan R. I. Cole and Nikki R. Keddie (New Haven: Yale University Press, 1986), 243.

7. For a study of this incident within the broader context of Islam in Saudi Arabia's political development, see James P. Piscatori, "Ideological Politics in Saudi Arabia," in *Islam in the Political Process,* ed. Piscatori, chap. 4; Farouk A. Sankari, "Islam and Politics in Saudi Arabia," in *Islamic Resurgence in the Arab World,* ed. Ali E. Hillal Dessouki (New York: Praeger, 1982), 178–195; and William Ochsenwald, "Saudi Arabia and the Islamic Revival," *International Journal of Middle East Studies* 13 (1981): 271–286.

8. Shaul Bakhash, *The Reign of the Ayatollahs: Iran and the Islamic Revolution* (New York: Basic Books, 1984).

9. Dilip Hiro, *Iran Under the Ayatollahs* (London: Routledge and Kegan Paul, 1985), 340.

10. Ibid.

11. This analysis of the Gulf crisis draws on John L. Esposito, "Islam in a World of Shattered Dreams: Islam, Arab Politics and the Gulf Crisis," *The World and I* (February 1991).

12. "Islam Divided," *The Economist,* 22 September 1990, 47.

13. Abdurrahman Alamoudi in *Washington Report on Middle East Affairs* (October 1990): 69.

14. *New York Times,* 4 October 1990.

15. *Herald* (September 1990): 30.

16. "The Gulf Crisis," *Aliran* 10:8 (1990): 32.

17. For a study of the role of the ulama in Saudi politics, see Joseph Kechichian, "The Role of the Ulama in the Politics of an Islamic State," *International Journal of Middle East Studies* 18 (February 1986): 53–71.

18. Judith Caesar, "Rumblings Under the Throne: Saudi Arabian Politics," *The Nation* 251:21, 762.

19. Ibid.

20. *Issues* 1:11 (September 1992): 2–3.

21. *Issues* 1:4 (January 1992): 7.

22. *Issues* 2:10 (October 1993).

23. *Issues* 1:6–7 1, 12.

24. *Forecasts* 1:0 (June 1995): 1.

25. *Shanti Communication News Agency* 63 (19 September 1995).

26. Aziz Abu Hamid as quoted in Robin Wright, "Experts Ask: Did Saudi Crackdown Light Fuse of Bomb? Motives: Critics Complain of Repression. But Anti-American Feelings Have Played a Role," *Los Angeles Times,* 15 November 1995.

27. Ibid.

28. Edward Cody, "Saudi Islamic Radicals Target U.S., Royal Family," *Washington Post,* 16 August 1996.

29. Munira A. Fakhro, "The Uprising in Bahrain," *Future Prospects for the Gulf* (Bellagio, Italy, 25–27 July 1995), 8.

30. Ibid. Many other sources list the number of signatories as 25,000. See, for

example, May Seikaly, "Women and Religion in Bahrain: An Emerging Identity," in *Islam, Gender, and Social Change,* ed. Yvonne Y. Haddad and John L. Esposito (New York: Oxford University Press, 1997), 2; and Parvez Syed, "Amnesty International Condemns Widespread Human Rights Violations and Calls for Investigations," in *Shanti Communication News Agency,* 28 September 1995.

31. "Translation of the Petition Being Submitted in October 1994," [n.p.], 1.

32. Seikaly, 2.

33. Amnesty International Report as quoted in *Voice of Bahrain* 46 (October 1994): 4.

34. *Shanti News,* 29 October 1995.

35. *Bahrain: A Human Rights Crisis* (New York: Amnesty International, September 1995), 3.

36. *Women in the Middle East: Human Rights Under Attack* (New York: Amnesty International, 1995), 13.

37. *Bahrain,* issued by the Bahrain Freedom Movement for Advancing Democracy and Human Rights in Bahrain, no. 45 (September 1995): 1.

38. Fakhro, 14.

39. *EIU Country Report,* 2d quarter 1995 (London: The Economist Intelligence Unit, 1995).

40. Peter Waldman, *Wall Street Journal,* 2 June 1995, as cited in Fakhro, 10.

41. "Arabia's Slow Pressure Cooker," *The Economist* (1992).

42. Nasser Sani, "The Kuwaiti Power-Sharing Experience," in *Power-Sharing Islam* (London: Grey Seal, 1993), 1–3.

43. See John O. Voll, *Islam: Continuity and Change in the Modern World,* 2d ed. (Syracuse: Syracuse University Press, 1994), chaps. 6–7; John L. Esposito, *Islam and Politics,* 3d ed. (Syracuse: Syracuse University Press, 1991); Nazih N. Ayoubi, *Political Islam: Religion and Politics in the Arab World* (London: Routledge, 1991).

44. Peter Waldman, "Unrest on the Nile: As Egypt Suppresses Muslim Brotherhood, Some Fear Backlash," *Wall Street Journal,* 8 December 1995.

45. Ibid.

46. John L. Esposito, *The Islamic Threat: Myth or Reality?* rev. ed. (New York: Oxford University Press, 1995), chaps. 5–6.

Part 2

Islam in the Political Process

4

Political Participation in Revolutionary Iran

Mohsen M. Milani

Is Islam compatible with political pluralism? This is one of the main questions addressed in the growing literature on Islam. Iran's experience in the past seventeen years can provide us with some tentative answers to this intriguing question. After all, Iran was the first country in the Islamic world to experience a popular revolution and the first in the modern age to establish an Islamic republic based on the direct rule of the ulama (clerics).

Twentieth-century Iran will be remembered for its restlessness and its many popular political movements—the Constitutional Movement of 1906–1911, the nationalist movement of the early 1950s, the Islamic revolution of 1979—that aimed, among other goals, to create a participatory political system where people could determine their own destiny.

Of those upheavals, the revolution in 1979 was by far the most consequential and the most popular. The level of political participation was astonishingly high during the revolutionary movement, which began in 1977 and ended when Mohammad Reza Shah Pahlavi was exiled in January 1979. People participated in demonstrations, public prayers, and poetry reading sessions. They formed political parties, published newspapers, occasionally resorted to violence, and staged paralyzing strikes. This was one of those rare moments when an entire nation felt it had taken charge of its own destiny.

But as the revolutionary fever subsided and the new Islamic system took root, old allies within the anti-shah coalition became new enemies, and the level of political participation fell substantially. Why was there so much political participation in the early days of the revolution and why did it fall off? How did the Islamic constitution of 1979 address the question of "popular sovereignty," or allowing people to determine their own destiny?

Mohsen M. Milani

What is the current level of political participation in Islamic Iran and how does it compare with that of the prerevolutionary days?

The central thesis of this chapter can be summarized as follows: Although political participation by the opponents of the Islamic Republic has been banned for the past fifteen years, a higher percentage of the population has been politically active in Islamic Iran than under the rule of Mohammad Reza Shah (1941–1979). The Islamic revolution has incorporated a relatively large segment of the population into the political process and has succeeded in institutionalizing its popular base of support. This phenomenon explains the Islamic Republic's remarkable resiliency to pressures from within and without.

Two main factors contribute to this high level of political participation: the Islamic constitution's embracing of "limited popular sovereignty" and the ongoing factional rivalry. Together these two factors are helping to develop a primitive pluralism among the governing elites. (I am not suggesting or implying that Iran is a pluralistic society.) Consequently, elections for the Majles and the presidency have not been interrupted during the past seventeen years, and the governing elites have had more room to maneuver, express their views, and build institutions than the elites of prerevolutionary Iran ever had.

Political Participation Defined

Political participation can be defined as "any activity by the private citizens designed to influence governmental decisionmaking."[1] It encompasses such activities as voting, lobbying, violence, riots, uprising, and revolution. In applying this definition, two caveats are in order. First, I refer here to "private citizens" as those who do not occupy any decisionmaking positions in the Iranian state. Second, I focus only on political participation that is "tolerable" to the leaders of the Islamic Republic. This is not to suggest that oppositional political activities do not exist in Iran or that they are unimportant. We have seen a number of such activities in the past few years, including the 1995 uprising in Qazvin, when the Majles refused to grant that city a province status, and the 1995 bombing of Imam Reza's shrine in Meshhad, which killed more than twenty people. Such events deserve study. Here, however, I concentrate on political participation that the government finds tolerable, because it reveals much about the nature of the new Islamic system and allows us to evaluate whether the Islamic Republic has expanded or contracted the scope of tolerable political participation that existed under the ancien régime. In such an evaluation, history is our best guide. And it is with history that our journey begins.

Patterns of Political
Participation in Prerevolutionary Iran

In Iran, the movement to expand the popular base of political participation has been slow; it all started more than a century ago. For much of the nine-teenth century, Iran's political system was corrupt, autocratic, and depen-dent on Russia and England. The Qajar shahs enjoyed unlimited power, refusing to recognize the distinction between the public and private domains: what they owned was theirs and what the state owned was also theirs. Politics was the exclusive business of the venal Qajars and their sub-ordinates.

The first crack in the Qajar's absolutism appeared in 1893 when Naser al-Din Shah was forced to cancel a lucrative tobacco concession he had granted to a British company. The fatwa by a marjae-taqlid (source of emu-lation), Haj Hassan Shirazi, against the use of tobacco gave legitimacy to the protest movement against the concession. The fatwa was so effective that even those close to the shah refused to indulge in smoking tobacco. But the popular base of the protest movement was confined to those adversely affected by the concession and to a few of the ulama.

Because that movement could not force the Qajars to change their modus operandi, Iran was plunged deeper into foreign debts, corruption, and arbitrary rule. Amid this sad state of affairs, the Constitutional Movement (1906–1911) flourished. It was a popular movement based on an alliance among the secular reformers, the merchants and asnaf (guilds), and a large segment of the ulama.

At the turn of the twentieth century Iran was slowly entering the age of mass politics. The Qajars were losing their monopoly over national politi-cal power as new groups entered the political arena. As political participa-tion increased, new newspapers appeared, secret and open associations were formed, the ulama mobilized the people from the pulpit, and the mass-es took sanctuary (bast) at the holy shrines to express their grievances. The first consultative body, the Majles, was formed and produced the country's first written constitution. Elections for the Majles were held, political par-ties were formed, and parliamentary factions debated critical issues.

Iran's entry into the age of mass politics, however, revealed the uneasy tension between Islam and popular sovereignty. The Persian constitution of 1906 came close to embracing "popular sovereignty" by admitting that "the powers of the realm are derived from the people" (Article 26). But it also proposed forming an "ecclesiastical committee," consisting of five ulama, with veto power over all Majles legislation deemed contrary to Islam. It guaranteed freedoms of assembly and press if they were not inimical to Islam.

This tension, however, was pushed to the sidelines; after 1911, the

Constitutional Movement suffered fatal blows, and by 1926, the new Pahlavi dynasty ascended to power. Reza Shah, the founder of the dynasty, was a ruthless nationalist who wanted to modernize Iran. During his brief rule (1926–1941), he laid the foundations of a modern economy and state. But Reza Shah blatantly violated the constitution, turned the Majles into a submissive body, and, unlike Ataturk in Turkey, failed to institutionalize what mass support he enjoyed by creating political parties. Nor did he allow others to form parties. In short, much was done for the people, but not by the people or in consultation with them.

With the forced abdication of Reza Shah in 1941, Mohammad Reza ascended to the throne. From 1941 until 1953, when the shah's power was at its nadir, the level of political participation reached a new zenith. New ideological parties were formed, recruiting people from all social classes. Activists published new newspapers, professionals and students formed associations, labor organizers revitalized their unions, and political debate became fashionable and free.

Iran was now truly in the midst of mass politics, and no one used it more effectively than Mohammad Mossadeq to enhance his popular political agenda. Relying mostly on middle-class support, the prime minister combined nationalism and mass politics to nationalize the British-controlled Iranian oil industry. Although he and his cohorts constituted a very small faction in the Majles, they relied on public pressure, mass demonstrations by their supporters, and an alliance with several leading ulama to pressure the landlord-dominated Majles to approve their innovative nationalization plan. Mossadeq's strategy worked, but only briefly. In 1953, he was overthrown by a CIA/MI6 operation, and Mohammad Reza Shah was returned to power. From that moment, the shah began to rule autocratically.

Mohammad Reza Shah was obsessed with modernization. He wished to be the king of a modern country, but he was determined to rule using a medieval system of governance. This is why he modernized the economy but failed to do the same for the political realm. That failure caused his downfall.

During his autocratic rule, the level of political participation was unusually low, and most people became politically passive and apathetic. The shah tried to create political parties. In 1958, he created a two-party system; in 1964, he dissolved them and created the Iran Novin Party. Finally, in 1975, he created the Rastakhiz Party and arrogantly ordered everyone to join or leave the country. Totally subservient to the monarch, and lacking any integrity, those parties failed to attract any significant portion of the population.

The shah also repressed all independent sources of power. He banned any political party that was not totally supportive of him and turned the Majles into a submissive body to approve and applaud his policies. Campaigns for the Majles became a farce: the shah chose the deputies before elections. Important questions about domestic or foreign affairs, such as the purchase of expensive military hardware, were never debated among the Majles deputies, nor were they discussed by the state-controlled media. Professional and student associations were either dissolved or brought under state control. Censorship was imposed with impressive efficiency. The shah made all important decisions, while millions of Iranians from all walks of life aspired to participate in the political process. The Islamic revolution was the manifestation of the desire of those deprived segments of the population to participate in politics and build a new society.

Islamic Innovations in Political Participation

During the last two years of the shah's rule, the general perception was that the monarch's power was somewhat diminishing because he was no longer receiving unconditional support from Washington. The shah's innate indecisiveness contributed to this perception, which precipitated the revolutionary movement. That period saw the highest level of political participation Iran has ever experienced. Because no one group could single-handedly overthrow the shah, sheer expediency led many groups to ally against him, creating a multiclass movement.

Political participation took many forms. Most were traditional: circulating protest letters to the shah, attending poetry sessions and demonstrations, and forming parties and professional associations. But the Islamists also used innovative methods to mobilize the masses, the most important of which was the manipulation of Shii symbols and rituals. Five such methods deserve mention here. First, the Shii tradition of commemorating the fortieth day after someone's death became more politically and emotionally charged as more and more protestors were killed in the anti-shah demonstrations. Second, public prayers mobilized people and demonstrated their unity of action. The first such public prayer session, held in mid-1987, was attended by thousands of people. Third, during the religious processions in the month of Moharram, the faithful commemorate the martyrdom of Imam Hossein through weeping and self-flagellation. In December 1978, the revolutionaries used those processions as a "walking referendum" to demand the end of the shah's rule. Fourth, when the military government of General Azhari banned assembly after dusk, the Islamic leaders urged the masses to go to their rooftops at exactly the same time and chant "Allah is great." This peaceful show of unity by millions of people demoralized the military. Finally, the ulama used cassette tapes of Khomeini's speeches to spread their gospel, effectively using modern equipment to spread a traditional religion. The protest movement was so effective that it took less than a year to overthrow Pahlavi's well-armed regime.[2]

Limited Popular Sovereignty in the Islamic Constitution

The Islamic constitution, drafted by seventy-three elected members of the ulama-dominated Assembly of Experts, was approved in a national plebescite in 1979, which was boycotted by many nationalist and leftist parties. Khomeini praised it as the "greatest accomplishment" of the revolution and a guarantee that the new order would forever remain Islamic.

In writing the constitution, the framers were pushed by two forces. First, they were determined to create an Islamic system in which the ulama enjoyed a dominant and secure position. They achieved this. Symbolic of this new power is the institution of the velayat-e faqih, the highest source of authority in Islamic Iran, whose unelected occupant enjoys extraordinary power, certainly more than the shah was granted in the 1906 constitution. Second, the framers faced mounting pressure to design a republic based on popular sovereignty. This was, after all, the raison d'être of the revolution. In the end, they created a system that is more Islamic than republican.

To create a system that is simultaneously Islamic and republican required some creative borrowing from the West and some modifying of the notion of popular sovereignty. After all, the Shii political theory of governance was not sufficiently developed to offer solutions to modern problems of governance. Hojatolislam Ali Akbar Hashemi Rafsanjani was quite candid about this shortcoming: "Where in Islamic history do you find parliaments, presidents, prime ministers? In fact, eighty percent of what we now have has no precedent in Islamic history."[3]

The framers also disfigured "popular sovereignty" by transforming it into what I call "limited popular sovereignty." It is based on five factors. First, the constitution states that "absolute sovereignty over the world belongs to God, and it is He who has placed man in charge of his social dignity." Second, in the constitution, power, the very essence of popular sovereignty, emanates from God, the faqih, the fuqaha (plural of faqih), and the people, in that order. Third, articles 6 through 8 stipulate that "the affairs of the country must be administered on the basis of public opinion expressed by means of elections or referenda" and grant the people the right to elect the president and the Majles deputies. At the same time, the unelected faqih and the Guardian Council are empowered to reject the credentials of any presidential and Majles candidates. Moreover, the Guardian Council enjoys veto power over all Majles legislation. Fourth, the power of the president, the only nationally elected figure of the Islamic Republic, is limited because the faqih is the commander of armed forces and can actually remove the president. Finally, while the constitution grants various freedoms, including those of the press and assembly, it also limits them if they are deemed inimical to Islam and to the republic.

The framers of the Islamic constitution were certainly not shy about admitting that popular sovereignty is not the foundation of the Islamic

Republic. Ayatollah Mohammad Hosseini Beheshti, architect and writer of the velayat-e faqih provision of the constitution, maintained that people's freedoms are limited by God's laws: a priori, sovereignty must be limited. Conceding that Islam is incompatible with popular sovereignty, he argued that once the people freely embraced Islam in April 1979, when they voted in a referendum to create the Islamic Republic, they must live within the boundaries of Islam interpreted by the ulama.[4]

The notion of limited popular sovereignty is, in fact, harmonious with the Shii hermeneutics and temperament. In Shiism, the truth is independent of the perception or the belief of the masses. This is why only the best of the ulama can surmise the Quran's batan (secret meaning), while the masses can digest the Quran's zaher (apparent meaning), and the faithful have to emulate a living ayatollah. There is an implicit assumption that the people cannot always distinguish good from evil. Mohammad Keyavosh, a deputy of the Assembly of Experts, echoed that view: "There are those who can easily deceive the people and dominate their lives and properties." He therefore justified strong intervention by the faqih and the Guardian Council in examining the credentials of candidates.[5] A host of Western thinkers, from Plato to Machiavelli, were generally pessimistic about the gullibility of the masses, as were many framers of the U.S. Constitution.

Patterns and Phases of Political Participation in Islamic Iran: Khomeini, Master of Mass Politics

There have been two distinct phases of political participation in revolutionary Iran. In the first phase, covering the first two years of the Islamic revolution, the level of political participation was the highest Iranians had ever seen. People formed hundreds of political parties and professional associations and published hundreds of new newspapers. They felt free. What permitted such participation was the intense struggle among competing groups for the ultimate control of the state. Khomeini emerged victorious from that struggle because he was the master of mass politics and institutionalized his popular support. In the second phase, covering the past fifteen years, all opponents of the Islamic Republic have been banned from political activity, and organizational political activity has been confined to those who do not question the legitimacy of the Islamic Republic and to factional rivalry among the governing elites.

The first two years of the Islamic revolution was the golden age of Iran's mass politics. No one understood better than Khomeini how to manipulate Iran's mass politics, whose fate was determined not in the corridors of governmental agencies but in the streets and by the crowds.[6] He who controlled the streets and the crowds was he who ruled. And it was Khomeini who controlled the streets. It was he who politicized millions of the "barefooted." It was he who, in the blink of an eye, could mobilize millions. Mossadeq, as I argued earlier, quite effectively used the crowds to enhance his agenda, but he was no Khomeini.

And it was Khomeini who institutionalized the very forces that make mass politics so powerful. He gradually incorporated all his supporters into a ministate he created, one that the regular state could neither control nor contain. This ministate had five pillars. The first was the Islamic Republican Party, Iran's largest political party, from whose ranks Khomeini appointed his "eyes and ears." The second pillar was the komites (committees), which sprang up everywhere, acting as a vigilante police. Third, the revolutionary courts imposed an Islamic system of justice. Fourth, the Revolutionary Guards, a militia of dedicated zealots, could neutralize any anti-Khomeini coup by the regular army. The last pillar was the Mostazefin Foundation, which inherited the massive fortunes of the Pahlavi Foundation.

Khomeini was the leader of this ministate; the lower classes were its soldiers, the Islamic Republican Party its brain, the komites its local police, the Pasdaran its army, the Revolutionary Courts its judiciary, and the Mostazefan Foundation its source of revenue. If revolutions are the explosion of political participation, then this ministate was the symbol of that explosion.

As if that ministate had not incorporated enough people into the political process, the war with Iraq allowed the pro-Khomeini forces to mobilize an ever larger portion of the urban and, especially, rural population. The war's impact on political participation was mixed. On the pretext of a war emergency, the government increased its repression of dissidents and imposed censorship laws. At the same time, the politicization of the lower classes was expanded to the rural areas as millions of young people were recruited for the war. Moreover, the war solidified the organic link between the ulama and the lower classes because the ulama administered the Basij (mobilization) organization, responsible for recruiting war volunteers.

While he encouraged his supporters to become "ever more present in the political scene," Khomeini used his ministate to crush his opponents and reduce political participation. Many of his opponents tried hard and sometimes violently to destroy him, but they were destroyed by Khomeini.

Medhi Bazargan's provisional government was the first victim of the ministate. Bazargan, appointed by Khomeini, was the first prime minister of Islamic Iran and founder of Iran's Freedom Movement. His was a good government for a wrong time, proposing reforms when the country was demanding revolution. Bazargan's powerlessness became embarrassingly visible when the militants who had stormed the U.S. Embassy ignored his demand to release the hostages. After he resigned, his Freedom Movement was reluctantly tolerated for a while. In the past decade, it has been banned from political activity.

Abolhassan Bani Sadr was next in line. The first elected president, with no party of his own, he aspired to be an imperial president. He tried to curtail the centrifugal forces of the revolutionary institutions when Khomeini was in fact controlling those very institutions. And he became entangled in a deadly war against the Islamic Republican Party without having the necessary resources to fight it. In that war, he formed an alliance with the armed Mojahedin-e Khaleq, an Islamic-socialist organization that enjoyed substantial support among the youth. After Bani Sadr was forcefully removed from office, two powerful bombs killed more than 100 people, including many top officials of the Islamic Republic. Blaming the Mojahedin and Bani Sadr for those and other acts of terrorism, the Islamic Republic responded violently by arresting and killing hundreds of the Mojahedin. In 1982, the Mojahedin hideout was discovered and their top leaders killed. Since that moment, the Mojahedin have conducted their activities outside of Iran. Today, their headquarters are in Iraq. Bani Sadr, no longer collaborating with the Mojahedin, resides in Paris.

The National Front, which enjoyed much support among the modern middle class, was easily defeated. A coalition partner in Bazargan's government, the National Front lost much of its power when he resigned. After halfheartedly supporting Bani Sadr, the National Front was barred from political activities in 1981.

The last serious hurdle in Khomeini's drive to control the state was Ayatollah Seyyed Kazem Shariatmadari. With impeccable religious credentials, he was the spiritual leader of the Moslem's People's Republican Party, which enjoyed substantial support among the Turks. Having issued a fatwa against the velayat-e faqih provision of the constitution, Shariatmadari was virtually placed under house arrest until his death in 1986. His party, accused of ties with the CIA, was banned from political activity in 1981.

Leftist parties were eliminated one by one. None of them enjoyed a large popular base of support, and all of them opposed in one form or another the Islamic Republic. The pro-Moscow Tudeh was the most powerful such party. Because it supported Khomeini, divided the left, attacked Bazargan and then Bani Sadr, and was used to improve relations with the Soviet Union, the Tudeh was tolerated until 1983 but then declared illegal. In fact, the Tudeh was the last non-Islamic party to be banned. The other leftist groups were all destroyed by 1982.

Thus, by 1983, all political parties, except the Islamic Republican Party, were banned from political activity. At the same time, a significant portion of the population had been integrated into the ministate and into the private foundations the pro-Khomeini forces had created. Political participation has now taken the form of involvement in factional politics.

Factionalism and Political Participation

There are genuine differences between the politics of imperial and Islamic Iran. Chief among them is the rivalry among factions in revolutionary Iran. It is because of factionalism that some primitive kind of pluralism among the governing elites is developing in Islamic Iran. It is also because of this factionalism that other trends are developing. Political institutions have acquired a degree of integrity and autonomy they never enjoyed under the shah's autocratic rule. Elections have become more important and established in Islamic Iran than they were in imperial Iran. The supporters of the Islamic Republic enjoy more freedom to debate important issues than the shah's supporters had under the monarchy. Powerful private foundations have grown within the civil society. And there are even some rumblings today about the need to create a multiparty system.

The emergence of factions in Islamic Iran was inevitable.[7] Shiism has traditionally been a polycephalic faith. The Shii ulama have always offered different interpretations of Islam, and the faithful have freely chosen their favorite clerics. Unlike Roman Catholicism, where we can speak of a church and a well-defined hierarchy of power, Shiism has neither a church nor an accepted hierarchy of power. Interestingly, the original Islamic constitution attempted to create a hierarchy of political and religious powers by insisting that the faqih was the country's highest religious and political authority. This is why the constitution stipulated that the faqih must not only be accepted by the majority of the people but must also be a marjae-taqlid. But this goal has not been achieved; even in the heyday of Khomeini's popularity, other grand ayatollahs, like Seyyed Kazem Shariatmadari and Mohammad Reza Golypayegani, enjoyed considerable mass followings of their own. Nor did the revision of the constitution after Khomeini's death in 1989 ameliorate the situation. Today the faqih no longer has to be accepted by the majority of people, nor is he required to be a marjae-taqlid. Because of this revision, in 1989, the Assembly of Experts could select as the new faqih Seyyed Ali Khamenei, who at the time was a hojatolislam, a rank lower than an ayatollah. Ayatollah Khamenei has publicly declared that he was not seeking religious leadership in Iran. This fact is testimony to the Islamic Republic's failure to render Shiism monolithic, as there are many people who follow not Khamenei but other ayatollahs in Iran and in Iraq. Therefore, factions and Shiism are inseparable, two sides of the same coin.

Factions were originally formed within the Islamic Republican Party. Three distinct factions have survived: the conservatives, the hard-liners, and the pragmatists. The conservatives, supported by the rich barzaaires, have championed the free enterprise system, opposed state ownership of the major industries, advocated for strict implementation of Islamic laws—especially those related to women and morality—and supported a cautious rapprochement with the West. The hard-liners, supported by the poor and the lower classes, have stressed the egalitarian aspects of Islam, as well as self-sufficiency, state ownership of major industries, export of the Islamic revolution, closer ties with the Islamic world, and no rapprochement with the United States. They are the champions of an Islamic "welfare state." Finally, the pragmatists have oscillated between the other two factions. Politically and socially more tolerant than the other factions, they drew their support from the middle class and the technocrats. Maintaining that feq (jurisprudence) is dynamic, they allow more latitude for innovative interpretations of Islam.

While Ayatollah Khomeini was alive, he kept those factions competitive, never allowing one to dominate or eliminate the other and always acting as the final arbiter of the factional feuds. Despite Khomeini's even-handed approach, differences among factions and their inability to achieve consensus reached such a critical level that, in 1987, Khomeini dissolved the Islamic Republican Party.

When factional rivalry operates in a system with multiple centers of power, institutional chaos is the inevitable result. This is exactly what Iran experienced during much of the 1980s. The Islamic Republic was explicitly designed so that no one branch of the government could dominate the others. It was built on institutional mistrust: making sure that the left hand never knew where the right hand was. This mistrust manifested itself in the lingering feud among the Majles, the executive branch, and the Guardian Council, leading to genuine gridlock. From 1982 to 1988, for example, the hard-line government of Mir Hossein Mussavi, and to a lesser extent the Majles, was frustrated with the many vetoes of the Guardian Council, which was packed with conservatives. The most notable example was the Guardian Council's rejection of the bill to nationalize foreign trade. To end this gridlock, Khomeini formed the Council for the Resolution of Differences in 1988. Empowered to have the final word about institutional disputes, it has somewhat improved the situation.

It is not only in the corridors of the Majles and the government agencies that factions compete to influence governmental policy. Factions have created and now control the private foundations; from there, they influence Iranian politics. Precious little is known about them. About a half dozen are quite influential, including the Mostazefan Foundation, the Fifteenth of Khordad Foundation, and the Martyrs Foundation. They are neither controlled by the government nor accountable to it. The office of the velayat-e faqih exercises some degree of control over them, although the extent of that control is not fully known.

The foundations perform a variety of functions, including supporting Islamic movements in other countries and organizing philanthropic activities inside and outside Iran. The Martyrs Foundation, for example, was created in 1980 to provide relief and support for the families of those who died in the revolutionary movement. As more and more men died in the Iran-Iraq war, the Martyrs Foundation grew in size and influence. Today it controls, among other things, the nation's largest medical facilities. The Mostazefan Foundation, whose assets are estimated in the billions, provides social services to the poor and needy.[8] It controls hundreds of factories, buildings, and companies in Iran and has substantial holdings in the West and in the Gulf.

The foundations have created an elaborate system that incorporates the lower classes into the political process. In addition to employing thousands of people, they provide all kinds of social services. The foundations have thus built a bridge with the needy and created a large and dependent constituency that they can quickly mobilize for such purposes as demonstrations and voting. Most foundations have their own publications, and a few of the more powerful ones control some dailies and magazines.

The foundations also influence both domestic and foreign policies of the government. Domestically the Martyrs Foundation has lobbied the government and the Majles to continue government subsidies and to increase government support for the families of the martyrs of the Iran-Iraq war. In 1990, the Fifteenth of Khordad Foundation, controlled by the hard-liners, influenced foreign policy. The government was negotiating with the Europeans to find "an honorable solution" to Ayatollah Khomeini's controversial fatwa, which sanctioned the killing of Salman Rushdie, the author of the *Satanic Verses*. At that sensitive time, the foundation announced a $2 million reward for anyone who would successfully execute the fatwa. For all practical purposes, the announcement, which received worldwide attention, derailed the negotiations. Recently, when some progress had been made toward resolving this nagging conflict, the foundation reminded everyone that the interest on the $2 million reward would be added to the original reward!

Factions and Political Discourse

Iran is not a static and closed society, as it is often portrayed in the mass media. Iran is a dynamic country, and there are both positive and disturbing trends developing within it.

The competition among the factions has given them more room to maneuver and express their views than the governing elites of prerevolutionary Iran ever had. In few Middle Eastern countries do the governing elites enjoy such space for political expression. This room for maneuverability has been visible in the Majles, in the mass media, and in the ongoing political discourse.

In revolutionary Iran, the faction that controls the Majles can exert a profound impact on politics. Since 1979, different factions have controlled the Majles. In the last Majles (1994–1996), for example, the conservatives constituted the majority. The orientation of the Fifth Majles (1996–1998) has yet to be decided because there are many "independents" among the new deputies.

With the exception of the Israeli Knesset and the Turkish parliament, Iran's Majles is arguably the most independent parliament in the Middle East and North Africa. The deputies engage in lively discussion about a host of substantive issues, from the impact of the Internet on politics to nationalizing the major industries. They also question and harshly criticize governmental policy and reject the credentials of government ministers. In 1993, after President Rafsanjani's reelection, the Majles rejected the credentials of his choice for the Ministry of Finance and Economy, Mohsen Nurbakhsh, a U.S.-trained economist. With the exception of the question of the velayat-e faqih, no other issue, including direct talks with the U.S. or governmental corruption, is off limits to the deputies. More important, the Majles has the final say on who gets what and how much, which is, after all, what politics is all about: it approves the government-submitted national budget but makes many changes. The Iranian Majles, in short, is no longer the rubber stamp it had become under the shah.[9]

The record of political discourse in revolutionary Iran has been a mixed one. There is censorship. In 1994, Ali Akbar Saedi Sirjani, a prominent and prolific writer with a unique knack for satire, died under mysterious circumstances while imprisoned by the government. Some of his books were banned. In 1995, a bookstore was set ablaze by the Ansar-e Hizbollah for selling a brief novel by an obscure young writer. The Hizbollah justified its action because the book was "derogatory" toward Islam. The public reaction to the bookstore burning was quite interesting. While the government explicitly condemned this act of "lawlessness," some newspapers and one ayatollah praised the Hizbollah for having drawn the red line beyond which freedom of the press was not to be tolerated. The pro-Hizbollah forces strongly condemned the minister of Islamic guidance for failing to censor the book.

But the existing censorship is far from the total censorship that existed under the Pahlavis.[10] Last year, a book entitled *Ma Che Qoun-e Ma Showdim?* (How Did We Become We?) became a best seller. Saddeq Ziba Khalam, a young U.S.-educated professor of political science at the University of Tehran, argues in this book that the main cause of Iran's underdevelopment is to be found in its domestic conditions. As long as Iranians blame imperialism and colonialism for their problems, he writes, they will not solve their problems. While this idea is hardly mind-shattering, the mere fact it could be discussed in a book published in a country obsessed with "anti-imperialism" is, indeed, interesting.

Or consider the case of Abdolkarim Soroush, the pen name for Hossein Dabbagh, a brilliant writer and thinker, well versed in Islamic his-

tory, the Quran, and Persian poetry.[11] In the early days of the revolution, he
was a member of the Committee of the Cultural Revolution, which purged
hundreds of educators. In the past few years, however, he has published
many books and articles implicitly but unmistakably questioning the very
foundation of the Islamic Republic. In his voluminous writings, Soroush
has raised important questions about the nature of Islam, its relations with
democracy, and other sensitive issues. His ideas are discussed by others;
here, however, I must emphasize two points. First, Soroush argues that
while Islam is based upon unchangeable principles, our interpretations of
those principles can and must change from time to time. Therefore, no one
can claim a monopoly over the "true" Islam. Thus, he has explicitly challenged the claim by the ulama that they are in fact the guardians of the
faith. To do so in a country run by the ayatollahs is something to ponder.
Second, Soroush advocates opening up the political process, maintaining
that a true religious state is based on democracy. He insists that Islam cannot and should not become an ideology serving the interest of a governing
elite. Again, his proposition implicitly rejects the very notion of the
velayat-e faqih, which is the foundation of the political system in Iran.

   Despite such criticisms of the very essence of the Islamic Republic,
Soroush was tolerated for a while—but not without being harassed. In Iran,
many of his lectures were interrupted by the Hizbollah, who accused him of
undermining the Islamic Republic and Islam. While some newspapers, like
Sobh, have staged an all-out propaganda war against Soroush, other magazines, like *Iran-e Farda* and *Keyan,* have been supportive of him.

   As late as June 1996, *Keyan* published one of Soroush's articles. That
Keyan could still do so is testimony to the existence of a space, albeit a
very small one, for the expression of views in Iran. True, the government
has used a paper shortage crisis as an effective way to limit the publication
of "unfriendly" newspapers. It is also true that government licenses to publish newspapers and magazines are not granted to the unfriendly elements.
But still, more than 400 newspapers and magazines are published in Iran
today, including more than six major dailies in Tehran alone. Some of them
openly criticize governmental policies and expose corruption. Others write
about secularism and religious pluralism. Of course, denigration of Islam,
the ulama, and the velayat-e faqih are not permitted and violators are
severely punished.

   In elections too we observe the same mixed signals. While elections
have been relatively free in Islamic Iran, the nominating process has been
quite restricted. The Guardian Council plays an important but indirect role
in the outcomes of elections. It consists of twelve men, six of them qualified ulama who are appointed by the faqih, and six lawyers nominated by
the supreme head of the judiciary and approved by the Majles. The
Guardian Council reviews the credentials of all candidates for the Majles
and president. It is in this process of screening and approving candidates
that the unelected members of this powerful organ influence Iranian poli-

tics. The elections for the Fourth Majles in 1992 illustrated the power of this council and its connection to factionalism.

More than 3,200 candidates filed applications with the Guardian Council for candidacy in the Majles in 1991. Many people argued that the Guardian Council should evaluate not only the professional but the ideological fitness of all candidates. The hard-liners, those critical of Rafsanjani's reform programs, were clearly the target of this campaign. After the screening, more than 1,000 candidates, or about 35 percent, were disqualified, many of them well-known hard-liners like Ayatollah Saddeq Khalkhali. The Guardian Council also disqualified many candidates for the fourth presidential election in 1994.

Once the screening procedures are completed, however, the candidates are relatively free to campaign as they wish. Despite occasional reports of gerrymandering and election fraud, the elections have been relatively free.

When campaigning, the candidates for the Majles and the presidency engage in lively and substantive discussions. Candidates receive endorsements from such powerful groups as the Combatant Ulama of Tehran, the Struggling Ulama, the United Societies of the Islamic Organizations, and the mujahidin of the Islamic Revolution. Candidates distribute position papers and receive endorsements from hundreds of professional and Islamic candidates. The more prosperous candidates occasionally use billboards to attract voters.

Whatever we say about elections in Iran, we cannot deny that to survive and remain legitimate, the government has had to become more concerned about public opinion. Elections are, after all, the best measure of public opinion.

Conclusion

According to the majority of the framers of the Islamic constitution in 1979, Islam and absolute popular sovereignty are incompatible. They believed that people are free to determine their own destiny provided they do not violate Islamic laws; hence my suggestion that the Islamic constitution is based on limited popular sovereignty. The experience of the Islamic Republic of Iran in the past seventeen years seems to confirm this proposition. It also refutes the suggestion that Islam is essentially "totalitarian." We should not, however, generalize about the Iranian experience, for there are many different interpretations of Islam's approach to popular sovereignty.

Until the Islamic revolution, there was a well-established pattern in Iran's popular political movements: the level of political participation increased during the heyday of such movements, which often flourished when the authority of the central government was weak or was perceived as weak, and it fell drastically as soon as the central government reimposed its despotic rule.[12] Although the level of political participation among the population has not been high in postrevolutionary Iran, it is still higher than what it was under the Pahlavi rule. More significantly, some kind of crude pluralism among the governing elites is developing in Islamic Iran. The three existing factions have demonstrated time and again that they can quickly unify to fight a common enemy. These factions, better than any other groups, know and defend their corporate interests. This elite pluralism has allowed limited political participation for those who do not question the legitimacy of the Islamic Republic. But this fragile elite pluralism is not based on a solid foundation and could disintegrate if the intrafactional rivalry becomes more intense and bloody.

As a result of the factional rivalry, Iran has had uninterrupted elections for the Majles and president for the past seventeen years. While the elections have been relatively free in Islamic Iran, the nominating process has been restricted. It must be kept in mind, however, that Iran does not live in a very "democratic neighborhood" and that its record of elections is not as awful as those of all its neighbors and virtually every other Middle Eastern country, except Israel and Turkey. The very suggestion of having elections, even the most tightly controlled, is not tolerated in most Middle Eastern countries run by emirs and kings. In those countries that have elections, presidents are sometimes elected for life, as in Iraq; and, more often, presidents win elections with more than 99 percent of the vote and face no opponents, as in Egypt. At least in Iran, after all the screening by the Guardian Council, Rafsanjani faced three opponents in the 1992 presidential election and he only received a little more than 63 percent of the vote.

The crude form of elite pluralism has also opened a space to express political views. This opening, small as it is, must not be quickly disregarded, but protected. It can be used, among other things, to slowly pressure the governing elites to open up the political process to those critical of the present regime.

The political history of Iran in this turbulent century shows that the drive to open up the political process and establish popular sovereignty can be derailed temporarily but cannot be suppressed indefinitely. The ultimate task confronting the Islamic Republic is to open up the system to the people who are not part of the existing factions without destroying the system in the process. This, I confess, is a daunting task. But who said it was easy to govern a complicated society like Iran's?

Notes

1. Samuel Huntington and Joan Nelson, *No Easy Choice: Political Participation in the Developing World* (Cambridge: Harvard University Press, 1976), 4.

2. For details, see Mohsen Milani, *The Making of Iran's Islamic Revolution,* 2d ed. (Boulder: Westview Press, 1994).

3. Cited by S. Bakhash, "Islam and Social Justice in Iran," in *Shiism, Resistance, and Revolution,* ed. Martin Kramer (Boulder: Westview Press, 1987), 113.

4. I have explained these problems in Mohsen Milani, "The Evolution of the Iranian Theocracy," *Iranian Studies* 26: 3–4 (Summer/Fall 1994): 359–374.

5. *Surat-e Mashruh-e Mozakerat-e Majles-e Barresi-ye Nahaie-ye Qanun-e Asassi-ye Johmhuri-ye Islami-ye Iran* [The Detailed Deliberations of the Proceedings of the Council on the Final Review of the Constitution of the Islamic Republic of Iran] 2 (Tehran, 1986): 1195.

6. Richard Cottam argues that U.S. policymakers have yet to understand the significance of Iran's mass politics. See his excellent book *Iran and the United States* (Pittsburgh: University of Pittsburgh Press, 1990).

7. On factionalism, see S. Akhavi, "Elite Factionalism in the Islamic Republic of Iran," *Middle East Journal* 41:2 (Spring 1987): 181–202; H. Amirahmadi, *Revolution and Economic Transition: The Iranian Experience* (New York: SUNY Press, 1990); and G. Rose, "Factional Alignment in the Central Committee of the Islamic Republican Party of Iran," in *The Iranian Revolution and the Islamic Republic,* ed. Nikki Keddie and Eric Hooglund (Syracuse, NY: Syracuse University, 1986), 45–55.

8. Robert Kaplan has written a short piece on Mohsen Rafiqdoost, who runs the Mostazefan Foundation, *Atlantic Monthly* (March 1996).

9. For the best study of the Majles, see Bahman Baktiari, *Parliamentary Politics in Revolutionary Iran* (Gainesville: University of Florida Press, 1996).

10. For a different interpretation, see two excellent articles: Ali Banuazizi, "Faltering Legitimacy: The Ruling Clerics and Civil Society in Contemporary Iran," *International Journal of Politics, Culture, and Society* 4 (1995): 563–577; and H. E. Chehabi, "The Impossible Republic: Contradictions of Iran's Islamic State," *Contention* 3 (Spring 1996): 135–154.

11. See, for example, Vala Vakili's excellent paper, "Soroush and the Islamic Republic," manuscript, March 1996.

12. The process of democratization has been slow everywhere. Democracy cannot be built overnight. It cannot be imported or exported, nor can it be imposed by military force. It has to be built slowly. Consider England, the world's oldest democracy. There, the process of expanding the electorate has been remarkably slow, as it has been in the United States. It took a religious split, a civil war, a royal beheading, and a military dictatorship by Oliver Cromwell before Parliament established its supremacy. In fact, this process took some 683 years, from 1215, when King John signed the Magna Carta, to 1689, when Queen Mary II accepted the supremacy of Parliament. Once Parliament became "sovereign," it took another 296 years to extend voting rights to all segments of the population who were eighteen years of age and older. In 1832, only 7 percent of the total adult population, mainly male large property owners, could vote; in 1866, voting rights were extended to some 16 percent of the population, which included parts of the working class; in 1884, they were extended to rural workers and miners; in 1918, they were extended to women over the age of thirty; in 1928, all women twenty-one or older could vote; finally, by 1960, all men and women over eighteen could vote.

5

Sudan:
Islamic Radicals in Power

Peter Woodward

Political Islam has been associated with Sudan particularly since 1989, for it was in that year that a coup led by Omer al-Beshir took place with the backing of the National Islamic Front. Subsequently the government has sought to effect a self-proclaimed Islamic revolution. Moreover, the would-be revolutionaries, like many revolutionaries, perceive their movement as having an impact not just on Sudan, but on the wider Islamic world as well.

However, such a claim to make Sudan a center for political Islam is not new to Sudan. As the Turco-Egyptian Sudan of the nineteenth century, it was the cradle of the revolt of Ahmed al-Mahdi from 1881 to 1885, which resulted in the establishment of an independent Islamic state under al-Mahdi's successor, the Khalifa Abdullahi, which survived until it was overthrown by the Anglo-Egyptian army at the Battle of Omdurman in 1898. The Mahdist state, as it is often known, perceived itself as a force to cleanse the Islamic world and sought unsuccessfully to invade Egypt as well as to fight its Christian neighbor, Abyssinia. The regime in power from 1989 has been aware of this parallel and has sought to appropriate the legacy of the Mahdist state for itself, though not without criticism from its numerous Sudanese opponents.

Political Islam is one side of a coin—the rise of movements that seek to take control of the state and then build it in the rulers' image of Islam. The other side of the coin, and one much older in central Sudan, has been the politics of Islam—the way in which a Muslim society has related to successive states that were not self-consciously "Islamic states," even though some of the rulers were themselves Muslims.

For a territory so close to the Arabian Peninsula, Islam was comparatively slow to penetrate Sudan. Though Egypt was an early conquest of the Arab/Islamic outpouring from Arabia, the middle reaches of the Nile were dominated until the fourteenth century by successive Coptic Christian kingdoms. It was only as they declined that the way opened for the slow and generally peaceful Arabization and Islamization of northern Sudan. From the sixteenth to the eighteenth centuries the Funj kingdom based on Sennar, south of Khartoum, did convert to Islam but was scarcely a militant Islamic state any more than its successor, the first "colonial" state established by the Turco-Egyptians in the early nineteenth century. However, Arabization and Islamization did not penetrate south of the thirteenth parallel: the areas later known as southern Sudan proved geographically inhospitable and populated by resistant communities.

The politics of Islam from the eighteenth century onward was a reflection of the growth of the Sufi orders, or turuq (singular tariqa), who came into Sudan and steadily grew in size. They were numerous and often constituted socioeconomic as well as religious societies.[1] One of the most prominent was that of the Khatmiyyah founded by Mohammed Osman al-Mirghani. He had arrived in Sudan in 1817, only shortly before the Turco-Egyptian invasion, but made good use of the opportunities afforded by the new rulers to develop the Khatmiyyah rapidly.[2] In much of northern Sudan, the turuq were to constitute what in modern day parlance might be labeled "civil society." As Cruise O'Brien has described the Sufi brotherhoods of Senegal, they "very seldom question the existence of the state. . . . Brotherhoods indeed need the modern state . . . they thrive on a recognised plural principle, while also lacking the requisite training to assume full control of the modern state."[3] Instead, the turuq worked with the political status quo, rather than seeking to achieve political power for themselves; and, as a result, the Khatmiyyah, in particular, was to be accused of collaborating with "colonial" authorities.

Many Sufi orders or brotherhoods opposed the rise of Mahdism in the late nineteenth century, regarding it as a seditious movement. The Khatmiyyah leaders went into exile in Egypt. The Anglo-Egyptian reconquest of Sudan allowed the Sufi turuq to reemerge and engage once more in informal relations with the new rulers as well as in rivalry with one another. What was to change the character of the politics of Islam in Sudan most unexpectedly under British rule was the rise of a reconstituted Mahdist movement.

The resurrection of Mahdism following its apparent defeat on the battlefield of Omdurman was a combination of ambiguous policymaking by the British rulers and the astuteness of Ahmed al-Mahdi's posthumous son, Abd al-Rahman al-Mahdi (later). Until World War I, Mahdism had been suppressed. Abd al-Rahman was kept in supervised obscurity, and the occasional claimants of the title of nabi isa (the one who would follow the Mahdi) in rural Sudan were vigorously repressed. However, the claim of the Ottoman sultan, as caliph of Islam, that Muslims should rise up against the infidel Western rulers during the war made the British in Sudan decide to rehabilitate Abd al-Rahman since Mahdism was historically anti-Turco-

Egyptian (i.e., Ottoman), and he was encouraged to tour his followers and promote their loyalty to the British. From that beginning Abd al-Rahman never looked back.[4] He combined the building up of his followers with the development of a range of commercial activities and by the 1930s had established a substantial movement, known informally as the neo-Mahdists.[5] However, he realized that he needed the British—both because he lacked the strength to challenge them directly and because they opposed the continuing claims of Egypt for a greater share of power in Sudan. The older Sufi turuq watched the new development with alarm, and only the Khatmiyyah was strong enough to engage in a rival pursuit of informal power. As well as appearing increasingly as two rival social groupings, often referred to as sects, the neo-Mahdists and the Khatmiyyah were rivals for the ear of the government and, increasingly, for the allegiance of the growing number of Western-educated Sudanese. The British attempt to balance neo-Mahdism with the Khatmiyyah further helped encourage the rivalry.

Although World War II contributed enormously to nationalism in Sudan, as elsewhere, the postwar movement was to be not a united secular movement, but one in which the Western-educated nationalist politicians of northern Sudan were mainly members of the neo-Mahdist Ummah Party or the Khatmiyyah-backed Unionists, later to become the National Unionist Party (so-called because of their links with Egypt, i.e., against Britain *and* the Ummah Party). That rivalry of Islamic movements, which also incited the alienation of southern politicians, was to be at the heart of party politics during the periods of liberal democracy in postindependence Sudan. When the system deadlocked itself and southern discontent grew, the military intervened on three occasions: in 1958, 1969, and 1989. Indeed, for the majority of the period since independence in 1956, Sudan has been under military rule.

It should be added that the implications for the broader region of northeast Africa were relatively slight. Sudan's long preoccupation with its own internal problems meant that it had few designs on others, though its own conflicts did spill over into neighboring states, especially in the form of refugees. In the 1970s and 1980s, Sudan was to become involved in Cold War manipulations extending from Libya to the Horn.[6]

In addition to the developing issue of Islamic politics, the question of the legal position of Islam had also been long-standing. The Funj kingdom had introduced the Maliki school of Islamic jurisprudence, while the Turco-Egyptian administration had used the Hanafi school of law. The rise of the Mahdist state saw the adoption of sharia, based on strict interpretation of the Quran and Sunnah. British rule brought English civil law and a new penal code based on it into use in India; Islamic law was left only for family and other personal affairs of Muslims, under the supervision of an established body of ulama (religious officials). In addition, there was local customary law.[7] This situation was maintained after independence, though the question of adopting an Islamic constitution was heard increasingly.

The Rise of Political Islam

It was after World War II that the influence of political Islam spread in Sudan, and though it was to become associated with the Muslim Brotherhood in particular, there was broader sympathy for its general thrust. Within the Unionists, there was concern for the crushing of the Muslim Brotherhood in Egypt by Nasser in 1954, whereas the neo-Mahdist movement was, by definition at least, sympathetic to the building of an Islamic state. However, the preoccupation with party rivalry, relations with Egypt, and the question of the south meant that constitutional debates were largely shelved until independence had been achieved, and even after the popular overthrow of Abboud's military regime in 1964. (Sudan had become independent with only a transitional constitution; its only "permanent constitutions" have been drawn up under military regimes.)

By the mid-1960s, the Muslim Brotherhood in Sudan was firmly established.[8] It had started in the late 1940s, partly as a response to the rise of nationalism and the Sudan Communist Party—for many years its bête noire—and partly as an offshoot of the older Muslim Brotherhood in Egypt. It attracted elements of the intelligentsia and became strong in the University of Khartoum. New students, particularly from the remoter parts of northern Sudan, such as the west (and therefore less involved in the riverain networks of the developing elite), were targeted for membership.

The Brotherhood really came to prominence with Abboud's downfall in 1964, when Sudanese politics appeared to be in the melting pot. It produced a dynamic leader in Hasan al-Turabi (grandson of a local religious leader), who had studied law at the University of London and at the Sorbonne before returning to Sudan in 1962. Once back at the University of Khartoum, he played an active part in the confrontations that sparked the 1964 uprising and was elected to parliament in 1965. Though the Islamic Charter Front, as the parliamentary party was called, had only five seats, its influence grew out of all proportion to its numbers as it pressed for the adoption of an Islamic constitution. However, a further military coup in 1969, initially with the support of the left, ended that campaign; leaders of the Muslim Brotherhood took refuge abroad, where they sought with other opposition politicians to destabilize the regime.

The attempted coup they staged in 1976 proved such a warning that President Jafar al-Nimeiri entered into secret negotiations that led, in 1977, to National Reconciliation with most of the northern opposition politicians, including the Muslim Brotherhood. Hasan al-Turabi rose to become attorney general, and the Muslim Brotherhood had, for the first time, won a foothold in government, which it was to exploit to the fullest.

Politically, Turabi's tactic was to compromise with Nimeiri's leadership, even though this was to bring him some criticism from within the movement. At the same time, he raised the pressure for an Islamic constitution, a project that appeared to achieve success when Nimeiri dramatically announced the adoption of the sharia in 1983.[9] Relations between Nimeiri and the Brotherhood nevertheless remained tense, and, fortuitously for the Brotherhood, they had been thrown out of power and Turabi detained just before the overthrow of Nimeiri by Sudan's second successful popular uprising in 1985. This helped the Brotherhood survive the downfall of its former patron, and it consolidated itself by winning fifty-one seats as the National Islamic Front (NIF) in the general election of 1986, making it a substantial third party in the renewed parliamentary politics. The new prime minister was Sadiq al-Mahdi of the Ummah Party (brother-in-law of al-Turabi), and the old pattern of unstable coalition governments soon returned.[10] The NIF was in and out of government before being discarded by Sadiq al-Mahdi early in 1989, apparently as he was pressed to a deal with the Sudan Peoples Liberation Army (SPLA). The SPLA had been increasingly successful in the war in the south, which had begun again in 1983 and was naturally opposed to the sharia, which remained on the statute books if not fully operative.

But behind the overt politics, the Muslim Brotherhood had also been busy for years building its support. The student body remained a fertile recruiting ground. Students were naturally attracted to ideology, and political Islam was one that had not yet had its chance in Sudan. (The Communist Party had been severely weakened by its association with Nimeiri from 1969 to 1971 and its subsequent suppression.) In addition, as the economy deteriorated from the late 1970s, the opportunities for the growing number of graduates declined, thus fueling discontent. Another growing constituency was small business. Because the big Sudanese commercial figures had long been linked to the old parties, the Muslim Brotherhood sought to develop among their smaller rivals. The mechanism was via the rise of Islamic banking. The Faisal Islamic Bank, founded in 1978 with the backing of Mohammed bin-Faisal, son of King Faisal of Saudi Arabia, attracted Sudanese and Arab investors with the very favorable terms offered by the government, targeting the small business sector.[11] It was followed by other Islamic banks and contributed to support for the Brotherhood and to the idea that there was an Islamic alternative to the old order. The third area in which the Brotherhood was building support was more covert. From 1977, in particular, it encouraged its supporters into various arms of the state where they were largely "sleepers," waiting for their moment to act. One of those institutions was the army itself. Long politicized, it was known that there were various factions within the army, and as the problems of parliamentary politics and war in the south grew in the late 1980s, there was inevitable speculation about another coup. It is widely believed that it was the possibility of Sadiq al-Mahdi abandoning the sharia for peace with the SPLA in the south that finally triggered a coup by a faction of political Islamists in June 1989.

Political Islam in Sudan Since 1989

At the time of the coup it was by no means clear what the consequences would be. While the Muslim Brotherhood was clearly well organized and had prepared its ground, ideologically it was far from certain what policies would be pursued, because the movement had never published a full and coherent program before seizing power. Rather, its thinking had been deduced largely from the scattered writings and speeches of its leader, Hasan al-Turabi.[12] While influenced by modern Islamic thinkers such as Hasan al-Banna and Abu al-ala Mawdudi, Turabi has always argued that intellectuals themselves, from whatever disciplinary background, should develop their own understanding of Islam, working from the application of the first principles of the Quran and sunna in the modern world. He is thus dismissive of appointed and official ulama, who he believes have been weak in Sudan; nor does he follow one of the long-standing Islamic schools of law. What he had to say before 1989 was generally regarded as liberal and, according to some of his critics, even heretical. His support for multiparty liberal democracy was made eminently clear in the 1986 elections (in which the other parties conspired to ensure that he did not win a seat). At the same time the NIF was seeking power through the ballot box as a long-term aim, it was also working to transform society from the bottom up, through such local activities as poverty alleviation and even famine relief. Organizations supported by the NIF included the Islamic Jihad Dawa, the Association of Southern Muslims, the Society for Enjoining Good and Speaking Against Evil, and the Islamic Africa Relief Agency. Such activities contributed to the wider goal of Islamic renewal, which sought to recapture the allegedly more authentic traditions of Islam in Sudan before they became overlain and corrupted with the superstitions and other-worldliness of Sufism. This renewed Islam is, in Turabi's view, what must be central to the broader Muslim community, the ummah, in the modern world. Among the more unorthodox views he has expressed is the importance of the role of women in the transformation of society, for which he has been criticized by more conservative thinkers.

However, as one of Turabi's followers made clear before the coup of 1989, far from relying on the long march of liberal democracy to achieve eventual power, the NIF leaders were preparing "to make a bid to control the state and impose their norms on society and hoped to succeed where their opponents had failed by defining a new Sudanese community based on Islam."[13] It is in this light that the developments in Sudan since 1989 must be seen.

The NIF-backed military rulers have been practicing a form of vanguardism that has a number of dimensions. The first has been the takeover of the state. The army itself has been extensively purged, with up to 40 percent of the officer corps dismissed (about 2,000 men). Attempted coups have been ruthlessly crushed, although intermittent reports of unrest in the army persist. At the same time, a number of new security networks have been established and an atmosphere of suspicion and repression has developed. Arbitrary detention and torture leading to mutilation and even death have been authoritatively recorded by Sudanese and international human rights organizations, including the Sudan Human Rights Organization (now forced into exile), Amnesty International, and the UN.[14] In addition, the regime has established its own Islamic force, the Popular Defense Force (PDF), numbering up to 150,000, to defend the National Salvation Revolution. PDF training has been made compulsory for higher education candidates and for civil servants. The judiciary, the civil service, and education have seen extensive resignations and purges.

Formal changes have also been made in the political system. Federalism has been introduced, with the number of states rising to twenty-six, allegedly with NIF control of top appointments in all areas. A "no-party" parliamentary system of a pyramidal character has been established, with power supposedly flowing up through the local councils and the states to the National Assembly. At the top, the Revolutionary Command Council (RCC) was dissolved in 1993, and Omer al-Beshir was formally made president. However, all but two of the old RCC were given seats in the twenty-member cabinet and the largest single identifiable allegiance of the cabinet was with the NIF.

In 1996, Sudan finally moved to "no-party elections." Omer al-Beshir was formally elected as president, officially winning 75 percent of the vote in defeating forty-one rival candidates for the post. Elections were also held for the National Assembly. Here it was reported that nearly 1,000 candidates competed for 264 seats, with eleven contests in the south being suspended due to the continuing civil war. It was estimated officially that there was a 60 percent turnout. Although it was a no-party election, it was claimed that a number of seats were won by individuals who had been leading members of the banned "traditional" parties. Among those winning seats in the National Assembly was Hasan al-Turabi, who was elected speaker (and, constitutionally, successor to President al-Beshir in the event of the latter's death in office).

In civil society, there has been a sustained attack on those often referred to in Sudan as the "modern forces": the professional organizations and the trade unions, which have long been regarded as relatively developed and dynamic in Sudan, having played a leading part in the popular revolts against military rule in 1964 and 1985. Perceived as bastions of Western liberal standards or, worse, as communists and Bathists of various hues, they have long contributed to a relatively free, pluralistic, and tolerant atmosphere in the country. In addition to dismissal and detention, many thousands of professionals and others have gone into exile, together with many former politicians. In their place, the regime has encouraged alternative bodies, often claiming that they are independent organizations. The previously free media have been totally commandeered and used for propaganda purposes.

In urban and rural areas, Popular Committees have been set up to operate in parallel with the local administration. Their significant powers include distributing rationed goods and acting as surveillance networks. Under their aegis, a plethora of local groups have been encouraged, including organizations for women and youth and various Islamic groupings, such as Jihad Dawa and the Holy Quran Society, though their levels of activity vary from one place to another.

On the policy front there has, of course, been a clear commitment to the sharia, with a revised version of the 1983 laws being introduced in 1991. There has also been a major drive toward Arabization and Islamization of education at all levels. There was a crackdown on women at work in the name of defending an Islamic conception of the family, and the numbers of women active in the professions dropped sharply. A conservative dress code for professional women and students was enforced, and some women were harassed in public places. The free movement of women was also restricted, requiring the permission of a male guardian or relative, if not his actual accompaniment.

In the south, the war with the SPLA has been prosecuted vigorously against a background of repeated failure in peace talks. Some NIF members advocated the abandonment of the non-Muslim south, but the war has been fought even more aggressively, with the participation of the PDF. After advances in the early years in power, there have been a number of setbacks since 1994. The war has also been accompanied by reports of forced Islamization and "ethnic cleansing," especially in the Nuba Mountains and Bahr al-Ghazal. The economy has been liberalized, meaning in practice that the influence of Islamic banks and businesses associated with the NIF has expanded. (However, international credit has been restricted as a result of Sudan's indebtedness and failure to reach agreement with the IMF.)

Given the restrictions of all kinds in Sudan, it is difficult to assess the effect of this Islamic vanguardism on the country. There are reports that the younger generation is more militantly Islamic, even to the point of criticizing NIF leaders on occasion. At the same time, there appears to be an awareness of the polarization of wealth in the hands of the regime's supporters while the real standard of living of most Sudanese continues to fall;

it is because the long decline of the Sudanese economy has not been arrested. Since 1992, there have been regular reports of demonstrations in a number of urban centers, though these were contained by the NIF's own security forces, often with loss of life. The demonstrations of September 1995 were the largest since the overthrow of Nimeiri ten years previously. As indicated, many hundreds of thousands have left the country, especially those with professional skills. (However, the opposition in exile has proven to be disunited and apparently incapable of mounting a major challenge.)

Regional and International
Dimensions of Political Islam

To determine how Sudan's attempt to build an Islamic state relates to the country's external environment, it is useful first to review the thinking of Hasan al-Turabi.[15]

Muslims, he believes, should relate to each other at a number of levels: from households and local communities to their country and to dar al-Islam, the Muslim Commonwealth. This is not to be regarded as a monolithic structure but as the entity to which Muslims aspire (and that can incorporate non-Muslims, as has always been required by Islam). The last great pan-Islamic enterprise, the Ottoman Empire, had finally succumbed to the "onslaught of European imperialism," which had also disestablished the sharia. However, pan-Islamism had been growing from the outset of that experience in the form of such developments as the revolt of Ahmed al-Mahdi and the teaching of Jamal al-Din al-Afghani. Later came movements such as the Muslim Brotherhood in Egypt and Jamaat-i Islami in the Indian subcontinent. However, in much of the Muslim world, imperialism had given way to a model of the nation-state that has been a "resounding failure." Nationalism and a range of other secular ideologies have all proven unsuccessful and have left deep disillusionment. That is the context in which Islamic revivalism has developed throughout the Muslim world to challenge the failure of the "national enterprise." True, the Organization of the Islamic Conference (OIC) has been established, but it is led by states that have remained manipulated by the West (as exemplified during the Gulf War) and is "politically impotent and totally unrepresentative of the true spirit of the community that animates the Muslim people." Instead of remaining within the present framework, "as Muslims tend towards their common ideals, they would per force move towards closer unity; and that would undermine the moral foundation and the positive structures of the present national state." Instead of this being achieved by force, it will come from the bottom up. "However once a single fully-fledged Islamic state is established, the model would radiate throughout the Muslim world" and it would become "a focus of pan-Islamic attention and affection." (Turabi has declared that he believes that Sudan is in the process of becoming such a beacon and that the country is being led in the right direction by a government in which he has in the past claimed to play no part, although in 1994 he was appointed to the Council of Justice overseeing inter alia the sharia.)

The modern world is increasingly international in most areas of life, and for Turabi this promotes pan-Islamic aspirations: "Muslims would for ever aspire to the ultimate ideal of the caliphate restored, of one central authority that holds the Muslim world community together." However, "countries may remain as areas of self-management for the full enrichment of Islam in the particular environment."

There may be those in the West, like Samuel Huntington, who perceive in political Islam a rival force with which there could be future conflict.[16] This however is not Turabi's proclaimed view. Muslims are not seeking confrontation, because "the present trends towards unity derive more from the inside revival of Islam, as spirituality for society, rather than from the excitation of Islam as the battle cry. . . . It is the common religious ideal, rather than the common enemy that draws the Muslims together." Pan-Islamism rallying the Muslim world will not be a threat to people of other faiths and cultures beyond dar al-Islam (or for minorities within it), but a "positive contribution to the human community in general."[17]

I have dwelt at some length on Turabi's views because he is projected as a leading figure in the international pan-Islamist movement and gave the talk at which these remarks were made three years after the coup of 1989 had allegedly set Sudan on the path to becoming an exemplary Islamic state.

Turabi's views were not just talk. In 1991, the Popular Islamic and Arabic Conference (PIAC) was established in Khartoum. Representatives of the pan-Islamic movement from a number of countries were invited, and Turabi was duly installed as secretary-general. The timing was directly related to the Gulf War, as the organizers felt that the time was right to seek the mobilization of pan-Islamists across the Islamic world in the face of the demonstration of Western might and the collaboration of many Middle Eastern governments with the United States and Israel. The PIAC was intended to develop as a vehicle for Islamic revolution, and Turabi was perceived as being at the center of a web that stretched out from Khartoum. He traveled widely to promote the cause, and while in Canada in 1992, he was seriously wounded in an assault by a Sudanese exile. He recovered sufficiently to continue his roving role, and it was even rumored in 1993 that he might move his center of operations to Switzerland for greater convenience. His activities, however, were not always appreciated in other Muslim countries, and, as a mark of their concern, the Islamic Conference Organization in 1992 cancelled a meeting of foreign ministers of Islamic states to be held in Khartoum. Sudan broke with the ICO and did not rejoin until 1994.

The PIAC's activities did not stop in the Islamic world. It was in keeping with Turabi's expressed views that he, as its secretary-general, should seek to enter into dialogue with the West, and particularly with Christian churches. Talks with British and U.S. government officials in 1992 did not achieve much progress, but with the Vatican relations grew. In February 1993, the pope made a brief stop in Khartoum while on an African tour and met with Omer al-Beshir; but he spent most of his short visit with the Catholic community, to whom he stressed his understanding of the suffering of many Sudanese. Although the pope did not meet Turabi then, contacts continued, and in October Turabi was granted an audience at the Vatican. Soon after, it was announced that diplomatic relations were being established between the Vatican and Khartoum. From the Vatican's perspective, it was doubtless a means to try to help Catholics in Sudan; Sudan, who claimed it as a degree of support for its approach to peacemaking in the south, also gained international recognition in its increasingly isolated position.

However, an attempt to achieve a similar rapprochement with the Anglican church later in 1993 backfired. The archbishop of Canterbury intended to visit both northern and southern Sudan, but a last minute breakdown over the arrangements for the northern leg resulted in his seeing only SPLA-held territory in the south—and a further deterioration in relations between Sudan and Britain. Nevertheless, the wooing of Christian churches outside Sudan continued, and a number were represented at Muslim-Christian conferences in Khartoum in 1993 and 1994. The archbishop of Canterbury finally made a brief visit to northern Sudan in 1995.

Turabi was also involved personally in the complicated relations between Sudan and France. While most Western powers have distanced themselves from Sudan, various contacts have been maintained with France, surfacing most dramatically with the handing over to France of the terrorist Carlos "the Jackal" in 1994. Behind this lay contacts that included French aerial intelligence assistance in the war in the south, suggestions of renewed French interest in oil in the south (where the oil company Total held a concession), and Sudan's influence with the Islamic movement in Algeria, which France believed could be used to its advantage. In contrast to the international coverage of Carlos, there was little comment when soon after Turabi made a quiet visit to Paris. However, following President Chirac's election in France, relations with Sudan became less active.

The Carlos incident reopened a discussion that has been particularly central to Sudan's regional and wider international relations, and that is the question of whether Sudan harbors international "terrorists" and, if so, for what purpose? There have been repeated reports of the presence of foreigners (referred to as "brothers in Islam" by the government). They include Iranians, Afghan veterans from various parts of the Middle East, and alleged members of groups such as Hizbollah of Lebanon, Islamic Jihad from Egypt, and HAMAS and the PLO from Palestine (members of these latter groups are referred to as "refugees," to whom Sudan generously offers its hospitality). Iranians and Afghan veterans in particular are believed to have been actively involved in various aspects of security, including training the People's Defense Forces (PDF) and leading them in the civil war. Among the "refugees" are alleged to be some who receive training at a number of secret camps and then return to their home countries, especially in North Africa, to commit acts of terrorism in the name of Islam. Accusations of this kind have been made by governments in Algeria, Egypt, and Tunisia, in particular, and in 1993, the United States added Sudan to its list of states actively supporting terrorism (Cuba, Iran, Iraq, Libya, North Korea, Syria). Sudan denied the accusation and may have handed over Carlos to try to improve its image: if so, it had the reverse effect, indicating that it does harbor internationally sought terrorists and reminding the international community that at least some are put to use training the PDF or the "refugees." A further abrupt reminder was given by the attempted assassination of President Mubarak of Egypt in Addis Ababa in 1995. It was alleged that Sudan was involved in training and equipping the would-be assassins and sheltering three escapees. Condemnation by the UN for failing to return the three to Ethiopia for trial led to moves to impose sanctions on Sudan.

Relations with African States[18]

The potential for tension between "Islamic" and "conventional" trends in foreign policy has been particularly marked in Sudan's relations with African neighbors to the east. Since the early 1960s, Sudan has been host to Eritrean liberation movements (as well as refugees). Later, the Eritrean People's Liberation Front (EPLF) assisted the formation of the Tigrean People's Liberation Front (TPLF). Sudanese security helped both these movements in the final assaults on the regime of Mengistu Haile Mariam, which resulted in his downfall in 1991 and led to the formation of the independent state of Eritrea and the establishment of governments both there and in Ethiopia based on the former liberation fronts.

These core groups in the interim governments in both Ethiopia and Eritrea consisted of former leftists who were still secularist in outlook and came from the traditionally Coptic Christian areas of northern Tigre on either side of the new international border. However, the PIAC, in particular, saw itself as promoting the substantial Muslim communities in the Horn of Africa, and at its first conference agreed to aid Oromiyyah Islamiyyah among the Oromo community in Ethiopia and Jihad Eritrea among the Muslims of western Eritrea. This provoked understandable alarm within the new governments and even public denunciation by Eritrean leader Issayas Aferworki. Sudan responded by seeking to placate Eritrea with a number of exchanges of visitors, including Turabi, and the expulsion from eastern Sudan of Jihad Eritrea (which took refuge in Saudi Arabia). However, tensions continued, with Eritrea still concerned over the activities of some Muslims in the new state and even lodging a complaint at the UN in 1994 and suggesting that Sudan was using remaining Eritrean refugees as hostages or recruits for the Islamic movement. Diplomatic relations between the two countries were broken, and Eritrea called openly for the overthrow of the regime in Sudan while hosting and supporting the Sudanese opposition in exile. Sudan, in turn, complained of Eritrea's position with regard to southern Sudan in the Intergovernmental Authority on Drought and Development (IGADD) peace initiative (in which Eritrea is a participant) and later complained of Eritrea's open support for the opposition in exile.

With regard to Ethiopia, it became clear that maintaining relations with the new government took precedence over being actively committed to the Islamists, especially as the Sudanese army was initially allowed access to western Ethiopia, which facilitated its attack on SPLA positions in eastern Equatoria. However, as relations with Eritrea deteriorated, so did relations with Sudan's close ally, Ethiopia. Following the attempted assassination of Mubarak, Ethiopia also joined the public condemnation of Sudan for supporting terrorism.

The PIAC's enthusiasm for promoting political Islam in the Horn did not face a similar dilemma in Somalia. There, both Sudan and Iran combined to encourage local Islamists, but in most areas, the fissures of clan and subclan division proved stronger than the call to unite under the banner of the common religion. Thus, although contacts were established and supplies passed (to the faction of Mohamed Aideed, among others), the influence of both Islamic states remained relatively small in comparison with the significance of the major Somali faction leaders.

On Sudan's southern flank, relations with Kenya and Uganda have been more problematic. The fall of Mengistu in Ethiopia had the immediate impact of weakening the SPLA: it lost its major source of supplies, fragmented into competing factions, and suffered a series of reverses at the hands of government forces. This made the SPLA factions (especially John Garang's "Mainstream") more dependent on East Africa, where there has long been a natural sympathy for southern Sudan's "African" fighters struggling against the forces of Islamism and Arabism. Continued supplies to the SPLA came to depend largely on the friendship of these two states, especially Uganda. Sudan, in return, sought to exert diplomatic pressure and threatened to encourage the two countries' Muslim minorities. (Muslims from Amin's regime are still in southern Sudan.) Kenya and Uganda, in turn, took the lead in involving IGADD in a further round of peace talks between the government and the SPLA. IGADD's involvement kept talks going and, in 1994, highlighted the differences between the SPLA factions and the government on the issue of the secularization of the state in Sudan or, failing that, the right of southerners to self-determination (with the implication of independence, as occurred in Eritrea). Uganda and Eritrea in particular seemed to support the SPLA on the issue; Sudan sought instead to construct its own internal peace process while still in contact with IGADD and prosecuting the war in the south, which it claims to have virtually won. However, this has proven premature and Garang's Mainstream SPLA has replied with renewed vigor since 1994, winning a number of engagements, with the government blaming increased foreign support for the SPLA.

Sudan's relations with its neighbors to the west and northwest, Chad and Libya, are not so much "African" or "Middle Eastern" as sui generis. The crux is really Chad; whereas in the south, the East African countries have played a significant role in the conflict in southern Sudan, it is Sudan that has been a major factor in the contest for power in Chad. In 1982, Husein Habre launched a successful attack from Darfur in western Sudan to take power in Chad; in 1990, he was ousted in the same manner by Idris Déby. But in both cases, Sudan was largely an instrument, albeit a willing one, because the real issue was Chad's position with regard to the aspirations of Libya. As well as the disputed Aouzou strip between Libya and Chad, there are historic links, while Colonel Qaddafi saw Chad as a center for wider penetration into Africa. It was when his protégé, Goukouni Oueddi, led the Government of National Unity (GUNT) in Chad that the United States, Egypt, and Sudan conspired to back Habre. After the downfall of Nimeiri, relations between Libya and Sudan changed, and the coup makers of 1989 allowed Libya a free hand to support Déby.

Political Islam has been only a minor factor in relations with Chad and Libya since 1980, though it has been present rhetorically. Relations with Déby have owed more to ethnic ties between those in government in Khartoum and Ndjamena; these ties are based in the Zaghawa, a people who straddle the northern Chad-Sudan border. In reality, France has long taken an active interest. France is encouraging Déby to develop a broader base by adopting democratization and also has a modus vivendi with both Sudan and Libya. As for Sudanese-Libyan relations, these cooled somewhat in the 1990s. Political Islam accounts for this in part, for it has become a theme of Qaddafi's Libyan opponents, though he, having his own interpretation of Islam, sees no room for their criticism. But probably just as important have been Libyan endeavors to improve relations with Egypt—which are far more important to Libya—at a time when Egyptian-Sudanese relations have been severely strained.

Relations with the Middle East

Mention of Egypt brings consideration of relations not only with a neighbor, but also with a major actor in Middle Eastern politics—a factor reflected in relations with Sudan. Relations between the two have always been of a special nature for both countries. Egypt, a former ruler of Sudan, has continued to regard the country as something of a southern hinterland; Egypt also has special concern for the Nile waters, which, though not rising in Sudan, flow most of their course there. From Sudan's viewpoint, one of the continuing points of reference in Sudanese politics for decades has been whether governments, parties, and politicians were broadly pro- or anti-Egyptian.

The agenda of political Islam adopted by the regime in power in Sudan since 1989 has put it in the anti-Egyptian camp. Egypt has denounced Sudan for supporting Islamic terrorists and Sudan has denied it, as seen above. Egypt, of course, finds it convenient to blame Sudan, and the roots of the movement in Egypt appear to be homegrown. Nevertheless, Egyptians have taken refuge in Sudan, including Umar Abd al-Rahman, a leader of the Islamic Jihad who later went to New York where, in 1996, he was jailed for his connections with the bombers of the World Trade Center. Some Egyptians do appear to have received a form of military training and to have tried to pass weapons (which have been easily available in Sudan in recent years) to Egypt.[19]

Yet the threat to Egypt from political Islam is only one aspect of the relationship between the two countries. The border dispute over Halayab, which has been dormant since 1958, has broken out once more. Its origin lies in ambiguity: the Anglo-Egyptian Treaty of 1898 set the border along the twenty-second parallel. However, for convenience, the barren Halayab region between the Nile and the Red Sea was administered from Sudan, even though it is north of the twenty-second parallel (most international maps show it as Sudan). Egyptian troops moved in 1958, and, though they were soon withdrawn, the issue was unresolved. It resurfaced in 1992, partly because of the deteriorating relations between the two countries, but more immediately because Sudan proposed to grant permits for mineral exploration on- and offshore. Once more Egyptian forces occupied Halayab, and shortly thereafter, Egypt invited international companies to bid for exploration. Sudan has sought to reverse the situation by popular occupation and international legal redress, but without success.

In other areas, too, relations have deteriorated over matters only partly concerned with political Islam. Egypt long retained a cultural and educational presence in Sudan, especially through the Khartoum branch of the University of Cairo and a network of schools. These were all closed in 1993, and Egypt has complained about the treatment of Egyptian nationals in the process. Sudan, in reply, has accused Egypt of seeking to be involved in Sudanese life, including political activities, and has pointed to such incidents as Egypt's hosting of John Garang, leader of the SPLA (Mainstream) and permitting various northern political exiles to operate freely. (Nimeiri was permitted to call for a popular uprising, apparently without any hint of irony.)

Egypt has also been concerned by the possible implications of the establishment of IGADD, especially if it might presage greater exploitation of the Nile waters by upstream states. In consequence, Egypt has secured observer status with IGADD but still sees Sudan as a potentially threatening force within it. At the same time, fears that a new regime in Sudan might permit the eventual secession of southern Sudan with possible implications for Egypt's water supply have introduced a note of caution into the latter's policy.

Sudan's other Middle Eastern neighbor is Saudi Arabia, and here too relations have been difficult. On the surface, this appears surprising, since Saudi Arabia was for years a backer of the Islamic movement in Sudan. In part, this was to contain the influence of Egypt, especially in the late 1970s, when Saudi Arabia's oil wealth was deployed both to support and to contain Egypt; since the days of Nasser in Yemen, an overmighty Egypt is to be prevented. From National Reconciliation in Sudan in 1977, money flowed to the Islamists from Saudi Arabia and the smaller Gulf states, most obviously to the Islamic banks.

However, after 1989, there was growing concern. Saudi Arabia presented itself as an Islamic state but now found it was increasingly castigated, first indirectly and later directly. Matters came to a head with Sudan's attitude toward the Gulf War, after which aid was sharply reduced and many of the numerous expatriate Sudanese in the kingdom were expelled. In 1994, a tycoon from Saudi Arabia, Osama bin Laden, who was living in Khartoum and was believed to be close to NIF business circles, was stripped of his citizenship by Saudi Arabia. Saudi Arabia also regularly hosted members of the Sudanese opposition and was, in turn, publicly accused by Sudan of supporting even the SPLA. Meanwhile, links between Sudan and the Islamist movement in Yemen have been increasing, possibly with the hope of influencing Yemen's relations with Eritrea.

For both Saudi Arabia and Egypt, Sudan is not just a neighbor, but a self-proclaimed Islamic state with a much broader agenda, and they are themselves major Middle Eastern actors. The agenda for Sudan has been seen as contributing to a possible domino effect of political Islam, which has been and remains a threat in much of North Africa. It also extends into Palestine in the form of HAMAS and even, some reports suggest, into secretive activities in Saudi Arabia itself.[20] In this view of political Islam versus the established order, including the Middle East peace process, Sudan has not been alone but has had some suspect allies, notably Iraq and Iran.

Sudan's involvement with Iraq grew notably in 1988 and owed less to ideology than Arab solidarity in the face of the SPLA's threat to the "Arab" north. Iraq, having just ended the long war with Iran, was in a position to supply much-needed arms, and Saddam Hussein was keen to promote himself in the Arab world. The coup of 1989 did not impede the flow of weapons; instead, it was to contribute to Sudan being one of the few states in the Middle East that refused to condemn Iraq's invasion of Kuwait. In fact, the government encouraged its supporters onto the streets for voluble anti-Western demonstrations. Such a posture angered Egypt and Saudi Arabia, and there were even threats of force should Sudan attempt to take any positive action to assist Iraq. (There were also exaggerated stories about Iraqi war planes or even Scud missiles having been sent to Sudan.) After the war, Iraq was in no position to support Sudan, and, instead, the Gulf Arab states cut aid as a punishment and expelled numbers of Sudanese working there. As already seen, Turabi personally denounced the Western action as a violation of the Muslim world and sought to capitalize on anti-Western sentiment in the region stirred up by the war.

Iraq's place as a friend and arms supplier was taken by its former foe, Iran. As the first of the modern wave of Islamic revolutions, Iran might appear to be an obvious ally for Sudan from 1989; however, while the Sudanese Muslim Brothers recognized the Iranian revolution, they also had their criticisms of it. In particular, as indicated, Turabi's concept of an Islamic state was not of a theocracy run by mullahs. Indeed, those to whom he felt closest had been the leaders of the Iran Freedom Movement, who were crushed as the revolution unfolded.[21] However, after the Gulf War, Sudan was isolated and in need of military support—and Iran proved willing to assist. From Iran's standpoint, it was an opportunity to demonstrate a continued commitment to political Islam, which was appealing particularly to more militant elements within the regime.

Iran, like Iraq before it, had weapons to spare. It also financed deliveries of new equipment from China, including aircraft (to replace the former assistance in the south from the Libyan air force). There were also military instructors with experience from the Iraq war and from the guerrilla wars against the Soviet Union in Afghanistan. In 1993, Sudan's armed forces and police were reorganized along the lines of the Iranian security forces. However, Iran had its own domestic problems and a declining economy. By 1994, enthusiasm for Sudan appeared to be waning.

In the international community, Sudan retained an isolated position. At the UN, it was shunned by most Arab states and remembered for its position in the Gulf War. It was also formally condemned for its human rights record by the UN special rapporteur (who was himself obstructed and then vilified by Sudan). The European Union also took a continuing interest and a comparable view. The United States maintained a similarly robust position. Certain members of the U.S. Congress and former president Jimmy Carter endeavored to pursue peace efforts, but to little avail. In 1993, the administration listed Sudan as a supporter of terrorism and a force behind the bombers of the World Trade Center. As a gesture of concern in 1994, the United States appointed a special envoy, Ambassador Melissa Wells, to seek to facilitate the peace process, though in practice this turned out to mean supporting the IGADD initiative. Following the attempt on

Mubarak's life, the United States was more open in depicting Sudan as a "pariah state" and in supporting Eritrea and Ethiopia in their open hostility to their western neighbor. Relations remained cool as well with the IMF, to which Sudan has a debt going back to the time of Nimeiri. It was suspended, and subsequent negotiations have proven difficult to the point of threats of expulsion by the IMF, which would be an unprecedented step.

Relations with most governments have reflected this growing international isolation. What is difficult to assess is Sudan's perspective on its external relations. The government frequently depicts itself as misunderstood and wronged and indicates that it would like to be less isolated regionally and internationally. This may be because of need: economic conditions remain troubled, there has been unrest, and the country is forced to rely heavily upon its security apparatus, because it remains a narrow-based regime.[22] Greater international support would be useful, especially with Sudan's project to realize its medium-sized oil potential, which requires foreign capital deterred by the country's relations with the IMF. There is too the view that Sudan has largely achieved the building of an Islamic state and that this should be recognized. An air of triumph emanates from Turabi, suggesting that the Islamic state is well advanced and the war in the south won, in spite of hostility from Sudan's enemies abroad. Turabi argues that it is now time for this to be recognized and for Sudan to take its place more actively in the international community. A third view would be that the Sudan government dissembles, that it outwardly adopts a posture of achievements at home and good intentions abroad but continues in its repressive and exploitative domestic policies, remaining as ready as ever to involve itself with the cause of political Islam internationally whenever such involvement is perceived as being in Sudan's interest.

Conclusion

For the first time since independence in 1956, Sudan has since 1989 sought to set itself up as a major actor in regional and international politics. It has acted as a mediator in the past, with the activities of Mohamed Ahmed Mahjoub at the Khartoum summit after the 1967 war, and Nimeiri's attempts in the first civil war in Lebanon, but on these occasions, it was the marginality and unobtrusiveness of Sudan that made it acceptable, rather than its pretensions to international leadership. In 1969, Sudan sought to be part of a new union with Libya and Egypt, but very much in the shadow of Nasser. Only since 1989 has it sought to become a guide to the Arab and Muslim world. This raises the question of whether the world of Islam is as Turabi depicts it and whether it is capable of attaining the Muslim Commonwealth for which he calls. It also brings into question the extent to which the self-proclaimed Islamic state erected in Sudan is the model to which others will rally. Certainly, attempts to persuade visitors to Sudan are offset, in part at least, by the hundreds of thousands who have left the country and tell a very different story to the outside world.

If the answer to such questions is in the negative, it leaves a very tragic picture of what has occurred since 1989. An Islamic state has been constructed by a degree of repression in the north and south unprecedented in Sudan's postindependence period. Real living conditions for most of the population have deteriorated, and many have left the country. Instead of becoming a beacon for political Islam, Sudan has become internationally isolated—as a reward for trying to attain the unattainable.

Perhaps there are parallels with the Mahdist state of the late nineteenth century, as the government likes to claim. The revolt of Ahmed al-Mahdi has been regarded as one of the great Islamic movements; and under the Khalifa Abdullahi there was a form of Islamic state building and an attempt to cleanse the Muslim world, beginning with an (unsuccessful) invasion of Egypt. Thousands of Sudanese died defending the Mahdiyyah at Omdurman. Yet it was also a time of great violence in the south and famine and impoverishment in much of the north; and while there were those outside Sudan who drew inspiration from the Mahdiyyah, most notably Sayyid Mohamed Abdille Husain in Somalia, regional and international forces combined eventually to bring about its downfall.

Notes

1. For a good example of the growth of a tariqa, see Awad al-Karsani, "The Majdhubiyya Tariqa," in *Two Sufi Tariqas in the Sudan,* ed. M. W. Daly (Khartoum: University of Khartoum, 1985).

2. For the fullest account, see John O. Voll, *A History of the Khatmia Tariqa in the Sudan* (Ph.D. diss., Harvard University, 1969).

3. D. C. O'Brien, "Islam and Power in Black Africa," in *Islam and Power,* ed. Alexander S. Cudsi and Ali Hillal Dessouki (London: Croom Helm, 1981).

4. Peter Woodward, "In the Footsteps of Gordon: The Sudan Government and the Rise of Sayyid Sir Abd al-Rahman, 1915–1935," *African Affairs* 84:334 (January 1985): 39–51.

5. For an example of this struggle for turf, see Awad al-Karsani, "The Establishment of Neo-Mahdism in the Western Sudan," *African Affairs* 86:344 (July 1987): 385–404.

6. For a broad discussion of Sudan's instability and its implications for its neighbors, see Peter Woodward, *Sudan 1898–1989: The Unstable State* (Boulder: Lynne Rienner; London: Lester Crook Academic, 1990).

7. For a full discussion of the development of Sudan's legal development, see Carolyn Fluehr-Lobban, *Islamic Law and Society in Sudan* (London: Frank Cass, 1987); and Herve Bleuchot, *Les Cultures Contre l'Homme: Essaie d'Anthropologie Historique du Droit Pénal Soudanais* (Aix-en-Provence: Presses Universitaires d'Aix Marseilles, 1994).

8. The fullest account of the rise of the Muslim Brotherhood in Sudan is

Abdelwahab El-Affendi, *Turabi's Revolution: Islam and Power in Sudan* (London: Grey Seal, 1991).

9. It appears that Nimeiri actually used people other than Muslim Brothers to draw up the sharia. Nevertheless, Turabi approved of it and encouraged his followers to attend the public amputations and executions. He fainted when he first witnessed one himself.

10. For a full description, see Kamal Osman Salih, "The Sudan, 1985–89: The Fading Democracy," in *Sudan After Nimeiri*, ed. Peter Woodward (London: Routledge, 1991).

11. E. Shaaeldin and R. Brown, "Towards an Understanding of Islamic Banking in Sudan," in *Sudan: State, Capital and Transformation*, ed. T. Barnett and A. Abdelkarim (London: Croom Helm, 1988).

12. A useful summary of Turabi's views is found in Tim Niblock, "Islamic Movements and Sudan's Political Coherence," in *Sudan: History, Identity, Ideology*, ed. Hervé Bleuchot, Christian Delmet, and Derek Hopwood (Reading, England: Ithaca Press, 1991). In 1989, a book (in Arabic) by Turabi did appear: Hasan al-Turabi, *The Islamic Movement in Sudan* (Khartoum: IRSS, 1989).

13. El-Affendi, 163.

14. Research in Sudan has been greatly constrained since 1989. As a consequence, a number of publications have appeared outside Sudan, mainly in English and Arabic, some clearly pro- or antiregime. What follows is indebted in particular to *Sudan Update*, which monitors, summarizes, and quotes a range of media sources.

15. The following material, including quotes, is taken from the printed handout of Turabi's address to the Royal Society of Arts (RSA), London, 27 April 1992.

16. Samuel P. Huntington, "The Clash of Civilizations?" *Foreign Affairs* 72 (Summer 1993): 22-49.

17. Turabi, RSA.

18. An earlier review of Sudan's external relations is in Charles Gurdon, "Sudan's Foreign Policy," *Sudan Studies* 12 (July 1992): 10–25. A more recent discussion of its position in the region is included in Peter Woodward, *The Horn of Africa: State Politics and International Relations* (London: I. B. Tauris, 1996).

19. Rashid Ghannouchi, leader of the al-Nahda Islamic movement in Tunisia, was another prominent figure helped by Sudan: he traveled on a Sudanese diplomatic passport until Sudan was pressured to withdraw it, after which he took refuge in Britain.

20. Turabi is a personal friend of PLO leader Yasir Arafat and has sought to mediate between the PLO and HAMAS, though without notable success.

21. El-Affendi, 146.

22. In 1992 and 1994, there were a number of reports of the possibility of a deal being struck with one or more of the opposition parties to broaden the regime.

6

Invidious Comparisons: Realism, Postmodern Globalism, and Centrist Islamic Movements in Egypt

Raymond William Baker

Prophetic Minorities in Our Late Modern World

Around the globe, in the West as well as in the Islamic world, prophetic minorities have spontaneously arisen, committed to the peaceful remaking of their own societies and of the modern world system originating in the "world revolution of Westernization."[1] With their creative, nonviolent actions—local but with global import, related but not coordinated, linked but not unified—these new social movements are inventing a postmodern global consciousness and a politics that act against the violence that has marred the revolution of Westernization.[2] Grounded in postmaterialist values, theirs, to borrow Inglehart's phrase, is a "silent revolution" in the human and planetary interest.[3]

In the Arab world, the human resources for new forms of cooperative action are emerging instead from the embattled institutions of civil society, with its efforts on behalf of popular participation and the curtailment of arbitrary power and from the centrist Islamic groups who have played so constructive a role in this new politics in the making. Yet, while CNN and the Western media generally have made the figure of Umar Abd al-Rahman, the inspirational leader of a criminal minority in Egypt, the symbol for Islamic groups worldwide, the great contemporary figures of Egyptian Islamic centrism, such as Yusuf al-Qaradawi, the late Muhammad al-Ghazzali, and Kamal Aboul Megd, are virtually unknown and almost completely unread and unheard of in the West.

Realism: Highlighting Violence

This distressingly lopsided knowledge of the Islamic awakening points to a general moral and intellectual failure of U.S. foreign policy decisionmakers and opinion leaders in the media and academia who continue to rely on an outmoded realist perspective, tied to the international state system, that cannot respond to the needs of our global age. This study questions the realist understanding of the meaning of the Islamic revival by examining the two most important competing frameworks for the analysis of international politics—realism and globalism—as each makes sense of the Islamic awakening in the late twentieth century.

My thesis is straightforward: It does make a difference if the unavoidable distortions of our representatives make the minority of radical and violent, fanatical elements the global icon for twentieth-century Islamic social movements rather than the majority of radical, yet creative and nonviolent, centrists. Dominant realist perspectives on international politics—U.S.-centered and focused on the "security dilemma"—have for the most part yielded characterizations of Islamic movements that are little more than incitements to violence against them. Alternative perspectives—world-oriented and anchored in human-centered global values like peace and social justice—have too rarely looked to the Muslim world for their "case studies."

With a focus on Egypt from a globalist perspective, this study contends that at the center of the worldwide Islamic awakenings is a moderate and humane vision that defies both the ravages of an imitative modernism linked to the violence of the worldwide revolution of Westernization and the even more destructive reactionary Islamic foundationalism that has coevolved with it.

The Islamic center is positioned between two forces: the discredited secular rulers who, in existing Arab states, lead corrupt and repressive regimes that preside over failed nationalist development projects; and the foundationalist Islamic militants who challenge them with growing effect. The pressures from the Islamic foundationalists are reactionary rather than simply conservative, in that they do not derive from a coherent Islamic tradition but from decontextualized and fetishized slogans and iconic fragments of such a tradition—such as the veil or the rallying call "Islam is the solution." Foundationalists, unconstrained by any sense of the historical integrity of the Islamic traditionalists, are peculiarly prone to violence to achieve their ends.[4]

The presence of centrist Islamists, in sharp contrast, opens up possibilities for creative interactions and perhaps even joint projects with those elsewhere around the globe who see as clearly the dangers of both the modernist project and the atavistic political forces that have emerged in reaction to it.[5] But why has the realist perspective so consistently concealed Islamic centrists and the possibilities for cooperation they offer?

Realists argue that, while a balance of power among competing national security states does not always secure peace and stability, it has guaranteed survival in the face of multiple threats. The realist perspective insistently directs our attention to those violent elements and groupings of the Islamic wave that pose a threat to Western interests. When we thought of ourselves locked in deadly combat with a superpower adversary out to "bury us," the realist focus on the security dilemma appeared to make good sense. The issues obscured by realism—the ecological health of the planet, peace in all parts of the globe and not just the center, the rights of women and human rights more generally, a just international economic order, values other than materialism and consumerism—simply seemed less important. With the end of the Cold War, these issues and values have asserted themselves. Transnational social movements preoccupied with questions of humane social orders and a healthy planet rather than the insatiable quest for "security" have arisen to challenge the foreign policy elites of national security states and the political ideologies that sustain them. This does not mean that the dangers of criminal violence, including criminal violence for political ends, can be ignored. It simply means that it must be kept in proper perspective.

The globalist perspective attacks all of the basic assumptions of state-centric realism.[6] The focus shifts from the states to transnational trends and movements that, according to the globalists, are bringing a global community into being. *Globalism,* as an idea, posits the real world of 5 billion people and the whole earth as a physical environment to be safeguarded and everyone living as world citizens, consumers, and producers connected but not united by a common interest.[7] The protean idea of globalism is, itself, one of the forces that have advanced the development of globalization. But it is only one such force. As important are the development of world-scale mass communications and information technologies; the proliferation of worldwide social movements; and international scientific, economic, and financial networks that link the peoples of the globe. The Muslim world too has felt and responded to these globalizing influences.[8]

While realism continues to dominate U.S. foreign policy formulation, most foreign affairs issues are now debated increasingly in terms of the clash of realist and globalist perspectives. A curious exceptionalism, noted but not explained earlier, marks Western and especially U.S. perspectives on the issue of our relationship with the Muslim world. Even our most lively and productive debates center on the security issue rather than on alternative ways of understanding Islamic movements: Is the Islamic threat a myth or reality?[9] The debate, quite apart from the position one takes, unavoidably produces texts suffused with the security concerns of the realist—are they exaggerated or reasonable, correctly targeted or misplaced?

Our present consternation with the perceived advance of Islam has deep historical roots. The world revolution of Westernization has always found in Islam a peculiarly recalcitrant opponent. As Wilfred Cantwell Smith reminds us, "Until Karl Marx and the rise of communism, the Prophet organized and launched the only serious challenge to Western civilization that it has faced in the whole course of its history."[10] Smith's prescient text goes on: "The Muslim challenge was flung with vigor, and was sweepingly successful in almost half of Christiandom. Islam is the only positive force which has won converts away from Christianity—by the tens of millions. It is the only force which has proclaimed that Christian doctrine is not only false, but repulsive."[11]

Today, especially now that communism has crumbled just about everywhere, Islam as a civilizational challenge looms large once again in the Western consciousness. Samuel Huntington has recovered this animus toward Islam, deeply embedded in the orientalist tradition, and harnessed it to his influential thesis that the coming century will be marked by a "clash of civilizations," with special attention to the possibility of danger from the Muslim world.[12] Huntington uses this freshly recycled formulation to argue for an aggressive and interventionist strategy to protect American interests—and, by direct implication, the security states linked to the United States in the Arab world—from the destructive Islamic tide.[13]

While Western commentators on Huntington's thesis have concentrated on its implications for U.S. global policy, the regional corollaries of the "clash of civilizations" have provoked the greatest interest in the Arab world and among Western media and academic specialists in the Middle East. Huntington's reworking of the state security perspective offers critical support to the repressive, pro-U.S. Arab state system, now justified by its role as a bulwark against "the return of Islam."

National security analysts, both in the United States and the Arab world, have spelled out the relevance of the Islamic threat along these lines.[14] Egypt's story, told in this way, can stand for the rest. An embattled regime, committed to peace with Israel and economic restructuring, confronts one battalion after another in the worldwide wave of Islamic fundamentalism. Exploiting the liberalizing policies of a president who would make Egypt part of the "Third Wave of Democratization," the Islamists have begun a two-pronged attack to turn Egypt into an Islamic state.[15] The militants, capitalizing on the short-term hardships of economic restructuring, have initiated an armed duel with the regime, hoping to provoke it into indiscriminate repression, which might spark mass upheaval on the Iranian model. While the militants fire away, their allied Islamic moderates, mouthing slogans of pluralism and democracy, undertake the systematic subversion of civil society, hoping to reach power through the ballot box so that the election that brought them to power will be the last. Faced with this pincer movement, the regime has no choice but to slow the move to democracy in order to contain the Islamic threat and preserve the democratic option for the long haul, while the Americans are "forced" to curtail their enthusiasm for the democratic experiment, reluctantly diverting funds from programs to support effective "governance and democracy" to incentives for the officer corps to ensure their loyalty to Mubarak.

More sophisticated variants of this realist imagining of Egypt's recent political history, while leaving in place the basic plot line of an underlying Islamic threat against the national security regime, introduce shadings to bring the story a bit more in line with the facts on the ground. The regime, for starters, is recognized as hopelessly corrupt and increasingly brutal. The realist perspective has an easy time tolerating state violence and official looting. Even instances of social violence, unconnected with the Islamic onslaught, can make their way into the more sophisticated realist vision. Do not such spontaneous eruptions of violence that have nothing or little to do with the Islamists—such as riots of ordinary citizens against the authorities in Abu Hammad and other sites in the delta—only reinforce the need for a strong state to maintain stability?[16] Clearly, by these lights, the strong state should seize the opportunity provided by the violent actions of the extremists to move against both wings of the Islamic wave. In such a context, it is much easier to justify trials in military rather than civilian courts, for example. The climate of crisis, requiring assertions of order, also makes easier restrictive revisions in the party law that governs both the formation and operation of political parties and changes in electoral rules in the syndicates, both transparently designed to undermine the Islamist moderates. From the realist perspective, there need be no embarrassment for all the corruption and repression, because, as Judith Miller advises, Egypt's case can easily be defended: "Washington can also say that the governments of Egypt . . . [and other allied states] are, for all their many, well-publicized failings, still more tolerant and less repressive than those that the Islamists *would most probably establish* in their stead."[17] It should be noted that such a speculative argument requires no documentation or evidence.

Globalism: Explaining Nonviolence

Like any other perspective, while the realist perspective spotlights some phenomena, it screens others from view. Which aspects of the Egyptian scene do we neglect when our attention is focused in this way on the security needs and antiterrorist campaigns of the existing regime?

Attention to the immediate violence of the Islamic extremists and our preoccupation with its explanation leads to the neglect of the structural violence built into the Arab political scene. When we do pay attention to the larger historical context in the ways a globalist perspective encourages, our efforts of more than a decade to explain the growing resort to terrorist violence in Egypt—and for that matter worldwide—seem somewhat misplaced. Given the extraordinary violence perpetuated against Westerners and non-Westerners alike by that preeminent globalizing force the "worldwide revolution of Westernization," as Von Laue named it, the puzzle that should command our attention is the emergence of peaceful, transnational social movements that aim to overcome the violent patterns everywhere associated with Westernization.

These movements first emerged as a major force in the West. In the face of a destructive, consumerist materialism and intolerable levels of violence in everyday life in the United States, the question that should command our attention is clearly the following: *How have powerful social groups in Western industrial societies dedicated to preserving the environment, securing the equality of women, and protecting human rights made themselves so powerful a moral force for peaceful transformation? What are the implications of the unexpected shifts in values that have transformed a significant minority in the West into prophets of a generous global consciousness?*

The parallel question about the emergence of nonviolent social movements in the global South, including the Muslim world, is even more compelling, just because the assault of Westernization there has been so traumatic. In a remarkably candid passage in *Preparing for the Twenty-First Century,* Paul Kennedy wrote of the impact of an expansionist Europe on the Islamic world:

> Sailing along the Arab littoral, assisting in the demise of the Mughal Empire, penetrating strategic points with railways, canals, and ports, steadily moving into North Africa, the Nile Valley, the Persian Gulf, the Levant, and then Arabia itself, dividing the Middle East along unnatural boundaries as part of a post–World War I diplomatic bargain, developing American power to buttress and then replace European influences, inserting an Israeli state in the midst of Arab peoples, instigating coups against local popular leaders, and usually indicating that this part of the globe was important only for its oil, the West may have played more of a role in turning the Muslim world into what it is today than outside commentators are willing to recognize. Clearly, Islam suffers many self-inflicted problems. But if much of its angry, confrontational stance toward the international order today is due to a long-held fear of being swallowed up by the West, not much in the way of change can be expected until that fear is dissipated.[18]

The physical onslaught in the nineteenth and first half of the twentieth century, characterized by Kennedy, was accompanied by an even more deadly cultural assault, which continues unabated today. The point is neither exaggerated nor easily explained away as simply part of a shared modern condition. Wilfred Cantwell Smith has given a classic expression to Western insensitivity on this issue:

The Arab increasingly lives in a world that he feels is not his own; that he can only partially understand, and certainly cannot control. Actually the whole of humanity lives in this kind of world in the twentieth century; all of us are faced with a modernity that undermines our past and challenges our survival. But few Arabs realize this; most see the novelty as alien, a disruption from outside, and see other human beings—particularly the West—not as sharing their distress but as inflicting it.[19]

What Smith, usually a more reliable guide in such matters, fails to understand is that it does make a difference if the modernist forces of disruption are internal versus external, originating from one's own society or from the outside. The issue here is one of power, and across the power divide, the common fate of Westernization nevertheless becomes a cultural weapon of the West. Moreover, we are misleading ourselves if we ignore the fact that the religious grounding of the world revolution of Westernization enables it to cut deeply and painfully into the cultural life of others who do not share the foundations we have chosen, with increasing shrillness, to identify as Judeo-Christian.

Can we really hope to understand the context for the Islamic revival with our studied indifference to the cultural forms of violence built into unequal power relations? Is it really helpful to ignore the implications of the loss for weaker peoples of the unviolated space to adopt one's inherited institutions to the pressures of modernity with some modicum of privacy, of the ability to plan one's future autonomously? What happens to an inherited cultural tradition when the cultural revolution of Westernization operates unhindered to undermine, weaken, and destroy indigenous cultural forms? What does it mean to a people, like the Egyptians, when their record of struggling with not one, but both, global models for development yields only more debt rather than development? What happens to the collective psyche of a small and dependent society when the United States carelessly radiates into the homes and hearts of its citizens the most superficial luxuries, its most vulgar and tasteless entertainment forms? What happens to the solidarity of a society when the largest dream of its best youth is to escape and to abandon the homeland for those fabled distant shores defined by the media? Coexisting with the intolerable results of these forms of violence are the often mindless outbursts of the extremists and radicals, the studied brutalities of the state, and spontaneous eruptions of social discontent.

Clearly, in a context marked by so much violence, the real mystery is not the origins of extremism. The puzzle that demands explanation is how, given such an environment, nonviolent social movements, including those with an Islamic character, have come to play such an important role in Egypt and other parts of the Arab Muslim world, advocating programs of peaceful reform. Who are the centrist Islamists who play a key role in promoting these movements and in articulating the policies they defend, and how can we learn to recognize them?

The Reform Policy of Egyptian Civil Society

A global vision, with its focus on the puzzling appearance of nonviolent social movements in a violent world, brings into view a neglected reformist policy perspective, with implications for U.S. policy. While the realists urge us to stand behind the repressive policy of the Egyptian regime, the globalists identify with reformist policy prescriptions that emerge from Egyptian civil society, where the centrist Islamists have a substantial presence.

With authoritarian regimes under attack from "people power" around the globe, it should come as no surprise that Egyptian reformist policy aims to curb the arbitrary power of the state. The planks of this policy entail the end of the presidential monopoly of power, legally enshrined in a constitution that must be changed if Egypt is to move in any meaningful way toward democracy; unrigged elections that will give opposition seats to more than a handful of the 440-member legislature; cessation of the encroachments on judicial independence; suspension of gross human rights violations; and the legalization of a centrist, nonviolent Islamic party, with the Muslim Brothers as the most obvious candidate. The reformists argue that such a reform policy, especially if combined with a serious campaign against corruption, might stem Egypt's slide into escalating violence and terror. The United States confronts more than one policy option in Egypt.

Recognizing the Centrists

The defining marker for the radicals is easy enough: they resort to violence. The recognition of the Islamic centrists or Wasittiyyah who speak as one voice from civil society and on behalf of its reformist stance poses special difficulties. What we are talking about is a fluid center that defines those who have responded with moderation to the violence of their age, drawing on the religious and cultural heritage of Islam to do so. While the legacy of the Muslim Brothers is important to all such groups, the Brothers cannot be assumed to exercise any consistent authority or control over those who see themselves as centrist. Moreover, the coordination among the groups is episodic and spontaneous. In identifying the centrists, a misplaced concreteness should be resisted. Rather than any rigid definition, the process of identification or, more precisely, recognition I have followed relies on the flexible notion of "family resemblances," i.e., a set of characteristics that, when found in some substantial combination, give a moderate appearance or character to the group.[20] To be considered centrist, a group need not display all these characteristics; rather, any group so identified as part of the Islamic Wasittiyyah will evince just enough of these characteristics to be recognizable as part of the larger family.

The identity as a centrist thus "emerges" from the presence of some combination of the ways of thinking and forms of behavior mentioned below:

- Advocacy of change through dialogue and debate rather than violence
- Support for civil society against the authoritarian state
- Devaluation of the role of a single figure in favor of collective leadership
- Marked tolerance for diversity of viewpoint, at both the elite and mass levels
- Enlargement of consciousness that transcends traditional national, sectarian, and other divisions
- Encouragement of social action with a populist thrust and a broadly social, rather than narrowly religious, cultural or political agenda
- Bestowal on politics of a sacred character, a spiritual dimension, that expresses itself through the building of the good Islamic community
- Translation of ethical and religious duties into principles of social responsibility and participation
- Definition of the sphere of significant social action as both local and transnational
- Openness to a global dialogue that seriously engages such questions as cultural authenticity, democracy, human rights, and the health of the planet and the welfare of all humankind in the late twentieth century.

In Egypt today, a number of clusters of nonviolent Islamist activists have arisen. Here I consider three that give a sense of the variety of groups that are recognizable by these "family resemblances":

First, the intellectuals and anti-Western young militants, many of whom were formerly on the left, who gravitated to the newspaper al-Shaab. When the Labor Party adopted an Islamist orientation, the party paper became a powerful voice of Islamic opposition under the energetic and frequently strident leadership of Adel Hussain in partnership with party leader Ibrahim Shukry. (The Labor Party registered 8 percent of the electoral vote in 1984 and 18 percent jointly with the Muslim Brotherhood as the Islamic Alliance in 1987.)[21]

The most militant and uncompromising of the three clusters considered here, the *al-Shaab* circle, has provided a high-profile platform for sharp attacks on the Egyptian role in the U.S.-sponsored peace process and the Middle East market concept, as well as a more general warning about economic and cultural dependency. During the Gulf crisis, *al-Shaab* pounded away at the Egyptian official failure to advance an Arab alternative to

the U.S. commitment to a military strike against Iraq.[22] As the crisis
unfolded, Hussain emerged as arguably the most active, vocal, and effective critic of government policy from an Islamist perspective. *Al-Shaab*
harshly attacked the Egyptian government's failure to back various diplomatic alternatives. When the regime failed to support efforts for a peaceful
resolution by the Jordanians, the Yemenis, the French, and the Russians—
virtually banning the word *negotiations* from the Egyptian official press—
the Islamist circle around Adel Hussain and Ibrahim Shukry mounted their
own mediation effort.[23] They were condemned and defamed in the government press for emerging as the sole force with a national platform calling
for negotiations and a peaceful Arab resolution of the crisis.[24] Reacting to
such arguments, government supporters labeled *al-Shaab* "an Iraqi publication in Egypt."[25] The political fallout for Hussain from these developments
included dissent within the Labor Party, strains with the Brotherhood in the
Islamic Alliance, and a brush with government repression, all culminating
in his arrest for a brief period in the winter of 1995.[26]

Second, the more varied constellation of Islamist activists who, follow-
ing the path laid out by the Muslim Brothers in the 1970s,[27] opted to work
within the professional associations and other civil society institutions to
realize their dream of a more just and humane Islamic society in Egypt.[28]
More of the traits of the Wasittiyyah can be seen in the impressive social
action of this larger and more diverse group. Many of the most influential
syndicate figures, like Essam al-Eryan of the Medical Association, are the
seasoned graduates of the important Islamic presence in university student
unions during the Sadat years.

Their peaceful brand of social activism grows out of the strategic decision of the Brotherhood in the Sadat years to work within the structures of
civil and state institutions.[29] Denied direct access to the political arena,
they have made the professional syndicates perhaps the most vibrant institutions of Egyptian civil society.[30] Building on the impressive record of
social action by the Brothers in the 1940s, the Islamists have worked to
extend medical insurance to syndicate members and their families, establish social and recreational clubs (and not just in large cities), increase the
stock of housing available to members at lower prices, and assist the families of those members arrested or otherwise detained by the regime.[31] By
such actions, the syndicate activists have renewed the legacy of social
Islam, pioneered by the Brothers, for a new generation of Egyptians.

Essam Eryan, in particular, has been instrumental in making the
Medical Association a national platform for dialogue and discussion of all
the key issues that confront the nation. Frequently providing a platform for
centrist intellectual figures, forums held in the syndicate on such key issues
of cultural politics as Islam and secularism or on such pressing political
concerns as the Egyptian role in the Gulf War have captured national attention. In the process, the Islamists have significantly transformed the associ-

ations themselves, making them the vehicle to extend the message of social Islam and to define its larger vision of centrist Islamic elements for Egyptian society. The extraordinary earthquake relief effort, spearheaded by syndicate activists, proved so effective in both these dimensions that the government felt called upon to criminalize relief efforts over which it did not exercise direct control, forcing the Islamists to lower their visibility.

But it is misleading, and certainly dangerous, for those involved to exaggerate the autonomy of the social space the syndicate activists have carved out. The lines between civil and state institutions are blurred in Egypt, and the regime retains substantial power to manipulate and control the syndicates. Given these limitations, the Islamists can hardly use the professional organizations to create a "countersociety" or to constitute themselves as a "counterelite," nor is it clear that such is their aim. Recent changes in the electoral laws in the syndicates, designed blatantly by the regime to curtail the Islamists, not to mention the arrest of Essam Eryan in the winter of 1995, have perhaps driven this point home.

Third, a small but enormously creative and outspoken group of religious intellectuals who have organized themselves loosely as a "school," with the aim of providing nonauthoritarian "right guidance" to the varied groupings of the Islamic body, including both the al-Shaab *and syndicate clusters.* The New Islamic trend, as these intellectuals call themselves, are a remarkable and diverse group of prominent religious intellectuals who have emerged as the most critical intellectual force in defining the Islamic Wasittiyyah. The major figures of the New Islamic "school" are Yusuf al-Qaradawi, Kamal Aboul Megd, Muhammad Selim al-Awa, and Muhammad al-Ghazzali. As a group, these figures have authored an entire library of books and articles—texts whose cross-references provide an effective web that binds them together and creates an intellectual and cultural space within which their adherents move. At the same time, several of the key figures in the group have a large mass following: when a Qaradawi or Ghazzali speaks publicly, he will draw crowds at times reaching over a quarter of a million.

In addition to their intellectual and cultural leadership, the New Islamists have either created or inspired a host of organizational innovations that have enriched the broad Islamic trend. From their fluid definition of their own group as an intellectual school (thus avoiding official attack as a party or faction), through their active involvement in the expanded public spaces created through the syndicate networks (where young and educated Islamists become acquainted with their thinking), to their own practice of issuing "statements" to the wider public on such pressing national issues as communal strife or Egypt's role in the Gulf War, the New Islamists have been creative agents in expanding the scope and richness of the legal political sphere. While their influence cannot be quantified, it is striking nevertheless that, when a group of moderate Islamists from the Brotherhood recently formed a party of the Islamic center in the wake of the depressing 1995 elections, their platform and initial statements bore the unmistakable imprint of New Islamist thinking on such crucial issues as the joint role of Christians and Muslims in the Islamic civilizational project and the need to democratize the political order. And when the government ended this brief chapter of moderate and legal initiative by arresting the leaders of the nascent Hizb al-Wasat on the absurd charge of "conspiring" to found a party, it was the New Islamist Selim al-Awa who offered the boldest condemnation of the government repression.[32]

Yet, despite the richness of their intellectual contributions and the creativity of their social interventions, all of these New Islamist figures—where the family resemblances of centrist Islamists occur in the most uncompromised form—are for the most part unread and unknown in the West.[33]

This intellectual school in moderate Islamic thought has several major characteristics that are underscored in *A Contemporary Islamic Vision,* the manifesto of the group written in 1982, but only published ten years later. It relies on a rational interpretation of the religious texts, the Quran and the Sunnah, and the large body of legal, social, and political thought in the Islamic tradition. Yet their orientation is not exclusively textual. The New Islamic trend is characterized by a deep concern for the plight of modern Egyptians and Muslims in areas related not only to their beliefs and religion, but also to their social, political, cultural, economic, and psychological well-being. At the same time, it regards the improvement of the plight of Egyptians and Muslims as linked equally and integrally to both a true revival of Islamic ideas, spirit, and way of life, and to a clear, rational knowledge and understanding of the modern world and the prerequisites for survival and success within it.[34]

The New Islamists thus speak from within the Islamic tradition to the issues of women and minority rights, of global human rights and the struggles for more just national and international orders.[35] In our troubled age, the New Islamists are convinced that the Islamic revival does have a message of universal importance, and they extend the invitation to a global dialogue on behalf of the humane principles that, in their view, all the great religious and cultural traditions share.

The New Islamists believe strongly that it is the duty of all Muslim leaders, thinkers, and intellectuals to face this challenge with creative solutions that embody the correct Islamic rules and principles. These creative resolutions to various problems challenging contemporary Muslim societies do not necessitate the complete overthrow of existing institutions and laws. Many of the laws in Egypt, for example, do not contradict Islamic law in the judgment of the New Islamists.[36] Furthermore, the New Islamists insist that those areas where changes must occur can and should be approached consistently and gradually, to avoid creating even greater havoc in society.

Belief in social Islam with its strong commitment to constructive social action is the distinguishing hallmark of the practical work of this intellectual school, which insists that direct social action is the duty of all those involved in the Islamic movement, including both the body and the leadership. They see worthwhile, practical activity as the correct path to spiritual and worldly salvation, as it were, even if the results are sometimes flawed or incomplete. The New Islamists call for a healthy, vibrant Islamic body that, in its own activities, will help create an open environment of tolerance, understanding, and, above all, dialogue that will yield a correct understanding of both Islam and the modern world, and that can guide the steps to renewal and change.

In the decade of the 1980s, the New Islamists registered their greatest success in advancing these goals. Without the advantages of a democratic political arena, this prophetic minority engaged in peaceful intellectual and political struggles aimed at creating an enlarged and tolerant Islamic consciousness open to the world. They intervened throughout the 1980s and into the first years of the 1990s as a force for moderation on a range of controversial public issues, ranging from communal strife to the war in the Gulf. In their public role and their most important publications, they articulated a strategic vision for a moderate and centrist orientation, deepening in the process their strong appeal to a mass following.

The New Islamists at the start of the decade seemed poised for a significant enhancement of their public role. The centrist Islam, for which they speak, asserted itself as a major and highly effective force, deeply rooted in Egyptian history and on the threshold of a revival that seemed poised to draw on the mid-century experience of the Muslim Brothers to write the second chapter of the social articulation of moderate Islam in twentieth-century Egypt. Unlike the ignorant militants, religious intellectuals such as Muhammad al-Ghazzali, Kamal Aboul Megd, Selim al-Awa, and Fahmy Huwaidy thrive in a climate of dialogue and democracy. At the same time, these New Islamist figures have the intellectual and moral authority to contain the appeal of the militants, while offering a vision far more compelling than anything the regime can advance.

But shadows hung over their achievements and, by the mid-1990s, these possibilities were overwhelmed by a climate of violence and repression. The fears to which Fahmy Huwaidy alluded in a guardedly optimistic assessment of the decade of the 1980s prove more justified than the hopes.[37] Violent extremists strike murderously at both civil society and the government to disrupt the emerging national dialogue. The regime, for its part, adopted a policy of sweeping repression. But the target was not simply the extremists. Seizing on the violence of the radicals as justification for a strike against the one force that can effectively challenge its legitimacy—moderate Islam—the regime struck at the Islamic Awakening in all its manifestations. The New Islamists too were targeted in a policy that limited their access to television and censored their writings in the mass press. Ominously, the charge is renewed by the regime that there is no real difference between moderates and extremists.

When the moderate Islamic groupings rather than the violent minority become the focus of attention, the startling conclusion unmistakably emerges that the real target of regime repression in Egypt is precisely these clusters of nonviolent Islamists who make a plausible claim to speak for the Islamic Wasittiyyah, rather than the terrorist minority. The anomaly of the assault on the moderates is screened by a security perspective that blurs all distinctions within the Islamic wave. From the contrasting globalist perspective, with its interest in values other than simply order and stability, these centrist Islamic groups emerge as the carriers of a project quite distinct from that of the criminal minorities who also carry an Islamic banner. Why has the regime targeted them so deliberately?

The answer is clear-cut: The well publicized radical assault, however deadly to the individuals caught in the crossfire, can be contained by the regime at relatively low cost, at least in the short run. Much more damaging to a dependent, corrupt, and unimaginative political order is the emergence of a social and political force, grounded in widely shared religious and cultural values, that by its very presence in the public arena constitutes a devastating critique of the existing system. To strike at the radicals, the regime argues, it must dry up the broad sources of the religious renewal in Egypt. In this way, a strategy of "drying of the springs," ostensibly aimed at the radicals, in fact legitimates an assault on the peaceful challenge represented by a centrist Islamic alternative that dramatizes regime failings and lack of legitimacy.

Conclusion: The Promise of Cooperative Engagement

The record of all three groupings of the Islamic Wasittiyyah considered here, though none more than the New Islamists, invites comparison with the work of the new social movements in other parts of the world. The parallels between the Islamic Wasittiyyah and such new social movements as Human Rights or the Greens include pragmatic and nonviolent ways of acting through loose networks of autonomous, grassroots, and nonhierarchical groupings rather than tight, organized structures. Relying primarily on a sense of personal responsibility for the common good, all these new movements are capable of spontaneous, autonomous actions outside official channels. While the agendas of the new social movements are always local, their struggles on behalf of humankind and the natural environment have transnational and global meaning, often understood explicitly in spiritual terms. Most striking in all cases is the capacity to invent and actualize new forms of political and social action for these larger purposes of "taking back" opportunities for personal and collective freedoms, lost to the dominant elites of the national security state system or simply to the ravages of reckless development that destroy human and natural communities.

If key elements of the Islamic Wasittiyyah—the New Islamists in the most compelling way—can thus usefully be recognized as part of the global phenomenon of new social movements, it makes sense to ask a question otherwise unthinkable in the present climate of hostility between Islamic movements and the West: *What effort of moral courage and intellectual imagination will it require to envision and implement cooperative projects between the prophet minorities of the West and those of the Islamic world?*

It is unfair, even invidious, to compare the centrist Islamists to the new social movements in the West. These Western movements have sprung from advanced postindustrial, and to some degree postmaterialist, conditions. They operate under relatively open political conditions, and their agendas and their priorities reflect those conditions. In contrast, the Islamic centrists wage their struggles in conditions of great vulnerability. We undoubtedly do violence to centrist Islamic activists and groups when we compare them with groups whose circumstances are so different.

But it is also important to recognize that the Islamic revival, in its moderate and peaceful expressions (such as the New Islamic Trend), is quite explicitly and courageously engaged in re-creating itself, rejecting a narrow and closed identity, and struggling to enlarge its consciousness to find its place in dialogue with an emerging global society—and in these ways refusing the limitations of its political environment.

A comparable refusal is required in the West. The terrible waste of time and talent necessary simply to soften the incitements to violence carried in prevailing Western characterizations of Islam and Islamic social movements has left too little energy for the positive tasks of building new forms of global dialogue and even cooperation with groups like the New Islamists, which offer our only hope to meet the world-scale dangers that threaten our planet and our species. This failure of mutual understanding points to the conclusion that, as a nation, we lack the cultural and intellectual resources to manage the new globalism peacefully. The recent resurgence of a virulent "realism" and self-righteous moralism feeds on a haunting sense of that incapacity. It drives us to build more high-tech prisons and erect higher barriers around our shores. It leads us to think that our leadership, displayed most recently in the Gulf War, in creating, marketing, and "testing" military technologies is the kind of leadership required for our global age.

This resurgent realism encourages us to see only a clash of civilizations, just when transnational social movements are making real the prospect of what Kamal Aboul Megd has called a global "dialogue of civilizations" in the human interest. The distortions of globalism may well expose our worldwide interests to unplanned dangers, will certainly loosen our control over other peoples' futures, and will inevitably lead to the creation of a world made less in our own image. But these are risks I believe we should bear, and encourage our children to bear, in the interest of a more vital and urgent search for ways to strengthen the "socio-political frameworks of human cooperation" on which the resolution of the global dangers that confront us depend: "That framework of peaceful interaction within global interdependence is still highly fragile; it cannot be taken for granted. Its preservation and improvement call for far larger resources of insight and perspectives than are currently available."[38]

Some part of our engagement with the world of Islam, with the prophetic minorities that have emerged there as part of new Islamic social movements, must be made part of our effort to promote, as Theodore Von Laue put it, "a peaceful collective transition to a global consciousness."[39]

Notes

1. The phrase is Theodor Von Laue's. See his magnificent *World Revolution of Westernization: The Twentieth Century in Global Perspective* (New York: Oxford University Press, 1987). While I do not accept Von Laue's underlying "culturalist" perspective, his conceptualization of the making of the modern world and the role violence has played in it, especially at the hands of "anti-Western, Westernizing" forces, has deeply influenced my thinking.

2. The most important of recent studies on the new social movements is Richard Falk, *Explorations at the Edge of Time: The Prospects for World Order* (Philadelphia: Temple University Press, 1992).

3. Ronald Inglehart has elaborated his "silent revolution" thesis in two important works, *The Silent Revolution: Changing Values and Political Styles Among Western Publics* (Princeton: Princeton University Press, 1977), and *Culture Shift in Advanced Industrial Society* (Princeton: Princeton University Press, 1990).

4. I owe the notion of foundationalism as a global, and not simply Islamic, phenomenon to Ferenc Fehrer and Agnes Heller, *The Postmodern Political Condition* (Oxford: Polity, 1988), 7–8. The feminist theorist Wendy Brown provides an interesting elaboration of the concept in "Feminist Hesitations, Postmodern Exposures," *Differences: A Journal of Feminist Cultural Studies* 3:1 (1991): 67–69.

5. Yusuf al-Qaradawi, in particular, has consistently called for such a global dialogue. See, among other works, his *Fiqh of Priorities,* especially 170–182.

6. I am aware that there are, in fact, two forms of globalism: corporate and grassroots, or globalism from above and below. For reasons of space, I am unable to develop that notion here. Those familiar with these distinctions will recognize that the globalism I speak of here is grassroots rather than corporate. In my view, the distinctions between corporate globalism and realism collapse from a normative vantage point that emphasizes values, precisely the stance taken here. For a brilliant summation of these considerations and a fine treatment of these distinctions, see Mel Gurtov, *Global Politics in the Human Interest* (Boulder and London: Lynne Rienner, 1988). The most up-to-date discussion of corporate globalism, not dis-

cussed here, is Richard J. Barnet and John Cavanagh, *Global Dreams* (New York: Simon and Schuster, 1994). While I start with Albrow's clear concepts of globalism and globalization, I have insinuated some postmodern extensions and cautions into my own formulations of these ideas.

7. Martin Albrow and Elizabeth King, eds., *Globalization, Knowledge and Society* (London: Sage Publications, 1990), 8.

8. Kamal Aboul Megd, *A Contemporary Islamic Vision: Declaration of Principles* (Cairo: Dar al-Shuruq, 1991), 13.

> The world is on the verge of a new age in the relationships among cultures and countries, where barriers are destroyed and where nations seek common interests to achieve a cultural rapprochement to serve the values of justice, peace, freedom and respect for human rights.
>
> In the midst of these continuous efforts, Islam is presented to the world as the antithesis of such effort and as unrelated to the values and principles which the new world is seeking. . . . Arabs and Muslims are pictured as strangers to this common humanitarian heritage. The matter reaches the point of picturing Arabs and Muslims as being an obstacle intellectually and historically on the road of this emerging humanitarian culture and a danger threatening its future.

9. The most cogent analysis of these dangers is by John L. Esposito, *The Islamic Threat: Myth or Reality?* rev. ed. (New York: Oxford University Press, 1995). The "myth" formulation is Esposito's, while Edward Said speaks of "The Phony Islamic Threat," *New York Times Magazine,* 2 November 1993.

10. Wilfred Cantwell Smith, *Islam in Modern History* (New York: New American Library, 1957), 110.

11. Ibid.

12. Bernard Lewis has popularized the notion of a "clash of civilizations," especially in his journalistic treatments of Islam and the West. Huntington, in turn, legitimated this thesis for security and policymaking circles.

13. See, in particular, the policy recommendations with which Samuel Huntington concludes his analysis in "The Clash of Civilizations?" *Foreign Affairs* 72 (Summer 1993): 48–49.

14. The classic in this genre is Judith Miller's "The Challenge of Radical Islam," *Foreign Affairs* 72:2 (Spring 1993): 43–56.

15. The phrase is taken from the title of Samuel Huntington's book *The Third Wave: Democratization in the Late Twentieth Century* (Norman: University of Oklahoma Press, 1991).

16. For an account of this and other such incidents of social violence not linked to the Islamists, see *al-Musawwar,* 21 August 1992.

17. Miller, 55 (emphasis added).

18. Paul Kennedy, *Preparing for the Twenty-first Century* (New York: Random House, 1993), 211.

19. Smith, 102.

20. I have borrowed this strategy of family resemblances from Terry Eagleton, who uses it for his discussion of the concept of ideology in *Ideology: An Introduction* (London: Verso, 1991), 222.

21. I have given a detailed account of this grouping and its role in public life in my essay in *The Gulf War and the New World Order,* ed. Tareq Y. Ismael and Jacqueline S. Ismael (Gainesville: University of Florida Press, 1994), 493–494.

22. Though widely debated at the time, it is now taken for granted in the stan-

dard accounts of the Gulf crisis that President Bush had early ruled out a peaceful resolution of the conflict by an Iraqi withdrawal from Kuwait for what he saw as national security reasons. See, for example, "The Persian Gulf," in *The Middle East* (Washington, D.C.: Congressional Quarterly, 1994), 118: "Perhaps the most important factor in the Bush administration's decision, however, was that many officials at the Pentagon and the White House and their Arab counterparts feared an Iraqi withdrawal from Kuwait almost as much as a war."

23. Magdy Hussein (on Algeria) and Adel Hussein (on Sudan) took positions that supported developments in those countries in contrast to the critical stance adopted by the mainstream Muslim Brothers. See Magdy Hussein in *al-Shaab*, 26 June 1991, and Adel Hussein in *al-Shaab*, 16 July 1991; for the Brothers' position, see *Rose al-Yusuf*, 29 July 1991.

24. Ahmed Abdullah, *Trilogies: The Second Gulf War: A Perspective from the Point of View of the Generation that Will Pay the Price!* (Cairo: Dar al-Arabiyah lil-Tibaa wa-al-Nashr wa-al-Tawzi, 1991), 14–19. Abdullah is a political analyst associated with the human rights perspective and human rights activism in Egypt and abroad.

25. Marwan Fouad, "Time to Get Their House in Order," *Middle East* 201 (July 1991): 19–20.

26. One important example of the repression is covered in "The Chief Prosecutor Decides to Jail Hussain for 15 Days," *al-Akhbar*, 28 January 1991. Adel Hussain gives his own version of government harassment in *al-Shaab*, 18 February 1991. As of March 1995, Adel Hussain was once again under arrest in Egypt on vague charges of supporting terrorism.

27. I have told this important and neglected story elsewhere. See Raymond William Baker, *Sadat and After: The Struggle for Egypt's Political Soul* (Cambridge: Harvard University Press, 1990), chap. 8, 243–270.

28. Real politics in Egypt is most alive and well, not in normal electoral channels and institutions (choked by authoritarian presidential rule), but rather in the key institutions of civil society, especially the middle class professional associations. For a representative discussion of these political spaces, creatively developed and used by Islamist activists among others, see Baker, *Sadat and After*, especially chap. 2, which focuses on the Bar Association. For an update on more recent developments in the association, including the rise of the Islamists as an organized and effective force in what was once the preserve of the liberals, see especially the interview with association leader Ahmed al-Khawaga in *Sabah al-Kheir*, 5 November 1992, and in *al-Alam al-Yawm*, 21 September 1992. For a centrist Islamist reading, see the account of Essam al-Eryan in *Rose al-Yusuf*, 28 September 1992.

29. This story is told in detail in Baker, *Sadat and After*, chap. 8, 243–270.

30. The role of several syndicates as a "political space" is examined in Baker, *Sadat and After*, chap. 2, 46–78.

31. Impressionistic evidence on the effectiveness of the Islamists in these realms of social welfare comes from episodic visits to actual sites and from press treatments like Ahmed Eddedin's survey "What the Islamic Trend Provides in the Syndicates," *al-Shaab*, 14 April 1992. Naturally, the Islamic press has delighted in such stories, but it is instructive that few critics, even the harshest, question the effectiveness of the Islamists in the social welfare sphere. The motives behind the activism, to be sure, are questioned.

32. See Muhammad Selim al-Awa's courageous article in *al-Shaab*, 6 April 1996.

33. Occasionally, a misleading article on Shaikh Muhammad al-Ghazzali will appear in the Western press, often comparing him in groundless ways with Iran's

Khomeini or, more ludicrously, with Shaikh Umar Abd al-Rahman, currently on trial in the United States for alleged links to violent, terrorist groups operating in Egypt and the United States. Ghazzali is in fact a major scholar, revered as such throughout the Muslim world, a central figure in moderate Islamist ranks, and quite frequently a target of attack from ignorant, extremist quarters.

34. This characterization draws from *Islam Without Fear,* a new book on the New Islamists I am writing with Karen Aboul Kheir for Harvard University Press.

35. For the most comprehensive collective statement on all these issues, see Aboul Megd, passim.

36. Kamal Aboul Megd gives the fullest elaboration of this view in an extensive interview in *October,* 8 July 1990.

37. Fahmi Huwaidi expresses these fears and his guarded hopes in his *al-Ahram* article of 2 January 1990.

38. Von Laue, xviii.

39. Ibid., xix.

7

Islamic Opposition in the Political Process: Lessons from Pakistan

S. V. R. Nasr

Since Islamic revivalism captured attention with the Iranian revolution of 1979, it has undergone change, not so much in what it seeks to attain but in the methods it is employing. The Islamic revolution in Iran cast Islamic revivalism as a revolutionary force, bent on the violent overthrow of the state and perpetual struggle against the West. Although many of the distinctive features of Islamic revivalism are still in place and some of its least savory characteristics have continued to surface—in Algeria, Egypt, and Lebanon most recently—significant changes have occurred during the past decade and a half. Increasingly, Islamic parties from Bangladesh to North Africa are looking to elections as the path to power. They have joined the political process and to varying degrees have interacted or coexisted with democracy. Some have even sought to accommodate democratic values at the doctrinal level.[1] In fact, in many instances, they have become the most visible champions of opening the political system before authoritarian regimes. It is for this reason that scholars and policymakers alike in the West have backed off from supporting democratization in the Muslim world, have openly supported those authoritarian regimes that claim to be threatened by Islamic revivalism, and generally have concluded that Islamic forces cannot exist in a democracy.[2] The conclusion in Western capitals has been that Islamic revivalism cannot and must not become a legal opposition.[3] It is apparent that Western observers do not take changes in the doctrine and practice of Islamic revivalism seriously and cannot envision a role for them in a democratic setting.

Islamic revivalism, however, is not new to the democratic process. There is a large body of evidence and relevant historical facts that are pertinent to the debates that today surround the place of Islamic revivalism in a democracy and its possible impact on it. These facts must be considered seriously. Some of the oldest expressions of Islamic revivalism, which were active long before Ayatollah Khomeini arrived on the scene, committed themselves to the political process early on and have participated in national elections since. They have been serving for some time now as legal oppositional forces. Clearly, this participation has not culminated in Islamic revolutions similar to the one witnessed in Iran. In fact, the state in these instances has not only remained intact, but has expanded its capacity and reach.

This implies that more attention should be paid to those factors that mediate the incorporation of Islamic revivalist movements in the political process, as well as to the terms under which they became a legal opposition. Focus here should not be only on the organizational features and ideology of Islamic movements, but also on how the state and its Islamic opposition negotiated the structure of their relations within the framework of the political process. In addition, scholarly analyses ought to critically examine both the extent of the impact of the Islamic revivalist movements on state policy and patterns of sociopolitical change once these movements join the political process, and the nature of the constrictions on the political maneuverability of Islamic movements pursuant to their political enfranchisement. The latter deserves particular attention. Thus far, most observers have been preoccupied solely with the impact of revivalism on politics, whereas participation in politics has had an equally important influence on the development of revivalist movements, which in turn conditions their political impact. The vicissitudes of this process can best explain the limitations Islamic movements face as they move beyond their status as legal opposition to capture power.

In this paper I examine these issues with reference to Islamic revivalism in Pakistan, with special focus on the development of the country's principal revivalist party, the Jamaat-i Islami (Islamic Party). Pakistan serves as a valuable case study of the inclusion of Islamic movements in the political process, offering insights into what might be expected from the proliferation of Islamic legal opposition movements in Muslim societies.

The Jamaat-i Islami and Islamic Revivalism in Pakistan

The Jamaat, formed in 1941, is one of the oldest Islamic revivalist movements.[4] The party's founder, Sayyid Abu al-ala Mawdudi (1903–1979), began to articulate a revivalist reading of Islam as early as 1932.[5] His works, which appeared in translation in the Arab world by the early 1940s, can be found today in more than twenty-two languages and in local editions in nearly every Muslim country. Mawdudi and the Jamaat are closely associated with the very rise of Islamic revivalism across the Muslim world. The Jamaat is also unusual in that it has been participating in the political process for close to five decades. The party moved to Pakistan in 1947, quickly joined the political process, and participated in the country's first elections in 1951. Since 1951, it has participated in all of Pakistan's six national elections and numerous other municipal and provincial elections. The party's politics and history provide analysts with a long and open account of revivalist activity in the political process.

There is little doubt that the Jamaat's main role in Pakistani politics has been one of dissent. Since 1947, the party has challenged various Pakistani governments on a host of issues, some Islamic and some secular. The Jamaat has demanded the Islamization of politics and social relations and sought to force governments to anchor state policy and institutions and constitutional debates in Islamic law. The campaign for Islamization took place in tandem with the demand for constitutional rights and democracy. In fact, the Jamaat's campaign soon served as the medium for articulation of diverse political views, and the party became the flag-bearer of civil societies and spearheaded their challenge to the state. Student, labor, clerical, women's, and professional associations formed by the Jamaat, or in cooperation with it, since the early 1960s have been instrumental in delineating a space for civil societies and limiting the scope of state authority.[6] They have also been important in harnessing popular discontent to launch prodemocracy agitations, most notably in 1969 against General Muhammad Ayub Khan's government and in 1977 against Zulfiqar Ali Bhutto's increasingly autocratic rule. In the same regard, the Jamaat has been an important voice in defense of civil liberties in Pakistan. The party was, in fact, one of the first political groups to form a civil liberties union, and throughout the 1960s and the 1970s, it was active in defending civil liberties.[7] During Pakistan's three constitution-making ordeals—1948–1956, 1962, and 1971–1973—the Jamaat demanded constitutional amendments and guarantees to limit exercise of arbitrary power by the executive. Most notably, it objected to those provisions of the Government of India Act of 1935 that gave the executive extraordinary powers and that were largely retained in the constitutions of 1956 and 1962.

The Jamaat's oppositional role also extended to economic issues. The party's challenge to the political establishment was not motivated by ideology alone, but also by political considerations that reflected the dynamics of its relations with the state. It has used diverse economic issues, with differing ideological implications, to challenge state authority. Two notable instances exemplify this point and elucidate the nature and scope of the party's dissent. First, the party strongly and successfully opposed Prime Minister Liaqat Ali Khan's land reform proposals in 1949–1951 because of their violation of Islamic law, which protects private property.[8] Mawdudi's views on this issue greatly differ from those of Ayatollah Khomeini, who initiated wholesale expropriation of private property after the Iranian revolution. Second, the Jamaat spearheaded, although this time unsuccessfully, the opposition to Prime Minister Moeen Quraishi's economic reform package in 1993.[9] Quraishi's reforms were designed to restructure Pakistan's economy and to cut public deficit and foreign debt by reducing imports and cutting subsidies. The austerity measures envisioned by the reform package were unpopular with Pakistanis of all hues. The Jamaat opposed Quraishi's plans and organized street demonstrations to stop them. By advocating a popular cause, the party's leadership hoped that the Jamaat would expand its base of support, especially among the poor. The party's politics had changed greatly since 1949–1951 when its opposition to land reform ran counter to the interests of the rural masses and proved politically costly.

Finally, the Jamaat has challenged the general direction of Pakistan's foreign policy, although it has also supported it in particular instances, especially during the Afghan war in the 1980s. The Jamaat since the 1950s, and especially since 1988, has strongly opposed Pakistan's close alliance with the United States. It opposed Pakistan's role in the Gulf War and expressed support for Iraq.[10] The party has also been vocal in regional issues. The Jamaat proved to be the principal obstacle to Zulfiqar Ali Bhutto's decision to recognize Bangladesh, which was postponed until 1974, when the government could bring the full force of the Islamic summit, which convened in Lahore that year, to bear upon the opposition. In a similar vein, the Jamaat has criticized Pakistan's policy on Kashmir. Since 1989, the Jamaat has mobilized popular support for Kashmiri freedom fighters and has sought to inform the government of popular sentiments through numerous demonstrations.

From all this, it is clear that the Jamaat's role as a legal opposition has been consequential in Pakistan's politics and has, in turn, determined the trajectory of the party's ideological and political development.

Two interrelated, although separate, factors have controlled the nature of the party's particular arrangement with the state. These factors have both set the pace for the party's inclusion in the political process and determined the extent of its impact on Pakistani politics. The first factor is the role of the judiciary in Pakistani politics, especially as the final arbiter in disputes between the state and its opposition. This fact underscores the importance of fair and consistent rule of law to the development of Islamic revivalism. The second is the manner in which the state has sought to confront the reality of Islamic activism in the political process. The first has guaranteed a space for Islamic activism in the political process, and the second has determined the nature of that activism and the scope of its influence.

The Judiciary and Political
Enfranchisement of the Jamaat

The Jamaat owes its inclusion in the political process largely to the role Pakistan's judiciary has played in that country's politics. Continuing in the

British tradition, and much like its Indian counterpart, the Pakistani judiciary has by and large maintained its independence from the executive branch and remained steadfast in protecting the rule of law in the country and institutionalized legal procedures. The judiciary has at times done the bidding of the powers that be—most notably in 1954, when it approved the decision of the governor general, Ghulam Muhammad, to dissolve the Constituent Assembly, and in 1979, when it sanctioned the execution of the former prime minister, Zulfiqar Ali Bhutto. Still, in comparison with its counterparts elsewhere in the Muslim world, the judiciary in Pakistan has displayed surprising independence of action. Between 1988 and 1994, for instance, the high courts in Pakistan have reviewed the executive's decisions in eighteen cases of dismissal of provincial and national assemblies. They have accepted only six of those decisions as legal and rejected twelve, half of which led to the restoration of the dissolved assemblies. The most notable case was the restoration of the National Assembly in 1993 after it was summarily dismissed by President Ghulam Ishaq Khan.[11]

The prominence of the judiciary, and its moderating influence on government behavior, is perhaps most clearly reflected in the fact that in 1995 Prime Minister Bhutto resorted to filing libel suits to silence her critics in the press rather than adopting censorship measures. Rulings by the judiciary were viewed by the government to be more legitimate in the eyes of the masses. The effect was, however, to dissuade the government from employing extraconstitutional policies to contend with dissent.

The judiciary's continued ability to check the abuse of power by the executive, although intermittent, has nevertheless been crucial to the openness of Pakistan's politics and to the political enfranchisement of Islamic parties such as the Jamaat. In fact, without the intercession of the judiciary, it is quite likely that the state would have effectively excluded the Jamaat and other Islamic parties from the political process. There are specific instances where this intercession occurred, directly influencing the balance of relations between the state and its Islamic opposition.

Twice Jamaat leaders were incarcerated by the government on the charge of undermining national security. In 1950, the Jamaat came under attack for questioning the Islamicity of the state and, more specifically, for questioning the government's right to support a jihad in Kashmir when it claimed to be observing a cease-fire with India. The government reacted by arresting Jamaat leaders and workers, confiscating the party's funds, and closing down its offices. In 1967, the Jamaat's leaders were imprisoned for questioning the government's right to declare the citation of the moon that marks the end of the holy month of Ramadan. Each time, the judiciary heard the appeal that was filed by the Jamaat and found the government's actions to have been unconstitutional. In 1950, the Supreme Court prevented the government from extending Mawlana Mawdudi's preventive custody without formally charging him with a crime and ordered him released. In

1967, the Supreme Court rejected the government's application of the Defense of Pakistan Rules to crack down on the Jamaat. It should be pointed out that the judiciary made these decisions in spite of considerable pressure from the government, which sought legal sanction for its actions. Moreover, in 1950, the government's perception of the Jamaat's threat to national security was shared by many among the general population who were also unsympathetic to the Jamaat because of its harangue against the Muslim League and its failure to support a jihad in Kashmir.

More important, in 1954, the Jamaat's leader, Mawlana Mawdudi, was arrested by the martial law administration in Punjab. The martial law had been declared in that province following two years of widespread disturbances by Islamic groups who demanded the declaration of the Ahmadi sect as a non-Muslim minority and the dismissal of Pakistan's Ahmadi foreign minister, Sir Chaudhri Zararullah Khan. Mawdudi was tried for sedition by a military tribunal after the declaration of martial law and sentenced to death. The Jamaat challenged the decision at the Lahore High Court and filed a habeas corpus petition. In 1955, the court reversed the sentences meted out by the military tribunal, which led to Mawdudi's release from prison.[12]

The most direct and blatant challenge to the Jamaat came in 1964. In that year, the secularist military regime of General Ayub Khan resolved to close down the Jamaat. Since 1961, the Jamaat had opposed a host of government reform measures, most notably the Family Law Ordinance of 1961, and had launched a nationwide campaign against Ayub Khan and his constitution of 1962. Jamaat's leaders were arrested and jailed; the party's publications were confiscated, its funds, property, and papers seized, and its offices closed down.[13] This was approximately when Nasser began to clamp down on the Muslim Brotherhood in Egypt, which led to the execution of Sayyid Qutb in 1966. Some in Ayub Khan's cabinet favored similar measures in Pakistan.

The Jamaat challenged the government's actions in provincial high courts. It won its case in the East Pakistan High Court and lost its case in the West Pakistan High Court. The government appealed the first decision and the Jamaat the second. The cases were referred to the Pakistan Supreme Court. After deliberations, and despite government pressure, the Supreme Court declared the banning of the Jamaat to have been illegal and ordered the party restored, its funds returned, and its leaders released from prison.[14] The judiciary's decision, snubbing a military government, which in turn, to its credit, accepted the verdict, has few if any parallels in other Muslim countries.

Through these actions, the judiciary helped negotiate a role for the Jamaat in the political process. By keeping the strong arm of the state at bay, and serving as a buffer between the state and the Islamic parties, the judiciary created a space for Islamic groups and parties, such as the Jamaat, in the political process, precluding their marginalization and radicalization. In the process, the Islamic movements, as the case of the Jamaat clearly shows, developed a healthy respect for an independent judiciary. Mawdudi's later works on the Islamic state clearly reflect this change in attitude.

The case of Islamic revivalism and the Jamaat in Pakistan show that the behavior of the state and, more to the point, the actions of various organs of the state—along with respect for and practice of the due process of law—do have an enduring and positive influence on the thinking and actions of Islamic groups.

One may also conclude from the above that the nature of Islamic activism is closely tied to the institutional structure of the state and the autonomy of its chief organizations, especially the executive branch.

The State and the Regulation of Islamic Activism

The second important factor that has controlled the Jamaat's inclusion in the political process is the manner in which the state has sought to contend with the Islamic factor in Pakistan's politics. Whereas the judiciary opened the door to Jamaat's political enfranchisement, state policy decided the nature and scope of its role in national politics.

Soon after Pakistan was created, the place of Islam in the national political discourse was put to debate. The secular political elite at first resisted giving Islam a role in national politics. However, a state built in the name of Islam and as a Muslim homeland, confronted with insurmountable ethnic, linguistic, and class conflicts, quickly succumbed to the temptation of mobilizing Islamic symbols in the service of state formation.[15] This tendency has only been reinforced over the years as the state has failed to address fundamental socioeconomic issues, carry out meaningful land reform, and consolidate power in the center. This has opened the door for Islamic parties to enter the fray. The incremental sacralization of the national political discourse has clearly favored a political role for those who claimed to speak for Islam and who advocate Islamization. Their activism, in turn, strengthened the impetus for Islamization.[16] The secular state resisted this trend only briefly. By 1949, the elite had accepted a political role for Islamic forces, compromising their original conception of Pakistan as a thoroughly secular state. In that year, the government adopted the Objectives Resolution, which was demanded by the Islamic forces as a statement of intent with regard to the future constitution. The resolution formally introduced Islamic concerns to constitutional debates and committed Pakistan to greater Islamization. Subsequent state policy, culminating in the constitution of 1956, only reinforced this tendency.[17] As a result, by the end of the first decade of Pakistan's existence, Islamic forces were fully included in its political process and had moved to appropriate the national political discourse from the state.

Although the state accepted a place for Islamic forces in national politics, it was not willing to abandon secularism, nor to permit any Islamization of society and politics outside the purview of its direct control. The state therefore resorted to regulating the flow of Islam in the political process, hoping to gradually negotiate arrangements with Islamic parties to that effect. Although the state never formalized a workable arrangement and was not able to avert frictions and confrontations, still it succeeded in retaining control over the flow of Islam in politics and limiting the scope of Islamization. The state oversaw the inclusion of Islamic forces into the political process by using regulatory arrangements. The manner in which these arrangements took form also accounts for the particular role Islamic parties have adopted in Pakistan's politics, the limits they have faced in their drive for power, and the structure of their discourse on politics and society.

The state has followed two general approaches to regulating Islamic activism. The first was directed at incorporating Islam into the state's discourse on sociopolitical change while simultaneously limiting the role of Islamic parties—the self-styled advocates of Islamization—in the political process. Here the state sought to appeal to the emotive power of Islam at the same time it sought to depoliticize it by limiting the political uses of faith by nonstate actors. This approach characterized the Ayub Khan and Zulfiqar Ali Bhutto periods (1958–1977). The second incorporated Islamic politics into the state's discourse by including Islamic parties in the political process and even in the running of the state, all with the aim of establishing control over them. This approach characterized the Zia ul-Haq period (1977–1988) and to a large extent characterizes the post-Zia period as well (1988–present).

The State's Islam and the
Marginalization of Islamic Parties, 1958–1977

During the Ayub Khan and Bhutto periods, the state acknowledged a role for Islam in politics, albeit begrudgingly.[18] Ayub Khan came to power at the helm of a military coup that sought not only to consolidate power in the central government, but also to modernize Pakistani society. Islam had no place in the general's vision of the future and could only serve as an obstacle to it. Hence, Ayub Khan initially tried to extricate Islam from politics. Soon after he assumed power, he charged the newly founded Bureau of National Reconstruction with formulating a new agenda for state construction, one that would be both secularizing and unifying—thus replacing Islam as the glue that kept Pakistan together.[19] However, the general found it impossible to undo the impact of a decade of gradual Islamization of national politics, especially as his autocratic style met with popular opposition and his plan of action raised the ire of various Pakistani ethnic groups, notably in East Pakistan. Ayub Khan was compelled to appeal to the emotive power of Islam to boost the legitimacy of the state. This change, of course, was most clearly evident during the war with India in 1965, when the general began to court the ulama and Islamic activists who had only recently been harassed by his regime and asked them to declare a jihad.

In sum, Ayub Khan's strategy amounted to merely limiting the scope of Islamic activism to the extent possible; more important, it moved to permanently marginalize, if not altogether banish, from politics Islamic political parties—the strongest and most visible of which was the Jamaat. To do so, Ayub Khan, and later Bhutto, floated their own interpretations of Islam—Islamic modernisms of sorts. The state thus looked to interpret Islam into quiescence, just as it appealed to its symbols and emotive power for legitimacy. Therefore, to the extent that Islam remained important to national politics, it was to serve modernization and social change. Central to this effort was the appropriation of the right to interpret Islam from the ulama and the Islamic parties, such as the Jamaat, and to wrest control of Islamic institutions from Sufi shrines to mosques and religious endowments.[20] This would make the state the chief spokesman for Islam and permit it to set the pace for the flow of Islam in politics. The state, in principle, conceded to a political role for Islam but only if it could control its interpretation, institutions, and politics.

As a result, the state used an Islamic rhetoric when necessary and paid lip service to Islamic ideals.[21] On 3 May 1959, soon after he consolidated power, Ayub Khan addressed a gathering of the ulama from both East and West Pakistan. In his speech, the general encouraged the religious leaders to interpret Islam in ways that would help the country's developmental agenda.[22] Soon thereafter, the Institute of Islamic Research, headed by Fazlur Rahman, later professor of Islamic studies at the University of Chicago, was charged with the task of formulating a modernist view of Islam. The government then proceeded to implement measures that clearly reoriented the state's policy on Islam to date and redefined the role of Islam in politics. The Family Law Ordinance of 1961, for instance, effectively secularized family law, precipitating a confrontation with the ulama and Islamic parties.[23] The constitution of 1962, in the same manner, removed "Islamic" from the official name of the state, which now became the Republic of Pakistan. By 1967, the government had introduced a host of bills to reform Islamic law and practice with the aim of accommodating the state's modernizing agenda.

The success of the state's policy depended on both a successful articulation of its interpretation of Islam, and its ability to effectively marginalize Islamic movements that could challenge its hold on Islam. Despite its efforts, the exclusionary approach to regulating Islam eventually failed. The failure was caused by both the shortcomings of the state's vision of Islam and its inability to maintain effective control over national politics. The result was a resurgence of Islamic activism, which drew power from social discontent to challenge both the state's authority and its vision of Islam. A number of factors were instrumental in undermining the state's project.

First, the Ayub Khan and, in the same vein, Bhutto governments were autocratic and followed economic policies that in different ways mobilized important segments of the population against the government. Ayub Khan's strategy for spurring industrial development led to corruption and flagrant income inequalities between social classes, economic groups, and, most ominously, the various provinces of Pakistan.[24] It led to mobilization of the industrial labor and the urban poor, led by the intelligentsia and ethnic parties. The outcome of the war of 1965 with India further eroded the authority of the regime. Bhutto's populism threatened the economic interests of the landowners of Punjab and Sind, the industrial elite, small landowners, shopkeepers, merchants, and the Muhajir community of urban Sind.

The opposition the policies of the two governments generated prevented them from consolidating power and effectively controlling national politics. In turn, parties such as the Jamaat found ample room to maneuver, established a base of support among dissident and prodemocracy forces, and were able to launch broadly based social movements.

Second, the Islamic pretense of the secular regimes was at no point convincing to the masses. The regimes' interpretation of Islam did not take root and was easily challenged by the ulama and Islamic activists. It was obvious to the few and sundry that the state was not serious about Islam and had no authority to interpret it. Ayub Khan's secular predilection and hostility to religion was well known; and Bhutto, who had been one of Ayub Khan's most secular lieutenants in the 1960s, had raised the ire of the masses with his open display of disregard for their religious sensibilities when he became prime minister in the 1970s.

The failure to convince the masses of the legitimacy of the state's Islamic policy opened the door for the Jamaat and its allies. The state had conveniently kept Islam in the political fray but, failing to retain control over its interpretation, had left its flank exposed to Islamic parties. The state, given the growing unpopularity of its economic and political policies, had only limited control over the activities of Islamic parties, who effectively mobilized Islam for purposes of political action. The coincidence of faltering state authority with the rise of Islamic activism undermined the regulatory arrangement that governed the relations between the two.

The change in the balance of relations between the state and the Islamic opposition is evident in the outcome of the following showdown over the right to interpret Islam. In 1966, two years before Ayub Khan left politics, his principal adviser on Islamic issues, Fazlur Rahman, presented a plan to resolve the dispute over the Islamicity of the banking system whereby only the real rate of interest would be counted as usury. The Jamaat and the ulama objected.[25] The debate came to a head in 1967 when the government declared that it would announce the citation of the moon at the end of the month of Ramadan, which traditionally marks the end of the period of fasting.[26] To add insult to injury, the government also claimed that it would use scientific methods to pinpoint the exact time of citation, methods that would not be available to the ulama, who had traditionally cited the moon and announced the end of the holy month. The government was not only appropriating the right to announce the end of Ramadan from the ulama but was doing so by the authority of its scientific know-how. Eight years after his rise to power, Ayub Khan was moving to once and for all assert the state's control over the right to interpret Islam and govern its sociopolitical functions. The ulama and the Jamaat refused to abide by the government's writ and resorted to agitations. By 1966, the Ayub Khan regime was weaker and more vulnerable. It had waited too long to assert its primacy in religious matters; its luster had long since been tarnished in the political arena. The dispute ended after the government capitulated and Fazlur Rahman resigned from government service.

Bhutto rose to power in the wake of the civil war of 1971, the loss of East Pakistan, and a humiliating military defeat. Bhutto also had an impressive mandate from the people of West Pakistan. Given this state of affairs, he was able to exercise effective authority in the political arena and to reinstate the regulatory arrangement that had controlled the flow of Islam in politics during Ayub Khan's rule. He couched his plans for Pakistan in religiously charged terms and symbols. Musawat-i Muhammadi (Muhammadan justice) became the hallmark of his populism as he replaced Ayub Khan's Islamic modernism with "Islamic socialism." For reasons explained above, Bhutto too was unable to retain control of this arrangement, which finally came apart in 1977. In fact, symbolically, Bhutto personally dismantled the regulatory arrangement under pressure from resurgent Islamic activism. He shelved Islamic socialism in a last-ditch effort to maintain control of the flow of Islam in politics and quickly adopted the demands of the Islamic opposition. He banned the serving of alcohol, ordered the closure of casinos and nightclubs, and banned gambling and all other social activities proscribed by Islamic law. He had hoped that by surrendering the right to interpret Islam to the Islamic groups he could mollify them. But Islamic parties, led by the Jamaat, were in no mood to be placated. Freed of the restrictions of state control, they were determined to use Islam to take over power. They continued their anti-Bhutto campaign, which came to an end only when the military staged a coup in July 1977.

Islamization and the Inclusion of the
Islamic Parties in the Political Process, 1977–1988

During the Zia period, the state adopted a radically different approach to managing the role of Islam in politics. Zia saw Islamic parties as distinct interest groups, whose power had risen considerably owing to their role in the anti-Bhutto agitations and the collapse of the two-decades-long containment strategy followed by the Ayub Khan and Bhutto regimes. His commitment to Islamic activism was by no stretch of the imagination as simple and straightforward as many have concluded. Rather, understanding both the limitations of the policies that his predecessors followed and the extent to which Islamic forces had gained in strength, he formulated his policies accordingly. As may be expected of any military ruler, Zia too sought to "depoliticize" Pakistani politics and to limit popular participation in it, regardless of whether that participation was Islamic or secular in nature. There was no doubt that with this aim in mind, although Zia was himself a devout Muslim, he would also look for ways to control Islamic parties and regulate the flow of Islam in politics. In fact, one can argue that the military coup of July 1977 was provoked directly by the collapse of the state's strategy of regulating Islam up to that point, and, as such, its aim was to prevent the Islamic forces from overwhelming the teetering state and to restore state authority before its Islamic opposition. In this sense, the July coup was similar to the Algerian coup of 1992 in its intent, although, as it will become clear, not in its methods.

General Zia sought to restore state authority by once again regulating the flow of Islam in politics and controlling the scope of Islamic activism. Interestingly, he did so by actively encouraging the inclusion of Islamic parties, such as the Jamaat, in the political process and by opening to them new avenues of activity. Zia not only relaxed restrictions on Islamic activism but also opened bureaucratic positions, state-led institutions, and even the military to Islamic activists. Ulama and leaders of Islamic parties joined the general's circle of advisers; four Jamaat leaders assumed ministerial positions in the 1977–1979 period. In addition, Zia placed the religious and ideological demands of the Islamic groups at the crux of state ideology and discourse on society and politics. Through these measures, Zia offered a power-sharing arrangement to the Islamic groups, in which the state would serve as the senior partner and the Islamic groups, led by the Jamaat, as junior partners.[27] Islamic parties would thus gain from state patronage; would find greater room for maneuverability in the bureaucracy, the military, and other government organs; and would enjoy a modicum of political activity, which, given the closed nature of the political system at the time, was important. The arrangement was made tenable by Zia's personal commitment to Islam, which was displayed in the concrete measures he undertook to implement an Islamization package from 1979 onward.

Consequently, Zia made no claims to interpreting Islam, nor did he seek to appropriate the right to interpret or represent Islam from its traditional spokesmen, as had his predecessors. Rather, he merely implemented an Islamization package that closely resembled the demands of the Jamaat and its allies, thus posing as the enforcer of a social code that was interpreted by Islamic activists. The Council of Islamic Ideology, an advisory body that deals with state policy, was staffed by members of various ulama groupings and Islamic parties. The council's seal of approval was secured for all aspects of the state-sponsored Islamization package, underscoring the fact that the regime was not responsible for interpreting Islamic dictums, but only for implementing them. As a result, Islamic activism lost its oppositional character and soon became an agent for implementing state policy.

The co-optation of Islamic forces, however, was not a halcyon affair, nor did it completely resolve the dilemma of controlling Islamization and its advocates. Zia proved willing to accept a greater sociopolitical role for the Jamaat and its allies and to give them considerable power and autonomy of action—but only in matters that were limited to religious questions. Hence, symbolic measures abounded—such as adding the adjective *Islamic* to the titles of a whole host of programs and institutions, giving greater lip service to Islam, restricting social activities of women and minorities, and implementing Islamic law in issues pertaining to personal conduct. The state, however, guarded its political and economic turf jealously. For instance, while Zia instituted a federal sharia court to review the compatibility of all laws with Islamic dictums, he was careful to exclude from the purview of the court's activities economic questions that would affect state policy.[28] Therefore, at a more fundamental level, the state kept Islamization at bay and ran its affairs with the aid of the same constellation of social classes and interest groups and in the same manner as it had since 1947. Moreover, the power and autonomy the Islamic parties enjoyed was limited by the state's tight control. Zia successfully resisted giving Islamic parties the handle to become empowered independent of his regime, and especially in lieu of his authority. Hence, he resisted holding elections during the months immediately following the coup when the Islamic parties may have fared well and found a base of support independent of his regime.

Meanwhile, through his patronage of Islamization, Zia gained legitimacy and institutionalized martial rule. He used the state's open advocacy of Islamization to control, and even silence, the Islamic parties, to repeatedly postpone elections, and to resist real economic and political changes or the meaningful restructuring of state policies. The fact that the state was so openly Islamic placed the Islamic parties in a very difficult position. Once the euphoria of state sponsorship of Islamization subsided, the Islamic parties understood that alliance with the military could be damaging to their long-term political interests but were unable to demand elections or to push for more rights and powers than the state was willing to give them. Zia's pro-Islamization strategy divided Islamic activities over the extent to which they ought to support this champion of Islam, even as he kept them under tight control and tarnished the popular image of Islam in politics. As a result, Zia deftly kept the Islamic parties in line without transferring real power to them.

Zia's strategy worked well in the short run but eventually proved unsuccessful. First, its use and abuse of Islam eventually scuttled the repository of Islam's popularity in the country and hence killed the proverbial goose that laid the golden egg. Second, Islamic parties—most notably the Jamaat-i Islami—eventually became tired of the limitations of their arrangement with the state. Islamic parties having suffered the brunt of the secularist autocracy of the Ayub Khan and Bhutto era were at first easily assuaged by Zia's strategy. The recognition and validation of the revivalist ideology Zia's Islamization package entailed and the prominence he gave to Islamic parties went a long way toward demobilizing them. In time, however, they began to demand more than just dabbling in Islamic issues and sought to extend their reach into political and economic matters of real concern to the state.

Although known primarily for their ideological demands, Islamic parties consisted of an array of social forces and smaller interest groups, civil societies, and unions, which behind the Islamic veneer of parties like the Jamaat had concrete socioeconomic and political agendas and demands for empowerment. A case in point is the Muhajir ("migrant") community of Sind that moved to Pakistan from India after the partition in 1947. Largely Urdu-speaking, they are the dominant force in the urban centers of Sind. Sindhis, who save for religion had little in common with the Muhajirs, have never been reconciled with their exodus, especially since Sind was not a stronghold of the Pakistan movement before 1947. As Sindhis expressed their political demands, which often ran counter to those of the Muhajirs, in ethnic and provincial terms, the Muhajirs turned to the unifying force of Islamic symbolism both to justify their presence in Sind and to override ethnic differences in the interest of a higher cause. Muhajirs had, therefore, traditionally dominated the leadership and rank and file of parties like the Jamaat and patronized the cause of Islam in national politics. Their close ties to Islamic parties did not mean that Islamization was their ultimate goal. Islamization was the means for transcending ethnic politics and its challenge to their interests, which were socioeconomic and political in nature.

General Zia was accommodating to the Jamaat and its allies on Islamic issues alone, but not on socioeconomic or political demands. For instance, Zia refused to repeal laws that were introduced during the Bhutto period to favor Sindhis at the expense of Muhajirs in the Sind bureaucracy and in the distribution of provincial resources.[29] As a result, the Muhajirs, much like other demand groups that formed the constituency of Islamic parties, did not realize their aims in Zia's Islamization. They either abandoned the Islamic parties altogether to form an ethnic party of their own, as did the Muhajir community, or they began to push the Jamaat and its allies for tangible results.

This led the Jamaat, and other Islamic parties, to distance themselves from the Zia regime and to join the national chorus for holding free and fair elections. They justified this new policy by claiming that Islamization could not be complete without democracy.[30] As important as Zia's contribution to Islamization may have been, his regime could now only further the cause of Islam by stepping aside. Implicit in this stance was an admission of error for having supported Zia in the first place and a desperate hope to regain control of the constituency whose support Islamization had once enjoyed.

These demands translated into tensions between the senior and junior partners, especially after it became clear that Zia had no intention of acceding ground. Meanwhile, with the passage of time, Islamic forces lost even more popular appeal. In the elections of 1985, Islamic parties performed poorly. The Jamaat, for instance, won only ten of the sixty-eight seats it contested in elections for the National Assembly. After the elections, despite the apparent centrality of Islam to national politics, secular political forces grew prominent. The landlord-dominated Muslim League formed the government, and the People's Party–led oppositional alliance (Movement for Restoration of Democracy) became the main contender for power. Even General Zia began to look to ethnic parties to bolster his regime. The decline in the fortunes of Islamic parties, their influence on the Zia regime notwithstanding, was now clearly evident.

The political hemorrhaging eventually compelled the Jamaat and its allies to draw back from their heretofore fecund arrangement with the Zia regime. That arrangement had been premised on the belief that the Jamaat was interested in Islam alone, but as a bona fide political party, the Jamaat ultimately showed that it was interested in power even more and would not stay happy with Islam alone. From 1986 on, as the Jamaat became more critical of the Zia regime, especially on Islamic issues that had been the linchpin of their relationship, it began to clamor for democracy and even entered into negotiations with anti-Zia forces.[31]

The Post-Zia Period, 1988–1996

Since 1988, when democracy returned to Pakistan, both Benazir Bhutto's Pakistan People's Party and Nawaz Sharif and the Muslim League have emulated Zia's strategy with some variations. Both parties have looked for a power-sharing arrangement with the Islamic parties and both have refrained from appropriating the right to interpret Islam for the state; but they have also sought to keep the state as the sponsor of Islamization. Given the legacy of the People's Party's relations with the Islamic forces, and Nawaz Sharif's close ties with Zia, the Muslim League enjoyed greater success in its dealings with Islamic parties. As far as the Islamic parties were concerned, the reasons they broke with Zia still applied. As the Jamaat's attitude indicates, the Islamic forces have not remained content with token Islamic measures and will accept a formal partnership with the state only if it will involve a real power-sharing arrangement.

The Jamaat joined the Muslim League–led Islamic Democratic Alliance, which emerged in 1988 to challenge Benazir Bhutto and the People's Party at the polls. Between 1988 and 1993, the Jamaat remained a mainstay of the alliance and Nawaz Sharif proved willing to promote Islamization, which culminated in the passage of a sharia bill in 1990. Much like Zia, however, Nawaz Sharif was willing to allow the Jamaat neither to influence economic, social, and foreign policy making, nor to expand its base of support independent from the Islamic Democratic Alliance. As a result, in 1993, the Jamaat informed the government that it wanted the ministries of foreign affairs, education, information and broadcasting, and finance—virtually the most important in the cabinet—and when Nawaz Sharif failed to deliver, it formally broke with the ruling alliance.[32] In the elections of 1993, the Islamic parties formed alliances of their own but did poorly. The People's Party and the Muslim League divided among them the bulk of the seats to the National Assembly.

Following the elections, the government of Benazir Bhutto has, despite ad hoc alliances, systematically avoided a formal arrangement with Islamic parties. In 1995, she in fact began to move in the opposite direction. On the eve of her trip to the United States, the prime minister began to characterize her government as a moderate Muslim one, besieged by radical religious pressure groups. In Washington, she proposed an alliance between her government and the United States to jointly confront radical Islamic activity—to build on the successful apprehension and extradition of Muhammad Ramzi Yusuf to stand trial in the United States for his role in the bombing of the World Trade Center in New York.

The Islamic parties found Bhutto's strategy to be a direct threat. They concluded that Bhutto was soliciting U.S. help in marginalizing parties that operate in the constitutional process.[33] The Islamic parties also viewed Bhutto's depiction of her government as a moderate Muslim one as reminiscent of Ayub Khan's and Zulfiqar Ali Bhutto's attempts to vest the state with the right to interpret Islam and control its flow in politics and society.

The deteriorating relations between the government and the opposition reached the point of rupture in October 1995, when the government announced that it had foiled a military coup plot that had the backing of certain Islamic groups. The Islamic parties dismissed the entire episode as a fabrication of the government to marginalize them and eventually to expel them from the political process. It remains to be seen whether, in the fragile political and economic climate of Pakistan, the state will arrive at a modus vivendi with Islamic forces; or will Islamic forces mobilize to challenge state policies?

The Implications of State
Strategies for Revivalist Politics

Although the oppositional role of Islam in Pakistan can be explained in terms of failures of state policies and the preponderance of socioeconomic crises, as is the case in other Muslim countries, the nature of Islamic activism has been decided in the context of the concord and conflict that state strategies to regulate Islam have entailed. I enumerate in this section the clearly discernible causal relations between state strategies and changes in the political attitudes and even ideology of Islamic parties, with reference to the case of the Jamaat.

In the first place, the state's Islamic policy, during the Zia period in particular, helped clarify the Jamaat's ultimate aims in the minds of its leaders and rank-and-file members. The state has, beginning with Ayub Khan's Islamic policy, legitimated and confirmed a role for Islam in the political process. The state has also increasingly acceded ground to Islamic forces, especially in the form of legislation inspired by Islamic laws. Still, the state has thus far managed to keep the Islamic parties, and the Jamaat in particular, away from altering fundamental socioeconomic and political structures. During the Zia period, by co-opting Islamic activism, the state also managed to effectively constrict the popular base of Islamic parties, which was reflected in national elections in 1985, 1988, 1990, and especially 1993, when the Jamaat and other Islamic parties contested the elections on their own. Pakistan may have become more Islamic during the Zia period, but the gains from it by the Jamaat and other Islamic parties have been quite modest.

As a consequence of state strategies to regulate Islam, especially during the Zia period, the Jamaat has been forced to confront fundamental questions regarding its role in politics. It has become clear that the Jamaat is more of a political party than an Islamic pressure group and as such is first and foremost interested in power. While during the Ayub Khan and Bhutto periods the party's political and religious aims coincided to obfuscate the real aim of its activism, the Zia period had the opposite effect. It essentially separated the party's religious aims—which the general served well—from its political interests—which he clearly hurt. The party's response to the apparent zero-sum choice was consequential. It finally chose to part with Zia to serve its political interests, although the general's

Islamization policy closely paralleled the Jamaat's own scheme. This realization, and the party's reaction to it, has had a profound impact on the
Jamaat's thinking and on that of its following and has reoriented the party
more effectively toward politics. Politics, rather than religion, impeded
Zia's regulation of Islamic activism.

Second, in addition to influencing the Jamaat's orientation, state
strategies have also influenced the content of its politics. The three decades
of experience with state management of the flow of Islam in the political
process have shaped the Jamaat's approach to political issues. It is in direct
reaction to state strategies that the Jamaat's views on democracy, good government, state power, economics, and a host of other social issues have
taken form. The Jamaat has imbibed certain values through its experiences
with the state as well as through its continued participation in the political
process. As a result, the Jamaat and its allies are far more committed to the
political process, and are far more mature politically, than revivalist parties
elsewhere in the Middle East and North Africa; and Pakistan has been able
to remain an open society and to produce a working democracy despite
Islamic activism.

Regulation of Islam and Political Change in Pakistan

The case of the Jamaat shows that inclusion of Islamic forces in the political process, and limits on the state's ability to crush them, can in fact serve
as an effective constraint on their growth. Although various strategies of
regulating Islam's flow in the political process have faltered, still their
cumulative effect has been to include Islamic groups in politics and to keep
the state from resorting to extreme measures in contending with its Islamic
opponents.

The results of six national elections in Pakistan attest to the constric-
tive impact of state strategies. In fact, the 1993 elections, which took place
after the Jamaat broke off its alliance with Nawaz Sharif's Muslim League,
show that Pakistan may be gradually approximating Israel's model.
Pakistan People's Party and the Muslim League have emerged as the two
major political parties, and the Islamic parties have been relegated to the
status of fringe parties. The Jamaat took part in these elections as the third
force in Pakistan's politics. In the same vein, Jamaat's leader, Qazi Husain
Ahmad, posing as a national leader, was exceeded in importance only by
Benazir Bhutto and Nawaz Sharif. In those elections, the Jamaat won only
three seats to the National Assembly, and Qazi Husain Ahmad failed to win
a seat. All Islamic parties put together won nine seats, trailing behind the
religious minorities.[34]

Yet another important consideration is the fact that the Jamaat's ability to act as a legal party for a sustained period of time, even if largely in dissent, has encouraged other Islamic parties to form and to enter the fray. This at first may have been a cause for concern, but it need not be so. The proliferation of Islamic parties since 1970 has, in one election after another, hopelessly divided the Islamic vote bank, at times to the benefit of secular parties. Routinely in national elections, the number of votes cast for parties with Islamic slogans has been far more impressive than the number of their seats in the National Assembly.

In the 1970 elections, in Punjab, Bhutto's People's Party performed very well, so much so that the province was later dubbed Bhutto's turf. Bhutto's success in Punjab owed to the fact that in the 82 electoral constituencies in that province, 260 candidates from Islamic and right-of-center parties and another 114 independent right-of-center candidates all appealed directly to Islam and divided the Islamic vote.[35] Similarly, in the 1993 elections, the Jamaat and two other Islamic coalitions divided the Islamic vote among themselves. They also took away votes from Nawaz Sharif's Muslim League to Benazir Bhutto's advantage. In at least ten constituencies, the votes cast for Islamic parties and the Muslim League exceeded those for People's Party candidates, but the seats went to the People's Party. Those ten seats may well have denied Benazir Bhutto her victory.

At a different level, continued participation in the political process has forced costly compromises, policy changes, and alliances on the Jamaat and its Islamic allies. These have tamed the revolutionary zeal of the Islamic forces and damaged their popular appeal. At times, the Islamic forces have been forced to reassess their ideological stance on particular issues, gradually routinizing their idealism in favor of greater pragmatism. In the process, Islamic forces have incorporated new ideals and policies into their ideology and praxis. They have learned from other political actors and have been compelled to respond to political imperatives and policy issues. Most notably, they have been forced to change in order to expand their base of support and to resolve costly contradictions in their doctrinal positions.

It is in this vein that the Jamaat has sought to accommodate traditional expressions of Islam, ironing out its differences with the various schools of Pakistani ulama, and move closer to popular Islam based in Sufism. Mawdudi's early work was critical of both the ulama and Sufis. Greater accommodation of traditional Islam was militated by the reality of the power and reach of the ulama and Sufi leaders in Pakistani politics. Similarly, the Jamaat has continuously sought to iron out the problem of accommodating democracy within the structure of its ideological perspective, which vests sovereignty in God. Continued participation in elections has highlighted contradictions between the party's ideological stance on democracy and the reality of its participation in it. The result has been revision and accommodation. In a system that includes and legitimates the Islamic opposition, the notion of an ideological cul-de-sac—an unbending outlook on politics that determines the behavior of Islamic groups—does not apply. Here, ideology, organization, and praxis all change in accordance with the pressures created by participation.

One can hardly underestimate the significance of these changes. Although they are largely tactical, and appear as subtle variations of doctrine and praxis, over time and cumulatively they recast revivalism. Such changes constitute what Martin Marty calls "epochal shifts."[36] Evidence shows that they can, and do, push revivalism to modernize, with the net effect of producing "controlled secularity,"[37] which Marty defines as "a complex set of radical religious changes, in which people set and think religiously in ways which differ from those of the past."[38] This is exactly what participation in the political process has entailed for the Jamaat. Continued inclusion in national politics can only hasten this process as it forces revivalism to confront problems and change course accordingly.

In 1995, fifteen of the Jamaat's senior leaders and chief ideologues defected from the party, arguing that the predominant attention being paid to political activities had detracted from the party's religious idealism. The crisis had followed the interruption of the sermon of Mawlana Gawhar Rahman (a senior conservative leader of the Jamaat) in the party's mosque in Lahore by noise from the neighboring bureau that was charged with producing music for the Jamaat's political rallies.[39] To succeed in the political arena, the party's activists are pushing for overtly pragmatic policy objectives and greater use of secular symbols and tools. As a consequence, gradually but surely, the party is drifting away from its original intellectual and ideological mainstay.

Finally, it is important to note that although the state's regulatory measures have failed to achieve their desired end, they have been successful in scuttling Islamic revivalism's political potential. Participation in the political process has averted radicalization of Islamic movements, and has also successfully restricted them to a small niche in the electoral arena. They can influence state policy but are not in a position to launch a successful bid for power.

While there are clear limits to applying elsewhere in the Muslim world the lessons of Pakistan's experience, the possibility should not be dismissed. Rather, the pattern of change in the politics of Islamic revivalism in Pakistan should broaden the scope of the debate on the place of Islamic forces in the political process as the legal opposition. There are other paths and outcomes conceivable in including Islamic actors in politics than those usually considered by specialists and policy makers. If nothing more, we have to make sense of the seeming paradox that one of the most Islamic countries is also one of the most open and democratic.

Notes

1. For more in this regard, see John L. Esposito and James P. Piscatori, "Democratization and Islam," *Middle East Journal* 45:3 (Summer 1991): 427–440; and Timothy D. Sisk, *Islam and Democracy: Religion, Politics, and Power in the Middle East* (Washington, D.C.: United States Institute of Peace, 1992).

2. See, for instance, Bernard Lewis, "Islam and Liberal Democracy," *The Atlantic* 271:2 (February 1993): 89–98.

3. The contour of this debate is presented in John L. Esposito, *The Islamic Threat: Myth or Reality?* rev. ed. (New York: Oxford University Press, 1995).

4. For more on the Jamaat, see Mumtaz Ahmad, "Islamic Fundamentalism in South Asia: The Jamaat-i Islami and the Tablighi Jamaat," in *Fundamentalisms Observed,* ed. Martin E. Marty and R. Scott Appleby (Chicago: University of Chicago Press, 1991), 457–530; Rafiuddin Ahmed, "Redefining Muslim Identity in South Asia: The Transformation of the Jamaat-i Islami," in *Accounting for Fundamentalisms: The Dynamic Character of Movements,* ed. Martin E. Marty and R. Scott Appleby (Chicago: University of Chicago Press, 1994), 699–705; Kalim Bahadur, *The Jamaat-i Islami of Pakistan* (New Delhi: Chetana Publications, 1977); and Seyyed Vali Reza Nasr, *The Vanguard of the Islamic Revolution: The Jamaat-i Islami of Pakistan* (Berkeley: University of California Press, 1994).

5. For a biography of Mawdudi, see Seyyed Vali Reza Nasr, *Mawdudi and the Making of Islamic Revivalism* (New York: Oxford University Press, 1996), 9–46.

6. Nasr, *Vanguard,* 116–218.

7. Mawdudi's regular attendance at the meetings of various civil liberties unions was even noted in diplomatic correspondences; see, for instance, U.S. Consulate General, Lahore, dispatch #189, 5/1/1952, 790D.00/5-152, National Archives, Washington, D.C.

8. Masudul Hasan, *Sayyid Abul Aala Maududi and His Thought,* vol. 1 (Lahore: Islamic Publications, 1984), 373.

9. Tahir Amin, "Pakistan in 1993," *Asian Survey* 34:2 (February 1994): 195.

10. Mumtaz Ahmad, "The Politics of War: Islamic Fundamentalisms in Pakistan," in *Islamic Fundamentalisms and the Gulf Crisis,* ed. James Piscatori (Chicago: American Academy of Arts and Sciences, 1991), 155–187.

11. Cited in Charles H. Kennedy, "Presidential–Prime Ministerial Relations: The Role of the Courts," paper presented at the conference "Politics of Social Change in Pakistan," Columbia University, 28 March 1994. For a general overview of the role of the judiciary in Pakistan's politics, see Paula Newberg, *Judging the State: Courts and Constitutional Politics in Pakistan* (New York: Cambridge University Press, 1995).

12. Nasr, *Vanguard,* 116–146.

13. Hasan, *Sayyid Abul Aala Maududi,* vol. 2, 169–170.

14. Ibid.

15. Seyyed Vali Reza Nasr, "Pakistan: Islamic State, Ethnic Polity," *Fletcher Forum of World Affairs* 16:2 (Summer 1992): 81–90.

16. See John L. Esposito, "Pakistan: The Quest for Islamic Identity," in *Islam and Development: Religion and Sociopolitical Change,* ed. John L. Esposito (Syracuse: Syracuse University Press, 1980), 139–162; and John L. Esposito, "Islam: Ideology and Politics in Pakistan," in *The State, Religion, and Ethnic Politics: Afghanistan, Iran, and Pakistan,* ed. Ali Banuazizi and Myron Weiner (Syracuse: Syracuse University Press, 1986), 333–369.

17. For more on the constitutional debates in the 1950s, see Leonard Binder, *Religion and Politics in Pakistan* (Berkeley: University of California Press, 1961).

18. For more on the Islamic policies of the two governments, see Mumtaz Ahmad, "Islam and the State: The Case of Pakistan," in *The Religious Challenge to the State,* ed. Matthew Moen and Lowell Gustafson (Philadelphia: Temple University Press, 1992), 239–267.

19. United Kingdom High Commissioner, Karachi, dispatch #INT.83/6/2, 3/10/1959, DO35/8949, Public Records Office, England.

20. Katherine Ewing, "The Politics of Sufism: Redefining the Saints of Pakistan," *Journal of Asian Studies* 42:2 (February 1983): 251–268.

21. Omar Noman, *Political Economy of Pakistan 1947–85* (London: KPI, 1988), 33–35.

22. The text of the speech is enclosed with United Kingdom High Commissioner, Karachi, dispatch #INT.48/47/1, 5/25/1959, DO35/8962, Public Records Office, England.

23. Fazlur Rahman, "The Controversy over the Muslim Family Laws," in *South Asian Religion and Politics,* ed. Donald E. Smith (Princeton: Princeton University Press, 1966), 414–427.

24. Khalid B. Sayeed, *Politics in Pakistan: The Nature and Direction of Change* (New York: Praeger, 1980).

25. Abu Tariq, ed., *Mawlana Mawdudi Ki Taqarir* [Mawlana Mawdudi's Speeches], vol. 6 (Lahore: Islamic Publications, 1976), 279–282.

26. *Pakistan Times,* 16 January 1967, 1.

27. See Seyyed Vali Reza Nasr, "Islamic Opposition to the Islamic State: The Jamaat-i Islami 1977–1988," *International Journal of Middle East Studies* 25:2 (May 1993): 261–283.

28. Ayesha Jalal, "The State and Political Privilege in Pakistan," in *The Politics of Social Transformation in Afghanistan, Iran, and Pakistan,* ed. Myron Weiner and Ali Banuazizi (Syracuse: Syracuse University Press, 1994), 178.

29. Nasr, "Pakistan," 86.

30. *Jasarat* (Karachi), 10 March 1990, 6.

31. Mujibul-Rahman Shami, "Jamaat-i Islami awr Peoples Party; Fasilah awr Rabitah, ik Musalsal Kahani," [Jamaat-i Islami and the Peoples Party: Distance and Relations, a Continuous Story] *Qaumi Digest* 11:2 (July 1988): 24.

32. *Newsline,* September 1991, 43.

33. *Resurgence* 4:3–4 (March-April 1995): 1–2.

34. Amin, "Pakistan in 1993," 195.

35. Sharif al-Mujahid, "Pakistan's First General Elections," *Asian Survey* 11:2 (February 1971): 170.

36. Martin Marty, *The Modern Schism* (New York: Harper and Row, 1969), 101.

37. Ibid.

38. Ibid., 108.

39. *Herald,* April 1995, 52–53.

Part 3

The International Relations of Political Islam

8

HAMAS: Legitimate Heir of Palestinian Nationalism?

Jean-François Legrain

Since the end of the 1970s, Islamism has become a major component in the social and political life of most Arab states. In Palestine, however, the particular circumstances of occupation delayed this ideological and political phenomenon. Indeed, until recently, the absence of a proper state made nationalist ideology exceptionally durable, allowing the Palestine Liberation Organization (PLO), the embodiment of nationalist identity in the quest for national liberation, to maintain itself as the undisputed "only legitimate representative of the Palestinian people." Although almost absent from the Palestinian public scene ten years ago, Islamism has now become a major political force in the West Bank and the Gaza Strip at the expense of the PLO. It has also shown itself to be a first-rate military force in terms of the number of operations it has carried out and its ability to identify and hit sensitive Israeli targets.

To accomplish this goal, the Muslim Brotherhood, the most popular Islamist organization in Palestine, had to end two decades of Islamic anti-Israeli inactivity. The 1987 explosion of the uprising (or intifada) left no other choice and, in 1988, the Brotherhood joined the active resistance against the occupation, an arena in which the Islamic Jihad trend had been a forerunner since the early 1980s. The Movement of Islamic Resistance (HAMAS), which was founded by the Muslim Brotherhood to mobilize the resistance, has profited from the union of patriotism (wataniyyah) and religion (dawa), blending moral and financial probity, military expertise, and political skill. Sixteen months after the signing of the Peace Accords in Washington on 13 September 1993, HAMAS imposed itself as the main opposition force to the Accords' terms of self-rule.

The evident success of HAMAS shows that the Islamist movement can no longer be analyzed as an epiphenomenon or the fruit of an ephemeral frustration. This chapter examines the context of the origins of the Islamist movement and explains how it took root in the political field and has endured within the framework of self-rule. Because the centrality of HAMAS is an established fact today, the analysis will also point to some of HAMAS's internal contradictions. The merging of political and military policies while reconciling Islamism with nationalism are highlighted as the sine qua non conditions of HAMAS's success in assuming the heritage of the former nationalist leader, the PLO.

The Establishment of the
Islamist Movement in the Political Arena

Protesting twenty years of Israeli occupation of the West Bank and Gaza, the intifada, a movement of violent and general anti-Israeli resistance, broke with the PLO's strategy of managing a "normalized" occupation of the territories, thereby ushering in a new era in the history of the Palestinian people. Under the auspices of the PLO, resistance existed, but only in specific conditions of time, place, and social group. Ending the occupation was conceptualized exclusively in military terms and therefore postponed, on the basis of successive Palestinian defeats. By contrast, the intifada planned the uprising of the whole society, seizing and appropriating the political initiative of the population inside the West Bank and Gaza, which had been, until then, left in the hands of the PLO leadership, located outside of the Occupied Territories.

In early 1988, the Unified National Leadership of the Uprising (UNLU), which had been established by second-rank followers of the PLO in Gaza and Jerusalem, began to give shape to this goal of seizing the political initiative. The UNLU had coined the catch phrases that defined the uprising as an antioccupation movement, "a revolt of stones and molotovs" restricted to the occupied territories that was to be based on civil disobedience and the demand that a Palestinian state be established alongside Israel.[1]

But even though the intifada, as a mechanism for political mobilization, emanated from nationalist ranks, the spark that ignited it came from the Islamists. Because of its numerous armed operations in 1986–1987 in the name of Islam, the Islamic Jihad movement constituted the major factor in transforming the passive suffering caused by the occupation into violent action against it.[2] The Islamic Jihad thus emphasized its founding principle: The Palestinian cause is central to the Islamist cause. Conceived in the late 1970s in Egyptian universities by Fathi Shiqaqi, a physician from Rafiah (south of Gaza), and Bashir Nafi, a biologist, Islamic Jihad considers Zionism and Israeli occupation an obstacle that cannot be ignored in the process of re-Islamization. Therefore, the destruction of Israel is an immediate and individual Islamic duty.[3] Based on the quranic commentary of

Shaikh Asad al-Tamimi, a former preacher at al-Aqsa mosque who has lived in Amman since 1967, Israel's destruction is as inevitable as the carrying out of divinely imposed religious duties by every believer.[4] Therefore, according to the Islamic Jihad, the liberation of Palestine is an immediate personal obligation (fard al-ain) for all Muslims, regardless of where they live. Because their lives are centered around a deeply rooted faith, Muslims do not need a sophisticated organizational apparatus to carry out acts of liberation. Rather, they are able to operate through very small and autonomous cells organized around a shaikh.

In its military strategies to achieve the Palestinian cause, the Islamic Jihad inside the Occupied Territories learned from the experience of detainees freed during the exchange of prisoners in May 1985 between Israel and the PFL-GC (Popular Forces of Liberation of Palestine–General Council) of Ahmad Jibril. Most of the Palestinian detainees were former activists of the PFL and members of an Islamic group (al-Jamaah al-Islamiyyah) that was founded by Jabr Ammar when he was in jail in the 1970s.[5] At the same time, outside the Territories, some high-ranking officers of Fatah independently set up the Islamic Jihad Brigades (Sarayat al-Jihad al-Islami), presumably without the knowledge of their superiors. Thanks to these experiences, in 1986 and 1987, the Islamic Jihad stepped up anti-Israeli military operations inside the Occupied Territories. The first serious act occurred on 15 October 1986, when a commando of the Jihad Brigades threw grenades at new recruits of an elite unit of the Israeli army at the Wailing Wall in Jerusalem. After six members of the Jihad escaped from Gaza's central prison in May 1987, several armed operations, including the assassination of the chief of the military police in Gaza, fueled a succession of massive popular anti-Israeli demonstrations. The killing of four Jihad militants on 6 October 1987 and the accidental death of Palestinian workers on 8 December 1987 are commonly held to mark the beginning of the intifada.[6]

Despite Israeli repression at the very beginning of the uprising and the hampering of its cellular and factional modes of operation, Islamic Jihad as an organization failed to become the catalyst for the reconciliation of patriotism and religion. In 1994, public opinion polls indicated that support for Islamic Jihad averaged about 2 to 5 percent. Fifteen years after its emergence, Islamic Jihad split into several rival organizations, of which only the Islamic Jihad Movement (IJM) in Palestine (Harakat al-Jihad al-Islami fi Filastin) has any real popular base in the Occupied Territories. It is also the only jihad organization that is still outside of the PLO's range. From its founding in the early 1980s, it was headed by Fathi Shiqaqi, who was deported by Israel in 1988 and assassinated in Malta in 1995.[7] This organization is opposed to the Oslo agreement, and it still conducts military operations against Israel.

All the other jihad organizations either disappeared or were merged into the PLO, according to a plan implemented by the Islamists and Fatah. The most significant military movement, the Islamic Jihad Brigades, was established in the mid-1980s by Hamdi Sultan al-Tamimi and Abu Hasan Qasim (Muhammad Al-Bhayss), two Fatah officers close to Abu Jihad (Khalil al-Wazir, the former second in command of the PLO, who was assassinated in Tunis in April 1988). Responsible for several deadly operations in 1986–1987, the Brigades almost disappeared after the assassination of their leaders in Limassol (Cyprus) in February 1988. Since then, headed by Jihad Amarayn, the Brigades were integrated into Fatah and seem to be dormant.

The Fighting Islamic Tendency (al-Ittijah al-Islami al-Mujahid) was founded by Munir Shafiq (an intellectual, a former Maoist from a Christian family, and former head of the Planning Center of the PLO) as the political wing of the Islamic Jihad Brigades and as the liaison with the Movement of Islamic Jihad in Palestine. It disappeared in 1988 after the assassination of the Brigades' leaders and after Shiqaqi claimed complete autonomy of decisionmaking. Munir Shafiq then became associated with HAMAS.

The Islamic Jihad Movement (IJM)–Jerusalem (Harakat al-Jihad al-Islami–Bayt al-Maqdis) is headed in Amman by Shaikh Asad al-Tamimi. Although Shaikh Asad played a part in its ideological formation, he failed to become an organizational leader when Fathi Shiqaqi left to found his own group. A personal friend of Yasir Arafat, Shaikh Asad served as an Islamic cautionary to Fatah's leader in the late 1980s and early 1990s and as a go-between with Abu Nidal's faction in Lebanon. The movement became inactive after condemning the Oslo agreement and freezing its participation with the PLO.

The Islamic Jihad Movement for the Liberation of Palestine–al-Aqsa Battalions (Harakat al-Jihad al-Islami li-Tahrir Filastin–Kataib al-Aqsa), which left the IJM–Jerusalem in the early 1990s, split into two factions: one, headed by Shaikh Fayiz Abu Abd Allah al-Aswad, who dismissed his rival Ibrahim Sirbil in 1992, operates from Gaza as a component of the PLO; the other one, resulting from the split that occurred in October 1994, was headed by Shaikh Husayn Anbar, who dismissed al-Aswad and criticized the financial and political conduct of the PLO from Khartoum and Algiers, although it did not withdraw from the organization. The short-lived Hizbollah-Palestine (Hizb Allah-Filastin), headed by Ahmad Muhanna, a former military officer of IJM in Palestine and then of IJM–Jerusalem, was a pro-Iranian and pro-Syrian group in the early 1990s.

Despite its small size and structural problems, since the mid-1980s, the Islamic Jihad movement has foreshadowed such current trends in ideology and mobilization as the retreat of Arab nationalism and the forging of new alliances between local patriotism and religion by committing itself militarily in the name of Islam. Consequently, the Islamic Jihad movement legitimated the Islamist movement as a whole through its links to patriotism (wataniyyah) rather than to nationalism (qawmiyyah).

By associating patriotism with religion, the Islamic Jihad cut itself off from the Muslim Brotherhood, for whom the re-Islamization of society is top priority, independent from the struggle against occupation.[8] At the end of the 1970s, the Islamic activism that appeared on the Palestinian scene was linked to the Jordanian and Egyptian Muslim Brotherhoods. The movement sought to reorganize society according to Islamic standards through the mosques, the universities, and an impressive number of charitable organizations. During the decade preceding the uprising, the Muslim Brothers established an extensive social welfare network in the Gaza Strip (charitable societies, dispensaries, kindergartens, sporting clubs, quranic schools, zakat [Islamic tithes] committees, etc.), from which Shaikh Ahmad Yasin, a former schoolmaster, emerged as a charismatic and influential leader. His Islamic Assembly (al-Mujamma al-Islami), founded in 1973, infiltrated the majority of mosques and came to control the Islamic University of Gaza. Religious associations were founded by the Muslim Brothers in the West Bank also, but they failed to establish a real network or to find their own leader; thus, the mosques remained in most cases under the control of the Jordanian ministry of awqaf (Islamic endowments). Prior to the intifada, the Brotherhood avoided confrontations with the occupying power and confined its political activities to the struggle against Palestinian "infidels," mainly the Communist Party. Fatah and Jordan encouraged this Islamist attack on the "left." Israel also had an interest in encouraging any division among the Palestinians.[9]

The Brotherhood maintained these policies until the intifada, although many people were reluctant to join an organization that required them to choose between religion and anti-Israeli activism. Whereas it was almost spontaneous at the beginning, once set in motion the uprising quickly became organized through local and regional committees whose mobilization capacity was, in most cases, able to overcome organizational fragmentation. The mobilization of the entire Palestinian society forced the Muslim Brothers to join the active resistance to the occupation. In these new conditions they had to recognize that their survival as a religious mobilizing organization depended on rejecting their former passivity and acknowledging patriotism as a prerequisite of any activity. HAMAS was therefore created.

The new organization was founded in two stages. In mid-December 1987, some prominent Muslim Brothers in Gaza decided, on their own initiative, to form a mobilizing structure called Harakat al-Muqawamah al-Islamiyyah (The Movement of Islamic Resistance, or HAMAS). This initiative appears to have been the work of people like Abd al-Aziz al-Rantisi, a physician working at the Islamic University of Gaza; and Salah Shahada and Yahya al-Sinuwwar, former student leaders at the Islamic University who were in charge of security matters in the Muslim Brotherhood. Although Shaikh Ahmad Yasin, the spiritual guide of the association in Gaza, apparently gave his approval, traditionalist hostility to any political move not directly connected to religious mobilization drove him to main-tain a clear distinction between this Islamic resistance and the Brotherhood. Two months later, however, in February 1988, the Brotherhood formally recognized The Movement of Islamic Resistance as its "strong arm." It is noteworthy that the acronym HAMAS dates from this very time.[10] It seems that this decision was made in Amman during a meeting between prominent Jordanian and Palestinian Muslim Brothers at the Islamic hospital. The Jordanian Brotherhood's spiritual guide, Shaikh Abd al-Rahman Khalifa, was present, as was the director of the hospital, Ali al-Hawamda, and par-liament members Ziyad Abu Ghanima, Hamza Mansur, and Hamam Said. Palestinians, of course, were also present, among them the official spokesman of HAMAS, Ibrahim Ghawcha, and the representative of the movement in Jordan, Muhammad Nazzal; from Gaza, the unofficial spokesman in the Occupied Territories, Mahmud al-Zahhar, a surgeon, and Abd al-Aziz al-Rantisi; and from the West Bank, probably Shaikh Jamil Hamami, a preacher from Jerusalem.[11]

Initiated by the operations of the Jihad and soon transformed into con-cepts by the followers of the PLO, the uprising owed its continuation to the presence of both nationalists and Islamists in the streets of Palestine. The Islamist militants were actively involved, despite their rejection of the ulti-mate political goal assigned to the intifada by the UNLU, i.e., the creation of a Palestinian state alongside Israel. Therefore, thanks to the wide and deeply rooted associative network put at the disposal of the intifada, politi-cal expertise, and a visibly growing military commitment, the Muslim Brotherhood, via HAMAS, managed as an organization to embody Islamic anti-Israeli resistance. This role grew because the PLO concentrated on the diplomatic process and left the conduct of the uprising and the armed mobi-lization since 1991 almost entirely to its shock troops, the Black Panthers of Fatah, the Fatah Hawks, the Red Eagles of the PFLP, and others, which were already distancing themselves from the political leadership. There is no doubt that this retreat gave opportunities to the armed wings of the Islamist movement—Kataib Sayf al-Islam and al-Quwah al-Islamiyyah al-Mujahidah (QASAM) of the Islamic Jihad, and Kataib Izz al-Din al-Qassam of HAMAS—to become more involved in the armed anti-Israeli resistance.[12]

Subsequently, the uprising began to change. Its daily struggle no longer followed the political and diplomatic lines of the project advocated outside the Occupied Territories. For the most part, actors in the West Bank and Gaza called for a reform of diplomatic initiatives (as demanded by the Democratic and Popular Fronts, or parts of Fatah and of the Palestinian People's Party, formerly communist), or even for their total termination (HAMAS, Islamic Jihad, and small organizations based in Damascus and not members of the PLO). New forms of violence concurrently emerged: first a "war of the knives" through an increased number of attacks against civilians, and then genuine guerrilla operations. The struggle also spread with operations carried out not only in the Occupied Territories, but also deep inside Israel.

Thus, while HAMAS was condemning the recognition of Israel as spelled out by the Palestinian National Council in 1988, calling for the liberation of Palestine "from the river to the sea," and carrying out an increasing number of military operations, the PLO withdrew from the field of violent confrontation, having failed to obtain concrete results subsequent to its political concessions. As a result, HAMAS succeeded in imposing itself as the legitimate alternative to nationalism.[13]

Islamism as a Response to the Washington Agreement

When the Israeli-Palestinian agreement secretly negotiated in Oslo was ratified in Washington on 13 September 1993, many commentators believed it to portend a decrease in HAMAS's influence; they attributed it to increasing Palestinian frustration over the deadlock of the Madrid peace talks. In their opinion, by signing the agreement, Israel had restored the PLO's political hegemony. The signing was followed by a short-lived euphoria. Fifteen months later, the PLO, or more properly Fatah, was discredited by the situation resulting from the ratification in Cairo on 9 February 1994 of the agreement on security issues in Gaza and the Jericho area, and 4 May 1994 implementation of Palestinian self-rule in those areas. Six months after the return of Yasir Arafat to Gaza, an increasing number of Palestinians believed that their administration was no longer able to defend their most elementary rights.[14] Henceforth the Islamist movement was deeply rooted in the political scene, and HAMAS, combining patriotism and integrity in an all-inclusive Islamic rhetoric, claimed to be the legitimate heir of PLO nationalism.

The Israeli army left no doubt about the increasing importance of HAMAS, even before the massive wave of military operations against Kataib al-Qassam. On 26 December 1993, General Matzan Vilnay, chief of the southern military region, speaking to a group of Israeli members of the Knesset visiting Gaza, estimated the population's support for HAMAS at 40 percent. An intelligence officer, believing this to be an underestimate, proposed a rate closer to 50 percent as more realistic.[15] Various elections held by student groups and professional organizations support the higher estimate. On 24 November 1993 at the elections for the student council at Bir Zeit University (2,536 registered), the HAMAS and the Popular and Democratic Fronts bloc won 52 percent of the vote against Fatah, the People's Party, and Fida (formerly the Democratic Front, Abd Rabbuh movement).[16] At the Islamic University of Gaza, on 5 and 6 November 1994, HAMAS received 91.5 percent of the vote and Islamic Jihad 7.7 percent; convinced of their defeat, the Fatah and PFLP blocs withdrew from the elections. Although an election tally at an Islamic university was not necessarily an accurate barometer of public opinion for the whole Strip, it is noteworthy that two weeks later, the Fatah bloc won the elections at al-Azhar University in Gaza (2,742 registered), their stronghold, with only 64 percent of the votes (1,764 votes), leaving 24 percent to HAMAS and 6 percent to the Islamic Jihad. Thus, in spite of Arafat's return to Gaza, Fatah failed to win new positions in Gaza's two most important universities.

Moreover, although elections had formerly been won exclusively in the academic arena, since the intifada, elections increasingly favored Islamist tickets, proving that support for Islamic groups has spread to almost all professional fields.[17] For example, on 28 January 1994, at the elections of the Gaza Engineers' Association (929 registered), the HAMAS and Jihad bloc won 46.7 percent of the votes, Fatah 43.95 percent, PFLP 6.5 percent, Arab Liberation Front (pro-Iraqi) 1.3 percent, and Fida 1.2 percent. In most of the professional and university elections held between 1989 and 1994, HAMAS and Fatah obtained almost the same results, i.e., around 40 percent each, reflecting the ability of each party to build alliances to ensure victory. By comparison, current opinion polls accord Fatah 40 to 43 percent of projected votes and HAMAS only 12 to 17 percent.[18] Experts emphasized that the differences in the results of professional elections can be explained by the prevalence among the total population of the traditionalists and/or older population who declare themselves either "independent" or support the existing power, whatever it may be. Fatah is still considered the existing power, but for how long?

The rising power of the Islamists is even more noticeable on the military front, where HAMAS and to a lesser—although not negligible—degree the Islamic Jihad gained a quasi-monopoly. Some of these operations, such as the killing in an ambush in December 1993 of the coordinator of the Israeli army's undercover units in the Gaza Strip, manifested undeniable military skill and expertise. By increasing the number of suicide operations, the Kataib al-Qassam of HAMAS (and QASAM of Islamic Jihad) brought a new type of warfare to Palestine. The fighters' resolve has rendered these operations, carried out mostly in Israel itself, very deadly and has raised a massive public reaction among both Israelis and Palestinians. As revenge for the Hebron massacre on 25 February 1994, when a Jewish settler killed thirty worshipers in the Patriarch mosque, the Kataib al-Qassam promised and carried out 5 anti-Israeli operations. The first occurred on 6 April, when 8 Israelis were killed and 19 wounded near the center of Afula (Galilee) in a suicide operation involving a bus. On 13 April, a bomb exploded in the central bus station of Hadera (Galilee), killing 6 Israelis and wounding 21 others. After a pause during the summer, al-Qassam began new operations on 9 October, when a commando raided a commercial street in Jerusalem, killing 2 passers-by and wounding 14 others. On 14 October, Corporal Waxman, who had earlier been abducted, was killed when the Israeli army raided the house in which he was detained. The last operation of the series was the most deadly: a 19 October bombing of a bus in the center of Tel-Aviv killed 23 persons and injured nearly 50.

The increase of HAMAS's power should be viewed in connection with the conditions under which the negotiation of the Israeli-Palestinian agreement was conducted. In this post–Cold War period, the Washington agreement formalized the balance of power between Israel and the Palestinians or, more generally, between the international community and the Arab world. One of the cosignatories of the agreement, Israel, was reputedly regarded as the winner, the other, the loser. But, after having publicly chosen the Palestinians as "partners," Israel returned to a strong line and offered no signs of goodwill. Therefore, because of the lack of broad consensus on the recognition of Israel in the present context, the Jewish state reinforced the Palestinian fear of seeing its leadership become the front line defense of the occupation, i.e., a supplementary militia matching Antoine Lahad's Army of South Lebanon.[19] Thus, HAMAS succeeded in gathering together those who opposed the Oslo process on the grounds that it would create Palestinian Bantustans, and those who still favor the process but believe Arafat has conceded so much that the predictions of those who reject it have been justified. The daily humiliations inflicted on the inhabitants of the Occupied Territories and on the PLO only strengthened HAMAS and its Kataib Izz al-Din al-Qassam, and the Islamic Jihad with its al-Quwah al-Mujahidah al-Qasam, which became spearheads of the Palestinian resistance.

None of the dates mentioned in the Washington agreement were honored by Israel: its army redeployments in Gaza and Jericho were delayed for more than five months; the redeployment in the West Bank and the elections of a Palestinian council of autonomy, both scheduled for July 1994, were still being negotiated in Cairo at the beginning of 1995. There was no end to repression: between 13 September and 30 November 1994, 164 Palestinians were killed by the army, among them many who had been placed by the government on the killing list of the "special units."[20] Although several hundred prisoners were freed, some 6,000 of them remained in detention centers. Colonization continued: around 470 hectares of land were confiscated per month from the beginning of the uprising; after the Madrid conference, the rate fell to 250 hectares per month but rose to 840 hectares after Oslo.[21] In 1993, according to the Israeli Bureau of Statistics, the Jewish population in the settlements in the West Bank (Jerusalem excluded) and Gaza increased by 9.3 percent (i.e., 115,000 settlers according to official estimates and 136,415 according to the settlers themselves); in East Jerusalem, occupied in 1967, the Jewish population (168,000) is now larger than the Palestinian (155,000). In Jerusalem, M. Meir Davidson, a former leading member of Ateret Cohanim, the movement for the colonization of the Muslim quarter of the Old City, was appointed to the town council at the beginning of 1994 as adviser for East Jerusalem affairs. Israel never abandoned its policy of collective punishment: the government repeatedly answered armed operations by sealing off the whole of the Occupied Territories, each time sending their precarious economy into free fall. Although the Hebron massacre was an individual act, it became for the Palestinians an official *casus belli* due to the massive repression by the Israeli army of the popular demonstrations that followed and the appropriation of a great part of the shrine to the benefit of the Jews.

Seen as a shelter for Palestinian dignity, HAMAS was viewed by large portions of the population as the voice of the Occupied Territories. This was a reaction to the political and diplomatic games that seemed to benefit the PLO leadership outside the Territories, but from which the Palestinians inside the Territories felt more and more excluded. At its beginning, the uprising had indeed been the appropriation by the population in the Territories of the political initiative. But by calling for negotiations as early as 1988, the underground UNLU gave this initiative back to the leadership in Tunis and to its official representatives inside the Territories, i.e., the pre-intifada establishment.[22] The Madrid and Washington negotiations maintained the illusion that the population inside the Territories was being heard, despite the fact that the real talks were taking place on a totally different basis, conducted secretly in Oslo between a handful of Yasir Arafat's personal representatives and the Israelis. Only a few days prior to the signing of the agreement did the population discover that its representatives in Washington were mere puppets. Later, when Arafat returned to Gaza with his old comrades, he was clearly reluctant to share power.

Therefore, for an increasing number of Palestinians—victims of daily difficulties under self-rule—Arafat, his team, and his police have been perceived as outsiders. HAMAS has taken advantage of this popular rejection of the PLO's operation under Arafat's guidance. More and more voices inside the organization have publicly denounced Yasir Arafat's disregard for institutional structures, since he rarely convenes them; when he does, it is only to ratify decisions he has already made. Growing public discontent was apparent, for instance, when Arafat called a meeting of the leadership in Tunis on 1 May 1994 to discuss the agreement he was about to sign in Cairo; both PLO executive committee members and leaders from the Occupied Territories boycotted the meeting. Since the assassinations of his companions in the struggle, founders of Fatah Abu Jihad (April 1988) and Abu Iyad (January 1991), Arafat has been acting on his own, surrounded by only a few advisers (Abu Mazin, Yasir Abd Rabbuh, Nabal Shaah, and Abu Ala). Internal criticism has undermined the cohesion of the structure but has not led Arafat to significantly change his modus operandi. For example, he has failed to act on the demand for democratic reforms presented in

April 1994 and later repeated by Haydar Abd al-Shafi, former head of the Palestinian delegation to the bilateral negotiations in Washington.

As a result, Yasir Arafat has seemed to be more and more isolated. Resentment reached even the most loyal among the leaders who were formerly outside the Territories, such as Mahmud Abbas (Abu Mazin), the main negotiator during the Oslo process, who refused any official involvement after Arafat's return to Gaza. Most of Arafat's companions, both from the diaspora and from the Occupied Territories, were reluctant to support an agreement they believed would produce a powerless Palestinian authority, given Arafat's habits and the terms imposed by Israel.

In the Occupied Territories, the internal crisis in Fatah sprang from the extensive restructuring of the political stage after six years of intifada. With the uprising, a new underground leadership emerged, comprising young, educated residents and refugees coming from towns, camps, and villages. The nationalist establishment—resident, urban, and largely concentrated in the Jerusalem-Ramallah-Bethlehem area—had formerly built its legitimacy on its privileged relationship with the leadership from the outside, thus confining itself to the fringes. In charge of establishing a structure of self-government, Fatah has resumed its established practice, aiming at controlling society by subduing its representatives. But, by appointing notables of the traditional establishment, such as Zakarya al-Agha in Gaza, to key positions, Yasir Arafat, disregarding the potential risk of the disintegration of his movement, excluded many young leaders who voiced their disagreement. Six months after the return of its president, Arafat's movement was nearly split. The Fatah internal elections were postponed in December 1994 after the first elections held in Ramallah in November put new leaders in office. (There is speculation that the Fatah leadership was not confident enough in the results of the forthcoming election.) Meanwhile, several violent incidents of infighting occurred in the Occupied Territories. Israeli demands concerning the exercise of self-rule and Fatah's internal dissension and inability to build a true and credible nationalist opposition enabled HAMAS to prosper, taking advantage of its own vitality and political skill.

Challenges to HAMAS

In such a context, HAMAS has had to diversify its role from within. Because its main support was drawn from a combination of a core of militants committed to the fight for an Islamic Palestine and individuals close to the PLO and independent movements, it, of necessity, assigned a lesser order of priority to religious and social concerns, although these elements have remained an important connection to the Muslim Brotherhood. Indeed, thanks to its pietistic past, HAMAS has the support of some of the most traditional elements of Palestinian society, which had previously been close to Jordan. However, granting autonomy to its "powerful arm" and allowing recruitment beyond the ranks of its traditional constituency created the risk for the Muslim Brotherhood of being challenged on its own ground. The growing challenge for HAMAS has undoubtedly been in the management of its internal diversity, on which the old guard and the younger generation have disagreed. The former, nostalgic for the internal coherence of the Muslim Brotherhood, regards diversity as a danger to the integrity of Islam and to the association, while the latter is more grassroots in its approach, promoting diversity as a source of enrichment. This became a dangerous challenge to the movement, which, at least in the beginning, was not able to assume the heritage of Fatah and the PLO without exacerbating its internal and long-standing contradictions.

Therefore, the behavior of HAMAS leaders should be viewed in terms of contradictions that have been part of the long history of the movement, rather than in terms of "finely calibrated political and military policy."[23] Historically, most HAMAS leaders stem from the Muslim Brotherhood, clinging to the centrality of religion. In their eyes, HAMAS's first priority is neither to seize administration of Palestinian policy from the PLO, nor to achieve the immediate liberation of Palestine. Shaikh Yasin's whole strategy can be viewed as pragmatism tied to the interests of the movement's religious imperatives (dawa). The spiritual guide of HAMAS considers patriotic struggle to be a simple means of reinforcing the legitimacy of his re-Islamization movement. Therefore, caution must be exercised in order to maintain its patriotic image, while avoiding any kind of repression that would imperil the Brotherhood's infrastructure.

Yet large parts of HAMAS's constituency no longer share this wait-and-see policy. Indeed, many younger members who joined HAMAS directly without being affiliated with the Brotherhood never adhered to this principle. The same contradiction can be observed between the leaders inside the Occupied Territories and their counterparts abroad. Most of HAMAS's representatives outside the Territories, such as Muhammad Nazzal in Amman, have different agendas, focusing instead on substituting their movement for the PLO, most often through a policy of radical refusal. Because they deal exclusively with states and organizations rather than interacting with the populace,[24] they have no need to organize religious activities.

For instance, during the Gulf War the leadership of HAMAS outside the Territories adopted the stance of the Jordanian Muslim Brotherhood, which aligned itself with Iraq and publicly distanced itself from its internal counterpart. After having shown some "understanding" vis-à-vis the Kuwaitis under occupation and having called for a vote on self-determination, HAMAS inside the Territories chose to remain silent on the crisis rather than aligning itself with public opinion and that of its Jordanian neighbors. The war itself enabled leaders both inside and outside the

Territories to speak in the name of the people, denouncing "the new Crusaders' aggression." Thus pragmatic leaders gave priority to preserving HAMAS's infrastructure. In this case, its opinion prevailed over the opinion of its radical challenger. This cleverness was later to be amply rewarded by the Gulf states, which maintained their financial support to the Islamist movement, while boycotting the PLO politically and financially.[25]

The Kataib Izz al-Din al-Qassam, for their part, have never agreed on these lukewarm historical and political activities. Because of the secrecy surrounding them, the detailed conditions of their birth and their operating mode are still unknown.[26] HAMAS's political leadership appears to have more symbolic than concrete authority over them. More than ever, they have pushed the uncompromising struggle against Israel, putting the Palestinian Authority (PNA) in an uncomfortable position at a time when many of HAMAS's political leaders want to transform their movement into an official political party. This kind of contradiction is not new. It dates back to the kidnapping and assassination of two Israeli soldiers, Sasportas and Saadon, in spring 1989. This twofold operation, claimed by the Kataib al-Qassam, was the first military action that clearly contradicted the primarily religious policy advocated by Shaikh Yasin. One of its first results was to shake the whole structure of the movement, following the massive Israeli raid against its supporters and the arrest of the shaikh himself, who was sentenced to life imprisonment. The Kataib conducted a similar military operation in December 1992 when it kidnapped Toledano, an Israeli border policeman. He was assassinated a few hours after Shaikh Yasin called on the abductors to keep him alive as an asset for negotiation. The operation led to the deportation of more than 400 so-called Islamists to Marj al-Zuhur in south Lebanon, which served to further destabilize the movement.

Kataib al-Qassam's increasingly dreadful operations deep inside Israel and against settlers at the fringes of Gaza gave Israel the opportunity to transform the political wing of HAMAS into its foremost enemy. Therefore, according to the Israeli view of the agreement, to achieve peace, HAMAS had to become the PNA's first target for eradication. Despite the fact that the HAMAS information office has always assumed its military operations to be on behalf of the Kataib al-Qassam, some of the political leaders inside, and even outside, the Occupied Territories kept a certain distance but did not condemn them. The most striking statement was made by Musa Abu Marzuq, head of HAMAS's political department, who lives in Amman, on the day of the Waxman abduction.[27] He announced his organization's agreement to a cease-fire with Israel in exchange for Israel's withdrawal from Gaza and the West Bank (including Jerusalem), the dismantling of the settlements, Israeli recognition of the right of return for the refugees, and the organization of free elections. Many younger supporters viewed Abu Marzuq's offer as an ideological deviation and demanded a quick "clarification," despite Shaikh Yasin's and Muhammad Nazzal's similar former declarations. The controversy died down when Abu Marzuq himself declared his statement had been misinterpreted. Some weeks later, on 2 June 1994, Gazan Islamist Shaikh Ahmad Bahar declared that resistance to occupation "does not have to be by armed struggle; it can be by words, opinions, and unifying people."[28] In October 1994, another HAMAS leader from Nablus, Shaikh Jamal Salim, speaking on Radio Israel in Arabic, suggested a mutual cessation of attacks against civilians.[29]

The same differences in the political behavior of HAMAS's leaders can be observed concerning the institutional relationship between HAMAS and the Jewish state. On 13 December 1993, for instance, General Doron Almog, commander of the Israeli army in the Gaza Strip, asserted upon taking office the previous week that he had met with "eminent HAMAS leaders" during the previous week. HAMAS denied this statement the next day in a leaflet issued in Gaza, stating that no meeting with an Israeli official was ever considered. A few weeks later, Mahmud al-Zahhar, former head of the information committee in Marj al-Zuhur, declared: "We have been told that army officers have met with HAMAS leaders before the deportation [in Marj al-Zuhur]; really, I have no objection to such meetings."[30] This declaration was made at the same time that the Kataib al-Qassam were increasing their anti-Israeli operations.

HAMAS's participation in the elections for the PNA was also a source of contradictory statements. Shaikh Hamid al-Bitawi, qadi of Tulkarm (northern West Bank), preacher in al-Aqsa mosque, president of the League of the Ulamas of Palestine, and former deportee to Marj al-Zuhur, was representative of the most open-minded trend, asserting unconditionally that "the Islamic movement will take part in the elections."[31] On the other hand, Shaikh Yasin, sending a series of letters from prison,[32] again displayed his traditional pragmatism, writing that "holding elections is now an issue for the Palestinians; the Islamists are divided between those supporting participation and those opposing it; as far as I am concerned, but only God knows, I consider it is better to participate than to abstain, providing that the Council be empowered with legislative privileges (tashri); as a matter of fact, we are opposed to what is happening in the streets, so why not express our opposition within the legislative institution which will de jure become in the future the authority representing the Palestinian people?" Such participation "will reassert the strength of the Islamic presence on the arena and will prevent it from losing ground because of its isolation." Ibrahim Ghawsha, spokesman for HAMAS in Amman and a negotiator representing the movement in the framework of the ten organizations opposed to the Washington agreement,[33] was compelled to take a harder stand when he claimed on 6 January 1994 in Damascus that Shaikh Yasin's words had been distorted and that HAMAS would not participate in prospective elections regarding autonomy. "Nevertheless," he added, "HAMAS will contin-

ue to participate in non-political elections." His stand on this matter was identical to that of Mahmud al-Zahhar, who stated that "we will participate in any election not connected with autonomy."[34]

Six months after Arafat returned to Gaza, HAMAS's behavior toward the PNA was essentially conciliatory, however rejectionist its public discourse. Despite occasional fighting and although the police killed 13 people and injured almost 200 others in Gaza on 18 November 1994, during a demonstration convoked by HAMAS, discipline prevented civil war. Every important conflict that occurred between the nationalists and the Islamists was followed by negotiations and agreement. It is to be noted that HAMAS never attacked Palestinian political figures, despite HAMAS's rejection of the Oslo agreement. To avoid problems for and with the PNA, HAMAS also refrained from attacking Israelis in Gaza. This attitude reflects an extreme realism vis-à-vis the autonomy. HAMAS accepted the Oslo agreement as a fact and is now forging the movement's new politics. Such pragmatism lends strength to the desire of some HAMAS leaders to transform the movement into an opposition party.

From 1984 to 1994 the Palestinian political scene was characterized by increasing polarization between nationalist and Islamist organizations. The Islamic Jihad, as a precursor, succeeded in reconciling Islam and patriotism, but failed as the organizational axis for this reconciliation and gave up this role to HAMAS during the uprising. The tremendous impact of the intifada on every aspect of the Palestinian situation was evident. Following the uprising, the Palestinian organizational, political, and military balances underwent a general restructuring: between the "inside" and the "outside"; between the youth of the UNLU and the established old guard; and between patriotism, nationalism, and religion. The Islamist movements clearly showed a greater ability than the nationalist organizations to profit from these new realities. Nevertheless, although the reconciliation of Islam with patriotism occurred on the level of ideology, the Islamist/nationalist dichotomy remained on the level of organization.

Furthermore, because there was no consensus, the signing of the Washington agreement increased the tensions within each movement, as well as between the main blocs. Six months after Arafat's return to Gaza, Fatah appeared doomed to split between the supporters of its president, to whom Israel and the international community have left no choice but to form the Palestinian equivalent of the Army of South Lebanon, in charge of policing and administrating Bantustan-like enclaves; and a bewildered grassroots constituency, who has decided to go back to the old principle of rejection, since occupation continues with no acceptable solution in sight. The Washington agreement could also lead HAMAS to split between its traditional advocacy of political participation in the higher interest of its religious activities and radical rejection of autonomy and support for an all-out armed struggle.

Therefore, the ground of the Palestinian political debate focused less on the conflict between nationalism and Islamism, and highlighted instead the controversy between the supporters of self-rule as it now exists and the partisans of radical change. This new fault line was evident in a mid-November 1994 public opinion poll conducted by the CPRS, which found 49.8 percent of the population in the Occupied Territories "accepting the PLO solution as the solution for the Palestinian cause" (i.e., establishment of two separate states in Palestine), and 38.7 percent "accepting the Islamic solution (that which is suggested by the Islamic movements and calling for the liberation of Palestine from the sea to the river)." When asked how they would vote if elections were held at that time, 42.3 percent said they would vote for Fatah's candidates, 17.4 percent for HAMAS's, and 3.7 percent for Jihad's. While 56.6 percent of the people supported armed operations against Israel, only 34.4 percent condemned them. Such figures indicate that HAMAS, as an organization, has not yet registered all its supporters. Considering the increasing rejection of the present terms of the self-rule, HAMAS will have to reconcile Islamism and nationalism if it wants either to replace the PLO or to become its new axis. Palestinian popular opinion seems to leave the door wide open for this task.

Conclusion

By August 1996, the pessimistic tone of the preceding discussion was corroborated by the manner in which the various agreements were implemented and by the measures taken by the new Israeli government. Official mutual recognition would not only have allowed Palestinians to recognize Israel's right to exist within Palestine (as Yasir Arafat, in his capacity as "representative of the Palestinians" did in the name of the PLO in September 1993), but also would have compelled Israel to recognize the national rights of the Palestinians within Palestine. By avoiding this official recognition, Israel still appeared to cling to the exclusivist ideals of Zionism, suggesting that the recent agreements constitute a means of continuing the occupation rather than ending it. Israel has indeed established its control over the Palestinians, no longer from within the populated zones through the presence of the Israeli army, but now from the outside, through the Palestinians themselves. Israel succeeded in this goal ten years after the failed endeavors of the Jordanians and the leagues of villages so precious to Ariel Sharon in the early 1980s. Confining the Palestinians in enclaves and intensified Jewish colonization of the Occupied Territories have replaced the expulsion of the Palestinians, which has become inconceivable in the present context.

For thirty years the Palestinians, under the PLO's leadership, built their national identity on recovering sovereignty over a shared land. By fos-

tering the "Bantustanization" of the Palestinians, the Washington agreement sanctioned the ideological, political, and military failure of the PLO while at the same time imposing it as the authority. Historically, the PLO regarded the recovery of the territory as top priority and the basis of Palestinian unity. Therefore the disappointment generated by the agreement shook the credibility of the PLO, leaving the field wide open for the Islamists to gain exclusive control as the sole potentially legitimate heirs, due to their successful fusion of nationalism and Islamization. Now facing the impossibility of recovering the territory and the threat of social disintegration, the religious ideology could prove to be the most efficient recourse, transforming Palestine from the symbol of Palestinian national identity to its place of fulfillment. Deriving its strength from its widespread associative, charitable, and cultural network, the Islamist movement may therefore be seen as the "natural" solution to social collapse.

Two years after Arafat's return to Gaza, as the limitations of the peace process have become clearer, the PNA, replacing right with might, capitalized on the exhaustion of the population and the threat of a civil war. It denied its challengers access to the political scene and the right to carry out military operations. As HAMAS and Jihad experienced severe joint Palestinian and Israeli repression, Arafat capitalized on the more conservative trends in society, bolstered by the January 1996 election of the Self-Rule Council, which was boycotted by both the Islamist and nationalist opposition, who regularly have strong showings in other elections. Despite its claim to be the legitimate successor of both the PLO and nationalism in political and military affairs, Islamism in this new context is prone to its former fundamentalist practices, aimed exclusively at religious and social goals. Therefore, it risks breaking along its old internal fault lines.

On ideological grounds, the return to religion, more than the recently adopted armed struggle, appears in HAMAS's literature as the preferred expression of jihad, as suggested by the slogan "Islam is the solution and the option." HAMAS is able to negotiate the recovery of Palestine in conjunction with the reconstruction of a unified society because this task is built into its own political and military structures. The normative discourse on the basic illegitimacy of Israel's existence and its inevitable destruction can be converted into various—even contradictory—daily practices, including a more or less temporary coexistence with the Israeli state.

Since about 1995, HAMAS has even demonstrated an ability to defer armed struggle, juxtaposing the heightened military activities of the Kataib al-Qassam with the declarations of Musa Abu Marzuq. Despite Israeli concessions to its demands, HAMAS's political command in the autonomous Occupied Territories has, since June 1995, kept its military wing and some of its representatives abroad at a distance, since it refused to assume responsibility for the three suicide attacks that occurred that summer. From August 1995 until January 1996 a truce was observed as negotiations were carried out between HAMAS, the PNA, and some Israeli authorities. The truce was broken on 5 January 1996, when Yahya Ayyache, the mastermind behind the most dreadful attacks of recent years, was assassinated. A small group from the region of Hebron—still under Israeli military occupation—decided, therefore, to split from both its political and military commands. Responsibility for the February 1996 attacks launched by the "cells of the martyr engineer Yahya Ayyache" in Askelon and Jerusalem was claimed by neither HAMAS nor the Kataib al-Qassam.

If permanent warfare with Israel can be considered by many Islamists, relationships with the PNA could also reach a state of normalcy where violence could be banned. Due to the Islamic interdiction against fitna (war between Muslims—Palestinian versus Palestinian in a civil war), and in spite of the repression it has endured, the Islamist movement has never begun a general, open struggle against Arafat's structures; quite the opposite: concerning matters within the jurisdiction of the PNA but without any link to the Israeli frame of self-rule, the Islamist movement did not hesitate to get involved in managing Palestinian affairs. For example, in January 1995, it accepted the appointment of one of its members, Shaikh Hamid al-Baytawi, as president of the official and recently created Islamic court of appeals.

This neofundamentalism to which Islamism was compelled to return after the "revolutionary option" reached a dead end exists outside the convulsive movements of some marginal cells. Its influence on society will therefore become clearer as the population derives new strategies against adversity from religion, having no recourse to any possibility of national liberation or real democracy. Because no Israeli concession on the question of Palestine is expected anytime in the near future, popular perceptions of the PNA's illegitimacy are bound to intensify in these "Bantustans of Allah" created by Israel with quasi-unanimous international assent.

Notes

1. Jean-François Legrain, *Les Voix du Soulevèment Palestinien 1987–1988* [The Voices of the Palestinian Uprising 1987–1988] (Cairo: Centre d'Etudes et de Documentation Economique, Juridique et Sociale [CEDEJ], 1991); Zeev Schiff and Ehud Yaari, *Intifada: The Palestinian Uprising, Israel's Third Front* (New York: Simon and Schuster, 1990).

2. Jean-François Legrain, "The Islamic Movement and the Intifada," in *Intifada: Palestine at the Crossroads,* ed. Jamal R. Nassar and Roger Heacock (New York: Praeger, 1990), 175–189.

3. Izz al-Din al-Faris and Ahmad Sadiq, "al-Qadiyya al-Filastiniyya Hiyya al-Qadiyya al-Markaziyya lil-Haraka al-Islamiyya" [The Palestinian Cause Is Central to the Islamic Movement], *al-Mukhtar al-Islami* 13 (June 1980): 28–41. For a history of the movement, see Movement of the Islamic Jihad, *Masirat al-Jihad al-Islami fi Filastin* [The Development of Islamic Jihad in Palestine] (Beirut: [n.p.], 1989); and Eli Rekhess, "The Iranian Impact on the Islamic Jihad Movement in the

Gaza Strip," in *The Iranian Revolution and the Muslim World*, ed. David Menashri (Boulder: Westview Press, 1990).

4. Asad al-Tamimi, *Zawal Israil, Hatmiyya Quraniyya* [The Destruction of Israel, Quranic Ineluctability] (al-Qahirah: al-Mukhtar al-Islami, 198-).

5. Muhsin Thabit, *Nashat al-Jamaa al-Islamiyya fi Sujun al-Ihtilal al-Israili* [Emergence of al-Jamaa al-Islamiyya in the Israeli Occupation's Jails] (n.p., n.p., n.d.).

6. The jihad historiography considers that the intifada began after its October operation; the PLO and HAMAS consider that it began only two months later, in spite of recurrent popular insurrections throughout the fall. The Islamic Jihad replies that, in any case, it started with the call for a general strike that immediately followed the December accident, a strike known as the first act of global mobilization in the uprising.

7. The "spiritual guide" of this movement, Shaikh Abd al-Aziz Uda, a former lecturer at the Islamic University of Gaza, is said now to mistrust Shiqaqi, who wants to create a new organization. (Ramadan Shallah, a former lecturer at the University of South Florida in Tampa and one of the founders of the movement, was elected the new head of IJM after the assassination of Shiqaqi in Malta in October 1995.)

8. Mohammed K. Shahid, "The Muslim Brotherhood Movement in the West Bank and Gaza," *Third World Quarterly* 10:2 (April 1988): 658–682.

9. Schiff and Yaari, 223–225.

10. Communiqué No. 4, 11 February 1988, Harakat al-Muqawama al-Islamiyya. *HAMAS* means zeal, enthusiasm; the term is not found in the Quran.

11. According to a personal anonymous source in Amman, September 1994. The traditional historiography of HAMAS as found in Ahmad Rashad, *HAMAS: Palestinian Politics with Islamic Hue* (Annandale, Va.: United Association for Studies and Research, 1993). Ziad Abu Amr, *Islamic Fundamentalism in the West Bank and Gaza: Muslim Brotherhood and Islamic Jihad* (Bloomington: Indiana University Press, 1994) never mentions this second meeting. This new information confirms my reading of the leaflets as found in *Les Voix du Soulèvement*.

12. It is essential to distinguish between *Qasam*, the acronym used by the jihad forces, which means oath, and *Qassam*, used by HAMAS to refer to the Syrian shaikh killed in 1935 by the British forces near Jenin; Qassam led a wide armed movement against the British and Jewish presence in Palestine.

13. Jean-François Legrain, "Palestinian Islamisms: Patriotism as a Condition of Their Expansion," in *Accounting for Fundamentalisms: The Dynamic Character of Movements*, ed. Martin E. Marty and R. Scott Appleby (Chicago: American Academy of Sciences, 1994).

14. See, for example, Edward Said, *Peace and Its Discontents: Gaza-Jericho 1993–1995* (London: Vintage, 1995); Naseer Aruri, "From Oslo to Cairo: Repacking the Occupation," *Middle East International*, 13 May 1994, 16–17.

15. Steve Rodan, "Peace Upsets Generals' United Front," *Jerusalem Post*, 11 February 1994.

16. In December 1994, due to this new *rapport de forces*, the university decided to end the former first-past-the-post system, which had guaranteed exclusive Fatah control of the council since its creation, and to institute proportional representation.

17. Jean-François Legrain, "Les Elections Etudiants en Cisjordanie (1978–1987)," in *Démocratie et Démocratisations dans le Monde Arabe*, ed. J. C. Vatin et al. (Cairo: CEDEJ, 1992); Mahmud al-Zahhar, "al-Haraka al-Islamiyya: Haqaiq wa Arqam, Bayna al-Haqiqa wa-al-Wahm" [The Islamic Movement: Realities and Figures, Between Truth and Fiction], *al-Quds*, 10 November 1992 (reprinted in *Filastin al-Muslima*, December 1992).

18. The Center for Palestine Research and Studies (CPRS) in Nablus publishes a monthly public opinion poll.

19. This fear is shared by Israel Shahak, "HAMAS and Arafat: The Balance of Power," *Middle East International* 468 (4 February 1994): 17–18. Edward Said, in *al-Ahram Weekly,* 7–13 October 1993, considers the Washington agreement as "an Instrument of Palestinian Surrender, a Palestinian Versailles." See also Jean-François Legrain, "De la Faiblesse de l'OLP, de la Sincérité d'Israel," *Le Monde,* 10 September 1993; Jean-François Legrain, "Gaza-Jericho, un Accord Contre la Paix," *Libération,* 7 March 1994; Jean-François Legrain, "Bantoustans Palestiniens et Terrorisme," *Liberation,* 26 October 1994.

20. Middle East Watch, *A License to Kill: Israeli Undercover Operations Against "Wanted" and Masked Palestinians* (New York: Human Rights Watch, 1993). During the same period, seventy Israelis were killed, proof of the increase of violence in the Territories.

21. Markaz Abhath al-Aradi, *al-Nashatat al-Istitaniyya wa-Musadarat al-Aradi fi-al-Diffa al-Gharbiyya* [The Settlement and Land Seizure Activities in the West Bank] (Jerusalem: Jamiyyat al-Dirasat al-Arabiyya, 24 January 1994).

22. Jean-François Legrain, "Le Leadership Palestinien de l'Intérieur" ("Document Husayni," Eté 1988), in *Etudes Politiques du Monde Arabe* (Cairo: CEDEJ, 1991).

23. This is the opinion of Graham Usher, "HAMAS Seeks a Place at the Table," *Middle East International,* 13 May 1994, 17–19, who also gives an excellent analysis of the recent situation.

24. HAMAS always claimed its lack of commitment in Jordanian affairs: the Islamist Palestinian mobilization in Jordan is officially left to the Jordanian Muslim Brotherhood.

25. Jean-François Legrain, "A Defining Moment: Palestinian Islamic Fundamentalism," in *Islamic Fundamentalisms and the Gulf Crisis,* ed. James Piscatori (Chicago: American Academy of Arts and Sciences, 1991).

26. Anonymous, "al-Majd li-al-Qassam" [Glory to Qassam], *al-Sabil* (Organ of the Islamic Action Front in Amman), 5–30 January 1993, lists twenty-six military operations led by them; the first one indexed took place in April 1988. The information office of HAMAS, in a document published in *Filastin al-Muslima,* January 1994, lists ninety operations with the same first listing. *Filastin al-Muslima,* November 1994, published a list made by al-Qassam of all its "martyrs"; the first one died in December 1990.

27. The interview was published by *al-Sabil,* Amman, 19–25 April 1994.

28. Quoted in *Middle East International,* 10 June 1994.

29. Quoted in *Jerusalem Post,* 24 October 1994.

30. *al-Nahar,* 10 January 1994.

31. *al-Nahar,* 2 January 1994.

32. *al-Nahar,* 1 November 1993.

33. Forming an opposition coalition since the Madrid conference in September 1991, ten organizations (four members of the PLO—Popular Front of George Habash, Democratic Front of Nayif Hawateh, Popular Struggle Front of Khalid Abd al-Majid, and the Liberation Front; the four members of the pro-Syrian National Salvation Front—Fath-Intifada of Abu Musa, Popular Front–General Commander of Ahmad Jibril, Saiqa of Isam al-Qadi, and the Revolutionary Communist Party of Urabi Awad; and HAMAS and the Movement of Islamic Jihad in Palestine of Fathi Shiqaqi) designated a central leadership composed of twenty members, on 5 January 1994 in Damascus, and a secretariat composed of ten members.

34. *al-Nahar,* 10 January 1994.

9

Arab Islamists in Afghanistan

Barnett R. Rubin

When a group of Muslim Arab immigrants were arrested for bombing New York's World Trade Center on 25 February 1993, investigations into their background pointed to a common link: most had participated in the war in Afghanistan.[1] News organizations seized on tenuous leads to see whether another Pulitzer Prize–worthy scandal might be uncovered. Did the CIA, in its all-out effort to oust the Soviets from Afghanistan, secretly train fanatical Muslim Arab terrorists who had now turned their U.S.-supplied weapons and skills on their former masters? More specifically, in return for services rendered in Afghanistan, had the CIA arranged entry to the United States for the group's spiritual leader, Shaikh Umar Abd al-Rahman, wanted in Egypt for authorizing killings by members of a radical Islamist group called al-Jihad? So charged, among others, President Hosni Mubarak of Egypt.

Similarly, when Saudi Arabia announced that it would execute four young men found guilty of placing a car bomb that exploded at a U.S.-run Saudi National Guard training center in Riyadh in November 1995 (killing five Americans and two Indians), the authorities first produced them on television. There they confessed to the bombing, and three of the four recounted their history of fighting in the Afghan jihad, where they learned both the ideological fervor and military skills they brought home with them.

To the surprise of no one who had followed Afghanistan before six Americans were killed in New York and five in Riyadh, the trail led back to Gulbuddin Hikmatyar, leader of the Hizb-i Islami (Islamic Party) of Afghanistan. Not that Hikmatyar or any other Afghan was even remotely implicated in this or any other act of violence outside of Afghanistan and its neighborhood;[2] and not that it had not been common knowledge among those who cared that Hikmatyar as well as other Afghan leaders who had not achieved his international bugbear status had been assassinating and terrorizing other Afghans for years; but all of the bombing suspects who had been to Afghanistan seemed to have worked with Hikmatyar's group. As had also been no secret for years, this was the group that had received the largest share of the U.S. and Saudi aid distributed to the mujahidin groups by Pakistan's Directorate of Inter-Services Intelligence (ISI).

U.S. and Saudi support for Islamist organizations that opposed Western policies and that also turned against Saudi Arabia in the 1990–1991 Gulf War grew out of the Cold War bipolar view of the world. This view affected all U.S. foreign policy thinking and was especially dominant in the security agencies, particularly the secret ones whose accountability was, to say the least, limited. Overt support for "right-wing authoritarians" against "left-wing totalitarians" was not so different from covert support for terrorists or Islamic extremists. The standard put-down of critics of this policy (worthy of inclusion in any updated edition of Gustave Flaubert's *Dictionnaire des Idées Reçues*) was, "Of course, he is not a Jeffersonian Democrat," implying that anyone who argued against arming political killers was naive and ethnocentric enough to think that in foreign policy one could collaborate only with eighteenth-century Americans (slave owners, by the way, so perhaps the remark is not as apt as it might be). Hikmatyar and his ilk were even helping us avenge Vietnam by carrying out the supreme Cold War goal: "killing Russians."[3]

On the other side, some of those ignorant of the situation in Afghanistan who have rushed to condemn a policy they ignored for years have extended their criticism to the whole Afghan resistance movement and the effort to assist it. It is worth remembering that the Soviet occupiers and their Afghan clients employed at least as much terror and violence as their most ruthless opponents.[4] The Afghans, who have suffered from these extremists more than anyone, do not constitute a "Terror Nation," as a CNN Special Report called it. To the extent that terrorists have found refuge and training in Afghanistan, the blame must go to all those who destroyed that country's fragile institutions, starting with the Soviet Union. Nor does experience of Afghanistan alone explain violence by some Islamists in Egypt, Algeria, Saudi Arabia, and elsewhere, despite the predictable attempts of ineffective, corrupt, or dictatorial governments to find external scapegoats for their problems.

In some quarters, the undifferentiated image of the "fundamentalist terrorist" seems to be replacing that of the "Soviet-inspired Communist" (or, in Moscow, "American imperialist") as the enemy image of our time. Then as now wise policy will take into account the real grievances that lead people to follow extremist leaders and will avoid labeling whole groups or nations with catchy slogans. As in the Cold War, simplified bipolar thinking can lead one into dangerous alliances. The forces of reaction that still excite fear in Moscow are the same ones the Yeltsin government relied on in the fight against "fundamentalism" in Central Asia and nationalism in the

Caucasus. A foreign policy that advances the interests of democracies requires a search for allies who share at least some democratic and liberal values. Between seeking nonexistent "Jeffersonian democrats" and arming "militarily efficient" extremists, other choices exist.

International Islamist Links
of the Afghan Islamic Movement

Since its founding, Afghanistan has been a Sunni Muslim state of the Hanafi fiqh. The first Afghan empire in 1721 originated in resistance against an attempt by the Safavids to force Shiism on Qandahar, and Afghanistan has always been strongly Sunni, despite the incorporation (after their brutal conquest in the 1880s) of the Imami Shia Hazara ethnic group and a few other Imami and Ismaili groups. Today these constitute perhaps 15 percent of the population.

Shiite Iran stood between landlocked Afghanistan and the Arab world, and most of the external influence on Afghan Islam came from either India or Central Asia, including the Naqshbandi revival, the movement of the mujahidin of Sayyid Ahmad Barelvi (which developed into today's Ahl-i Hadith), and finally the Jamaat-i Islami of Sayyid Abu al-ala Mawdudi. Sufism of various types was widespread in Afghanistan. The rulers' legitimacy was proclaimed by the Mujaddidi family, heads of the Naqshbandi order, and the royal clan intermarried with both the Mujaddidis and the Gailanis, chiefs of the Qadiri order.

The links to the Arab world that contributed to the development of Arab participation in the Afghan jihad were initiated by the Afghan state in its quest for Islamic legitimacy. Afghan rulers feared privately (or poorly) educated ulama attached to tribes as well as ulama educated in British India or subsequently Pakistan because of their penchant for preaching jihad against the government, as a result of either "ignorance" or British/ Pakistani gold. Since at least the late nineteenth century, Afghan governments had denounced such movements as "Wahhabi," linking them to the anti-Sufi Salafi movement of Muhammad ibn Abd al-Wahhab. They in turn linked "Wahhabism" to Britain and Western imperialist interests. Afghanistan's communist president, Najibullah, used identical rhetoric against the mujahidin a century later.[5]

Nonetheless, the government required a corps of competent and loyal ulama to administer the judicial system, whose relation to Hanafi jurisprudence was essential to state legitimacy. It therefore established a faculty of theology at Kabul University in collaboration with Egypt's al-Azhar University.[6] In conjunction with the founding of various faculties, nearly all with foreign sponsorship, Afghans who were to become professors received scholarships to study at the sponsoring institutions. Thus, for example, in the early 1970s, half of the teachers in the theology faculty had degrees from al-Azhar.[7]

In turning to al-Azhar, the regime undoubtedly had in mind the Azhar of, among others, Muhammad Abduh, whose version of Islamic modernism legitimated the same type of rule by secular figures, seemingly Western reforms of customs, the pursuit of modern professions, and the combination of Western, traditional, and Islamic legal sources that the Afghan monarchy sought to promote. A number of prominent figures of the old regime indeed brought exactly such views back from Cairo. Sending students into the turbulent Islamic milieu of Cairo in the 1950s and 1960s, however, inevitably brought the young Afghan scholars into contact with the Muslim Brotherhood and the exciting new writings of the Brotherhood's most charismatic thinker, Sayyid Qutb.

The expansion of the state funded by foreign aid created new elites, who organized political groups. Some of these groups adopted revolutionary ideologies; they sought to seize control of the state in order to transform society. The would-be revolutionaries of Afghanistan, as much as those of France, Russia, and China, "precipitated out of the ranks of relatively highly educated groups oriented to state activities or employments . . . and from among those who were somewhat marginal to the established classes and governing elites under the Old Regimes."[8] Like revolutionaries elsewhere, they also included many who had studied abroad, an experience that provided a first-hand encounter with foreign models of modernity and a perspective from which to criticize their own society.

Most studies of revolutionary "counterelites" during the Cold War adopted the same bipolar view as the policymakers, equating revolutionaries with communists or leftists, foreign education with "Western" education, and cosmopolitanism or modernization with Westernization. In Afghanistan, however, as in the rest of the Islamic world, Islamic revolutionary ideas (Islamism) competed with Marxism, creating two distinct and opposed tendencies among the disaffected, with different international ties as well.

The Islamic movement in Kabul had roots in the 1950s, when a group of students and teachers at the faculty of theology, including some who had contacts with the Muslim Brotherhood while studying in Egypt, began meeting to study how to refute the arguments put forward by the Marxists on campus.[9] After 1965, as the university expanded rapidly with provincial recruits, a newly invigorated Islamic movement gained influence among students under the name of the Muslim Youth Organization (Sazman-i Javanan-i Musulman).[10] Around the beginning of 1973, the movement began to register its members and formed a leadership shura (council).[11] The first meeting of the shura took place in the home of Burhanuddin Rabbani, then a junior professor of the sharia faculty, who was elected leader and chairman of the leadership council. Ghulam Rasul (later Abd al-Rabb al-Rasul) Sayyaf, also a lecturer at the sharia faculty, was elected deputy leader.[12] All three had studied at al-Azhar. Gulbuddin Hikmatyar, a former student of the engineering faculty, was in jail for having ordered the murder of a Maoist student and was not present at the meeting, but he was to be in charge of political activities together with another jailed activist (since killed). The council later selected the name Jamiat-i Islami (Islamic Society) for the movement.[13] Two-thirds of the members of the Islamic movement's shura and about two-fifths of all the early leaders had advanced Islamic educations.[14] The top three leaders and the official in charge of cultural affairs had all studied at al-Azhar or in Saudi Arabia.

After a coup d'état in 1973 that initially brought more pro-Soviet elements into the government, the Islamic movement's main activists fled to Peshawar. "Signs of differences" had appeared among them since at least the early 1970s, and in 1975, this movement also split in two, becoming the Jamiat-i Islami, still led by Rabbani, and the Hizb-i Islami (Islamic Party), led by Hikmatyar.[15] After the 1978 coup, another group, led by Mawlawi Yunus Khalis, broke with Hikmatyar and formed another Hizb-i Islami. (The two are referred to as Hizb-Hikmatyar and Hizb-Khalis.)

The Islamists had been in contact with the Egyptian Muslim Brotherhood and had regular contact with the Pakistani Jamaat-i Islami, but at first they had no formal links with either.[16] Although their opponents called them "Ikhwanis" (and this was an accurate depiction of their ideology), according to Roy, the Egyptian Ikhwan did not organize formal branches outside the central Arab world.[17] The writer who seems to have influenced them the most was Sayyid Qutb, who was executed by Nasser about the time that the Islamic movement began to grow on the Kabul campus. Both Rabbani and Khalis translated his work in the 1960s.[18]

I have no evidence that the Afghan Islamists received outside financial support as long as they were in Afghanistan. In exile, however, the Islamists set about their search for foreign aid. In 1974, Rabbani spent six months in Saudi Arabia. The Saudis provided assistance for the first year of exile, probably through the Muslim World League (Rabitat al-Alam al-Islami), but after 1975 and Daoud's shift toward the shah's Iran and the Saudis, they stopped their aid.[19]

The programs of Hizb and Jamiat clearly show the influence of Qutb and Mawdudi, particularly in their use of the term jahiliyyah (pre-Islamic ignorance or barbarism) to describe Western or communist societies.[20] Qutb was the first to extend this term to societies of nominal Muslims not governed entirely by Islam.[21] Qutb's views, never adopted by the mainstream of the Ikhwan, led to the practice of takfir, declaring as unbelievers people who are Muslims by customary criteria (Muslim father, profession of the faith, prayer, etc.). According to Roy, the split between Jamiat and Hizb, in addition to its ethnic, personal, and organizational causes, recapit-

ulated the split in the international Islamist movement over takfir. Roy
claims that Hizb-i Islami took the more extreme position. The evidence of
these documents and some others partly supports this claim.[22] Hizb
described Afghan society as fundamentally un-Islamic,[23] though its leader's
pragmatism is far more ruthless than his ideology (alliances with communist army officers and militia leaders against Islamist rivals).

The question for many Islamists in the Arab world, whether to concentrate on the seizure of power from above (à la Lenin) or the Islamization of
society from below (à la Gramsci), had little resonance in Afghanistan in
the 1980s. Faced with a military occupation by an atheist power, Muslims
had to engage in jihad, which in itself Islamicized society. Even before this
period, however, Hizb-i Islami of Afghanistan clearly sided with the political activists: "Without a complete reform of the system of government, no
individual reform is possible," states its program.[24]

The Islamists were as a whole the least Westernized (or Sovietized) of
the Afghan elites. Their education embodied the Islamist slogan "Neither
East nor West." Not a single one of them had been educated in the Soviet
bloc or in non-Islamic Third World institutions like the American University of Beirut or Indian universities; a sole individual of secondary importance had a master's degree in engineering from the United States, reflecting the U.S. sponsorship of Kabul's faculty of engineering. Their only significant international ties were with the Islamic ummah.

International Networks:
Saudi Salafis, Muslim Brotherhood, Jamaat-i Islami

By the time the Soviets invaded Afghanistan, the Afghan Islamists were
already connected to an international network that included both radical
Islamists in the Arab world and the U.S. security establishment. The key
links at the center of this network were the Saudi monarchy and the
Pakistani military regime of Zia ul-Haq, the pillars of U.S. security policy
in the Gulf. The development of the Islamic networks in the Afghan war
resulted largely from the policies of the United States and these two
Muslim states.[25]

Despite the increasing (private) Westernization of behavior in Saudi
Arabia, the monarchy's legitimacy rested on its alliance with possibly the
most conservative religious establishment in the Islamic world. The rise of
the dynasty of ibn Saud consisted of the classic combination of a tribal
chief and a charismatic preacher, in this case Muhammad ibn Abd al-
Wahhab. Ibn Abd al-Wahhab preached return to the early days of Islam, to
the original, former (Salafi) practice of the faith—before Sufism, excessive
tolerance for non-Muslims, and other foreign practices had polluted the
ummah. His views were in a way a precursor of Sayyid Qutb's. The Saudi

monarchy claimed that the Quran was their only constitution and based the judicial system on the Hanbali school of jurisprudence, known as the strictest of the four Sunni schools.

Nonetheless, the Saudi use of Islam in international relations was not a pure outgrowth of their ideology. It was aimed at two rivals in the Muslim world: secular Arab nationalism, especially in its leftist, anti-imperialist, Soviet-leaning forms (as represented by Nasser); and the Iranian revolution, which was both revolutionary and Shia.

A principal organization used by the Saudis in this struggle was the Rabitat al-Alam al-Islami, founded in 1962.[26] This organization financed the printing of Qurans and other religious literature; it supported Islamic centers in various parts of the world, including the United States. It did not specifically try to spread Salafi Islam, but the conservative preaching that it favored was in the Salafi tradition.

At the time the Rabita was founded, the Saudis were engaged in a direct military struggle with Nasser in Yemen, and it is reasonable to suppose that this organization was intended to strengthen their alliance with the Ikhwan against their common enemy. Although the Brothers' revolutionary and anti-imperialist orientation was anathema to the Saudi monarchy, their opposition to "communism," of which Nasserism was for them only a local variant, made them allies. The evolution of the wing of the Brothers led by Hudaybi and then Talamasani, rejecting Qutb's teaching and favoring a strategy of Islamicizing society from below rather than seizing political power (what Roy calls "neo-fundamentalism," in distinction from Islamism) fit well with the Saudi strategy.[27] This strategy also made them amenable to Anwar al-Sadat in the 1970s, as he purged Nasserites from the state and attempted to use the Islamists against the leftists on the street and the university campuses. This strategy of Sadat enjoyed the support of Saudi Arabia and the United States.[28] Saudi Arabia, via the Rabita, is thought to have supported Muslim Brotherhood activity throughout the Arab world. In return, the Ikhwan never tried to organize a branch, even clandestinely, in Saudi Arabia.[29] In South Asia, the Saudis supported the Jamaat-i Islami of Pakistan, whose more conservative approach was already closer to their views.

After the Iranian revolution, the Saudis increased their activity as, for the first time, another state contested their position as the leading Muslim state. The jihad in Afghanistan arrived at the right time for this effort, and much of the Saudi effort there must be understood as directed at establishing a militant Sunni Islamist movement, anti-Shia to an extent that Afghan Sufi-impregnated Islam had never been, and under their patronage.

Among the Islamists themselves, the Muslim Brotherhood and the Jamaat recognized each other as peers in leading the movement; each was associated with one of the movement's founding thinkers. The Ikhwan, however, had a committee organized to oversee its international activities since the 1940s. This committee remains dominated by Egyptians; sources mentioned by Roy claim that in 1990 it had one non-Arab member, Abd al-Rabb al-Rasul Sayyaf.[30]

In the 1970s, after the OPEC price rises and the division of Pakistan, Pakistan and Saudi Arabia became closer in foreign policy. At the same time, the Jamaat, while deprived of any direct access to the state under the regime of Zulfiqar Ali Bhutto, had been pursuing a policy of recruiting sympathizers in the military. The Pakistani officer corps had been undergoing a social change that replaced the more aristocratic officers recruited and trained by the British for their colonial army (the archetype of which was Ayub Khan) with more middle-class Punjabis from rural or provincial families, a social group much more amenable to Islamist appeals.[31] One such officer, the chief of army staff, General Zia ul-Haq, seized power in a coup in July 1977. As he sought a way to legitimate his rule, he seized on "Islamization" in the fall of 1979, for which reason he enjoyed the support of the Jamaat. At the same time, the U.S. government (especially after the election of President Ronald Reagan a year later) was eager to build up his regime as a partner to Saudi Arabia in both the Gulf and in resisting the Soviets in Afghanistan.

Under the Nixon doctrine, the United States sought regional partners in the Third World. After the loss of the shah's Iran, a principal regional partner, Saudi Arabia and Pakistan replaced that partner in the region. The Saudi government supported Zia ul-Haq financially (as did the United States); the Saudis also supported the Rabita, which funded both various branches of the Muslim Brotherhood and the Jamaat-i Islami, which in turn supported Zia ul-Haq. These networks were reflected in the cooperation that later developed among the intelligence agencies of the three countries, with the Jamaat as principal local implementing partner and activists from the Rabita, Muslim Brotherhood, and other Arab Islamist organizations in supporting roles. This form of collaboration between governments and nongovernmental organizations (NGOs) is usually ignored by analysts of the topic.[32]

Besides these mainstream groups, the international Islamist movement included a variety of splinter factions of more extreme orientation. While they differed on many counts, they generally accepted one version or another of Qutb's teaching, including the idea that Muslims were obligated to wage armed jihad against all regimes that did not fully implement Islam, and that many of those commonly labeled Muslims were in fact unbelievers or, worse, apostates. There were at least as many variations on these themes as on the Trotskyite idea of the degenerate workers' state, and this account cannot do them justice.[33] These groups' relation to the main Muslim Brotherhood organization varied from country to country; in some they were part of it, in others opposed. The Arab world, especially the youth of Egypt, generated many such groups in the 1970s and 1980s. In Pakistan, the only kindred group seems to have been the well-established Ahl-i Hadith, which was much more akin to extreme Salafi teachings (rejection of the schools of fiqh in favor of direct reference to Quran, Sunnah, and hadith, opposition to Sufism and the adornment of tombs rather than working for the seizure of state power). Ahl-i Hadith, which had also received the support of the Saudi religious establishment for decades, established several madrasas in northwest Pakistan and one (ironically enough in a town called Panjpir, or five pirs) in Kunar province of Afghanistan. These were the border areas to which Barelvi's followers had made hijra. The Afghan Ahl-i Hadith movement later brought Salafi fighters and money from the Gulf to join the jihad there.[34]

The Arab Role in Aid to the Mujahidin

Once the Communists seized power and, later, the Soviets invaded, a far broader section of the Afghan population supported jihad, whereas under the old regime the Islamists had been a tiny isolated group. Nonetheless, the more mainstream nationalist and traditionalist groups failed to form equally effective groups in the jihad, partly because of the opposition to them by Pakistan (Afghan nationalists had irredentist claims against Pakistan), and partly because aid to the resistance primarily mobilized the international networks described above with which the Islamists were already articulated. All of these Islamic networks combined with U.S., Pakistani, and Saudi intelligence agencies to form the network that supported the mujahidin. Arab Islamist volunteers played an important role in this system; they were not merely incidental or members of a parallel system.

Of course, just as support for the Afghan resistance crossed the political spectrum in the United States (as shown by the unanimous congressional votes approving more aid to the mujahidin than the CIA requested), so support for the jihad crossed the Islamic spectrum in the Middle East. Nonetheless, among U.S. personnel involved directly with the Afghan war effort as volunteers (rather than officials), one could note a disproportionate number of right-wingers, ranging from extreme conservatives to a few genuine nut cases. These were the people in the United States who responded most viscerally to an armed struggle against the Red Army. Similarly, among the Arabs and other Muslims who provided various forms of aid to the Afghans, a disproportionate number came from extreme groups who longed for armed jihad and found it in Afghanistan. Both President Anwar al-Sadat and Shaikh Umar Abd al-Rahman supported the mujahidin, but it was the latter who said, "When the Afghans rose and declared a jihad—and jihad had been dead for the longest time—I can't tell you how proud I was."[35]

The Soviet invasion of Afghanistan violated basic norms of international conduct and law, appeared (if deceptively) to pose a threat to the oil resources of the Gulf, and placed the first Muslim state to join the modern state system under the occupation of an avowedly atheist power. The West (led by the United States), the Islamic world (led by Saudi Arabia), and China gave substantial and growing support to the Pakistani effort to aid the mujahidin. Various agencies of the Iranian government also aided Shia mujahidin parties who followed the line of Khomeini.

The Pakistani ISI, which administered the distribution of the aid, insisted on controlling and directing the military operations of the mujahidin. The ISI tried to control military operations through a form of brokerage based on the distribution of weapons to parties and small groups of fighters. This means of control favored those commanders who conformed to Pakistan's military and political goals.[36]

To implement this system of brokerage, the ISI distributed weapons not only for use in operations, but also (and in greater quantity) as the reward for carrying them out. For instance, for each plane confirmed downed by a Stinger, the commander responsible received two more missiles.[37] Hence, downing a Soviet plane took at least three missiles: one that was fired and two that were delivered as a reward. And Stingers were the most closely held and strictly controlled weapon. This tactic is the traditional one used in the "tribal" policies of governments; it both corresponded to and stimulated the tribal norm of competing for influence by obtaining resources from external patrons. Together with the even more profligate Soviet aid, this program made Afghanistan into probably the world's largest recipient of personal weapons during the late 1980s and left it by 1992 with more such weapons than India (the world's largest arms importer during the same period) and Pakistan combined.[38]

U.S. aid grew from $30 million in 1980 to over $600 million per year by 1986–1989. Saudi and other Arab aid matched or slightly exceeded the U.S. share.[39] The Chinese mainly sold weapons to the CIA. The agencies that managed this immense flow of money and arms were the CIA, the ISI, and the Saudi General Intelligence Agency (al-Istakhbarah al-Ammah). The Afghan operation became the single largest program of each of these agencies.

In Saudi Arabia, besides the "official" aid overseen by Istakhbarah (headed by Prince Turki al-Faisal Saud), there were several other major aid sources. The Rabita funded many schools and madrasas for refugees, especially those of Hizb-i Islami, for which it supplied many of the educational materials. The Afghanistan support committee headed by Prince Salman ibn Abd al-Aziz, governor of Riyadh, funded the Arab volunteers recruited by the Muslim Brotherhood who worked for Sayyaf's party and other groups and went to fight alongside the mujahidin in Afghanistan. Salman's committee may well have funded the volunteers who later blew up the training center in the city he governed. The Islamic Salvation Foundation, created by Osama bin Laden, who had made billions in construction in

Saudi Arabia, provided aid to favored Afghan groups as well as to Arab volunteers. Until at least 1988, and perhaps as late as 1990, bin Laden worked closely with Prince Turki.[40]

Besides the Saudi sources, other Arabs also gave money. The Salafis in Kuwait were a particularly important source of contributions, either to Sayyaf or to various support committees. The Muslim Brotherhood in its various offices also collected funds, as did many other offices, such as the now notorious Al-Kifah Refugee Center in Brooklyn. The Arab volunteers and the Muslim Brotherhood workers coordinated their activities through several offices. The NGOs working with refugees and in cross-border civilian projects formed the Islamic Coordination Council in Peshawar, headed by Abdullah Azzam, a Palestinian educated at al-Azhar who was assassinated with two of his sons by a car bomb in Peshawar on 24 November 1989. Abdullah Azzam was also described as a "guide to hundreds of Arab Mujahedeen in Afghanistan."[41]

After Abdullah Azzam's assassination, Hizb-i Islami published the following biography as part of his obituary:

> Born in a Palestinian village, Sella Haressiyya, in 1941, Abdullah Azzam completed his early education at his native village. He graduated in theology from Damascus University in 1966 and then joined Al-Azhar University in Cairo to get his M.A. and Ph.D. degrees. He joined the well-known Islamic movement operating throughout the Arab world, Al-Ikhwanul Muslimoon, took part in the struggle against Zionist hegemony, and participated in the 1967 Arab-Israeli war.
>
> After the war he emigrated from the West Bank to Jordan. At the Jordanian University in Amman, he started his professional career as a lecturer of theology. Abdullah Azzam's difficulties increased with every passing day. He became disappointed in his profession, in the political set-up of his country, in the Palestinian leadership for their secular attitudes, and in the narrowness of his platform for addressing the Muslim Ummah. In view of this, he may have been relieved rather than grieved when, after one of his usual fights with the authorities, he was dismissed from his University position. He knew it was useless to protest or to try to reverse the decision, as it enjoyed the blessings of higher circles. So he packed up his belongings and departed for Saudi Arabia where he hoped to fare better in his search for a suitable climate for his ideology.
>
> In 1980 while in Saudi Arabia, Abdullah Azzam had the opportunity of meeting a delegation of Afghan Mujahideen who had come to perform Haj. He soon found himself attracted to their circles and wanted to know more about the Afghan Jihad. When the story of the Afghan Jihad was unfolded to Abdullah Azzam, he felt that it was this cause of the Afghan people for which he had been searching for so long. He arranged visits to Afghanistan where his impressions about the Afghan Mujahideen were confirmed beyond doubt. He shifted to Pakistan and started delivering lectures at the Islamic University, Islamabad [this university, where Ramzi Ahmad Yusuf, charged with planning the bombing of the World Trade Center, had a network of contacts, was run by Jamaat-i Islami and funded by Rabita]. He later decided to devote himself fully to the cause of the Afghan people, and settled in Peshawar. . . .

He has participated in Jihad and has helped others to participate with either their services or their financial contributions. He has established the Islamic Coordination Council which includes nearly 20 Islamic organizations working in support of the Afghan Jihad, offering services inside and outside Afghanistan in the fields of education, health, relief, social care, and the like, administered by efficient staff stationed in numerous places in the liberated areas and refugee camps. . . .

Dr. Azzam left behind . . . a Mujahida wife. . . . She has her own Jihad activities in the refugee camps in Pakistan—ten schools and a nursery and a sewing and training center for widows and sisters of Shaheed [martyrs].[42]

With his connections to the Ikhwan, Saudi Arabia, Rabita, and Jamaat-i Islami, Abdullah Azzam embodied the Islamist networks supporting the mujahidin.[43]

These networks were fully incorporated into the aid effort. In 1978, when the Saudis first wanted to resume aid to Afghan opponents of the new communist regime, they approached the Jamaat for guidance and used it as their channel. The military officers who ran the arms pipeline in the ISI and who dominated the Pakistan refugee administration at least in the early years of the war were largely (although not all) militants of Jamaat and supporters of Hizb-Hikmatyar. Throughout the war, Saudi government funds were vital to the purchase of weapons, and private Arab funds became vital for that purpose when the U.S. Congress began cutting back the U.S. contribution after the Soviet withdrawal. From the beginning, private Arab funds (like those from bin Laden) and Arab volunteers were essential to keeping the system for transporting arms running.

The arms pipeline consisted of three parts.[44] First, the CIA (using Saudi and U.S. funds) bought weapons from China, Egypt, Israel, and elsewhere.[45] Second, once the weapons had arrived in Pakistan, the ISI took custody. They trucked the weapons to the depots controlled by the mujahidin groups in the border region. The CIA paid for these transport expenses through monthly deposits into special accounts in Pakistan.[46] In addition to weapons, the mujahidin needed food, clothing, and other supplies, also paid for from the CIA accounts.

These funds frequently ran short, and only "Arab money saved the system."[47] This money, however, benefited only the Islamist groups integrated into the international networks, not the more nationalist and traditionalist groups who arrived only after the communist coup in April 1978.

Third, it was the responsibility of the parties to distribute the weapons to commanders and oversee their transport into Afghanistan. Transport was left to the private sector.[48] Attempts to build up a centralized supply network would have interfered with the flourishing businesses of both Afghans and Pakistani Pashtuns from the tribal territories who had converted their previous smuggling and trucking operations into far more profitable ones related to the transport of weapons and drugs. The transport of weapons was extremely expensive; in 1986, it cost $15 to $20 per kilogram to move supplies from Pakistan to north Afghanistan, amounting to $1,100 for one mortar or $65 for one bomb. Total transport costs ran to $1.5 million per month.[49] To pay these costs, the Saudi Red Crescent maintained offices in the border regions funded by the Saudi Afghanistan Support Committee. These offices were staffed by Arab volunteers. They gave the Afghan Islamist parties 100 percent of estimated transport costs plus an extra 5 percent for contingencies, while they gave the traditionalist-nationalist parties only about 15 percent of total costs.[50]

The volunteers seemed to have considerable discretion over whom to fund. In the fall of 1986, when Rabbani took time out from leading a mujahidin delegation to the UN General Assembly to meet President Reagan (which Hikmatyar had refused to do the previous year), the volunteers cut off funding for Jamiat's transport for several weeks. They also tried to pressure Jamiat to expel female European medical personnel working in north Afghanistan for Médecins Sans Frontières (MSI) or Aide Médicale Internationale.

The aid went disproportionately to those parties favored by the Islamist network, and these parties (in particular those of Hikmatyar and Sayyaf) provided training for Islamist militants. In 1980, the Pakistani military regime officially recognized six Islamic parties as representatives of the refugees and mujahidin. (Pakistan later added a seventh party, that of Sayyaf, because of its Saudi support.) This system served several Pakistani goals. Pakistan feared losing control over the Afghan refugees and the military and political conduct of the war to any unified organization of Afghans.[51] General Zia, then the chief martial law administrator, had been a military adviser in Jordan during "Black September" in 1970, when the PLO nearly overthrew King Hussein.

Furthermore, to guard against Pashtun nationalism, Pakistan insisted that only religiously oriented parties and leaders could operate on its soil. The Saudis largely treated Afghanistan as a religious issue and deferred to their own religious establishment, which preferred the Islamists, and particularly the Salafis among them. Aid to the Afghan jihad both helped to legitimate the Saudi regime at home and in the Islamic world, and it provided a diversion for activist Islamists who might otherwise have focused their energies on their own country, as, indeed, they later did.

In addition to weapons, the ISI also provided training. Brigadier Yousaf claims that 80,000 mujahidin passed through courses between 1983, when the program was expanded, and 1987.[52] According to some reports, these training camps also included members of Jamaat and some of the Arab volunteers. Some of the mujahidin parties also set up their own training camps in the border area; both Hikmatyar and Sayyaf commanders appear to have trained Arab, Kashmiri, and other volunteers. While these camps were not supposed to include active-duty Pakistani officers, some retired ISI or other military personnel did take part.

Next to the decision to recognize the parties and require membership in them as a condition for receiving aid, the allocation of resources among them was the most controversial aspect of the operation. The Islamists consistently received more than the traditionalist-nationalists. According to Brigadier Yousaf, in 1987 the Islamists received over two-thirds of all weapons, with Hikmatyar's party receiving the most. Amazingly, Sayyaf's party, with virtually no social base in the country, received more than any traditionalist party and almost as much as Jamiat. In addition, these same parties received virtually all the private Arab money.

The ISI claimed that its decisions reflected objective analysis of military effectiveness, not political favoritism toward Hikmatyar and Sayyaf. Even if one accepted this dubious claim, there is still no doubt that the Arab donors decided on the basis of political preference. Since the old-regime parties did not receive Arab cash to pay for the transport of weapons or the operation of offices, they often sold weapons to pay these expenses. This contributed to the ISI's opinion that they were corrupt.

Besides its political bias, the ISI advocated a purely military, or even tactical, view of the war, which developed out of the history of the Pakistan military. The Pakistan military viewed "politics" as antithetical to government or policy. Its generals had never accepted orders from political leaders, whom it regarded as having no legitimate role in security issues, let alone war. Hence, the Pakistan army took a rather different view of the relation of politics to war than such strategists as von Clausewitz and Mao Tsetung.[53] The ISI claimed that its strategy during the Soviet occupation was to inflict maximum military damage on the Soviet forces in Afghanistan, period. Many in the Reagan administration and U.S. Congress endorsed this view, adding to it a desire to punish the Soviets for U.S. losses in Vietnam.

The ISI regarded itself as the general staff of the war, planning and commanding the actions of the mujahidin. The ISI would plan operations, pick targets, and promise commanders and parties extra weapons allocations for carrying them out. It also sent advisers inside Afghanistan to oversee key operations. In its view, those fighters who best succeeded in carrying out ISI-planned operations deserved the most support. Those parties with a high level of outside funding, weak links to the local society, more educated commanders, and ideological proximity to the ISI ended up being most effective by these criteria.

The ISI explicitly excluded the extent of the parties' political support among Afghans or potential for establishing a stable government as criteria for receipt of aid. As Brigadier Yousaf proudly wrote, "My critics were taking into account political considerations and biases which, as a soldier, I was fortunately able to ignore."[54] A commander's success in mobilizing a large coalition, setting up a civil administration replacing the state in a region of the country, or attracting support and defectors from Kabul city or the regime army were all considered irrelevant.[55] Links to local society might hinder mujahidin from attacking the ISI's designated targets either to avoid reprisals on the civilian population or to preserve assets such as bridges or oil pipelines that served local communities as well as the regime. An Afghan commander who developed his own political-military organization in Afghanistan might develop strategic priorities different from "headquarters" in Rawalpindi. The ISI regarded such upstarts as a general might view a lieutenant who organized his own general staff. It would then support that commander's rivals or subordinates in order to weaken him or pressure him into accepting ISI directions. It is hardly surprising that no unified Afghan national organization or leadership developed out of this system.

The lack of links to local society became a positive virtue of the most radical Islamists and, especially, the Arab volunteers in the eyes of the ISI and CIA after the Soviet withdrawal. Once the Soviets were gone, many of the less ideological mujahidin considered that jihad was over; they became more concerned with their local rivals and with making money through smuggling, the drug trade, and other activities. They also began to reach accommodation with cotribals or coethnics in the government.[56] Especially after the failed attack on the city of Jalalabad in March-June 1989, they resisted efforts by the ISI and CIA to get them to attack targets in their area. The more "conventional" army of Hikmatyar raised in the refugee camps, especially from the Arab-funded Hizb schools, and the Arab volunteers whose only goal in Afghanistan was to perform jihad, had no such distractions. According to former Pakistan ambassador to the United States Abida Hussein, by the time of the November 1991 offensive against Gardez, Paktia, the vast majority of the "mujahidin" taking part were Arab and other non-Afghan volunteers.[57]

Early in the 1980s, Sayyaf's party was the main one favored by private Arab donors and volunteers. This organization was linked to virtually no social networks in Afghanistan, but its leader spoke excellent Arabic, supported Salafi Islam, and proved adept at raising millions of dollars in the Gulf. Sayyaf had too few commanders for them to figure significantly in any of the available data sets on commanders from the mid-1980s, but the head of the ISI's Afghanistan operation during 1983–1987 claimed that Sayyaf received 17 to 18 percent of the weapons distributed among the seven parties in 1987. Arabs affiliated with his party distributed large amounts of cash to commanders who would join them.[58] As an opponent of nationalism and supporter of pan-Islamic ideals, Sayyaf strongly supported the participation in the resistance of Arab and other Islamic volunteers, who swelled his ranks and created considerable friction with the Afghan mujahidin. Only the Arab-funded commanders of Sayyaf and, later, the Salafi organization Jamaat al-Dawa paid wages to the mujahidin.[59]

Arab Islamist money was also behind the role of Sayyaf and his party members in mujahidin "interim governments" supported by Pakistan and the United States. When under ISI and U.S. pressure the seven leaders agreed to an "interim government" in June 1988, the list showed considerable deference to Saudi sensitivities, as Saudi princes agreed to pay the "government" $1 million per month.[60] The prime minister was a "Wahhabi," a member of Sayyaf's party. Again, when a Pakistani-convened shura appointed by the seven parties met to choose the Islamic Interim Government of Afghanistan (IIGA) in February 1989, the government it chose resulted from ISI and Saudi manipulation of the shura's electoral process. On the first day of the shura, when the chairman tried to push through a resolution making Sayyaf's deputy the president, the body rose in protest, claiming they did not want a "Wahhabi" president.[61] According to U.S. diplomats, the Saudi intelligence service ultimately spent $26 million during the shura. Others claim that each of the 519 delegates received at least $25,000.[62] Sayyaf finally became prime minister in deference to the Saudis, who promised to fund a conventional "Islamic army" for the government if their sect were adequately represented.[63] For several years afterward, U.S. policy insisted on treating the IIGA as the "most representative group of Afghans," despite the well-known circumstances of its creation.[64]

After the end of the Gulf War in 1988 and the Soviet withdrawal in February 1989, Iran became much more assertive in supporting the Shia mujahidin parties and demanding that they receive significant representation in any interim arrangement. Saudi pressure helped keep the February 1989 shura from including any Shia representatives, and frustrating Iran's aims became a still more central aim of Saudi policy. For this purpose they increasingly turned to Hikmatyar, with his superior organization and military power. This money flowed not only through official channels but through the Jamaat and a group of retired ISI officers led by former ISI director General Hamid Gul, after Prime Minister Benazir Bhutto forced him to retire from the army in early 1992. The ISI and CIA also exerted themselves to persuade or pressure the Afghan groups to unite. For this purpose they enlisted such figures as Abdullah Azzam and Shaikh Umar Abd-al-Rahman.

In the summer of 1989, however, the global strategic situation was changing. As the Soviet threat receded, the U.S. State Department began to challenge the large share of aid that went to Hikmatyar and Sayyaf as well as the sole use of the Peshawar parties as conduits for assistance. In the fall of 1989, a new decision defined the goal of U.S. policy not only as "self-determination" for Afghanistan, but as seeking a negotiated political settlement that would lead to the "sidelining of extremists," including Najibullah, Hikmatyar, and Sayyaf. The United States engaged in a two-track policy, beginning a diplomatic dialogue with the U.S.S.R. on a UN-sponsored political settlement, while trying to improve the military performance of the mujahidin.[65] In an attempt to keep the two tracks from contradicting each other, the United States also decided that no weapons paid for by its funds would be given to Hikmatyar or Sayyaf, who opposed such a settlement. They would mainly go to regional or local military shuras inside Afghanistan.[66] Saudi and other Arab funds, however, took up the slack in aid to the mujahidin "extremists," so this policy made little if any difference on the ground. The operations wing of the CIA, which maintained close links with the ISI and the Saudi Istakhbarah, looked with skepticism if not hostility on the new policy. In practice, the continued U.S. maintenance of the arms pipeline continued to strengthen the Afghan groups that U.S. policy was allegedly aimed at weakening.

During this period, political "unity" of some sort among the mujahidin groups was a major goal of U.S.-Pakistani-Saudi policy. Arab supporters of jihad gained a new role as promoters of unity, especially between the feuding Islamists, Hizb and Jamiat. In July 1989, in the so-called Farkhar Valley or Takhar incident, a Hikmatyar commander captured and killed a group of Massoud's commanders as they were returning from a key strategy meeting. Massoud later captured the commander responsible and hanged him and his brother after a trial by ulama. This incident led Hikmatyar to suspend participation in the IIGA (its president, Sibghatullah Mujaddidi, called him a murderer and terrorist in press interviews, so this was perhaps understandable).

Abdullah Azzam traveled to the north after this incident in an attempt to make peace between the two: "He believed that one of the most serious designs of the enemies of Jihad was the conflict between the Hizbi-Islami and the Jamiat-i-Islami resulting in the Takhar incident." He brokered an agreement between Rabbani and Hikmatyar that "was concluded in the night before his assassination."[67] In 1990, after the assassination of Abdullah Azzam, Abd al-Rahman was invited to Peshawar, where his host was Khalid al-Islambouli, brother of one of the assassins of Sadat. Two of Abd al-Rahman's sons participated in a 300-man detachment of the Egyptian al-Jamaat Islamiyyah that fought in eastern Afghanistan's Nangarhar province. On this trip, reportedly paid for by the CIA, Abd al-Rahman preached to the Afghans about the necessity of unity to overthrow the Kabul regime.[68]

Arab Volunteer Fighters

I do not know when the first Arabs actually began to receive military training and to fight in Afghanistan. Before the Soviet withdrawal, while the role of the Arab volunteers in humanitarian aid was common knowledge, and a little investigation revealed how key they were to the logistics system, one heard very little about their actual fighting. Osama bin Laden in an interview said that the Afghans originally told him that they needed only financial assistance, not volunteers. He ascribed his decision to join the fighting to personal religious and political concerns, not the needs of the Afghan effort. He emphasized (as did many of the mujahidin) the personal obligation (fard al-ain) of every Muslim to participate in jihad as well as the need to prepare himself to defend Mecca and Madina from the "Jews."[69]

By the late 1980s, however, hundreds, then thousands of Arab youth, largely recruited from the extremist fringes of the Islamic movement, came to Afghanistan to perform jihad. The ISI used Saudi funds to construct a large base for one Sayyaf commander, Mawlawi Arsala Rahmani, near Urgun, Paktika.[70] Hundreds of Arab "mujahidin" trained there.

The Arab volunteers also set up their own training programs and camps in eastern Afghanistan. One, in Jaji, Paktia province, was named Maasadat al-Ansar. It was constructed with the help of Osama bin Laden and hosted several hundred volunteers from Saudi Arabia, Egypt, Yemen, Syria, Algeria, Libya, and Morocco in 1988. The Arabs were described as working with Hikmatyar and Sayyaf.[71]

In 1989, after the Soviet withdrawal, as mujahidin forces in eastern Afghanistan concentrated in provincial centers and other towns abandoned by the Soviet and regime troops, both foreigners and Afghans became more aware of the presence of Arab fighters.

Some stories came from Kunar province, where mullahs trained at the Saudi-funded Ahl-i Hadith madrasa at Panjpir had founded a few principalities. Northern Nuristan came under the control of Mawlawi Afzal, who founded the Dawlat-i Inqilabi-yi Islami-yi Nuristan (Islamic Revolutionary State of Nuristan), generally called the Dawlat (state). The Dawlat received direct financial support from some Salafi religious groups in Kuwait and Saudi Arabia. There had been no government presence in the area since 1978, however, so the opportunities for becoming either ghazi (a killer of unbelievers in jihad) or shahid (a martyr in jihad) were slim; few if any Arab fighters joined Mawlawi Afzal.

The first widely circulated reports of Arab fighters came from the Kunar River valley in the southern part of the province, which had been the scene of many heavy offensives as the Soviets tried to relieve the isolated garrisons along the Pakistan border, which were supplied by air. Jamil al-Rahman, another Panjpir-educated mullah, from the Safi tribe of Pashtuns, had originally joined Hikmatyar. He left Hizb-Hikmatyar in 1985 to form a strict Salafi party, the Jamaat al-Dawa ila al-Quran wa Ahl al-Hadith.[72] This group was hardly known outside of Kunar until the government evacuated several areas, including the provincial center (Asadabad, known as Chaghasarai in Pashto), which were then overrun by mujahidin in the fall of 1988.

These mujahidin included several hundred Arabs fighting with Jamaat al-Dawa, which Afghans generally referred to as "the Wahhabis." Jamaat al-Dawa set up its own shura, separate from the seven parties; in the summer of 1989, it allied with Hizb, when the latter suspended participation in the IIGA. It took over the principal mosque in the city, where worship was now conducted according to the rite of Ahl-i Hadith, which differed from the Hanafi traditions.[73] Most notoriously, mujahidin reported that Jamaat al-Dawa applied a version of the takfir doctrine: they treated Afghans living in government-controlled areas as unbelievers to whom Muslims should apply the laws of futuhat (conquest), including execution of adult males who resisted and enslavement of women and children.[74] Stories circulated of videotaped executions of captured members of tribal militia, of rapes, and of captured women being sold in Peshawar and sent to the Middle East. To some extent, Afghans may have been trying to blame offenses committed by a variety of groups on this deviant one, and particularly on the Arab foreigners. Jamaat al-Dawa also opposed accepting aid from non-Muslims;[75] its mujahidin attacked Western journalists and relief workers, including some traveling under the protection of commanders of Hizb-i Islami. Isolating the mujahidin and Afghanistan from any Western contact has proven to be a goal they share with other Arab volunteers.

With extensive support from Saudi and Kuwaiti private sources, Jamaat al-Dawa grew to be even more powerful in the area than the seven parties. Increasing numbers of Arabs came to fight in its ranks. Nonetheless, it soon retreated into preaching orthodoxy rather than pursuing a political strategy—that is, it retreated from "Islamism" to "neo-fundamentalism."[76] Its militants spent their time knocking down flags and monuments erected over tombs and opposing other "non-Islamic" Afghan customs, often connected with Sufism.

The money supporting this group largely came from the Saudi Afghanistan support committee, but it seems that Prince Salman was not necessarily more aware of where the money was going than Dan Rather was of the tactics of some of his cameramen in Afghanistan. Some Saudis who were concerned that this group was detracting from jihad tried to convince Prince Salman to stop funding it and give the money he collected to Hikmatyar or Rabbani.

Perhaps more typical were the more politically minded Arab mujahidin who formed their own groups in eastern Afghanistan or fought with Hikmatyar or Sayyaf groups. Their number at the time of the fall of the Najibullah government in 1992 is usually given as about 5,000. Whereas the Arabs in the Salafi groups seemed largely to come from the Gulf countries, those with Hikmatyar came from the countries with more politicized Islamic movements, including Algerians, Palestinians, Sudanese, and Egyptians. Some came for long periods of time, others for short stints. Some travel agents organized two- or three-week jihad tours, and students could spend their school vacations participating in jihad in Afghanistan. Khashoggi reported in 1988:

> "Visiting" Mujahedeen include students and employees who arrive during their summer or annual vacations. More than 500 youths have so far come here as "visitors" from Saudi Arabia and they stayed for two or three weeks, during last mid-year school break. Military training programs are arranged for these visitors in camps like Sada along the Afghan border. After training they move to camps like Maasada and Meeran Shah and usually take part in the night watch and reconnaissance in the company of highly trained personnel.[77]

The conflict in the Islamic world over the approaching Gulf War in late 1990 and early 1991 temporarily weakened the financial support for the Arab volunteers and their sponsors. Open conflict broke out between those groups, such as Jamaat al-Dawa, who were close to Saudi and Kuwaiti Salafis, and those allied with the Muslim Brotherhood and the Islamist takfir groups. The Salafis supported Saudi Arabia, whose invitation to U.S. and other Western forces was opposed by the radical elements of the Afghan mujahidin, in particular Hikmatyar and Sayyaf, the Jamaat-i Islami of Pakistan, key mujahidin supporters in the Pakistani military and ISI, and the other Arab volunteers.[78] The civilian government of Pakistan, along with the nationalists and moderates among the mujahidin, supported the U.S.-Saudi position. The Saudis had made arrangements to transport 2,000 mujahidin to Saudi Arabia to offer symbolic support to the U.S.-led coalition, but the project was repeatedly held up by objections from radical mujahidin groups and Pakistani military officers, including the chief of army staff, General Mirza Aslam Beg. The Saudis at least temporarily cut off funding to Hikmatyar and some other groups, though they started funding them again a few months later. At the local level, the Gulf War broke the alliance in Kunar between Hikmatyar and Jamil al-Rahman. A battle in the summer of 1991 ended in August when an Egyptian gunman assassinated Jamil al-Rahman.

The Arab volunteer fighters came to international attention once again after the security belt around Kabul had been breached in April 1992 by Massoud and Hikmatyar, and other mujahidin also started to flow into Kabul, set up checkpoints, and engage in looting. These guerrillas included Arab Islamists. They made even more difficult the problem of negotiating over power sharing with the newly mobilized Shiite population of Kabul. During the spring and summer of 1992, Shiite mujahidin armed by Iran, who controlled about one-fourth of Kabul city, repeatedly clashed with Sayyaf and other Salafi mujahidin aided by Arab volunteers. By October, hundreds of civilian hostages taken in these clashes in June were still missing.[79]

Until Hikmatyar fled before the new movement of the Taliban (Islamic students) in February 1995, reports continued to circulate of Arabs fighting for him in the battle for Kabul. Sayyaf's group switched sides and allied with Rabbani in January 1993, when Hikmatyar signed an agreement with Hizb-i Wahdat, the unified Shia party sponsored by Iran. Massoud's forces in Kabul repeatedly captured Arabs and Pakistanis fighting for Hikmatyar. In 1993, Massoud circulated videotapes of two Algerian prisoners. In February 1995, his forces captured a nineteen-year-old Palestinian who said he had been recruited by Hizb-i Islami in Saudi Arabia. His original group of recruits included three men from Yemen and two from Saudi Arabia. They all received three months of military training.[80]

The support for these efforts seemed no longer to come from Saudi Arabia or Pakistan (not to mention the United States). Saudi Arabia ended official funding of these networks during the Gulf crisis. After the bombing of the World Trade Center, pressure on Pakistan to shut down the networks intensified. By some reports, the unwillingness of the government of Prime Minister Nawaz Sharif to arrest and deport some of the Arabs was one of the factors leading to his dismissal by President Ghulam Ishaq Khan in April 1993. (Nawaz Sharif was politically allied with the Jamaat at that time, and his director of ISI was a sympathizer of the Islamists.) In early 1994, Saudi Arabia confiscated the assets and revoked the citizenship of Osama bin Laden, who settled in Khartoum, with occasional visits to Afghanistan.

But the networks established under the aegis of these states during the war, now nourished by private donations and the drug trade, continue to function. Veterans of the war in Afghanistan appear to form the core of the Armed Islamic Group in Algeria (the group responsible for the most assassinations), as well as the armed groups of the most extreme Islamists in Jordan, Yemen, Egypt, Gaza, Saudi Arabia, and elsewhere. One of the units of the Palestinian Islamic Jihad Group is now named after Abdullah Azzam.

Besides fighting, Arab NGOs associated with the Islamic Coordination Council are active in relief and reconstruction efforts in many parts of Afghanistan, especially in Jalalabad and Kunduz, where activists are also providing military aid and training to refugees from the Tajik civil war. Their attempts to exclude Western organizations from Afghanistan have led to a number of clashes. Some charge that Arab Islamist extremists were responsible for the killing of two UN expatriates and two Afghan UN employees near Jalalabad and of two UN High Commissioner for Refugees (UNHCR) expatriate staff near Kunduz in February 1993.

Arab Islamists in North Afghanistan and the Tajikistan Conflict

The Arab activity in Kunduz is particularly important, though it does not seem to involve a large number of people. About half of the estimated

60,000 refugees from Tajikistan who remained in northern Afghanistan by summer 1993 were in the Kunduz area.[81] The Islamic Renaissance Party (IRP) established its exile headquarters in Taliqan, the administrative center of neighboring Takhar province and of Ahmad Shah Massoud's Supervisory Council of the North.[82]

Kunduz has been nominally under the control of a shura, dominated by Jamiat and Sayyaf commanders. The governor of Kunduz, Haji Rahmatullah, a member of Jamiat, exercises little real power. The administrative center of the province, Kunduz city, was controlled by Amir Chughai, a commander of Sayyaf's party until his death in fighting during the summer of 1995. Since November 1993, however, control of the city has changed hands several times, as the former communist general turned Uzbek warlord, Abdul Rashid Dostum, has repeatedly attacked it. Russia and Uzbekistan are anxious to wipe out this base of support for the Tajikistan Islamic resistance.

According to reports in early 1994, the most powerful people in Kunduz were a small group of Arabs who have set up an office of the Islamic Coordination Council. They derived their power from the fact that they are the only source of aid for the Tajik refugees and the shura. Those whose nationalities could be identified (by their Arabic accent and dialect) seem to be Algerian, probably members of the Armed Islamic Group.[83] In early 1996, their influence seemed to have diminished, as they had far less money to distribute, apparently because of a crackdown on their fund-raising in their homelands.

The Tajik refugees do not receive regular assistance from UNHCR, whose office in Kunduz is staffed only by local employees and occasional UN volunteers. UNHCR withdrew its international staff from Kunduz in early 1993, when guerrillas attacked a UNHCR convoy of refugees moving from Kunduz to rejoin family members in Camp Sakhi and two staff members were killed. At around the same time, two UNHCR international contract employees and their Afghan driver and translator were assassinated near Jalalabad. UNHCR pulled virtually all international staff out of posts in Afghanistan at that time.

In March 1993, Kunduz shura leader Amir Chughai expelled the Afghan UNHCR team leader from Kunduz city. Thereafter the refugees received assistance only from representatives of Arab Islamist groups. They transported supplies to Kunduz from Peshawar. In early June 1993, one observer stated that the Arabs had not supplied food to the refugees in May, claiming that a new law in Saudi Arabia restricting donations to foreign organizations had dried up their resources. This law aimed at ending the donation of zakat (Islamic taxes often collected in mosques) to revolutionary Islamic groups not approved by the Saudi government and was adopted partly in response to the World Trade Center bombing.

Other reports from Kunduz, however, indicated that Arab donations for weapons and military training of IRP fighters continued. Perhaps 3,000 to 5,000 members of the IRP were undergoing military training by Afghan mujahidin in different parts of Kunduz and Takhar. The Arab Islamists are still part of the same network as before, including some political forces in Pakistan. In March and April 1993, General (ret.) Hamid Gul, former chief of ISI, and Qazi Husain Ahmad, emir of the Jamaat-i Islami, visited the IRP headquarters in Taliqan. In 1994, the Russian-supported government of Tajikistan reported capturing a few Arab fighters participating in operations with the Tajik Islamic resistance movement.

The Arab Islamists and their Pakistani supporters also supplied the refugees with a hospital, medicines, housing, and food. They have resisted the intrusion of the UN and Western relief organizations into the area.

Nonetheless, subsequent incidents may hold out some lessons. In November 1993, Médecins Sans Frontières (MSF) returned to Kunduz with support from the Soros Foundation and the European Community Humanitarian Organization to aid Tajik refugees. The Afghan shura welcomed them, and the governor immediately authorized them to work. As soon as they arrived at the hospital, however, they were rudely expelled by an Arab NGO worker, apparently an Algerian from the Islamic Coordination Council. Repeated appeals to the shura were fruitless, as the Arabs were paying all the bills. The Tajik doctors, certainly no "fundamentalists" or Islamists, were also reluctant to work with the MSF staff, for fear that they would lose their Arab funding, which had proven much more dependable than the intermittent presence of Western organizations. After weeks of negotiations, however, Abbas, the Algerian head of the ICC office in Kunduz, agreed to allow MSF to work there after being assured that they would stay for six months and were sincerely trying to give aid, not undermine the Arabs politically. In addition, and very important, the new policies of the governments of Pakistan and Saudi Arabia restricting the activities of these groups had placed them in some financial difficulties. There were rumors that they were unable to pay some debts to the bazaar.[84] When I visited these same areas in 1996, Western visitors were more welcome, and the Tajik refugee leaders appealed for more external aid, from whatever source.

In this case, a combination of pressure, the offer of an alternative source of aid, and patient negotiation eventually led to an agreement on cooperation. Unfortunately, the main warring Islamist political groups in Afghanistan as well as the more traditionalist Taliban can still collect and use funds without obstacles, and the international community is not providing Afghans with any reliable alternative to the aid provided by the Arab Islamists. Under these circumstances, their influence will inevitably grow in Afghanistan, and perhaps beyond.

Do these groups constitute a threat of terrorism to the whole world? Of course, some of the returning "Afghanis" have been dissatisfied with the moderation of groups at home and have turned to violence.[85] A few who returned to New York may have bombed the World Trade Center and planned other terrorist acts. Some of the returnees to Saudi Arabia bombed the training center in Riyadh and may be responsible for the attack on the U.S. barracks in Khobar in June 1996. The training these militants received in Afghanistan may have made them militarily more effective, though the car bombs used in the attacks were never used in Afghanistan, to the best of my knowledge. The violence in Egypt, Algeria, and elsewhere is due mainly to the political and social blockage experienced by the youth of those countries, not a handful of activists returning from Afghanistan. The principal victims of the extremists among the Afghan Islamists and their Arab supporters remain the people of Afghanistan themselves. Afghans yearn to recover their country for themselves and to end the day when its territory is merely a field for the battles of others.

Notes

1. Much of this chapter has appeared in another form in Barnett R. Rubin, *The Fragmentation of Afghanistan: State Formation and Collapse in the International System* (New Haven: Yale University Press, 1995).

2. Afghan volunteers (ethnic Tajiks) have apparently fought with some Islamic guerrillas in Tajikistan. Hikmatyar also rented 1,000 of his fighters from the Jalalabad area to the government of Azerbaijan to help it resist ethnic Armenian forces covertly backed by the Armenian government. In late 1994, Hikmatyar withdrew the fighters in protest when Baku permitted the opening of an Israeli diplomatic mission. Some of the Afghans reportedly joined the fighting in Chechnya rather than return home.

3. I heard this view expressed by government officials myself. For quotations from the late director of the Central Intelligence Agency, William Casey, and U.S. congressman Charles Wilson (D.-Tex.) see Mohammad Yousaf and Mark Adkins, *The Bear Trap: Afghanistan's Untold Story* (London: Mark Cooper, 1992), 63, 79.

4. Jeri Laber and Barnett R. Rubin, *A Nation Is Dying: Afghanistan Under the Soviets* (Evanston: Northwestern University Press, 1988).

5. The attempt to label Islamic movements "Wahhabi" has an interesting history in late and post-Soviet Central Asia as well. The Tajikistan Islamic opposition is called Wahhabi by the same officials who accuse Iran of supporting it. In a 13 May 1993 interview, officials of the Tashkent municipal government regretted that they had accepted Russian scholars' classification of Islamic movements as Wahhabi. On 17 May 1993, the deputy mufti of Kyrgyzstan, a Naqshbandi from Daghestan, told a U.S. delegation that Wahhabism was started by a British intelligence agent. This is a common theme in Iranian writing on Wahhabism (see Olivier Roy, *L'Echec de l'Islam Politique* [Paris: Editions du Seuil, 1992], 158). The career of "Wahhabism" as a political label for international conspiracy deserves a study of its own. As the Afghan war shows, however, Western powers have indeed at times used militant Islam, including its Salafi varieties, against their opponents.

6. Louis Dupree, *Afghanistan,* 2d ed. (Princeton: Princeton University Press, 1980), 598.

7. Marvin G. Weinbaum, "Legal Elites in Afghan Society," *International Journal of Middle East Studies* 12 (1980): 48.

8. Theda Skocpol, *States and Social Revolutions: A Comparative Analysis of France, Russia and China* (Cambridge: Cambridge University Press, 1979), 165. For a review of a variety of studies of revolutionary counterelites, see Robert D. Putnam, *The Comparative Study of Political Elites* (Englewood Cliffs, N.J.: Prentice-Hall, 1976), 170–172.

9. Sayyed Musa Tawana, "Glimpses into the Historical Background of the Islamic Movement in Afghanistan: Memoirs of Dr. Tawana, Part 4," *AFGHANews* 5 (15 May 1989): 5ff. Tawana's articles give the views of Jamiat-i Islami on the early years of the Islamic movement (though in a dispute with Rabbani he has since abandoned Jamiat and joined Abdul Rashind Dostum's organization). For a brief summary of its rival Hizb-i Islami's view, see Farshad Rastegar, "Education and Revolutionary Political Mobilization: Schooling Versus Uprootedness as Determinants of Islamic Political Activities Among Afghan Refugee Students in Pakistan" (Ph.D. diss., University of California, Los Angeles, 1991), 112.

10. For a participant's memoir of this period, also from the Jamiat viewpoint, see Mohammad Es'haq, "Evolution of Islamic Movement in Afghanistan, Part 1: Islamists Felt Need for a Party to Defend Islam," *AFGHANews* 5 (1 January 1989), 5, 8.

11. Ibid., 8; Sayyed Musa Tawana, "Glimpses into the Historical Background of the Islamic Movement in Afghanistan: Memoirs of Dr. Tawana, Part 1," *AFGHANews* 5 (1 April 1989), 6–7. This article contains a detailed account of the meeting.

12. "Ghulam Rasul," meaning slave or worshipper of the Prophet, was Sayyaf's given name, a common one in Afghanistan. In line with Salafi teachings he later changed it to Abd al-Rabb al-Rasul, or "worshipper of the Master of the Prophet."

13. Tawana, "Glimpses, Part 4," 5, describes the choice of name. Hizb claims that "Jamiat" was the name only for the professors' association, not the whole movement.

14. For details on the data set and statistical tables, see Barnett R. Rubin, "Political Elites in Afghanistan: Rentier State Building, Rentier State Wrecking," *International Journal of Middle East Studies* 24 (1992): 77–99; or Rubin, *Fragmentation of Afghanistan,* chap. 4.

15. Tawana, "Glimpses, Part 4," 5.

16. According to Tawana (ibid.), they chose the name *Jamiyyat* (or Jamiat) for the movement "because it resembled the word 'Jamaat' in the name of 'Jamaat Ikhwan Muslemeen' of Egypt and 'Jamaat Islami' of Pakistan but was also distinct from both."

17. Roy, *L'Echec de l'Islam Politique,* 141–145.

18. Olivier Roy, *Islam and Resistance in Afghanistan* (Cambridge: Cambridge University Press, 1986), 70.

19. Mohammad Es'haq, "Evolution of the Islamic Movement in Afghanistan, Part 4: Life in Exile from 1975 to 1978," *AFGHANews* 5 (15 February 1989), 6; Roy, *Islam and Resistance,* 76–77.

20. For this use of the term *jahiliyyah,* see *Fishurdah-yi hadaf va maram-i Jamiyyat-i Islami-yi Afghanistan* [A Summary of the Aims and Program of the Islamic Society of Afghanistan] (Peshawar?: n.p., 1978 or 1979?), 8; *Maram-i Hizb-i Islami-yi Afghanistan* [Program of the Islamic Party of Afghanistan] (Peshawar?: n.p., 1986–1987), vi.

21. Hamied N. Ansari, "The Islamic Militants in Egyptian Politics,"

International Journal of Middle East Studies 16 (1984): 140. See also Roy, *Islam and Resistance*, 77–78.

22. The fullest analysis in English of the ideological dimensions of the split is in Rastegar, "Education and Revolutionary Political Mobilization," 115–127.

23. "The way of life of the people is not established on the basis of its beliefs [in Islam]" (*Maram-i Hizb*, v). The economic system of Afghanistan "is a summary of all the corruptions, tyrannical practices, and injustices of all the un-Islamic orders and systems" (ibid., 38).

24. *Maram-i Hizb*, vii. All translations from party programs by the author.

25. As Roy argues more generally (*L'Echec de l'Islam Politique*, 138), "L'évolution de l'islamisme ne relève pas seulement de facteurs idéologiques, mais s'inscrit aussi dans les jeux géostratégiques du monde musulman. Il est clair aujourd'hui que l'islamisme n'a pas modifié en profondeur ce contexte géostratégique, dominé par les stratégies d'Etats et non par des mouvements idéologiques et transnationaux."

26. Ibid., 148.

27. On these developments, see Gilles Kepel, *Le Prophète et Pharaon: Aux Sources des Mouvements Islamistes,* 2d ed. (Paris: Editions du Seuil, 1993).

28. Ibid.

29. Roy, *L'Echec de l'Islam Politique,* 142.

30. Ibid., 143. Afghan sources have independently repeated this claim to me, but I have no firm evidence to back it up.

31. Stephen P. Cohen, *The Pakistan Army* (Berkeley: University of California Press, 1984), 55–74.

32. See, for instance, *Our Global Neighborhood: The Report of the Commission on Global Governance* (Oxford: Oxford University Press, 1995), 253–262, which discusses "Global Civil Society," including NGOs, as a force for peace and human rights.

33. Kepel, *Le Prophète et Pharaon,* describes the Egyptian ones in some detail.

34. Roy, *L'Echec de l'Islam Politique,* 152.

35. "Talk of the Town," *New Yorker,* 10 January 1994 (interview by Marianne Weaver). For a similar statement by Shaikh Abdullah Azzam, see Jamal Khashoggi, "Arab Mujahedeen in Afghanistan-II: Masada Exemplifies the Unity of Islamic Ummah," *Arab News,* 14 May 1988, 9.

36. For a fuller description, see Rubin, *Fragmentation of Afghanistan,* 196–201.

37. Yousaf and Adkins, *Bear Trap,* 177.

38. Ian Anthony, Agnes Courades Allebeck, Gerd Hagmeyer-Gaverns, Paolo Miggiano, and Herbert Wulf, "The Trade in Major Conventional Weapons," in *SIPRI Yearbook 1991: World Armaments and Disarmament* (Oxford: Oxford University Press, 1991), 199, 208; Patrice Piquard, "Pourquoi le Chaos Afghan Peut Faire Exploser l'Asie Centrale," *l'Evènement du Jeudi,* 13 January 1993, 7.

39. Yousaf and Adkins, *Bear Trap,* 77.

40. On bin-Laden, see Jamal Khashoggi, "Arab Youths Fight Shoulder to Shoulder with Mujahedeen," *Arab News,* 4 May 1988, 9; and "Arab Veterans of Afghanistan Lead New Islamic Holy War," *Federal News Service,* 28 October 1994. The former article includes a photograph of bin Laden inside Afghanistan.

41. Khashoggi, "Arab Mujahedeen-II."

42. "Sheikh Abdullah Azzam Is Martyred," *Mujahideen Monthly* 4 (January 1990): 10–11. Azzam told Khashoggi ("Arab Mujahedeen-II") that it became too difficult to perform jihad in Palestine because of Israeli security measures: "I later searched for another place where I could perform this Ibadah (devotional service) of

Jihad. I couldn't find a better place than Afghanistan where the battle is apparently between Islam and atheism. No doubt about it."

43. According to Roy (*L'Echec de l'Islam Politique,* 150), Azzam considered Muhammad Abu al-Nasr, leader of the Egyptian Muslim Brothers, as his "spiritual guide."

44. Yousaf and Adkins, *Bear Trap,* 97–112.

45. Both China and Egypt manufactured versions of the Kalashnikov rifle and the SAKR ground-to-ground missile. Israel had captured many Soviet-manufactured weapons in Lebanon in 1982.

46. Many of these accounts were in the Bank of Credit and Commerce International.

47. Yousaf and Adkins, *Bear Trap,* 106.

48. Roy, *Islam and Resistance,* 163–164.

49. Yousaf and Adkins, *Bear Trap,* 106.

50. Interview with logistics officer of a traditionalist-nationalist party, Khyber Agency, Pakistan, February 1989. According to a National Islamic Front of Afghanistan (Gailani) commander of Pashtuns in Kunduz province, "In NIFA party there is no transportation cost for mujahedin. . . . Usually weapons of NIFA and Professor Mojaddedi are sold because of this transportation cost" (files of Cash for Food Program, Swedish Committee for Afghanistan, Peshawar).

51. Riaz Mohammad Khan, *Untying the Afghan Knot: Negotiating Soviet Withdrawal* (Durham: Duke University Press, 1991), 73.

52. Yousaf and Adkins, *Bear Trap,* 117.

53. According to ibid., 209, "General Akhtar [director of ISI] was conscious that if political activities were initiated before the capture of Kabul it would so weaken the Jehad that a military victory might prove unattainable."

54. Ibid., 105.

55. Apparently the same views existed among "American observers," presumably the CIA. (Farid Abolfathi, "A Reassessment of the Afghan Conflict, 1978–1988," prepared under contract for the U.S. Government [Fairfax, Va., March 1989] derides such views on pp. 3–43.)

56. For a detailed analysis, see Rubin, *Fragmentation of Afghanistan,* chap. 11.

57. Talk at Columbia University, December 1991.

58. In February 1989, in Nangarhar, I stayed one day with an Ahmadzai nomad commander of NIFA, who recounted how "Arabs" from Sayyaf's party had offered him huge amounts of money to join. "I spit on their shoes," he said. "They think jihad is a business." Later I heard he had taken their money and joined Sayyaf for a while. He subsequently went back to Gailani.

59. In the summer of 1989, when the Qandahar commanders' shura refused to carry out the ISI's plan to attack the city, the ISI brought two commanders from Wardak (an area populated by different Pashtun tribes than those in Qandahar) to carry out the attack. According to one Qandahari, "They paid each of their mujahidin Rs. 500 per day, plus Rs. 50,000 in case of death and Rs. 20,000 in case of injury [Rs. 20 then equaled about $1]. This created a terrible reaction. It was not jihad but a mercenary war. People began to ask themselves, is this still jihad?" (interview, Arlington, Va., May 1990.)

60. *The Independent,* 13 September 1988.

61. Interview with several delegates at the shura.

62. Interview with U.S. diplomat in Riyadh, 20 March 1989; Richard Cronin, *Afghanistan After the Soviet Withdrawal: Contenders for Power* (Washington, D.C.: Congressional Research Service, May 1989), 7.

63. *The Independent,* 2 February 1989.

64. Assistant Secretary John Kelly, Testimony Before the Sub-Committees on Europe and the Middle East and Asia and the Pacific, Committee on Foreign Affairs, House of Representatives, 7 March 1990.

65. For details, see Barnett R. Rubin, *The Search for Peace in Afghanistan: From Buffer State to Failed State* (New Haven: Yale University Press, 1995); and Rubin, "Post–Cold-War State Disintegration: The Failure of International Conflict Resolution in Afghanistan," *Journal of International Affairs* 46 (Winter 1993): 469–492.

66. *Washington Post,* 9 September 1989; *New York Times,* 19 November 1989.

67. "Sheikh Abdullah Azzam Is Martyred," 11.

68. "Arab Veterans."

69. Khashoggi, "Arab Youths Fight."

70. Yousaf and Adkins, *Bear Trap,* 182.

71. Khashoggi, "Arab Youths Fight," 9.

72. The name means "Group for the Call to the Quran and People of the Hadith."

73. This created much bitterness among the local Afghan population, as if the Islam for which they had fought and died for over a decade was not Islamic enough.

74. "Actions of the Pakistan Military with Respect to Afghanistan: Human Rights Concerns," *News from Asia Watch,* 27 February 1989; this was based on my own reporting from Peshawar and Nangarhar.

75. Hikmatyar has taken this position verbally at times, but in view of the massive aid he received from the United States, Afghans did not take his statements on this subject too seriously.

76. Roy, *L'Echec de l'Islam Politique.*

77. Khashoggi, "Arab Youths Fight."

78. Roy claims that Rabbani supported the Saudis (*L'Echec de l'Islam Politique*). This seems to have been the case when he talked to Saudis and Americans, but he also signed a document opposing the U.S.-led coalition that was issued by a Jamaat-convened international conference in Lahore. Rabbani explained to U.S. diplomats that he had to do so out of Islamic solidarity.

79. *Guardian,* 14 October 1992.

80. Reuters, Kabul, 10 February 1995.

81. The rest were near Mazar-i Sharif, in an area largely controlled by former communist Uzbek militia leader Abdul Rashid Dostum. On Tajikistan see Barnett R. Rubin, "The Fragmentation of Tajikistan," *Survival* 35 (Winter 1993/94): 71–91; and Olivier Roy, *The Civil War in Tajikistan: Causes and Implications: A Report of the Study Group on the Prospects for Conflict and Opportunities for Peacemaking in the Southern Tier of Former Soviet Republics* (Washington, D.C.: United States Institute of Peace, December 1993). I visited all of these camps (as well as one run by the Iranian Red Crescent Society) in North Afghanistan in January 1996.

82. *Washington Post,* 29 April 1993.

83. Khashoggi ("Arab Mujahedeen-II") reported in 1988 that Massoud had an Algerian assistant.

84. Interview with MSF doctor, 28 February 1994. Abbas was also the name of the Algerian reported to be aiding Massoud in 1988.

85. Roy, *L'Echec de l'Islam Politique,* 147.

10

Islamists and the Peace Process

Yvonne Yazbeck Haddad

The signing of the Peace Accords between the Palestine Liberation Organization and the state of Israel was staged as an occasion for great celebration by the U.S. government and highly acclaimed in the U.S. media. The mainline media did not publish or welcome comments from skeptical observers. The virtual blackout of critical commentary by the media was reminiscent of coverage of the intifada[1] and, more particularly, of Operation Desert Storm, when only official or quasi-official spokespersons were allowed to interpret events, blocking out any questions regarding the conduct of that foreign policy.[2] Only recently, with the Peace Accords running into obvious difficulties and obstructions to their implementation, have the media begun to raise serious questions and even publish some revisionist commentary.

While some elements within the Islamist movement assumed a cautious initial response to the peace process, they questioned several issues concerning its provisions. These included such questions as: Given the prevailing political and economic conditions in the area, is this a just peace that will restore equity to the oppressed Palestinians? Are the Peace Accords legitimate? Did Yasir Arafat have the right to sign away the rights of the Palestinian and Muslim people in the Holy Land? And what are the consequences of such an agreement since the Muslims are not participating in setting the agenda? For most Muslim commentators, any accord that does not provide for the total Israeli withdrawal from all Occupied Territories, including Jerusalem, and does not provide for the right of the Palestinians to return to their land and establish a state with Jerusalem as its capital, will not be considered a just peace. Consequently, it is bound to perpetuate discord in the area.[3]

The real question was whether Israel actually would provide a just peace and a comprehensive reconciliation, or whether the Declaration of Principles (DOP) was primarily a means of liquidating the Palestinian cause. From the Islamist perspective, Israel has never expressed an interest in having a fair solution to the problem it initiated by its insistence on creating a state exclusively for Jewish people. Those elements within the Islamist movement who were reluctant to condemn the peace process at first, because of the manner in which it was packaged and sold to the Arab world as a means of empowering the Palestinian people in their own nation, have become increasingly cynical. They have noted that the packaging of the Accords to the Israeli public was different from the way it was presented to the Palestinians (apparently promising the liquidation of the Islamic resistance) and that the way in which things are actually unfolding is more attuned to the Israeli scenario as articulated by Benjamin Netanyahu on the ABC television program *Nightline* than to Palestinian aspirations.[4]

Others, both within the Islamist movement and the secularist allies of the PLO, immediately proclaimed the Peace Accords to be unacceptable. The restrictions appeared to them to provide for an unjust solution that could not under any circumstances form a stable foundation for a lasting peace. The Accords in their view address Israeli security concerns at the expense of justice for the Palestinian people. The consensus of the opposition commentary on the Declaration of Principles, whether secularist or Islamist, has been that it is a bad deal, a virtual sellout. The more the details of the DOP became available, the more they were met with disbelief from various sectors of Palestinian, Arab, and Muslim society. While some had been initially willing to concede that Arafat had no option but to accede to Israeli demands since the Israelis drove a very hard bargain and basically made no concessions, the majority believe that what he accepted is a major humiliation, a surrender to Israel. As Edward Said, a former member of the Palestine National Council, put it: "Let us call the agreement by its real name: an instrument of Palestinian surrender, a Palestinian Versailles."[5]

Initial Islamist Assessment

One of the first written responses outlining objections to the Accords appeared in the spring 1994 issue of *Inquiry*. In an editorial, Professor Sami Al-Araian of Tampa, Florida, gave sixteen specific objections. Here is a brief summary of Professor Al-Araian's basic points:

1. The agreement changes the conflict "from a struggle against occupation, racism, displacement, economic exploitation and the future of a national liberation movement with regional and international implications, to a mere internal problem, to self-rule of a 'foreign' population with all political, economic and military cards in the hands of the Israelis" (p. 8).

2. The powers given to the administrative council are restricted to six service-type areas, which only exacerbates Palestinian fears that the aim of this agreement is simply to relieve the Israeli army from having to rule the Palestinians "without giving up the claims over the land, water, and ulti-

mate sovereignty over the territories." He worries that in the end the result will look much like the black Bantustan townships in South Africa under the apartheid system (p. 8).[6]

3. The greatest deception is the expectation that Israel would withdraw from the territories. The actual title of that particular article in the Accords is called "Redeployment of Israeli Forces." It was anticipated that UN Resolutions 242 and 338 would be implemented, in which international law would be upheld forcing Israel to give up land it acquired through war. Instead, Israel holds on to the land it seized (p. 8).[7]

4. Seven decades worth of struggle on the part of Palestinians for their land has resulted in Israeli withdrawal (or redeployment) from less than 1.5 percent of Palestine (p. 8).

5. The Palestinian demand to halt the construction of settlements, at least the building of new ones, in the Occupied Territories has been totally ignored (p. 9). Since his writing, there have been numerous reports of continued Israeli expansion of settlements.

6. The status of Jerusalem, so important as a holy city to both Muslims and Christians, has basically been ignored in the agreement, with the acknowledgment that its status would be negotiated later. "What else," asks Al-Araian, "could the Palestinians possibly give the Israelis for them to give up part of Jerusalem?" (p. 9).[8]

7. There is no attempt in the Accords to address the issue of the fate of 4 million Palestinians living as refugees in the diaspora. This goes against UN resolutions acknowledging the right of Palestinians to return to their homeland or to be compensated. Thus, by definition the Accords lack the support of two-thirds of all Palestinians. "While Israel prepares to absorb as many as 2 million Russian Jews and U.S. Jewish settlers, it continues to deprive the true owners of the land, the Palestinians, from living there" (p. 9).

8. The PLO negotiating team has failed to deal specifically with the more than 13,000 Palestinians who are imprisoned or detained in Israeli jails (p. 9).

9. It also has failed to deal with the status of the million Palestinians living in occupied lands since 1948 who would remain under the control of Israel, "undesirables in their own lands simply because they are not Jews" (p. 10).

10. In Al-Araian's view, the Accords represent a grave security risk for all Palestinians because they are not granted constitutional, political, or human rights. Arafat's job of taming the Palestinian resistance and stopping the intifada serves to safeguard Israeli (especially settler) interests at the expense of the Palestinians. Palestinian communities are thus at the mercy of the army and the armed settlers anywhere, including Gaza and Jericho (p. 10).

11. While political matters were left vague, economic issues were

spelled out expansively. The objectives of certain ventures and projects are clear: the domination and control of Palestinian economic development, the continuation of Palestinian cheap labor, the expansion of Palestinian consumers, and the inclusion of a much larger market in the Arab world through a small segment of Palestinians acting as agents and middlemen for Israeli products (p.10).

12. The treaty is based on integration of the Zionist regime into the region, a new Middle East order with Israel at the center, sharing the water resources and raw materials of the Arab countries (p. 10). "Acceptance of this agreement simply guarantees the strategic imbalance of power in favor of Israel and preserves its hegemony and strategic control" (p.11).

13. The Accords suggest that international and Islamic support for Palestine and the solution of its problems is undercut (p. 11).

14. It also weakens the position of many non-Zionist Jews (whom Al-Araian says are few but vocal) who have supported Palestinian rights (p. 11).

15. Inherent in the agreement is that the Israelis are magnanimous enough to satisfy the Palestinians without tying them down to any acceptable outcomes. However, nothing in the history of the conflict or in current Israeli behavior or rhetoric portends such an outcome (p. 11).

16. Secret negotiations, like the one concluded in Oslo, do not earn the trust and support of the people. They represent an agreement forced on the weaker party, which is then coerced into making painful, unacceptable, and illegal concessions. No single person (i.e., Arafat) should have the right to make such a major decision on behalf of a people. No individual has the right to deprive future generations of their God-given rights (p. 12).

Islamist critique notes that the Peace Accords took care of several of Israel's concerns. It gave Israel the responsibility for Israelis in the Occupied Territories, kept Jerusalem out of the area of self-government, recognized the right of Israel to exist in secure borders, ended armed resistance, abrogated thirty-three articles from the Palestine National Covenant that called for the eradication of Israel, and altered the core principles of the Palestine Liberation Organization.[9]

Critique of the Accords

The growth of public support for Islamists in the Muslim world is due in no small part to their ability to present themselves as a reaction against the disempowerment of Muslim people and their dismemberment into nation-states. A major theme of Islamist literature is the perception that, since the time when nation-states were carved out by European colonialists, the dominant world order has sought to control Muslim nations and make them subservient to foreign interests. A predatory relationship between strong Western elements and Muslims has rendered Muslims weak and subject to "forces of hate."[10] The perception is that Muslims have been victimized by Jews and Christians over the centuries, by the Crusades, the Reconquista, European colonialism, Christian missionaries, communism, Zionism and the latest outrage, ethnic cleansing in Bosnia. The last is seen as one more manifestation of European efforts to eradicate a Muslim population, in this case from Eastern Europe.[11]

Islamists also identify a double standard operating in the Western framing of events in Israel/Palestine. For example, they note that attacks on Israeli soldiers by Palestinian freedom fighters are portrayed as terrorist activities, while raids by Israeli death squads liquidating members of the Palestinian resistance are justified as security measures. Muslims are depicted as enemies of peace, while the assassin Greenberg was simply called a lunatic.[12] Thus, the person who defends his homeland is a "terrorist," and the killing of Palestinian civilians by Israelis is described by the euphemism "administrative measures."

With the signing of the Accords, Islamists grumble, anyone who agrees to the normalization is deemed "realistic" and the peace is defined as the "peace of the brave." The term *salam,* peace, is repeated day and night over the media. People read it until it sinks into the consciousness and programs the brain, and whoever disagrees with it is called "the enemy of peace."[13] Thus, one reads about

> bridges of peace, fruits of peace, seeds of peace, year of peace, the victims of peace, the society of peace, the hope of peace, the dimension of peace, gifts of peace, goals of peace, umbrella of peace, peace efforts, meaning of peace, peace initiative, opposition to peace, torpedo the peace, impediments to peace, the essence of peace, the structure of peace, peace arrangements, desire for peace, peace experiment, priorities of peace, lessons of peace, results of peace, spoils of peace, peace disaster, tools of peace, mechanics of peace, reality of peace, peace covenant, obligations of peace, the future of peace, the peace imperative, demands of peace, justification of peace, opportunities for peace, goal of peace, cold peace, destruction of peace, slippery peace, undulations of peace, the climate of peace, the peace of the brave.[14]

Despite the rhetoric of peace and its benefits propagated by the governments of the area as the peace process has unfolded, from an Islamist perspective, its weak points and structural fault lines have become evident. Criticism of the Accords as well as of Yasir Arafat has become increasingly more open and more vocal. This criticism has been aggravated by the treatment Arafat received from both Rabin and Clinton (and, more recently, from Netanyahu). Since it appears that all of them treat him with palpable disdain, Arabs ask, why should his own people look up to him? On the one hand, his power and jurisdiction are restricted insofar as he is seen to be nothing more than a mayor. On the other hand, the Clinton administration has echoed what is perceived as unjustified and unreasonable expectations insisted on by Israel that Arafat has to eradicate the HAMAS movement in areas under his jurisdiction in Gaza, even though Israel, with its vastly superior military strength and security apparatus, failed to even penetrate it during all the intifada years.[15]

Reservations about the Peace Accords among Islamists also stem from what is seen as the growing atmosphere of demonization of Islam in the West. Samuel Huntington's article "The Clash of Civilizations?" in *Foreign Affairs* has received extensive commentary. It taps into a reservoir of fear and apprehension that the war against Islam in the West has not ceased but has just taken new forms.[16] Thus, what appears to be an attempt to convince the United States and Europe that after the fall of the U.S.S.R. there is a new enemy, Islamic fundamentalism, which is equally as threatening as communism was for four decades, seems to be taking hold. Islamists see this as playing into the prevailing negative atmosphere in relation to Islam, reflected in the growing body of literature demonizing Islamists by a variety of interests both in Muslim countries and in the United States. This attitude is evidenced in quotations from U.S. officials, "policy wrongs," beltway experts, and columnists in the U.S. press, as well as from the Israeli government and academy and from Arab governments who do not tolerate any kind of opposition. It was well summed up by Ari Goldman in a recent book review in which he noted that the best-known Hebrew word in the English language is *shalom,* while the best known Arabic word is *jihad.*

Islamist literature takes very serious note of the intensified and sustained emphasis on the threat of Islam in the speeches of Israeli leaders. They see this as an effort by the Israeli government to sell itself as the guardian of U.S. and Western interests in the region. The late Israeli prime minister Yitzhak Rabin, in what appeared to be a concerted effort to sell Israel in Washington, said that the United States must support Israel in order to combat the Islamists, the enemies of peace who also threaten Arab regimes in the area, including Algeria, Egypt, and Tunisia. The Islamist press notes that in March 1994, Rabin reportedly depicted the Islamists as a cancer and proposed to the Clinton administration that the two countries cooperate in fighting them. Haim Hertzok is reported to have said that, while the world today is concerned about the atom bomb and weapons of mass destruction in the region, a more sinister and dangerous development is the growth of Islamic fundamentalism. Shimon Peres told a White House audience that the United States must increase its aid to Israel because it is engaged in a war against Islamic extremism.[17]

The timing of the Peace Accords has been a major factor in the difficulty many Arabs have had in accepting it, regardless of efforts by various governments to make it palatable. It came so soon after Operation Desert

Storm and the collapse of the myth of Arab unity that many are full of fore-boding. They recall examples from Islamic history when some Muslim leaders, seeking to advance their own interests over those of their people, formed alliances with foreign enemies against Muslim rivals. During the Crusades, because the Western principalities managed to ally themselves with some Muslim leaders against others, the Crusaders were able to survive for a century in the area. In Andalusia (Spain), rivalry between Muslim princes and alliances they formed with non-Muslims in their struggle against one another led to the Reconquista, the final demise of the Muslim presence in Western Europe. In the eyes of some Islamists, all of these alliances and their historical consequences appear to have been ignored by the Arab and Muslim nations who allied themselves with the United States in Operation Desert Storm. The signing of the Peace Accords can thus be projected as portending consequences parallel to those of past history. They can only further the disintegration of the Arab and Muslim nations.

The legacy of the Gulf War is still fresh in Arab memory. Fatwas warning of alliances with the United States were not heeded by heads of Arab and Muslim states who commissioned counter-fatwas to legitimate their participation. They believed that if they cooperated with the West, they would reap great benefits. They gambled that if they proved themselves to be reliable allies working for U.S. interests, they would be raised from the subservient status of client states. They had assumed that their cooperation with the West would prove that Arabs can make reliable allies for the United States in the area, thereby precluding the U.S. need for Israel. They had not, however, counted on the election of Bill Clinton to the presidency of the United States and the subsequent assignment given to Dennis Ross at the State Department and Martin Indyk at the National Security Council to design and implement policy in the area. The Peace Accords are thus seen as having been engineered and implemented under the auspices of operatives noted for their partiality to the state of Israel (both being senior distinguished alumni of the Israeli lobby) with a vested interest in implementing Israeli plans in the area. More than ever before, U.S. foreign policy in the Middle East is perceived as having been subordinated to Israeli interests. The Israeli plans for the area have always been seen to have been developed at the expense of the Palestinian people. Meanwhile, the Gulf states who allied themselves with the United States have been rendered financially bankrupt and dependent for their survival and security on Western support. Other Arab regimes increasingly appear to owe their very survival to U.S. largess rather than to the will and support of their own people.[18]

Israelis have insisted that the signing of the Peace Accords means the implementation of policies that Islamists see as resulting in what is actually a Palestinian defeat. This has been described under the euphemism "normalization," which for Islamists is unacceptable. The Arabic word for "normalization" is *tatbi,* which means "to tame, domesticate, break in, train, leave one's stamp on." It connotes a master imposing a reality on an obedient subservient client, rather than the negotiation of a new reality by two equals. It affirms an image of a winner and a loser. Thus, while some Islamists have agreed that some kind of reconciliation may be in order at present, "normalization," which in the Arabic connotation of the word would mean subservience to Israeli interests, has to be resisted at all costs.[19]

Islamists continue to call for a rejection of the Clinton administration's policy for normalization. Clinton appears to link the defense of the Gulf Cooperation Council with the implementation of peace with Israel. He is perceived as "confronting all Muslims in all parts of the world by forcing them to have a peaceful coexistence with the Israeli enemy," with the implication that U.S. pressure will focus on those who oppose it. Terrorism, which Clinton insists must be eradicated before the peace process can bear fruit, seems to Islamists to carry a one-way definition. For Clinton, it is perceived to mean that there is no limitation on Israeli enjoyment of their occupation of Palestine; peace in his view is seen by Islamists to mean the killing of innocent Muslims, the raping of their women, and the expulsion of children, as is evident in Bosnia and Herzegovina. And normalization for Clinton seems to mean closing off the past and refusing to deal with the injustices, while opening a new page on the future means no remorse for the treatment of Palestinians and no restitution for their losses. "Is the past that is to be forgotten that of Israel's occupation of Palestine and the expulsion of about four million Palestinians and killing of thousands of innocent people, the jailing of thousands in Israeli prisons and the raping of women?"[20]

Islamists have taken note of the speed with which the rewriting of history to serve the interests of Israel has taken place. One of the by-products of the peace process, for example, is the revision of history textbooks that has been imposed on the United Nations Relief and Works Agency (UNRWA) schools. References to Jewish expansionist plans in the area and the religious history of the Jews have been deleted. The word *Palestine* has been removed from maps in the geography textbooks. Passages making reference to "martyrs of the intifada" or "the aggression of the occupation forces over the holy places of Islam" have been deleted.[21]

Even the venue for the signing of the Accords, Madrid, proved to be a negative one for Islamists, evoking images of the victimization of Muslims at the hands of Europe. Muslims smarting from the 500-year celebration of the fall of Granada and the eradication of Islam from Western Europe found it a grim irony that this should be the location of the "imposed" peace agreement.

The Arabs once claimed that [Palestine] is their primary issue. . . . Today, on October 30, 1991, they compete to attend its funeral at the American Peace Conference in the capital of Spain, a fact that has a lacerating significance. It represents America's humiliating slap of its Arab allies and commemorates a similar historical event. At the same time, [the Peace Conference] can be considered as an appropriate gift to Spain on the eve of its festivities celebrating 500 years of the collapse of the last Islamic kingdom in al-Andalus in 1492.[22]

The Economic Provisions

While some people in the Arab world seemed initially to welcome the alleviation of the miserable conditions of the Palestinians under the occupation, increasingly they see that the economic attachments to the Accords are a sellout. The Palestinians are perceived to be relegated to the role of peddling the Israeli economy to other Arab states. As soon as the Declaration of Principles was signed, several magazines and newspapers in the Gulf began calling for normalization of relations with Israel by urging the end of the Arab economic boycott of Israel.[23] (Some elements of the Kuwaiti press had wanted to end it right after the liberation of Kuwait as a way of getting back at the Palestine Liberation Organization and the Jordanian government and people because of their support of Iraq during the Gulf War.) One Islamist noted that among the newspapers calling for the end of the boycott was the Kuwaiti daily *al-Siyasa,* which was one of the leaders in the attack against Anwar al-Sadat after Camp David for "opening the door to surrender." He noted the irony that these same newspapers were now motivated by vengeance rather than the interest of the Muslims. Along with favoring a lifting of the current boycott, they have now declared Sadat a "hero of peace," ahead of his time, misunderstood by the Arabs.[24]

The Islamist response to ending the boycott has been very negative from the outset, describing this prospect as leading to Israeli domination of the economies of the region.[25] Islamists note that there is a structural imbalance in the economies of Israel and the surrounding Arab countries. While Israel has a superior advanced industrial and technological base, the Arab economies are dependent economies. Some are basically agrarian, others have the oil produced for them, while still others are dependent on tourism. The Israeli economy is about $60 billion, while that of all the surrounding Arab nations together is $15 billion. This could only serve Israeli policies in the area. As a writer for *al-Mujtama,* the Kuwaiti weekly published by the Islah Party, comments, "The Israeli goals in the region for half a century can now be realized through economic activity. . . . The goal of realizing the Zionist Jewish legitimacy in the land of the ascension of the Prophet to heaven is followed by the realization of peace with the Arabs, which they thought could come about through military action and the breaking of the will of the Arab nation by attacking the Islamic doctrine."[26]

Another source of aggravation was the Middle East economic summit convened in Casablanca in 1993. For Islamists, this meeting served in effect to give credibility to the claim that Israel is in the process of creating a new identity for the area. An editorial in *al-Mujtama,* for example, claimed that the conference was "one hundred percent produced and directed by Israel. It is apparent that with the help of the United States and certain Arab elements, Israel seeks to firmly fix a new identity for the area. This will entail 'melting Arabism,' fighting Islam and declaring that the area be called 'Middle Eastern' [rather than Arab], with its citizens conversant in Hebrew, French, English and Arabic, the languages of the conference."[27]

The editorial reported that there was an imbalance in the power of representation at the Casablanca conference as well as in the number of projects discussed. It reported that one-third of the delegates were Israeli and that they submitted 150 projects, while Egypt, Jordan, and Morocco, in an effort to please the United States, submitted fifty projects, all predicated on cooperation and joint sponsorship with Israel. According to this editorial, the Israeli projects were aimed at subsuming all Arab economic potential under Israeli hegemony. Israel thereby would become the economic heart of the Middle East, thus realizing its dream of becoming "Greater Israel."[28] In the opinion of the writer of this editorial, the "cunning of the Jews" will turn against them, a consequence of their evil. He warned that this, however, will be realized only when the ummah is awakened from its slumber and becomes fully cognizant of its repression and returns to its identity and religion, and to the extent that the people have the will to be ready to recover the holy places and defend al-hurumat, the sacrosanct.[29]

The tone with which Yitzhak Rabin addressed the Arab delegates at the Casablanca conference was interpreted to be both arrogant and filled with enmity. His declaration that Jerusalem is the eternal capital of Israel was seen as an insult to the Muslims in attendance. His agenda was declared by these observers as a clear realization of the Israeli dream of the "New Middle East," which they noted not incidentally is the title of the new book by Shimon Peres.[30] Rabin is depicted as having talked about the "grafting of the Arab and Muslim umma on the skin of the Jewish state." He did not accuse his opposition of terrorism or of destroying the peace process, but focused on the importance of the Middle East market and the restructuring of the Middle East according to the U.S. strategy, which guarantees Israeli superiority and the flow of cheap oil.[31]

Peres's book has thus become of great concern to many Arabs in the Middle East. Quotations from it are used to justify the fear of Israeli hegemony in the area. Its goal is described as "a realization of Arab surrender which is the most important goal of Zionism."[32] Peres is faulted for asking the Arab nation to forget its history, "to bury our memory, confiscate our consciousness and stop our heartbeat." This at a time when he considers

"Zionist myths about the Land of Return to be a permanent reality."[33] Peres notes that Israel sought peace because of four realities that have materialized in the area: (1) Islamic fundamentalism, the genie that has come out of the bottle and turned into a giant; (2) the realization that missiles can reach inside Israel as proven during the Gulf War; (3) the intifada—the Palestinian will to resist the occupation; and (4) recognition of the importance of demographics and the fact that the population bomb threatens the future of Israel. Peres is depicted as rejecting Israeli accountability for the Palestinian refugees and blaming the United Nations for their misery. Had not the United Nations provided for them, they would have disappeared into other nations. He insists that along with economic power, Israel must also have nuclear capacity.[34]

Peres's plans are perceived as aimed at aborting any future united Arab or Muslim economic projects.[35] Integrating Israel into the "New Middle East" means a permanent sectoring of Arab nations from the rest of the Muslim world, a deepening of the rift between their interests, and a victory for the West, which wants to see a permanent fragmentation of the area. The economic project for the Middle East is perceived as an economic threat to Arabs because of Israeli superiority in technology and agriculture and the possibility of Israel completely undermining the Arab market.

> The failure of this project has been witnessed before when Sadat thought that by making peace with the Jews, wealth and luxury would spread to all sectors in Egypt . . . however, Egypt, after many steps taken on the road to surrender (*istislam*) has fallen in the web of the economic octopus and political subordination. The Egyptian individual did not reap anything except poverty, deprivation, unemployment and dispersal, as well as massacres we witness daily between the government and what it calls "fundamentalism" which is used by Israel to distort the pure image of Islam.[36]

The Legitimacy of Making Peace with Israel

The current discussion vis-à-vis the legitimacy of signing a peace treaty with Israel echoes the debates that followed the Camp David agreement. At the time, the Azharite professor Abd al-Wahab Khallaf issued an opinion in support of Anwar al-Sadat's policy legitimizing the peace. His justification was the Quranic verse "And if they veer towards peace, then you do likewise" (S. 8:61). Other fatwas sanctioning the Camp David accord were also issued by Shaikh al-Azhar as well as other Egyptian religious leaders. These fatwas were seen by Islamists at the time as an example of the ulama's subservience to the regime.[37] There was a general rejection of the interpretation and justification for peace provided by these fatwas, based on the belief that Israel has not sought peace but hegemony and legitimation of its appropriation of the property it had won by war. The Jordanian mufti at

the time, Shaikh Abd Allah al-Qalqili, issued a fatwa banning reconciliation, cooperation, or the forming of coalitions with Israel. He noted that
there is disagreement among the ulama over the issue. One group bases its
opinion on the verse quoted above, as well as citing the example of the
Prophet Muhammad in his treatment of the Meccans at Hudaybiyyah.
Rather than fight them, the Prophet contracted a peace treaty. Such a treaty
is predicated on the belief that cooperation under the prevalent circumstances was in the public interest, maslaha, of the community, or that it was
by darura, necessity, since he could not defeat them. For al-Qalqili, the
Hudaybiyyah truce is not applicable in the current conditions since the
Israelis are occupiers of land. He notes that reconciliation can take place
with an enemy who already has legitimate possessions, power, and land
that it had sought to augment or protect through war. Peace in this case
would involve the recognition that the aggressor is now restrained from his
greed. Peace is not possible, however, with one who had no legitimate right
to the land to begin with. Since Israel is the aggressor, having confiscated
the property of others and robbed them, to make peace on these terms without restitution would be simply to surrender. Religion does not allow granting Israel the land and keeping the Palestinians without a homeland, its
people in dispersion. As the Quran says, "God forbids you friendship with
those who fought you in your religion and expelled you from your homes.
He who seeks to be their friend is of the oppressors" (S. 60:13).[38]

Therefore, Islamic responses to the issue of whether the peace with
Israel outlined in the current accords is legitimate vary considerably. On the
one side are those who feel that sulh, reconciliation, not salam, full peace,
can be justified with the proper interpretation, whereas others reject it cate-
gorically. In December 1994, for example, the mufti of Saudi Arabia, Abd
al-Aziz bin Baz, argued that Palestinians have the right to aid from their
fellow Muslim nations in getting rid of the Jews, whom he calls the "enemies of God." Muslims, therefore, are bound in duty to do jihad against
God's enemies, the Jews, until God gives them victory by expelling the
Jews from the Palestinian nation. But bin Baz went on to insist that an
alternative to expulsion is sulh, reconciliation or temporary peace, between
Palestinians and Jews, particularly since the continuation of war would
bring great harm and injury to Palestinian men, women, and children, an
unacceptable condition according to Islamic law. Citing the precedent of
the Prophet, he said that sulh is acceptable because it is in the interest of
Palestinian security and it does give them some rights. Asked whether
Muslims outside Palestine should support the opponents of peace or the
PLO, he urged all to accept sulh and to cooperate so as not to shed more
blood.[39]

The controversial nature of this fatwa generated heated response. It
was condemned in a mosque rally during early January by Said Ramadan
al-Buti, dean of the sharia college at the University of Damascus. The most

notable refutation of bin Baz's opinion is the fatwa issued by the Egyptian scholar Yusuf al-Qaradawi, of the University of Qatar, who in the late 1980s had said that recognition of the Zionist entity or giving up any part of Jerusalem is "a betrayal to God, his messenger and the trust given to Muslims."[40] He has continued this theme in his opposition to the Peace Accords. Shaikh bin Baz, he says, is wrong in his interpretation. While agreeing that sulh is appropriate if the enemy "veers toward peace," he insists that such is not the case with Israel today. "The usurping Jews have not sought peace on any day. How can one consider the Jews to be seeking peace after they have usurped the land, spilled blood, displaced the people and expelled them unjustly from their homes?" Israel has appropriated Haifa, Jaffa, Akka, Lodd, Ramleh, Beer Sheeba, and even Jerusalem. The "usurper" cannot be considered as moving toward peace unless he returns what he has appropriated. Recognition of a usurper's right to land, implied in a temporary peace or sulh, is therefore wrong and must be opposed.[41]

The fallout from this debate received top billing in many newspapers in the Arab world that faulted bin Baz as catering to the Saudi authorities in order to justify their policies. In January of 1995 bin Baz responded to al-Qaradawi by reiterating the same themes. "*Sulh* or truce does not necessitate loving or even liking the Jews," he said. "It is for security reasons on both sides." Sulh allows for both trade and diplomatic exchange. The Prophet, for example, had made sulh with the Jews of Medina, traded with them, talked with them, and invited them to God. But when the Banu Nadir tribe betrayed him, he expelled them. When the Qurayza tribe reneged on the treaty and collaborated with the Meccans against the Prophet he fought them, killed their warriers, and took their women and children. Does such a peace mean affirming the rights of the enemy in their usurpation of the land of Palestine today? "No, it is not an eternal possession but a temporary one until the truce comes to an end or the Muslims are empowered to expel them by force from Muslim land," bin Baz insists. But, he adds, what obtains in the agreement between the PLO and "the Jews" is not necessarily valid for other nations. Each country should decide whether or not to have relations with Israel.[42]

Many have assumed that Palestine and the Peace Accords are a matter of concern only to Arab peoples and nations.[43] In fact, Muslims from a range of countries have expressed their fears for the future of the Palestinian state on repeated occasions. In 1988, for example, when the Palestine Liberation Organization made one of the first moves toward peace by recognizing the state of Israel, a fatwa was issued whose signatories included eleven Egyptians, seven Kuwaitis, six Indians, six Palestinians, four each from Afghanistan and Sudan, three each from Syria, Lebanon, Iraq, and Turkey, and one each from Pakistan, Oman, Guinea, Jordan, Tunisia, Algeria, Malaysia, Morocco, and the Comoro Islands.

We the undersigned declare in this document to all Muslims during these difficult times that of all humanity the Jews are the most severe in their enmity to the believers. They have usurped Palestine and violated Muslim land, dispersed its people and desecrated its holy places. They will not cease until they eradicate the religion of Islam and the existence of Muslims in every place.

We declare, according to the covenant we have made with God that Jihad is the only means of liberating Palestine and that it is not permissible under any circumstances to recognize Jewish sovereignty over any part of the land of Palestine. No one person or organization has the right to confirm Jewish tenure of the land of Palestine or cede any part of it to them, or affirm any right for them in it. Such a recognition is treason against God, the Prophet and the trust the Muslims have been given for its protection.[44]

Islamist rejection of the Accords is not restricted to the Arab world. For example, after the signing, Nejmeldin Erbakan, leader of the Welfare Islamic Party in Turkey said: "This agreement is an ugly example of the arrogance of the world. It shows that the US is ready to do anything to please Israel." And on 16 September 1993, at the time of the final formulation of the Peace Accords, Iran's Ayatollah Khameini asked,

Is it peace for someone to engage in a tyrannical act, force the tyrannized person to accept that tyranny without any yielding from the oppressor and without reducing his injustice? Or is it a disgrace, a surrender to tyranny? This is the act which is forbidden and condemned by the holy sharia of Islam. Today they are celebrating, thinking that the issue of Palestine is over. I say that the issue of Palestine is not over. They should not make a mistake. The issue is not over. There is no change in the issue. The issue of Palestine is still here as it has always been.[45]

In light of Jordan's special agreement with Israel, members of the Islamic Front have expressed their own particular set of responses to the Peace Accords, given the importance of the Palestinian constituency in the country as well as their legitimacy as participants in the Jordanian democratic process. From the beginning they recognized three options: opposing the peace process, supporting it, or being impartial or unconcerned about it. In general, they have rejected it on the grounds that it acquiesces to Israel's interests and terms, at the same time that they express their opposition mainly through democratic rather than violent means.[46] According to their critique, Israel insisted on control of the land of all Palestine; refused the repatriation of Palestinian refugees; wanted the establishment of a Palestinian self-government that is not independent and has no authority over its land, foreign policy, defense, or judiciary; and insisted on keeping Jerusalem out of the negotiations.

The Islamic Front has made clear its opposition to the project by issuing declarations, holding symposia, writing articles for the press, raising consciousness, and putting pressure on the parliament. The leadership of the Islamic Front did not expect to halt or impede the process for the following reasons: (1) The Front would need a parliamentary majority, which it did not have nor did it expect to have in the foreseeable future. This restricted their operations to political opposition using the media and public pressure. Their efforts have centered on the battle to resist cultural and economic normalization with Israel. (2) They are aware that the peace process is proceeding under heavy pressure from outside forces and that normalization is a consequence of U.S. hegemony and its ability to pressure and force, of Israeli superiority and its ability to threaten and steal, and of the disunity and disintegration of the Arab ranks and the economic and political weakness of the Arab nations.[47] The Arab nations find themselves in a situation in which all they can hope for is to lessen the losses, to achieve some benefits, and to limit or better the conditions. Thus, the goal of the opposition is to attempt to keep the government from giving up too much and to achieve at least a few results.[48]

Abdal-Majid Dhanibat of the Jordanian Muslim Brotherhood described in an interview the strong opposition his organization has to the Jordanian-Israeli Accord. We shall continue to oppose all future efforts at normalization and Judaization by all the means available to us, he said. These treaties do not represent the people nor are they bound by them. "Our battle with the Jews is a long battle and needs patience and rational assessment. . . . Our role is to raise consciousness about the danger of the next phase and to secure the umma from the plagues and viruses of the Jews by propagating and deepening Islamic consciousness because we know that Islam is the only thing capable of withstanding their expansionist, colonial and racist project. Just as Islam was instrumental in liberating the Muslim people from the attacks of the Crusaders and the Tartars, it will be the axis for the liberation of this umma."[49] Jordanian Islamists focus on the fact that the right of militant resistance in the Occupied Territories is guaranteed under various international treaties for all people under military occupation. They see the Israelis as extremists, since "they are a conquering oppressive authority; in fact, since the beginning, they have been the living model of extremism in their settlements and colonization policies."[50]

Some Jordanians are betting that time and timing are on the side of the Arabs. Efforts are therefore aimed at postponing the agreement. What follows in the way of political, cultural, and economic normalization may tilt the balance in favor of the Arabs in the future, such as a weakening of U.S. hegemony, or a separation between Western and Israeli interests, or a move toward more Arab unity and cooperation so that they could dictate their own interests and respect their own rights. This is perceived as possible given the growth in the deficit in the U.S. budget, increasing economic problems in the United States, and the possibility of competition for U.S. hegemony by growing powers in Asia or Europe, especially Germany. It is bolstered by the feeling that no matter what the circumstances, Arabs must not abandon their rights to their land. There is no option but to resist and reject, despite the fact that it may lead to further losses.[51] Some also feel that once Israel finds itself in the sea of Arabs who are well trained, it will recognize what a small minority in the area it really is.[52]

Others have a different perception, namely that time is not on the side of the Arabs. Every delay in making peace leads to further losses and decreases Arab options while strengthening the Zionist entity. This is supported by a look at the progression of Palestinian losses from 1948 through 1967, as well as Israeli occupation of Lebanese land and the potential for further occupation of other Arab land. It is bolstered by the awareness that Arabs do not possess the power to bring about a different solution. A third opinion proceeds on the assumption that the Zionist entity gains its power because of Arab weakness and disunity. From this perspective, the only option is to focus on an Arab renaissance, ignoring the peace process or at least remaining partial toward it. This approach seeks the unity of the Arab people, development, and coordination and support for the Palestinians in resisting occupation and normalization.[53]

It is obvious, then, that across the Muslim world there is a profound feeling of cynicism about the peace—its quality and its outcome. Is it a peace the Arabs can enjoy? Is it even one they can live with? What is the peace, and what is the wellbeing that Arabs shall enjoy with Israel? The questioning comes as a reaction to President Clinton's continued affirmation of his unequivocal support for Israel. He is perceived to be willing to use the logic of force to get the countries in the region to have relations with Israel in what has been dubbed the "counterfeit peace." Islamists question why the Clinton administration is not willing to build the economies in the area in cooperation with other Arab, Muslim, or friendly countries without "having to fall into the lap of the murderers and the spillers of Muslim blood, the rapers. How could we trust those Jews and entrust them with our affairs?"[54]

To some extent the Islamists are increasingly exhibiting a kind of victim mentality. From this perspective, the Islamist sees himself as a member of a community singled out for oppression and dehumanization because of his belief.[55] Those who have robbed him of his land, his dignity, and his future have been the ones who have advised him not to wallow in his feelings of victimhood. Rather he should give up his hope for a better Arab/Islamic future and participate in fashioning a secure economic future for the oppressor. His struggle against the oppressor is considered illegitimate, while surrender and defeat are declared acceptable. Tawfiq al-Wai, a regular feature writer in *al-Mujtama,* has expressed the extreme pain of those who feel deeply betrayed by the Accords:

Who will stifle the scream of the oppressed? Who can stop the cry of the one who has been robbed and whose property has been declared legitimate [for the thief]? Who can stop the mourning for the one that is murdered? Who can halt the struggle of the terrorized nations? What should the Muslim do when his blood is devalued, his dignity wasted, his reputation sullied, his wealth stolen, and his land robbed? What does the Muslim do when his tongue is severed, his bones crushed, his doctrine ridiculed? [What does he do] when they ask him to abandon his religion when he believes in its veracity, to abandon his path which he believes is the right one, and to renege on his allegiance which is part of his being? What does the Muslim do when he is sold in the market of slavery, butchered in the market of subservience and buried in the garbage heaps of history? What does this defeated, helpless, distraught, and wounded one do?[56]

Increasingly, the dominant discourse in the Islamist press refers to the Peace Accords as surrender, or istislam, not peace, or salam.[57] *Al-Mujtama* faults the leadership of the Arab world for agreeing to unacceptable terms. For example, that the signing of the peace agreement between Jordan and Israel required heavy military protection of the participants is perceived as an acknowledgment by those engaged in the process of the fact that the public rejects the agreement. Further proof that the agreement was in the interest of Israel is the fact that all members of the Knesset except three voted for it, and the three Knesset members who disagreed did so because they were eager to get even more concessions from the Palestinians: "The leaders of the Arabs came singly or in groups seeking [Israel's] forgiveness for the past, granting them gifts and privileges which are the rights of the Arab nation, its firm foundation, its land, its heritage and the product of the struggle of the forefathers. It is as though these foundations of the nation have become the private property of the leaders to dispose of as they please through gifts or by leasing [of land]."[58]

To Islamists, it is both disconcerting and galling that the Arab leaders appear to be following a policy of surrender, abandoning Arab rights to the whole land of Palestine and acquiescing to Israeli occupation of the land in terms of the 1967 border. Few make reference anymore to the "crimes of the Zionist gangs" of the twenties, the thirties, and the forties, the usurpation of Palestinian land, or the travesty of the establishment of the state of Israel.

Peace cannot be made through agreements based on deception, fraud, and the theft of people's rights. . . . The rejection of the noble Egyptian people of the Camp David Agreement signed by Sadat with the Jews fifteen years ago and their boycott of all forms and kinds of efforts at normalization affirm that this struggle which the nation is embarked on with Zionism is a struggle for existence, for identity and for survival, a struggle prescribed to persist from generation to generation until God gives the victory to this nation, even after a hundred years.[59]

According to a recent article in *al-Mujtama,* essential for victory are those things that can return Arab countries to unity and, therefore, to strength. This means a return to the common elements that have always bound the community together: religion, language, civilization, and history. History demonstrates that small bands of people have always been able to unite themselves into political, economic, and military entities; so too can the Muslims, who in the past have joined together to defeat more powerful enemies, such as the Crusaders, the Mongols, the Tartars, and European colonialists, "the grandchildren of the Crusaders." The article goes on to affirm that "anything founded on falsehood is invalid; agreements based on deceit, fraud, theft and robbery and loss of rights cannot see the light of day. The imperative of victory is an imperative for the nation, even if it takes time."[60]

There seems to be a growing consensus even outside Islamist circles that real peace cannot be established until there is justice. For Arabs, that includes "the immediate implementation of international decisions which include total Israeli withdrawal from all occupied Arab territory in Palestine, in South Lebanon and the Syrian Golan and the assurance of the right of the Palestinian people to return to their land, to self determination and to establish an independent state on their land whose capital is Jerusalem, as well as the respect of the right of the Lebanese people to total control of their national land. The establishment of a just, comprehensive and stable peace in the area is a necessary condition to the realization of development and equality."[61] The perception is that, in the Oslo protocol, Arafat agreed to end the intifada, but did not insist on the end of Israeli occupation of Palestine.[62] This, then, is one of the major points of contention between Arafat and the Islamists, who insist that resistance to occupation is a god-given right. In fact, the Quran clearly justifies the taking of arms in jihad as a response to aggression, especially in the case where people are expelled from their homes because of their religious affiliation.

Islamists who initially took a wait-and-see attitude increasingly have come to recognize that the dangers and pitfalls they feared are materializing. As the months pass, they have become aware of Israeli reluctance to withdraw from the Occupied Territories. As one Islamist put it, they are attempting "to extract the last drop of dignity from the Palestinians." And the passage of time has "proven," to the satisfaction of those who from the start were convinced that it was a bad deal, that they were right to mistrust the "machinations of the Crusader-Zionist" coalition against Islam.

Islamists feel that the discourse on the peace process has moved to a new stage. No longer "a dialogue of the deaf" as it was termed for a while, in which neither side hears the other, it now seems to have taken the form of one party's insistence that the perceptions of reality and hopes of the other are not only insignificant but have no legitimacy and therefore must be eradicated as negative thinking. Islamists are concerned that anyone who raises an issue about the Accords is identified as "an enemy of peace" or "enemy of Israel." Increasingly, the Accords seem to conjure up images of decay, death, and destruction.[63] One woman likened the situation to a crumbled and moldy cake that has been covered with luscious icing. While members of the U.S. administration and the U.S. press focus on the icing, marveling at the mastery of crafting an attractive product, the Palestinians live in the rotten crumbled pieces, wondering what the peace has wrought. Another depicted it as a rusty hunk of a car that is sprayed with a beautiful coat of bright paint. While the observers admire the shining color, the rust continues to destroy the core. Still another talked about the beautifully decorated mummy whose core is not only dead but devoured by worms.

Given these perceptions, it is difficult to imagine that the Peace Accords, viewed as they are by Islamists and increasingly by others in the Arab world to be founded on unjust presuppositions and developed on the basis of unjust arrangements, can actually lead to peace. Only when the true interests of the Palestinian people are served—not merely those of Israel and the West—will there be enthusiastic support from the citizens of those countries who are the neighbors and economic partners of Israel/Palestine, as well as from the Palestinian people themselves.

Notes

1. Jim Lederman, *Battle Lines: The American Media and the Intifada* (Boulder: Westview Press, 1992).

2. Hamid Mawlana, George Gerbner, and Herbert I. Schiller, *Triumph of the Image: The Media's War in the Persian Gulf—A Global Perspective* (Boulder: Westview Press, 1992); Douglas Kellner, *The Persian Gulf TV War* (Boulder: Westview Press, 1992); Perry M. Smith, *How CNN Fought the War: A View from the Inside* (Secaucus, N.J.: Birch Lane Press, 1991).

3. Hamid al-Ghabid, executive secretary of the Organization of the Islamic Conference, in an interview with Muhammad al-Abbasi, "al-Khilafa al-Islamiyya Qamat bi-Himayat Masalih al-Muslimin," *al-Mujtama,* 24 January 1995, 23; cf. "Hasilat Ittifaq Washington Sifr Bad Am Min Tawqiih wa al-Tasarufat al-Israiliyya Lam Tataghayyar Bad al-Insihab," *al-Sharq al-Awsat,* 24 September 1994; Jawad al-Hamad, "Ma Alladhi Yadfauna ila Rafd al-Ittifaq al-Filastini al-Israili," *al-Hayat,* 25 October 1993.

4. In an interview, the Islamist Palestinian intellectual Munir Shafiq said, "The Accords that the regimes are signing with the Zionists realize peace for Israel and calamity for the Arabs." Ali Rashid, "al-Ittifaqat Allati Tuwaqqiuha al-Anzima ma al-Sihuniyya Tuhaqqiq al-Salam li-Israil wa al-Karitha li al-Arab," *al-Mujtama,* 14 February 1995, 36. Cf. Fahmi Huwaidi, "Imma al-Mustawtanat wa Imma al-Salam," *al-Majalla,* 3–9 April 1994, 38–39; "Rabin li-Arafat: Imma HAMAS Aw al-Salam," *al-Quds al-Arabi,* 15–16 October 1994; Abraham Tal, "La Majal li al-Tafawud wa al-Sulh ma al-Haraka al-Islamiyya Bal Yajib al-Tahaluf Maa al-Duwal al-Mujawira Li Iqtilaiha min al-Judhur," *al-Quds al-Arabi,* 19 October 1994; Ahmad Yusuf, "al-Islamiyyun wa Marhalat Ma Bad al-Ittifaq," *Filastin al-Muslima,* June 1994; "HAMAS li-Arafat: Alayka al-An an Takun Ma Shabika wa-

Illa," *al-Ufuq*, 11 May 1994; "Abbas Zaki, Istratijiyya Duwaliya li-Tatwi al-Filastiniyyin," *al-Aswaq*, 24 September 1994.

5. Edward Said, "The Morning After," *Inquiry* (Spring 1994): 20; cf. Uri Davis, "The Declaration of Principles Evokes a Palestinian Nightmare: Not Once Is the Word Sovereignty Mentioned," *Inquiry* (Spring 1994): 34.

6. Davis, 34.

7. "al-Bayan wa al-Tasrihat Lam Tatadaman Itirafan bi-Qarar 242 Aw al-Tanazul An Barnamaj al-Haraka wa-Thawabitiha al-Islamiya al-Asila," *al-Sabil* 1:27 (26 April–2 May 1994).

8. A commentary in *al-Mujtama* suggests similar concerns in relation to Jerusalem: "The problem of Jerusalem is no more an issue for the vanquished who lie prostrate before 'Israel' and its schemes. They have become servants of its designs and expansionist goals. . . . Jerusalem is not an issue except for the children of the stones who have raised high the head of the nation and humiliated the Jews. . . . They unequivocally believe that what is lost is a right behind which stands a fighter (*mujahid*), not a negotiator (*mufawid*)." "al-Quds Lam Taud Qadiyyatukum Ayyuha al-Munhazimun," *al-Mujtama*, 1 November 1994, 4.

9. Samir Ahmad al-Sharif, "al-Sharq al-Awsat al-Jadid," *al-Insan* 3:12 (October 1994): 7.

10. Recently, there has been a heightened apprehension of what is termed as the scheming of the Orthodox church against Islam, given the attempts of "Islamic" cleansing in Bosnia and Chechnya. Muhammad al-Abbasi, "al-Tahaluf al-Urthuduxi al-Alami al-Jadid," *al-Mujtama*, 14 February 1995, 20–23. Cf. "In recent days, the West has started to triumphantly declare that in today's world, Arabs do not matter. For them Muslims also do not matter and they would like to keep it that way. The media and Western political and propaganda machines are assiduously asserting that Islam is incompatible with civilization. Their main points are that Islam lacks democracy, is devoid of compassion and has no rights for women." Abdurrahman Abdullah, "The Final Battle for the Soul of Afghanistan," *Inquiry* 1:3 (June 1992): 19.

11. One author described the minarets of Yugoslavia in the following words: "They remain a living testimony to the glorious and often forgotten Islamic heritage, the last remnant of Europe's indigenous Muslim population, a people, a society, a civilization possibly on the verge of extinction. This is not a fate different from that experienced by the indigenous Muslims of Sicily, Italy, Spain, Portugal, Hungary, Malta, etc. many centuries earlier." Saffet Catovic, "Europe's Islamic Heritage in Jeopardy," *Inquiry* 1:6 (January 1993): 28. Cf. Ahmad Yahya al-Fai, "al-Umam al-Muttahida wa Dawruha al-Mashbuh," *al-Mujtama*, 24 December 1993, 64. Cf. Ahmad Mansur, "Sarajevo Hiya Akbar Mutaqal li al-Ibada fi al-Alam," *al-Mujtama*, 24 January 1995, 24–26.

12. "The demonstrators in Moscow are criminals and in Peking are freedom lovers; the Kurds in Iraq are victims, in Turkey, they are professional criminals. These are the contradictory depictions that have made the word 'extremist' predominantly a kind of political curse word rather than a name for anyone in particular." Abd al-Baqi Khalifa, "al-Tatarruf: Mafahimuh . . . Asbabuh . . . Nataijuh . . . Ilajuh," *al-Mujtama*, 23 November 1993.

13. Muhammad al-Rashid, "Salam ya Salam," *al-Mujtama*, 31 January 1995, 17.

14. Ibid.

15. "al-Quds Lam Taud Qadiyyatukum Ayyuha al-Munhazimun," *al-Mujtama*, 1 November 1994, 4.

16. Abd Allah al-Shaykh, "Sira al-Hadarat . . . wa Dawr al-Islam," *al-Mujtama*, 8 February 1994, 20–24.

17. *al-Mujtama*, December 1993. For an assessment of the role of Zionism in impeding the understanding of the Islamist program, see "al-Sahayina Yushawwihuna Surat al-Amal al-Islami wa-Mashariuna Tashhad ala Tabiat al-Amal al-Ighathi Alladhi Taqum bih," *al-Mujtama*, 27 December 1994, 44–45.

18. Shafiq, "al-Ittifaqat," 36–38.

19. "Naiban Kuwaitiyyan Yarfudan al-Tatbi Maa al-Yahud," *al-Mujtama*, 22 November 1994, 8.

20. "Hal Satuthmir Ziyarat Clinton bi-Tatbi al-Alaqat al-Khalijiyya al-Israiliyya," *al-Mujtama*, 15 November 1994, 18.

21. "Hadhf Faqarat An al-Sira al-Arabi- al-Israili min Kutub Madrasiyya Mutamada Lada Wakalat al-Ghawth," *al-Mujtama*, 15 November 1994, 22.

22. Idris al-Kettani, *Banu Israil fi Asr al-Inhitat al-Arabi* (Rabat: Maktabat Badr, 1992), 3.

23. For example, *al-Majalla*, the Saudi weekly published in London, initially wrote an editorial welcoming the economic ventures and called for the end of the Israeli boycott since it promises the economic development of the area.

24. Adil al-Zayid, "La wa Alf La," *al-Mujtama*, 14 December 1993, 14.

25. Atif al-Jawlani, "Izalat al-Muqataa al-Arabiyya al-Iqtisadiyya li-Israil Ala Ras al-Awlawiyyat al-Amrikiyya," *al-Majalla*, 8 February 1994, 36. For a slightly different interpretation, see Salim al-Huss, "al-Iqtisad al-Israili Huwa al-Aqwa wa Yusawi Adaf Majmu al-Iqtisad al-Lubnani wa al-Suri wa al-Urduni," *al-Majalla*, 26 June–2 July 1994, 46–47.

26. Athar al-Ittifaq, *al-Mujtama*, November 1993, 30.

27. "Matami Israil wa Iradat al-Shuub al-Muslima," *al-Mujtama*, 8 November 1994, 5; cf. "Makasib Israil fi Mutamar al-Dar al-Bayda," *al-Mujtama*, 8 November 1994, 24–25.

28. "Matami Israil," *al-Mujtama*, 5. Cf. "al-Mutamar al-Iqtisadi li al-Sharq al-Awsat al-Khutwa al-Raisiyya li-Iqamat Israil al-Kubra," *al-Mujtama*, 25 October 1994, 24–26; Badr Muhammad Badr, "Khubara al-Iqtisad al-Siyasi Yuhadhdhirun min Awaqib al-Mutamar al-Iqtisadi li al-Sharq al-Awsat," *al-Mujtama*, 25 October 1994, 27–28; Muhammad Dalbah, "Hal Tatahaqqaq Ahlam 'Israil' al-Iqtisadiyya Bad Mutamar al-Ahlam fi Dar al-Bayda?" *al-Mujtama*, November 1994, 34–37; "Takris li al-Haymana al-Sihyuniyya Ala Muqadarat al-Alam al-Arabi," *al-Mujtama*, 8 November 1994, 28.

29. "Matami Israil," 5.

30. Shimon Peres (with Arye Naor), *The New Middle East* (New York: Henry Holt, 1993).

31. Muhammad Jamil, "Israil Tasa li-Tahqiq Hilm Hertzl bi-Iqamat al-Suq al-Sharq Awsatiyya," *al-Mujtama*, 15 November 1994, 32; Ihsan Ali Abu Haliqa, "al-Suq al-Sharq-awsatiyya Arabiyya . . . la Mafarr," *al-Majalla*, 29 January–4 February 1995, 61.

32. Samir Ahmad al-Sharif, "al-Sharq al-Awsat al-Jadid," *al-Insan* 3:12 (October 1994): 6.

33. Ibid.

34. Ibid., 7.

35. Ibid., 8.

36. Ibid.

37. For a discussion of the issues and a refutation of these fatwas, see Asad Bayyud al-Tamimi, *Zawal Israil Hatmiyya Quraniyya* (Cairo: al-Mukhtar al-Islami, [n.d.]), 143–150.

38. "Mufti al-Mamlaka Yuharrim al-Sulh Ma al-Yahud," *al-Sabil* 1:43 (29 August 1995): 8.

39. *al-Muslimun* 10:516 (23 December 1994).

40. Yusuf al-Qaradawi, 20 September 1993.

41. *al-Mujtama,* 10 January 1995.

42. *al-Muslimun* 10:520 (20 January 1995).

43. In an interview, Zuhair al-Ubaidi of the Lebanese Islamic Front said that all Arabs regardless of their political allegiance reject this humiliating sulh that is being contracted between the Zionist enemy and governors of the Arabs. The people reject this sulh of defeat, a sulh of surrender because there is a historical, deep-rooted enmity with a state that has been aggressive. The peace to be sought will restore the land and the dignity to the Palestinian and Arab people, and at the forefront is the city of Jerusalem. "The Israeli lobby is pressuring America into pressuring us into signing. We should not surrender to the Israeli and American threat." Zuhair al-Ubaidi, "al-Ittifaq Maa al-Kiyan al-Sihyuni La Yulzimuna bi-Ay Hal min al-Ahwal" (filed by Muslih al-Habahiba), *al-Sabil* 1:43 (29 August 1994): 25.

44. *Fatwa Ulama al-Muslimin bi Tahrim al-Tanazul an Ay Juzin min Filastin* (Kuwait: Jamiyyat al-Islah, 1990), 16–17.

45. Ayatollah Khomeini, 16 September 1993.

46. Fahmi Huwaidi, "al-Usuliyyun Yuridun Hallan," *al-Majallah,* 11–17 December 1994, 42.

47. Ibrahim Gharaybeh, "Hawl al-Tajriba al-Siyasiyya li-al-Haraka al-Islamiyya fi al-Urdun," *al-Insan* 3:12 (October 1994):20.

48. Ibid.

49. "Nuarid al-Ittifaqiyya wala Nataqid Annana Sanastadim Maa al-Sultat al-Urduniyya," *al-Mujtama,* 1 November 1994, 36.

50. Fahmi Huwaidi, "al-Usuliyyun Yuridun Hallan," *al-Majalla,* 11–17 December 1994, 43.

51. Gharaybeh, "Hawl al-Tajriba," 21.

52. Ibid. In an interview, Abd Allah Ali al-Mutawi, president of the Islah Party of Kuwait, said, "The peace Treaty with Israel is a sad matter. . . . These treaties will not benefit anyone save Israel." He affirmed that "all of Palestine including Jerusalem is Islamic land. It is a trust for every Muslim." Yusuf Abd al-Rahman, "Alladhina Taawanu wa Alladhina Yanwun al-Taawun Maa al-Yahud Mukhtiun wa-Muhasabun Amam Allah," *al-Mujtama,* 20 December 1994, 16.

53. Gharaybeh, "Hawl al-Tajriba," 22.

54. "Hal Satuthmir Ziyarat Clinton bi-Tatbi al-Alaqat al-Khalijiyya al-Israiliyya?!" *al-Mujtama,* 15 November 1994, 18.

55. For a selection of papers presented to the Conference on Islamic Jurisprudence at the Islamic University of Imam Muhammad Ibn Saud in 1976, see *The Intellectual Invasion and Anti-Islamic Attitudes* (Riyad: Imam University Press, 1984); cf. Najib al-Aqiqi, *al-Mustashriqun* (Beirut: [n.p.], 1937); al-Jundi, *Afaq,* 20–22; al-Bahnasawi, *al-Ghazu,* 111–147; Anwar al-Jundi, *al-Alam al-Islami wa-al-Istimar al-Siyasi wa-al-Ijtimai wa-al-Thaqafi* (Cairo: Dar al-Kitab al-Misri, 1970); Abd al-Munim Nimr, *al-Islam wa-al-Gharb Wajhan li-Wajh* (Beirut: al Muassasah al-Jamiiyah lil-Dirasat wa-al-Nashr wa-al-Tawzi, 1982); cf. al-Tamimi, *Zawal Israil,* 7–28; Ali Abd al-Halim Mahmud, *al-Ghazu al-Fikri wa al-Tayyarat al-Muadiya li al-Islam* (Riyad: Imam Muhammad bin Saud University, 1984); Ziyad Muhammad Ali, *Ida al-Yahud li al-Haraka al-Islamiyya* (Amman: [n.p.], 1982), 21; Abd al-Halim Uways, *Al-Muslimun fi Marakat al-Baqa* (Cairo: Dar al-Itisam, 1979); Hassan Muhammad Hassan, *Wasail Muqawamat al-Ghazu al-Fikri li-al-Alam al-Islami* (Mecca: [n.p.], 1981); Abd al-Halim Mahmud, *al-Ghazu al-Fikri wa-Atharuhu fi al-Mujtama al-Islami al-Muasir* (Kuwait: Dar al-Buhuth al-Ilmiyah, 1979); Muhammad Muhammad Husayn, *Husununa Muhadada min Dakhiliha* (Beirut: [n.p.], [n.d.]); Ali Muhammad Jarisha and Muhammad Sharif al-Zaybaq,

Asalib al-Ghazu al-Fikri li-al-Alam al-Islami (Cairo: Dar al-Itisam, 1977); Mustafa al-Rafii, *al-Islam wa-Mushkilat al-Asr* (Beirut: [n.p.], 1972); Muhammad al-Ghazali, *Kifah Din* (Cairo: [n.p.], [n.d.]); Muhammad Faraj, *al-Islam fi Mutarak al-Sira al-Fikri al-Hadith* (Cairo: [n.p.], 1962); Muhammad Jalal Kishk, *al-Ghazu al-Fikri* (Cairo: [n.p.], 1975); al-Jundi, *Afaq,* especially 19–27; Anwar al-Jundi, *Al-Islam wa al-Istimar* (Cairo: [n.p.], 1948); Mustafa Khalidi wa Umar Farrukh, *al-Tabshir wa-al-Istimar fi al-Bilad al-Arabiyya: Arad li-Juhud al-Mubashshirin Allati Tarma Ila Ikhda al-Sharq lil-Istimar al-Gharbi* (Beirut: Al-Maktabah al-Asriyah, 1957); Ibrahim Khalil Ahmad, *Al-Istishraq wa-al-Tabshir wa-Silatuhuma bi-al-Imperialiyya al-Alamiyya* (Cairo: [n.p.], 1974); Abd al-Rahman Habnakat al-Midani, *Ajnihat al-Makr al-Thalatha wa-Khawafiha: al-Tabshir- al-Istishraq-al-Istimar* (Damascus: [n.p.], [1395AH]).

56. Tawfiq al-Wai, "al-Kifah al-Haram . . . wa al-Inhizam al-Mubah," *al-Mujtama,* 15 November 1994, 37.

57. See for example: "Dawa li al-Taawun," *al-Majalla,* 29 November 1994, 4; cf. "Masirat al-Istislam . . . wa Nuhud al-Umma min Kabwatiha," *al-Mujtama,* 1 November 1994, 5.

58. "Masirat al-Istislam," 5.

59. Ibid.

60. Ibid.

61. *Declaration of Peace for the Advancement of the Arab World,* Arab Regional Preparatory Meeting for the Fourth World Conference on Women, Beijing, 1995, 10.

62. Shafiq, "al-Ittifaqat," 38.

63. Muhammad al-Rashid, "Salam ya Salam," *al-Mujtama,* 31 January 1995, 17.

11

Relations Among
Islamist Groups

John Obert Voll

Major linkages exist among activist Muslims in the contemporary world. The movements and organizations of political Islam maintain a variety of connections that have an important impact on their development. The links that gain the most attention in the world news media are those that involve dramatic acts of destruction and conflict. However, these "terrorist networks" are not the most profoundly significant linkages in terms of the major political transformations that are taking place in Muslim communities around the globe. Great networks of intellectual and ideological exchange are transforming the very foundations of the worldviews of political Islam in its many different forms. It is important to cope with the dangers of the "terrorist" linkages, but it is even more important to understand the role of the more profound linkages in the contemporary dynamics of the world of Muslims.

These linkage networks take many different forms and are international in their scope. The networks are not limited to a single region, not even the Middle East, and are in many ways global in their nature and impact. An analysis examining linkages among activist Muslims of the 1990s that ignores New York City, Kuala Lumpur, London, and Nigeria simply is not talking about the actual world of political Islam.

In addition, a discussion of linkages among Islamically activist groups that treats those linkages and their appearance as a startling new phenomenon in the history of Islam is simplistic and current events–oriented to a degree that opens the way for significant misunderstanding of the dynamics of political Islam in the world today. Contemporary electronic communications have created an astoundingly integrated new world, and that new world does have an impact on linkages among Islamically activist groups. It is possible, for example, to issue the call globally for volunteers for jihad in Bosnia and Kashmir through E-mail. We are, in fact, living in a "new world order," however that phrase may be understood. But the phenomenon of linkage among actively committed Muslims who want to change their society did not begin with E-mail or with the utilization of cassettes by organizers of the Islamic revolution in Iran. Such linkages are almost as old as the history of Islam itself.

The Basic Historical Experience

It is nothing new in the history of the Islamic world for there to be important networks of inspiration and mutual support among activist movements of Islamic revival. Throughout most of Islamic history, groups and individuals have interacted and provided effective aid to each other. At the same time, there is also a long history of fear by governmental organizations that such networks exist and represent a threat to some established order or another.

Both of these dimensions need to be clearly discussed and viewed from a realistic rather than an alarmist apocalyptic perspective. Such networks do, in fact, exist and are effective in a number of ways. At the same time, under normal conditions, such networks do not represent "the end of civilization as we know it" or threats that are of the same magnitude as global nuclear destruction in the days of the Cold War.

It is worth noting some of the grand historic precedents for current concerns and current activities. In medieval times there was a relatively continuing concern about the possibility of Shii revolutionary movements that might be able to overthrow the established order of the Sunni caliphate. Given the chronic inability of such revolutionary movements to succeed in the early Islamic centuries, the impression is somewhat justified that Sunni establishments were paranoid about these movements. It is clear that whatever threat may have realistically existed, revolutionary Shiism never succeeded in overthrowing the dominant Sunni establishments in the majority of the Islamic world.

At the same time, it is also necessary to remember many clear examples that show the real existence of a dangerous and widespread revolutionary underground. In the tenth century, an interregional Ismaili Shii revolutionary movement succeeded in moving from bases in Yemen to taking control of large parts of North Africa and establishing the great Fatimid state centered in Cairo.[1] Later, a particular sect of Ismaili Shiis that became known as the "Assassins" were effective political killers. They succeeded, in the era of the Crusades, in murdering a number of major political leaders even though their particular movement never won control of any state.[2]

In the eighteenth century, there were some scholars who interacted through networks of scholarly communication.[3] These scholars did not have a single ideology or represent a specific detailed school of thought.[4]

However, it is clear that they did communicate with one another and represented an interesting pattern of interregional communication of individuals from Morocco and West Africa to China and Southeast Asia. A number of movements of activist reform were associated with individuals in this network and, in later years, there were people who viewed at least parts of the network as being a concrete threat to existing political systems. One might see the common usage of the label "Wahhabi" in the nineteenth (and even the twentieth) century as an example of such a movement—and the mistaken impressions about such a movement, since few Islamic activist movements in the eighteenth and nineteenth century were directly organized by or directly inspired by the Wahhabis of the Arabian Peninsula.[5] (Instead, the Wahhabis were simply a part of the broader interactions of many different individuals and groups.)

In the modern context, it is worth mentioning the perceptions of the nineteenth-century activities of the Sanusiyyah Tariqah and the spread of the Salafiyyah modernism of people like Muhammad Abduh. The Sanusiyyah was a widespread and expanding Islamic organization in Africa. Sanusis came into contact with French imperial expansion in a number of places, and some French imperial analysts began to feel that there was an enormous pan-Islamic, anti-French movement that was coordinated by some secret Sanusi intercontinental inner circle.[6] That the Sanusiyyah represented an important pattern of international linkages is undeniable. That they represented an international conspiracy capable of significantly weakening Western civilization was the product of Orientalist paranoid illusions. (This does not, of course, mean that specific Sanusi groups were not security threats to specific French interests in particular places.)

A more effective international network of linkages was the Salafiyyah movement, inspired by the Islamic modernist teachings of Muhammad Abduh.[7] In a variety of ways, through publications, itinerant scholars, and utilization of the full range of modern communications media available early in the twentieth century, this movement had a major impact throughout the Islamic world. It helped shape the emerging expressions of "public Islam" in Southeast Asia and provided the foundations for important developments in North Africa.[8] In terms of having an international influence and impact, both short-term and long-term, the Salafiyyah movement is of much greater significance than the pan-Islamic movements so feared by British and French intelligence agencies in the first three decades of the twentieth century.[9]

The much-feared pan-Islamic political movement failed quickly, if it ever really existed in the organizational forms described by imperial intelligence officers. However, while such reactionary movements blustered and fizzled, the Salafiyyah effectively changed the worldview of the intellectual and political elites in the modern Muslim world from southeast Asia to

northwest Africa. To see the truly important regional and international linkages of political Islam in the first quarter of the twentieth century, one
should not look at the feeble attempts to create them by the heirs of Jamal
al-Din al-Afghani and the Ottoman sultan Abd al-Hamid II, who are often
identified as the main figures of the pan-Islamic movements of the late
nineteenth and early twentieth centuries. Instead, one should look at movements like the Salafiyyah, which did not throw bombs and murder people
but, instead, changed the worldviews and ideologies of the majorities.

The historical heritage of the Islamic world emphasizes that Muslims
have interacted in many different ways. These linkages have often been a
significant dimension of the broader interactions within the Islamic world.
But frequently, the most important linkages have not been the spectacular
or dramatic ones representing the actions of a few extremists or reflecting
the particular perspectives of security-conscious observers. Instead, at
times, the really important linkages have been those that have gradually
transformed the basic foundations of discourse. In this sense, the real
Salafiyyahs have been more important than the imagined Sanusiyyahs. This
emphasizes the importance of recognizing the many different types of linkages in the contemporary Islamic world.

Institutions and Organizations of Linkage

Contemporary Muslims throughout the world participate in many different
types of international and regional linkage patterns. There is a very important aspect of these linkages that is well known and obvious but often
ignored in discussions of international linkages in the Islamic world. The
structures of Islamic faith are built on the assumption that there exists an
interregional and international community, or ummah. A Muslim cannot be
a Muslim in isolation. There is a communal dimension to the basic requirements of the faith just as there is an individual dimension. Muslims from all
parts of the world are *required by their faith* to get together and work
together through interregional linkages.

The longest-standing and most explicitly commanded linkage is the
requirement of pilgrimage (hajj) to Mecca for each believer, if it is at all
possible. From the earliest times of Islam to the present, there have been
"international" organizations and networks for the purpose of bringing people together on the hajj. Ultimately, it was not some secret revolutionary or
fundamentalist organization that brought Malcolm X to Mecca in the
1960s—it was the centuries-old pattern of Muslims going on pilgrimage.
By the time Malcolm X went on hajj, there already existed international
linkages that made it possible for American Muslims to go on pilgrimage.[10]
The pilgrimage experience may have revolutionary consequences in the life

of the pilgrims and their communities, but even this is a long-standing historical phenomenon.

There is also a long-standing phenomenon of international travel by Islamically committed scholars and preachers. The Prophet Muhammad is reported to have told Muslims to "seek knowledge, even as far as China," and Muslim scholars and preachers have been grand travelers over the centuries.[11] In this context, it is no more surprising to find Hasan al-Turabi of Sudan traveling to Afghanistan than it was to find the fourteenth-century teacher Ibn Battuta traveling to the Maldives. If one concentrates on the gunrunners, murderers, and military mercenaries, one may, like the French imperial intelligence officers, miss the really important linkages that are transforming the contemporary Islamic world.

The terrorist linkages do exist, and for specific tactical responses in particular situations, they cannot be ignored. However, it would be a mistake to identify these as being the most important linkages for the majority of Muslims in the major countries of the world. It would also be a mistake to develop policies based on the assumption that "fundamentalist" political Islam is basically identical with the structures of the terrorist linkages. Such an assumption is comforting to social scientists in both the West and the Muslim world who maintain the simple faith that all of the religious revivalism visible in the contemporary world is simply a blip in the long-term and ultimate triumph of Western-oriented secularism and who for more than a decade and a half have periodically announced the end of the religious resurgence only to be disappointed by new developments.[12]

The large-scale (and truly significant) regional and international linkages among Muslims in the contemporary world are not small networks of terrorist cells. Often they are not seen as being part of a narrowly defined, and therefore unrealistic, political Islam. However, they are in the forefront of the process of worldview transformation among Muslims in every part of the world and, at minimum, provide the foundation for the more overtly political movements.

What Are Some of the Linkages?

There are many different types of linkage networks. Probably the most important, in many ways, is the most informal. A global informal community of scholar-activists and intellectuals utilize modern transportation and communication media to move rapidly around the world. Like scholars in almost any other field, contemporary Islamist scholars attend conferences, give speeches, participate in discussions, write articles and books, and engage in many other activities. Through these interactions there is emerging a global Islamist perspective that is creating a common conceptual basis for the exchange of ideas. There is no single emerging "Islamic fundamentalist ideology," and even political allies like Rashid al-Ghannouchi of Tunisia and Hasan al-Turabi in Sudan do not present the same programs. It is important to emphasize that there is no ideologically monolithic, global Islamist movement. However, there is an emerging Islamic perspective that makes it possible to discuss politics—and economics and society—in a way that does not depend on the assumptions of Western secularist academic social science discourse. This is an important dimension of the emergence of political Islam in the last years of the twentieth century.

In the development of this political Islam, there have been some individuals of international significance. One good example is Khurshid Ahmad, the Pakistani economist.[13] He has a "home base" in the largest Islamist organization in South Asia, the Jamaat-i Islami, and is politically influential on the national political scene in Pakistan. However, for many years he has been on the international lecture circuit and has· helped raise the Islamic consciousness of young Muslims in Malaysia, South Africa, Great Britain, the United States, and many other places. His visits to Muslim groups in South Africa helped define the nature and goals of the emerging Muslim Youth Movement, and in Malaysia he was an important element in bringing together the leader of the activist Islamic student movement with leaders of the majority Malay political party. He was a major figure in the establishment of the Islamic Foundation in Great Britain, which has been in the forefront of publishing works that help define the role of Muslims as minorities and Islamist classics like Abu al-ala Mawdudi's commentary on the Quran. These activities help create a cosmopolitan global set of linkages that are crucial in defining the worldview foundations for political Islam in many different areas. Khurshid Ahmad is only one of a relatively large number of internationally and globally active Muslim intellectuals who are important links in the cosmopolitan networks of the contemporary Islamic world.

A second and more formal type of institution in this discourse-creating set of linkages is the "international Islamic university" and the Islamic "think tank." These institutions have become important contexts within which Muslim intellectuals from many different parts of the world interact and create a shared conceptual foundation for debates about political Islam. In the faculty of the International Islamic University in Malaysia are Muslim scholars from the United States, Sudan, Pakistan, and many other countries. In their classes and international conferences, they provide contexts within which cosmopolitan Islamist concepts can be further defined and developed.

One of the best examples of the Islamic think tank is the International Institute of Islamic Thought (IIIT) in Virginia. Here scholars from throughout the Islamic world have been working on a broadly conceived project called the "Islamization of Knowledge."[14] One of the important individuals in defining that project was Ismail al-Faruqi, a Palestinian Muslim who taught for many years at Temple University in Philadelphia. IIIT publishes a monograph series and *The American Journal of Islamic Social Sciences,* and, as one looks at the authors in these publications, it is clear that there are important international linkages among Muslim scholars and that these linkages play an important role in the definition of political Islam throughout the world.

Interregional Islamic Organizations

Interregional organizations of a more activist nature are also important parts of global linkages. One of the oldest such organizations is the Muslim Brotherhood, which was established in Egypt in the 1920s. The Brotherhood and the Jamaat-i Islami, which originated in South Asia under the leadership of Mawlana Mawdudi, are still highly visible organizations whose structures are those of more modern-style associations.

Interregional activist groups are not unique to the modern era, nor do they exist only in the structural format of a modern association. The older Sufi brotherhood or tariqa organization also provides an example of such structures. In the eighteenth century, the Naqshbandiyyah Brotherhood provided important links by which Ma Ming-hsin, a Chinese Muslim revivalist, could travel across central and south Asia, stay and study in Yemen, and then complete the pilgrimage and return to China, where he led a major Naqshbandiyyah Islamic revivalist effort.[15] In the twentieth century, groups like the Naqshbandiyyah provided important means of linkage in Muslim societies in the former Soviet Union and were a significant element in maintaining a sense of Islamic political identity in the face of communist suppression.[16]

The Muslim Brotherhood experiences remind us of a number of important analytical issues in understanding interregional linkages in political Islam. There are many different "national" organizations of the Muslim Brotherhood, some of which have existed for many decades. These national Brotherhoods have had associations and contacts with the original Brotherhood in Egypt,[17] and some were established as a result of the work of people who had studied and worked in Egypt with the Egyptian Brotherhood. However, these national Brotherhoods also represent distinctive, and organizationally independent, associations that operate within the broader worldview perspective represented by the Egyptian Brotherhood and that has been most visibly articulated by the Egyptians. However, the various Muslim Brotherhoods throughout the Arab world in particular did not and do not represent a single, clearly structured organization. Instead, they represent a general, shared perspective that includes a wide diversity of approaches and positions.

The cases of the Muslim Brotherhoods in Syria and Sudan are important examples of the nature of international linkages in the style of political Islam represented by the Muslim Brotherhood tradition. The organizer of the Muslim Brotherhood in Syria[18] was Mustafa al-Sibai, a scholar from a prominent Syrian family who studied in Egypt and worked closely with the Egyptian Brotherhood. He returned to Syria and maintained close ties with the leadership of the Egyptian Brotherhood. However, the Syrian Brotherhood as it developed in the 1940s and 1950s under his leadership was an independent coalition of Islamically oriented groups, some of whom had been in existence before the formal establishment of the Brotherhood. In this context, it would be incorrect to see the Syrian organization as simply a branch of the Egyptian Brotherhood and somehow basically an Egyptian import.[19] Even in the days of the Egyptian-Syrian union under Nasser in 1958–1961, when the two branches of the Brotherhood shared the experience of persecution by the emerging Arab socialist regime, there does not appear to have been significant cooperation or coordination of efforts between the two branches.

The experience of the Muslim Brotherhood in Sudan emphasizes even more the diversity of approaches represented by groups identified as the Muslim Brotherhood. Although Egyptians had some role in the 1940s in helping organize some small Islamically oriented groups among Sudanese students, the leading Islamic groups in Sudan were of local origin, and many of the prominent figures, even in the early days, had not studied in Egypt. Hasan al-Turabi, who was to become the most noted and visible of the Sudanese Brotherhood leaders, studied in Khartoum and then London and Paris. The various Islamic groups in Sudan in the early 1950s worked together to coordinate their activities and created a single organization, but the choice of "Muslim Brotherhood" as the name of the new organization was hotly debated at the organizational conference in 1954. The simple organizational forms that were formally adopted were those of the Egyptian Brotherhood, but in fact the actual operational structure was strongly influenced by the structures and experiences of the Sudanese Communist Party as well.[20] Over the years, the Sudanese Brotherhood has operated in a way that has been distinctly independent from Egyptian control or even influence. During the 1970s and 1980s, when the National Islamic Front (NIF) was emerging as a major political force under Turabi's leadership, there was little evidence of important organizational ties with the Egyptian Brotherhood. Even in the development of ideological positions, while Sudanese intellectuals were clearly aware of the writings of important Egyptians like Sayyid Qutb, the positions of Sudanese Brotherhood leaders like Hasan al-Turabi were significantly different from both mainstream and radical Egyptian Brotherhood positions.[21]

International Relations and Organizations

In the 1990s, there are other important forms of international linkages in political Islamic terms. As formally Islamic states have been created, particularly in Iran and Sudan, they have developed links that are similar to those developed by other states with shared interests and ideologies. As a result, since the establishment of the NIF-influenced (or NIF-controlled) government in Sudan in 1989, there have been a series of trade agreements, visits by delegations, exchanges of personnel and expertise, and other intensifications of relations between Sudan and Iran. As the United States began a major effort to isolate Sudan diplomatically and economically and continued its "containment policy" toward Iran, the importance of Sudanese ties with Iran increased and, unless there is a significant change in U.S. policy, the tendency to make the ties even closer will be strengthened.

Sudanese-Iranian relations illustrate a broader tendency of states that identify themselves in some way with the Islamic tradition to see that tradition as one basis for international cooperation. Thus, although the Economic Cooperation Organization (ECO)—founded by Turkey, Iran, and Pakistan and expanded in 1992 to include Muslim republics of the former Soviet Union—does not explicitly identify itself as an organization for Muslim cooperation, the Islamic dimension in the societal identities of all parties provides some basis for a sense of the utility of cooperation. This was clear in the speech by Iranian president Akbar Hashemi Rafsanjani opening the ECO summit in February 1992 and in comments by other leaders and the news coverage of the conference.[22] Clearly the ECO is not a "fundamentalist Islamic" organization, but it represents an important international political initiative and has the potential for being the largest Muslim regional organization in the world. In this sense, it is a very important part of the picture of regional and international linkages within the framework of political Islam.

The largest explicitly Islamic international organization is the Organization of the Islamic Conference (OIC). This is also not a "fundamentalist" Islamic organization but is clearly one of the significant institutions of global political Islam. It was established in 1969 by a group of Muslim states following an attack by an arsonist in Jerusalem on al-Aqsa mosque, which at that time had just recently come under Israeli control. The OIC is an interstate organization that holds regular summits and meetings of high-level officials.[23] It seeks to mobilize efforts of Muslims around the world and has dealt with many political issues. It provided collective official responses to many world crises and had some success, for example, in helping reduce the conflict between Philippine Muslims and their government.[24]

In many ways the OIC presents the official voice of the states in the

Muslim world. Membership and participation in the OIC is accepted as recognition of the Muslim nature of the state. As a result, there was controversy in Turkey regarding Turkish participation in the OIC because of the officially secular nature of the Turkish state. Similarly, Nigerian participation roused a storm of opposition from non-Muslim Nigerians.

The OIC is a global formal network of official linkages among states in which the majority of the population is Muslim. However, a large number of international associations and organizations represent important networks of activities by Muslims in many different fields of action. An important earlier pioneer in the field is the World Muslim League, founded in 1962 with Saudi support. The League brought together a number of existing transnational groups and was, during the 1960s, an important vehicle for opposing the emerging radical socialist ideologies of the Bath Party and Gamal Abd al-Nasser in Egypt. After the establishment of the OIC, the League concentrated its efforts on cultural affairs and support for Islamic missionary activities.

Some of the largest of the international and transnational Muslim associations are what might be called "sectarian" associations, like the large missionary organizations of the Ahmadiyyah, whose origins were in Pakistan but whose members now number many thousands in Africa, Europe, North America, the Middle East, and South Asia. Some of the international organizations represent important special groups. International associations of Muslim students and youth are perhaps the most important of these. The World Assembly of Muslim Youth (WAMY) was established in 1972, with Saudi support, to provide means for support for Muslim youth groups around the world. WAMY was, in some ways, an outgrowth of the worldwide federation of associations of Muslim students, the International Islamic Federation of Student Organizations (IIFSO), which had been established in a series of meetings in the late 1960s. The IIFSO was strongly influenced by the development of the Muslim Student Association of the United States and Canada and has been an important part of the developing global networks of interactions among Muslims.

All of these major international and transnational groupings reflect the dynamics of the "Islamic resurgence" of the late twentieth century, but none represents a militant or an explicitly Islamist orientation. Instead, they are a continuation of the traditions of intersocietal connections among Muslims within the Islamic world.

At the level of more explicitly Islamist international linkages, it is worthwhile to note the creation of the organization of the Popular Arab and Islamic Conference (PAIC) under the leadership of Hasan al-Turabi in Khartoum. The PAIC held its second international meeting in early December 1993, and delegates came from some sixty countries. Representatives of most major Islamically oriented organizations attended, including the current emir of the Jamaat-i Islami of Pakistan, Qazi Husain

Ahmad, and representatives of HAMAS, the Islamic Salvation Front of Algeria, the Muslim Brotherhood of Jordan, and Hizbollah of Lebanon. The congress provided the venue for major efforts to mediate between conflicting groups within the Islamic world and showed at least the potential for international Islamic diplomatic and negotiating coordination. PAIC committees and delegations worked to find a common ground between Yasir Arafat (and the Palestine Liberation Organization) and HAMAS over the issue of negotiations with Israel; to find a way to bring the fighting factions in Afghanistan together; and to initiate a dialogue between Iran and Iraq that could be based on Islamic grounds rather than opening the way for outside forces to increase existing Muslim divisions.

The concept of holding a grand pan-Islamic congress is not a new idea, and it is important to note that such grand congress schemes in the early twentieth century did not produce any significant, long-term results.[25] It remains to be seen whether the "congress format" is an effective mode of operation in the present context of heightened Islamic awareness and increased importance of Islamic perspectives in the global political arena. It is clear that the PAIC meeting in 1993 was larger and more important than any of the early pan-Islamic congresses.

Linkages and Terrorism

Some of the most important concerns in this subject of linkages relate to the relationships between international networks in the framework of political Islam and terrorism. Because of the nature of the subject, this dimension of linkages is the most difficult to analyze because of the secret and covert nature of the groups and activities involved. At the same time, it is a subject of major significance that, like other aspects of the subject of linkages, is complex and does not represent a homogeneous set of phenomena.

It is clear that a number of organizations in the Islamic world utilize methods of violence and military operations as a part of their programs to destroy or transform the status quo of their societies. For the most visible of these groups, whether they are identified as "terrorists" or "freedom fighters" or by some other label depends more on the perspectives of the observer than the characteristics of the particular group. During much of the 1980s, for example, for many Western observers, someone who placed a bomb in a market in Kabul was a legitimate "freedom fighter" or opponent of aggression, while someone who placed a bomb in a market in Algiers, Beirut, or Cairo was a "fanatic terrorist." For purposes of this discussion, one may simply speak of these as "militant" groups, recognizing that this is an arbitrary label for those nonstate groups that utilize violence or military operations in pursuit of their goals.

One type of linkage pattern involves large militant groups and governments. Some militant Islamist groups are relatively large and have a degree of international visibility and recognition. Among these, we would include the Hizbollah in Lebanon, HAMAS, the Iranian mujahidin, the mujahidin organization in Kashmir, and, until recently, the various Afghan mujahidin groups. For each of these organizations, there is an international network of supporters that may include states as well as individuals. The Islamic Republic of Iran, for example, has long been supportive of the Hizbollah in Lebanon, and the United States provided significant support for Afghan mujahidin and now provides at least some asylum for the Iranian mujahidin.

The list of states that provide support for such groups is relatively long and difficult to define. The list of states supporting terrorism compiled by the U.S. State Department shows some of the problems in this area of defining linkages. The State Department report "Patterns of Global Terrorism 1992," for example, stated that "in 1992 the Government of Sudan continued a disturbing pattern of relationships with international terrorist groups," but explicitly stated that there "is no evidence that the Government of Sudan conducted or sponsored a specific terrorist attack in the past year."[26] Yet, less than six months after the publication of that report, Sudan was added to the State Department list, with no new documentation given to tie the Sudanese government to any terrorist activity. The point here is not either to agree or to disagree with the U.S. policy, but rather to point out the difficulty of identifying specifically concrete international linkages in cases where such linkages are denied.

In these relationships, there are also the important "gray areas" in addition to the issues of direct support. In particular, a vexing issue is the degree to which allowing an organization to maintain offices and providing asylum represents support of the organizational activities. The U.S. State Department report identified the fact that elements of the Abu Nidal organization and HAMAS "continue to find refuge in Sudan" as evidence of Sudan's support for "radical Arab terrorist groups."[27] However, by this same criterion, the United States might be charged with supporting the militant antigovernment Iranian mujahidin organization.

A second type of linkage involves support for less visible, smaller, and more openly terrorist organizations, like the various jihad groups in Egypt. In this area, Sudan again provides an important case study. The Egyptian government charges Sudan with training and actively inciting antigovernment terrorist acts in Egypt. Recently, for example, Egyptian newspapers published reports that terrorist training camps in Sudan had been photographed by Egyptian security organizations. It was stated that these camps were run by military personnel from Iran and Afghanistan, but it was reported that the actual sites had not yet been identified.[28] As a result, the charges join a long list of reports of such activity that have never been publicly verified.

As one looks at the accounts of the development of the most important of these small militant groups in Egypt, it seems clear that they are authentically local in inspiration and early development. The important study by Gilles Kepel, for example, examines the process by which the major modes of Muslim extremism were firmly articulated and set before the Iranian revolution had taken place.[29] Shaikh Umar Abd al-Rahman neither needed nor received aid or inspiration from Iran or Sudan when he developed the ideological foundations for the militancy of the jihad and the Jamaat Islamiyyah in the early 1980s. He was already an established teacher who, early in his career, had criticized the socialism of Nasser and during the 1970s had begun to develop a reputation for strict Islamist positions.

In this context, the groups who attacked tourist buses and threatened all foreigners in Egypt and who are the source of the terrorist bombings do not require non-Egyptian sources of inspiration or support to be credible. They are part of a long-standing indigenous tradition. In the absence of concrete and explicit—and publicly documented—evidence that their activities result from Iranian or Sudanese agents, militant terrorism in Egypt remains best understood in its local context rather than in the context of some global conspiratorial organization. The same must be said for those convicted of the bombing of the Trade Center in New York City and of plotting to bomb many major facilities in New York. The importance of specific local conditions must never be forgotten as we try to understand the militant terrorists of the world.

What we can say for sure about the relationship between international linkages and the small-scale groups of militants relates to the broader context. There were murderous militant and Islamically oriented groups in the 1940s, 1950s, and 1960s. However, the global ideological climate at those times was very different from that of the 1990s. In the early post–World War II era, extremist critiques of the status quo were more likely to express their protest in Marxist or materialist than in religious terms. Even the non-terrorist revolutionary opposition followed this tendency. Thus, in Sudan, the largest and most effective antisystem political movement in the 1960s was the Sudanese Communist Party, not the Muslim Brotherhood.[30] In the arena of militant activism, when terrorism was utilized as a tactical option by Palestinians, it was done by the Marxist extremists like the Popular Front for the Liberation of Palestine and the Popular Democratic Front for the Liberation of Palestine. There was no major activist, Islamically oriented Palestinian group in the late 1960s.[31] The most effective revolutionary opposition was articulated in the language of Marxism and Western radicalism in the 1960s.

The situation has now been transformed. Materialist and secularist radicalism has been significantly weakened throughout the world. Secularism is now the basis for the language of most of the conservative political establishments, and the failure of radical socialist and Marxist regimes has created a real disenchantment with that style of revolutionary activism. In many different societies, the older religious traditions of discourse have been revitalized and now provide in new forms the basis for the articulation and organization of revolutionary opposition to existing establishments and conditions.

In the transformation of the nature of protest and revolutionary ideologies, the international linkages have been of crucial importance in the emergence of the new political Islam. Support for small militant groups by various governments and larger networks of military supply and support for more established groups certainly have an important role in developments in such specific locales as Lebanon, Kashmir, Iraq, as well as elsewhere. However, if one wants to look for the specific reasons for militant, activist terrorism in Egypt, one should not look for a secret terrorist training camp in Sudan but should examine the conditions in Egypt. It is not necessary to have a copy of some secret Iranian payroll to understand the difficulties of secular governments in Algeria and Tunisia. The National Islamic Front government in Sudan did not come to power as a result of some international conspiracy.

The most influential international linkages among Islamically committed activists are not the relatively small networks of support for "terrorist" groups. It is the nonviolent linkages of scholar-activists and the great networks of intellectual exchange that have the greatest significance in the 1990s for the nature, development, and power of political Islam.

A revitalization of Islamic discourse and a reassertion of Islamic identity are the major features of the emergence of political Islam as a major force in the contemporary world. This new discourse is the result of the really effective and revolutionary linkages among Muslims—intercontinental, international, and intersocietal. These are the important networks at the end of the twentieth century just as they were at the beginning of this century. It was Muhammad Abduh and the Salafiyyah who changed the worldview of public Islam and not the ineffective plots of the political descendants of Jamal al-Din al-Afghani or the activities of the Sanusis that were so much feared by the imperial intelligence services. The really effective Islamist linkages today are those that are changing the whole worldview of political Islam. It is important to recognize the distinctive challenges posed by these linkages rather than to concentrate so much on the specific actions of terrorists that the broader transformations taking place are not recognized.

Notes

1. A helpful introduction to the world of these interregional conspiratorial networks is the chapter "Ubaydallah al-Mahdi, Founder of the Fatimid Empire in

Africa," in *Makers of Arab History,* ed. Philip K. Hitti (New York: St. Martin's Press, 1968).

2. Two important studies of this movement are Bernard Lewis, *The Assassins* (London: Weidenfeld and Nicolson, 1967); and Enno Franzius, *History of the Order of Assassins* (New York: Funk and Wagnalls, 1969).

3. See, for example, the discussions in John O. Voll, "Muhammad Hayyat al-Sindi and Muhammad ibn Abd al-Wahhab: An Analysis of an Intellectual Group in Eighteenth Century Madina," *Bulletin of the School of Oriental and African Studies,* 38:1 (1975): 32–39; John O. Voll, "Hadith Scholars and Tariqahs: An Ulama Group in the 18th Century Haramayn and Their Impact in the Islamic World," *Journal of Asian and African Studies* 15:3–4 (July-October 1980): 264–273.

4. See, for example, the analysis in Ahmad Dallal, "The Origins and Objectives of Islamic Revivalist Thought, 1750–1850," *Journal of the American Oriental Society* 113:3 (July-September 1993): 341–359, which makes the important point that the major intellectual trends of the late eighteenth century did not represent one monolithic ideological position, which few contemporary scholars would argue, but rather identifies "four major intellectual trends of Islamic thought" of the era. However, he tends to ignore the point that the major figures in these important intellectual trends were part of a large historical network of people who had contacted and interacted with each other.

5. Wilfred Cantwell Smith, for example, noted this problem in his discussion of the so-called Wahhabis in South Asia. See Wilfred Cantwell Smith, *Modern Islam in India* (Lahore: Minerva Book Shop, 1943), 1, 188–190. There is a continuing tendency in the late twentieth century to call Islamic revivalists in Central Asia "Wahhabis" because they may have received some financial support from Saudi Arabia or simply because they advocate a more strict adherence to a literal interpretation of the Quran.

6. A good summary of the French imperial sources for the history of the Sanusi can be found in the important study by Knut S. Vikor, *Sufi and Scholar on the Desert Edge: Muhammad b. Ali al-Sanusi (1787–1859)* (Ph.D. diss., University of Bergen, Norway, 1991), 5–9.

7. For the basic ideas of this school of thought, see Albert Hourani, *Arabic Thought in the Liberal Age 1789–1939* (London: Oxford University Press, 1962).

8. See, for example, the discussions in John Obert Voll, *Islam: Continuity and Change in the Modern World,* 2d ed. (Syracuse: Syracuse University Press, 1994), in the Salafiyyah entry in the index of that book, discussing developments in North Africa, West Africa, and Southeast Asia.

9. A good example of the kind of speculation by imperial intelligence services about the widespread nature of the pan-Islamic threat can be seen in the report on pan-Islam by C. A. Willis that appeared in *Sudan Monthly Intelligence Report* 328 (November 1921). A complete set of these reports was available in the Sudan Collection of the University of Khartoum Library.

10. This organization and the procedures are well described in Malcolm X, *The Autobiography of Malcolm X* (New York: Ballantine Books, 1973).

11. An important collection of studies on this subject is Dale F. Eickelman and James Piscatori, eds., *Muslim Travellers: Pilgrimage, Migration, and the Religious Imagination* (Berkeley: University of California Press, 1990).

12. Examples of such announcements of the end of the Islamic resurgence can be found in John Yemma, "Militant Islam Facing Backlash in Middle East," *Christian Science Monitor,* 12 March 1981; Elie Kedourie, "Islamic Fundamentalism—an Idea Whose Time Has Gone," *Daily Telegraph,* 27 August 1985; Shireen T. Hunter, "Islamic Fundamentalism: Currently on the Wane,"

Christian Science Monitor, 2 December 1985; Fouad Ajami, "Bush's Middle East Memo," *U.S. News and World Report,* 26 December 1988–2 January 1989, 75. A presentation of this position in more general and theoretical terms can be found in Donald Eugene Smith, "The Limits of Religious Resurgence," in *Religious Resurgence and Politics in the Contemporary World,* ed. Emile Sahliyeh (Albany: State University of New York Press, 1990).

13. For a discussion of this figure, see John L. Esposito and John O. Voll, "Khurshid Ahmad: Muslim Activist-Economist," *Muslim World* 80:1 (January 1990): 24–36.

14. The basic agenda for this project was set forth in Ismail R. Faruqi, *Islamization of Knowledge: General Principles and Work Plan* (Herndon, Va.: International Institute of Islamic Thought, 1987).

15. A helpful introduction to this important but little-known figure is A. D. W. Forbes, "Ma Ming-hsin," vol. 5, *The Encyclopedia of Islam,* new ed. (Leiden: E. J. Brill, 1983), 850–852.

16. Alexandre Bennigsen and S. Enders Wimbush, *Mystics and Commissars: Sufism in the Soviet Union* (Berkeley: University of California Press, 1985), passim.

17. The best study of the establishment and early development of the ideology and organization of the Muslim Brotherhood in Egypt remains Richard P. Mitchell, *The Society of the Muslim Brothers* (New York: Oxford University Press, 1969).

18. A helpful Islamist account of the history of the Syrian Brotherhood is Umar F. Abd Allah, *The Islamic Struggle in Syria* (Berkeley: Mizan Press, 1983), especially chap. 3.

19. Ibid., 90–91.

20. This process is discussed in Turabi's account of the history of the Sudanese Brotherhood in Hasan Turabi, *Harakah al-Islamiyyah fi al-Sudan* (Cairo: al-Qari al-Arabi, 1991), 27–30.

21. See, for example, the important analysis of Turabi's positions in Abdelwahab Affendi, *Turabi's Revolution: Islam and Power in Sudan* (London: Grey Seal, 1991), especially 179–180 and the conclusion.

22. See, for example, the text of President Rafsanjani's speech and other materials in Foreign Broadcast Information Service, FBIS-NES-92-032 (18 February 1992) and FBIS-NES-92-033 (19 February 1992).

23. A helpful discussion of the organization in its Islamic context can be found in Abdullah al-Ahsan, *Ummah or Nation? Identity Crisis in Contemporary Muslim Society* (Leicester: Islamic Foundation, 1992).

24. Ibid., 113–122.

25. Two important studies of this experience are Martin Kramer, *Islam Assembled: The Advent of the Muslim Congresses* (New York: Columbia University Press, 1986), and Jacob M. Landau, *The Politics of Pan-Islam* (Oxford: Clarendon Press, 1990).

26. U.S. Department of State, *Patterns of Global Terrorism 1992,* Publication (DOS) No. 10054, April 1993, 3–4.

27. Ibid.

28. This report was distributed through an E-mail network reporting mid-February newspaper accounts in Egypt, especially *al-Ahrar.* A similar report in *al-Wafd* (Cairo) said that settlements in the Shandi area of northern Sudan, which the Sudanese government identified as agricultural projects, were terrorist training camps. See FBIS-NES-94-024 (4 February 1994).

29. Gilles Kepel, *Muslim Extremism in Egypt: The Prophet and Pharaoh,* trans. Jon Rothschild (Berkeley: University of California Press, 1985).

30. An important study of the Sudan Communist Party is Gabriel Warburg,

Islam, Nationalism, and Communism in a Traditional Society: The Case of Sudan (London: Frank Cass, 1978).

31. See, for example, the careful and comprehensive analysis of Palestinian organizations in the late 1960s written by William B. Quandt in Part 2 of William B. Quandt, Fuad Jabber, and Ann Mosely Lesch, *The Politics of Palestinian Nationalism* (Berkeley: University of California Press, 1973).

General Bibliography

"Abbas Zaki, Istratijiyya Duwaliya li-Tatwi al-Filastiniyyin." *al-Aswaq,* 24 September 1994.

Abbasi, Muhammad. "al-Tahaluf al-Urthuduxi al-Alami al-Jadid." *al-Mujtama,* 14 February 1995, 20–23.

Abd Allah, Umar F. *The Islamic Struggle in Syria.* Berkeley: Mizan Press, 1983.

Abd al-Rahman, Yusuf. "Alladhina Taawanu wa Alladhina Yanwun al-Taawun Ma al-Yahud Mukhtiun wa-Muhasabun Amam Allah." *al-Mujtama,* 20 December 1994, 16.

Abdullah, Abdurrahman. "The Final Battle for the Soul of Afghanistan." *Inquiry* 1:3 (June 1992): 19.

Abdullah, Ahmed. *Trilogies: The Second Gulf War: A Perspective from the Point of View of the Generation that Will Pay the Price!* Cairo: Dar al-Arabiyah lil-Tibaa wa-al-Nashr wa-al-Tawzi, 1991.

Abolfathi, Farid. "A Reassessment of the Afghan Conflict, 1978–1988." Prepared under contract for the U.S. Government. Fairfax, Va., March 1989.

Aboul Megd, Kamal. *A Contemporary Islamic Vision: Declaration of Principles.* Cairo: Dar al-Shuruq, 1991.

———. Interview in *October,* 8 July 1990.

Abu Amr, Ziad. *Islamic Fundamentalism in the West Bank and Gaza: Muslim Brotherhood and Islamic Jihad.* Bloomington: Indiana University Press, 1994.

Abu Haliqa, Ihsan Ali. "al-Suq al-Sharq-awsatiyya Arabiyya . . . La Mafarr." *al-Majalla,* 29 January–4 February 1995, 61.

Abu Tariq, ed. *Mawlana Mawdudi Ki Taqarir* [Mawlana Mawdudi's Speeches]. Vol. 6. Lahore: Islamic Publications, 1976.

"Actions of the Pakistan Military with Respect to Afghanistan: Human Rights Concerns." *News from Asia Watch,* 27 February 1989.

Affendi, Abdelwahab. *Turabi's Revolution: Islam and Power in Sudan.* London: Grey Seal, 1991.

Ahmad, Ibrahim Khalil. *al-Istishraq wa-al-Tabshir wa-Silatuhuma bi-al-Imperialiyya al-Alamiyya.* Cairo: [n.p.], 1974.

Ahmad, Mumtaz. "Islam and the State: The Case of Pakistan." In *The Religious Challenge to the State,* ed. Matthew Moen and Lowell Gustafson. Philadelphia: Temple University Press, 1992.

———. "Islamic Fundamentalism in South Asia: The Jamaat-i Islami and the Tablighi Jamaat." In *Fundamentalisms Observed,* ed. Martin E. Marty and R. Scott Appleby. Chicago: University of Chicago Press, 1991.

———. "The Politics of War: Islamic Fundamentalisms in Pakistan." In *Islamic Fundamentalisms and the Gulf Crisis,* ed. James Piscatori. Chicago: American Academy of Arts and Sciences, 1991.

Ahmed, Abdelkader Sid. "La Crise de l'Etat Redistributeur au Maghreb." Paper presented at the conference "Le Maghreb Après la Crise du Golfe: Transformations Politiques et Ordre International," Granada, November 1991.

Ahmed, Rafiuddin. "Redefining Muslim Identity in South Asia: The Transformation of the Jamaat-i Islami." In *Accounting for Fundamentalisms: The Dynamic*

Character of Movements, ed. Martin E. Marty and R. Scott Appleby. Chicago: University of Chicago Press, 1994.

Ahsan, Abdullah. *Ummah or Nation? Identity Crisis in Contemporary Muslim Society.* Leicester: Islamic Foundation, 1992.

Ajami, Fouad. "Bush's Middle East Memo." *U.S. News and World Report,* 26 December 1988–2 January 1989, 75–78.

Akhavi, S. "Elite Factionalism in the Islamic Republic of Iran." *Middle East Journal* 41:2 (Spring 1987): 181–202.

Alamoudi, Abdurrahman. In the *Washington Report on Middle East Affairs* (October 1990): 69.

Albrow, Martin, and Elizabeth King, eds. *Globalization, Knowledge and Society.* London: Sage Publications, 1990.

Ali, Ziyad Muhammad. *Ida al-Yahud Li al-Haraka al-Islamiyya.* Amman: [n.p.], 1982.

Amin, Tahir. "Pakistan in 1993." *Asian Survey* 34:2 (February 1994): 195.

Amirahmadi, H. *Revolution and Economic Transition: The Iranian Experience.* New York: SUNY Press, 1990.

Amnesty International Report. As quoted in *Voice of Bahrain* 46 (October 1994).

Anderson, Lisa. "Democracy Frustrated: The Mzali Years in Tunisia." In *Middle East and North Africa: Essays in Honor of J. C. Hurewitz,* ed. Reeva Simon. New York: Middle East Institute, Columbia University, 1989.

———. "Lawless Government and Illegal Opposition: Reflections on the Middle East." *Journal of International Affairs* 40:1 (Winter/Spring 1987): 219–232.

Ansari, Hamied N. "The Islamic Militants in Egyptian Politics." *International Journal of Middle East Studies* 16 (1984): 123–144.

Anthony, Ian, Agnes Courades Allebeck, Gerd Hagmeyer-Gaverns, Paolo Miggiano, and Herbert Wulf. "The Trade in Major Conventional Weapons." In *SIPRI Yearbook 1991: World Armaments and Disarmament.* Oxford: Oxford University Press, 1991, 197–279.

Aqiqi, Najib. *al-Mustashriqun.* Beirut: [n.p.], 1937.

"Arab Veterans of Afghanistan Lead New Islamic Holy War." *Federal News Service,* 28 October 1994.

"Arabia's Slow Pressure Cooker." *The Economist* (1992).

Aradi, Markaz Abhath. *al-Nashatat al-Islamiyya wa-Musadarat al-Aradi fi-al-Diffa al-Gharbiyya* [The Settlement and Land Seizure Activities in the West Bank]. Jerusalem: Jamiyyat al-Dirasat al-Arabiya, 24 January 1994.

Arjomand, Said. *The Turban for the Crown: The Islamic Revolution in Iran.* New York: Oxford University Press, 1988.

Aruri, Naseer. "From Oslo to Cairo: Repacking the Occupation." *Middle East International* (13 May 1994): 16–17.

"Athar al-Ittifaq." *al-Mujtama,* November 1993.

Auda, Gehad. "Egypt's Uneasy Party Politics." *Journal of Democracy* 2:2 (Spring 1991): 70–78.

Ayubi, Nazih N. *Political Islam: Religion and Politics in the Arab World.* London: Routledge, 1991.

Badr, Muhammad Badr. "Khubara al-Iqtisad al-Siyasi Yuhadhdhirun Min Awqab al-Mutamar al-Iqtisadi lil-Sharq al-Awsat." *al-Mujtama,* 25 October 1994, 27–28.

Bahadur, Kalim. *The Jamaat-i Islami of Pakistan.* New Delhi: Chetana Publications, 1977.

Bahrain. Issued by the Bahrain Freedom Movement for Advancing Democracy and Human Rights in Bahrain, no. 45 (September 1995): 1.

Bahrain: A Human Rights Crisis. New York: Amnesty International, September 1995.

Baker, Raymond William. "Imagining Egypt in the New Age: Civil Society and the Leftist Critique," and "Islam, Democracy, and the Arab Future: Contested Islam in the Gulf Crisis," in *The Gulf War and the New World Order,* ed. Tareq Y. Ismael and Jacqueline S. Ismael. Gainesville: University of Florida Press, 1994.

———. *Sadat and After: The Struggle for Egypt's Political Soul.* Cambridge: Harvard University Press, 1990.

Baker, Raymond, and Karen Aboul Kheir. *Islam Without Fear.* Cambridge: Harvard University Press, forthcoming.

Bakhash, Saul. "Islam and Social Justice in Iran." In *Shiism, Resistance and Revolution,* ed. Martin Kramer. Boulder: Westview Press, 1987.

———. *The Reign of the Ayatollahs: Iran and the Islamic Revolution.* New York: Basic Books, 1984.

Baktiari, Bahman. *Parliamentary Politics in Revolutionary Iran.* Gainesville: University Press of Florida, 1996.

Banuazizi, Ali. "Faltering Legitimacy: The Ruling Clerics and Civil Society in Contemporary Iran." *International Journal of Politics, Culture, and Society* 4 (1995): 563–577.

Banuazizi, Ali, and Myron Weiner, eds. *The State, Religion, and Ethnic Politics: Afghanistan, Iran, and Pakistan.* Syracuse: Syracuse University Press, 1986.

Barkey, Henri, ed. *The Politics of Economic Reform in the Middle East.* New York: St. Martin's Press, 1992.

Barnet, Richard J., and John Cavanagh. *Global Dreams.* New York: Simon and Schuster, 1994.

Barnett, T., and A. Abdelkarim, eds. *Sudan: State, Capital and Transformation.* London: Croom Helm, 1988.

"al-Bayan wa-al-Tasrihat Lam Tatadaman Itirafan bi-Qarar 242 aw al-Tanazul An Barnamij al-Haraka wa-Thawabitiha al-Islamiya al-Asila." *al-Sabil* 1:27 (26 April–2 May 1994).

Beblawi, Hazem, and Giacomo Luciani, eds. *The Rentier State.* New York: Croom Helm, 1987.

Becker, David. "Bonanza Development and the New Bourgeoisie: Peru Under Military Rule." In *Postimperialism: International Capitalism and Development,* ed. David Becker, Jeff Frieden, Sayre Schatz, and Richard Sklar. Boulder: Lynne Rienner, 1987.

Becker, David, Jeff Frieden, Sayre Schatz, and Richard Sklar, eds. *Postimperialism: International Capitalism and Development.* Boulder: Lynne Rienner, 1987.

Bennigsen, Alexandre, and S. Enders Wimbush. *Mystics and Commisars: Sufism in the Soviet Union.* Berkeley: University of California Press, 1985.

Bennoune, Mahfoud, and Ali el-Kenz. *Le Hasard et l'Histoire: Entretiens avec Belaid Abdesselem.* Vols. 1 and 2. Algiers: ENAG Editions, 1990.

Bill, James A. "Resurgent Islam in the Persian Gulf." *Foreign Affairs* 63 (Fall 1984): 108–127.

Binder, Leonard. *Religion and Politics in Pakistan.* Berkeley: University of California Press, 1961.

Bleuchot, Hervé. *Les Cultures Contre L'Homme: Essaie d'Anthropologie Historique du Droit Pénal Soudanais.* Aix-en-Provence: Presses Universitaires d'Aix Marseilles, 1994.

Bleuchot, Hervé, Christian Delmet, and Derek Hopwood, eds. *Sudan: History, Identity, Ideology.* Reading, England: Ithaca Press, 1991.

Brahimi, Abdelhamid. *L'Economie Algérienne: Défis et Enjeux.* Algiers: Dahlab, 1992.

———. *Justice Sociale et Développement en Economie Islamique.* Paris: La Pensée Universelle, 1993.

Brown, Wendy. "Feminist Hesitations, Postmodern Exposures." *Differences: A Journal of Feminist Cultural Studies* 3:1 (1991): 67–69.

Buchanan, James M. "Rent Seeking and Profit Seeking." In *Toward a Theory of a Rent-Seeking Society,* ed. James M. Buchanan, Robert D. Tollison, and Gordon Tullock. College Station: Texas A&M University Press, 1980.

Buchanan, James M., Robert D. Tollison, and Gordon Tullock, eds. *Toward a Theory of a Rent-Seeking Society.* College Station: Texas A&M University, 1980.

Burgat, François. *The Islamic Movement in North Africa.* Austin: Center for Middle East Studies, University of Texas, 1993.

Caesar, Judith. "Rumblings Under the Throne: Saudi Arabian Politics." *The Nation* 251:21, 762.

Cantori, Louis, ed. "Overview: Democratization in the Middle East." *American-Arab Affairs* 36 (Spring 1991): 1–2.

Catovec, Saffet. "Europe's Islamic Heritage in Jeopardy." *Inquiry* 1:6 (January 1993): 28.

Cesari, Jocelyne. "L'Etat Algérien Protagoniste de la Crise." *Peuples Méditerranéans* 70–71 (1995).

Chase-Dunn, Christopher K. *Global Formation: Structures of the World Economy.* Cambridge, MA: B. Blackwell, 1989.

Chaudry, Kiren Aziz. "The Price of Wealth: Business and State in Labor Remittance and Oil Economies." *International Organization* 43:1 (Winter 1989):101–145.

Chehabi, H. E. "The Impossible Republic: Contradictions of Iran's Islamic State." *Contention* 3 (Spring 1996): 135–154.

"The Chief Prosecutor Decides to Jail Hussain for 15 Days." *al-Akhbar,* 28 January 1991.

Cody, Edward. "Saudi Islamic Radicals Target U.S., Royal Family." *Washington Post,* 16 August 1996.

Cohen, Stephen P. *The Pakistan Army.* Berkeley: University of California Press, 1984.

Cole, Juan I. R., and Nikki Keddie, eds. *Shiism and Social Protest.* New Haven: Yale University Press, 1986.

Commission on Global Governance. *Our Global Neighborhood: The Report of the Commission on Global Governance.* Oxford: Oxford University Press, 1995.

"Constitution of the Islamic Republic of Iran." *Middle East Journal* 34 (1980): 185.

Cook, Miriam A., ed. *Studies in the Economic History of the Middle East from the Rise of Islam to the Present Day.* Oxford: Oxford University Press, 1970.

Cottam, Richard. *Iran and the United States.* Pittsburgh: University of Pittsburgh Press, 1990.

Cronin, Richard. *Afghanistan After the Soviet Withdrawal: Contenders for Power.* Washington, D.C.: Congressional Research Service, May 1989.

Cudsi, Alexander S., and Ali Hillal Dessouki, eds. *Islam and Power.* London: Croom Helm, 1981.

Dahl, Robert. *Polyarchy: Participation and Opposition.* New Haven: Yale University Press, 1971.

———. *Regimes and Oppositions.* New Haven: Yale University Press, 1973.

Dalbah, Muhammad. "Hal Tatahaqqaq Ahlam Israil al-Iqtisadiyya Bad Mutamar al-Ahlam fi Dar al-Bayda?" *al-Mujtama,* November 1994, 34–37.

Dallal, Ahmad. "The Origins and Objectives of Islamic Revivalist Thought, 1750–1850." *Journal of the American Oriental Society* 113:3 (July-September 1993): 341–359.

Daly, M. W., ed. *Two Sufi Tariqas in the Sudan.* Khartoum: University of Khartoum, 1985.

Davis, Uri. "The Declaration of Principles Evokes a Palestinian Nightmare: Not Once Is the Word Sovereignty Mentioned." *Inquiry* (Spring 1994): 34.

"Dawa Lil-Taawun." *al-Majalla,* 29 November 1994, 4.

Dazi, Mehdi. "Informal Economies in Algeria: Path and Pattern." In *Informal Economies in the Middle East and North Africa,* ed. Dirk Vandewalle. Forthcoming.

Declaration of Peace for the Advancement of the Arab World. Arab Regional Preparatory Meeting for the Fourth World Conference on Women. Beijing: 1995.

Dessouki, Ali E. Hillal, ed. *Islamic Resurgence in the Arab World.* New York: Praeger, 1982.

Difraoui, Abdelasiem. "La Critique du Système Démocratique par le Front Islamique du Salut." In *Exils et Royaumes: Les Appartenances au Monde Arabo-Musulman Aujourd'hui,* ed. Gilles Kepel and Rémy Leveau. Paris: Presses de la Fondation Nationale des Sciences Politiques, 1994.

Dupree, Louis. *Afghanistan.* 2d ed. Princeton: Princeton University Press, 1980.

Eagleton, Terry. *Ideology: An Introduction.* London: Verso, 1991.

Eddedin, Ahmed. "What the Islamic Trend Provides in the Syndicates." *al-Shaab,* 14 April 1992.

Eickelman, Dale F., and James Piscatori, eds. *Muslim Travellers: Pilgrimage, Migration, and the Religious Imagination.* Berkeley: University of California Press, 1990.

EIU Country Report, 2d Quarter 1995. London: The Economist Intelligence Unit, 1995.

Elsenhans, Hartmut. "Algeria: The Contradiction of Rent-Financed Development." *Maghreb Review* 14:3–4 (1989): 226–248.

Entelis, John. *Algeria: The Revolution Institutionalized.* Boulder: Westview Press, 1986.

Eryan, Essam. Account in *Rose al-Yusuf,* 28 September 1992.

Es'haq, Mohammad. "Evolution of the Islamic Movement in Afghanistan, Part 1: Islamists Felt Need for a Party to Defend Islam." *AFGHANews* 5 (1 January 1989): 5, 8.

———. "Evolution of the Islamic Movement in Afghanistan, Part 4: Life in Exile from 1975 to 1978." *AFGHANews* 5 (15 February 1989): 6.

Esposito, John L. *The Iranian Revolution: Its Global Impact.* Gainesville: University of Florida Press, 1990.

———. *Islam and Politics.* 3d ed. Syracuse: Syracuse University Press, 1991.

———. "Islam: Ideology and Politics in Pakistan." In *The State, Religion, and Ethnic Politics: Afghanistan, Iran, and Pakistan,* ed. Ali Banuazizi and Myron Weiner. Syracuse: Syracuse University Press, 1986.

———. "Islam in a World of Shattered Dreams: Islam, Arab Politics and the Gulf Crisis." *The World and I* (February 1991).

———. *The Islamic Threat: Myth or Reality?* Rev. ed. New York: Oxford University Press, 1995.

———. "Pakistan: The Quest for Islamic Identity." In *Islam and Development: Religion and Sociopolitical Change,* ed. John L. Esposito. Syracuse: Syracuse University Press, 1980.

————, ed. *Islam and Development: Religion and Sociopolitical Change*. Syracuse: Syracuse University Press, 1980.

Esposito, John L., and James P. Piscatori. "Democratization and Islam." *Middle East Journal* 45:3 (Summer 1991): 427–440.

Esposito, John L., and John O. Voll. *Islam and Democracy*. New York: Oxford University Press, 1996.

————. "Khurshid Ahmad: Muslim Activist-Economist." *Muslim World* 80:1 (January 1990): 24–36.

Etudes Politiques du Monde Arabe. Cairo: CEDEJ, 1991.

Ewing, Katherine. "The Politics of Sufism: Redefining the Saints of Pakistan." *Journal of Asian Studies* 42:2 (February 1983): 251–268.

Fai, Ahmad Yahya. "al-Umam al-Muttahida wa Dawruha al-Mashbuh." *al-Mujtama*, 24 December 1994, 64.

Fakhro, Munira A. "The Uprising in Bahrain." Future Prospects for the Gulf. Bellagio, Italy: 25–27 July 1995.

Falk, Richard. *Explorations at the Edge of Time: The Prospects for World Order*. Philadelphia: Temple University Press, 1992.

Fanon, Franz. *The Wretched of the Earth*. Harmondsworth, England: Penguin Books, 1967.

Faraj, Muhammad. *al-Islam Fi Mutarak al-Sira al-Fikri al-Hadith*. Cairo: [n.p.], 1962.

Faris, Izz al-Din, and Ahmad Sadiq. "al-Qadiyya al-Filastiniyya Hiyya al-Qadiyya al-Markaziya lil-Haraka al-Islamiyya" [The Palestinian Cause Is Central to the Islamic Movement]. *al-Mukhtar al-Islami* 13 (June 1980): 28–41.

Faruqi, Ismail. *Islamization of Knowledge: General Principles and Work Plan*. Herndon, Va.: International Institute of Islamic Thought, 1987.

Fatwa Ulama al-Muslimin Bi Tahrim al-Tanazul An Ay Juzin Min Filastin. Kuwait: Jamiyyat al-Islah, 1990.

Fehrer, Ferenc, and Agnes Heller. *The Postmodern Political Condition*. Oxford: Polity, 1988.

Fishurdah-yi Hadaf va Maram-i Jamiyyat-i Islami-yi Afghanistan [A Summary of the Aims and Program of the Islamic Society of Afghanistan]. [Peshawar?]: [1978 or 1979?].

Fluehr-Lobban, Carolyn. *Islamic Law and Society in Sudan*. London: Frank Cass, 1987.

Forbes, A. D. W. "Ma Ming-hsin." *The Encyclopedia of Islam*. Vol. 5: 850–852. Leiden: E. J. Brill, 1983.

Forecasts 1:0 (June 1995): 1.

Fouad, Marwan. "Time to Get Their House in Order." *Middle East* 201 (July 1991): 19–20.

Franzius, Enno. *History of the Order of Assassins*. New York: Funk and Wagnalls, 1969.

Fukuyama, Francis. "The End of History?" *National Interest* 16 (Summer 1989): 3–18.

Ghabid, Hamid. "Hasilat Ittifaq Washington Sifr Bad Am min Tawqiih wa al-Tasarufat al-Israiliyya Lam Tataghayyar Bad al-Insihab." *al-Sharq al-Awsat*, 24 September 1994.

————. Interview with Muhammad al-Abbasi in "al-Khilafa al-Islamiyya Qamat bi-Himayat Masalih al-Muslimun." *al-Mujtama* 25:1135 (24 January 1995): 23.

Gharaybeh, Ibrahim. "Hawl al-Tajriba al-Siyasiyya lil-Haraka al-Islamiyya fi al-Urdun." *al-Insan* 3:12 (October 1994), 20.

Ghazzali, Muhammad. *Kifah Din*. Cairo: [n.p., n.d.].

————. *Our Beginning in Wisdom.* Trans. Ismail R. al-Faruqi. Washington, D.C.: American Council of Learned Societies, 1953.

Goldberg, Jacob. "The Shii Minority in Saudi Arabia." In *Shiism and Social Protest,* ed. Juan R. I. Cole and Nikki R. Keddie. New Haven: Yale University Press, 1986.

"The Gulf Crisis." *Aliran* 10:8 (1990): 32.

Gurdon, Charles. "Sudan's Foreign Policy." *Sudan Studies* 12 (July 1992): 10–25.

Gurtov, Mel. *Global Politics in the Human Interest.* Boulder and London: Lynne Rienner, 1988.

Haddad, Yvonne Y., and John L. Esposito, eds. *Islam, Gender, and Social Change.* New York: Oxford University Press, 1997.

"Hadhf Faqarat An al-Sira al-Arabi- al-Israili Min Kutub Madrasiyya Mutamada Lada Wakalat al-Ghawth." *al-Mujtama,* 15 November 1994, 22.

"Hal Satuthmir Ziyarat Clinton bi-Tatbi Ma al-Yahud." *al-Mujtama,* 15 November 1994, 18.

Hamad, Jawad. "Ma Alladhi Yadfauna Ila Rafd al-Ittifaq al-Filastini al-Israili." *al-Hayat,* 25 October 1993.

"Hamas li-Arafat: Alayka al-An An Takun Ma Shabika wa-Illa." *al-Ufuq,* 11 May 1994.

Hamrouche, Mouloud, as quoted in *Le Monde,* 7 June 1991, 4.

Harakat al-Muqawama al-Islamiyya. Communiqué No. 4, 11 February 1988.

Harik, Ilya, and Denis Sullivan, eds. *Privatization and Liberalization in the Middle East.* Bloomington: Indiana University Press, 1992.

Harrold, Deborah. "Economic Discourse in Algeria: Economists Circle the State." In *North Africa: The Political Economy of Development and Reform in a Changing Global Economy,* ed. Dirk Vandewalle. New York: St. Martin's Press, 1996.

Hasan, Masudul. *Sayyid Abul Aala Maududi and His Thought.* Vol. 1. Lahore: Islamic Publications, 1984.

Hassan, Hassan Muhammad. *Wasail Muqawamat al-Ghazu al-Fikri Lil-Alam al-Islami.* Mecca: [n.p.], 1981.

Herald (September 1990): 3.

Herald (April 1995): 52–53.

Hermassi, Elbaki, and Dirk Vandewalle. "The Second Stage of State-Building in North Africa." In *State and Society in North Africa,* ed. I. William Zartman. Boulder: Westview Press, 1992.

Hiro, Dilip. *Iran Under the Ayatollahs.* London: Routledge and Kegan Paul, 1985.

Hirschman, Albert O. *The Passions and the Interests: Political Arguments for Capitalism Before Its Triumph.* Princeton: Princeton University Press, 1977.

Hitti, Philip K. *Makers of Arab History.* New York: St. Martin's Press, 1968.

Hourani, Albert. *Arabic Thought in the Liberal Age 1789–1939.* London: Oxford University Press, 1962.

Hudson, Michael C. "The Islamic Factor in Syrian and Iraqi Politics." In *Islam in the Political Process,* ed. James P. Piscatori. Cambridge: Cambridge University Press, 1983.

Human Rights Watch/Middle East. *Human Rights Abuses in Algeria: No-One Is Spared.* New York: Human Rights Watch, 1994.

Hunter, Jane. "World Trade Center: 240 Years." *Middle East International,* 10 June 1994, 13–15.

Hunter, Shireen T. "Islamic Fundamentalism: Currently on the Wane." *Christian Science Monitor,* 2 December 1985.

Huntington, Samuel P. "The Clash of Civilizations?" *Foreign Affairs* 72 (Summer 1993): 22–49.

———. *Political Order in Changing Societies.* New Haven: Yale University Press, 1968.

———. *The Third Wave: Democratization in the Late Twentieth Century.* Norman: University of Oklahoma Press, 1991.

Huntington, Samuel, and Joan Nelson. *No Easy Choice: Political Participation in the Developing World.* Cambridge: Harvard University Press, 1976.

Husayn, Muhammad Muhammad. *Husununa Muhadada Min Dakhiliha.* Beirut: [n.p., n.d.].

Huss, Salim, "al-Iqtisad al-Israili Huwa al-Aqwa wa-Yusawi Adaf Majmu al-Iqtisad al-Lubnani wa-al-Suri wa-al-Urduni." *al-Majalla,* 26 June–2 July 1994, 46–47.

Hussein, Adel. *al-Shaab,* 18 February 1991.

———. *al-Shaab,* 16 July 1991.

Hussein, Magdy. *al-Shaab,* 26 June 1991.

Huwaidi, Fahmi. *al-Ahram,* 2 January 1990.

———. "Imma al-Mustawtanat wa-Imma al-Salam." *al-Majalla,* 3–9 April 1994, 38-39.

———. "Rabin Li-Arafat: Imma Hamas aw al-Salam." *al-Quds al-Arabi,* 15–16 October 1994.

———. "al-Usuliyyun Yuridun Hallan." *al-Majallah,* 11–17 December 1994, 42.

Ibn Khaldun. *Muqaddimah.* Trans. Franz Rosenthal. New York: Pantheon, 1958.

Ibrahim, Saad Eddin. "Anatomy of Egypt's Militant Islamic Groups." *International Journal of Middle East Studies* 12:4 (December 1980): 423–453.

———. "Egypt's Islamic Activism in the 1980s." *Third World Quarterly* 10:2 (1988): 632–658.

Inglehart, Ronald. *Culture Shift in Advanced Industrial Society.* Princeton: Princeton University Press, 1990.

———. *The Silent Revolution: Changing Values and Political Styles Among Western Publics.* Princeton: Princeton University Press, 1977.

Intellectual Invasion and Anti-Islamic Attitudes. Riyadh: Imam University Press, 1984.

"Islam Divided." *The Economist,* 22 September 1990, 47.

Issues 1:4 (January 1992): 7.

Issues 1:11 (September 1992): 2–3.

Issues 2:10 (October 1993).

Issues 1:6–7 (March-April 1992): 1, 12.

Jackson, Robert H., and Carl G. Rosberg. "Why Africa's Weak States Persist: The Empirical and Juridical in Statehood." *World Politics* 35:1 (1 October 1982): 1–25.

Jalal, Ayesha. "The State and Political Privilege in Pakistan." In *The Politics of Social Transformation in Afghanistan, Iran, and Pakistan,* ed. Myron Weiner and Ali Banuazizi. Syracuse: Syracuse University Press, 1994.

Jamil, Muhammad. "Israil Tasaa li-Tahqiq Hilm Hertzl bi-Iqamat al-Suq al-Sharq al-Awsatiyya." *al-Mujtama,* 15 November 1994, 32.

Jarisha, Ali Muhammad, and Muhammad Sharif al-Zaybaq. *Asalib al-Ghazu al-Fikri Lil-Alam al-Islami.* Cairo: Dar al-Itisam, 1977.

Jasarat, 10 March 1990, 6.

Jawlani, Atif. "Izalat al-Muqataa al-Arabiyya al-Iqtisadiyya li-Israil Ala Ra's al-Awliyyat al-Amrikiyya." *al-Majalla,* 8 February 1994, 36.

"Jerusalem Is Israel's, Rabin Says." *International Herald Tribune,* 29 May 1995.

Jerusalem Post, 24 October 1994.

Jundi, Anwar. *Afaq Jadida Lil-Dawa al-Islamiyya Fi Alam al-Gharb.* Beirut: [n.p.], 1984.

———. *al-Alam al-Islami wa-al-Istimar al-Siyasi wa-al-Ijtimai wa-al-Thaqafi.* Cairo: Dar al-Kitab al-Misri, 1970.

———. *al-Islam wa al-Istimar.* Cairo: [n.p.], 1948.

Kapil, Arun. "Islamic Economics: The Surest Path?" *MESA Bulletin* 29:1 (July 1995): 22–24.

———. "Les Parties Islamistes en Algérie: Eléments de Présentation." *Maghreb-Machrek* 133 (July-September 1991): 103–111.

Kaplan, Robert. "Mohsen Rafiqdoost." *Atlantic Monthly* (March 1996).

Karl, Terry Lynn. *The Paradox of Plenty: Oil Booms and Petrostates.* Berkeley: University of California Press, forthcoming.

———. "The Political Economy of Petrodollars: Oil and Democracy in Venezuela." Ph.D. diss., Stanford University, 1982.

Karsani, Awad. "The Establishment of Neo-Mahdism in the Western Sudan." *African Affairs* 86:344 (July 1987): 385–404.

———. "The Majdhubiyya Tariqa." In *Two Sufi Tariqas in the Sudan,* ed. M. W. Daly. Khartoum: University of Khartoum, 1985.

Katouzian, Homa. "The Aridosolatic Society: A Model of Long-Term Social and Economic Development in Iran." *International Journal of Middle East Studies* 15 (1983): 259–281.

Kechichian, Joseph. "The Role of the Ulama in the Politics of an Islamic State." *International Journal of Middle East Studies* 18 (February 1986): 53–71.

Keddie, Nikki. "Introduction: Deciphering Middle Eastern Women's History." *Women in Middle Eastern History,* ed. Nikki Keddie and Beth Baron. New Haven: Yale University Press, 1991.

Keddie, Nikki, and Beth Baron, eds. *Women in Middle Eastern History.* New Haven: Yale University Press, 1991.

Keddie, Nikki, and Eric Hooglund, ed. *The Iranian Revolution and the Islamic Republic.* Syracuse: Syracuse University, 1986.

Kedourie, Elie. *Democracy and Arab Political Culture.* Washington, D.C.: Washington Institute for Near East Policy, 1992.

———. "Islamic Fundamentalism—an Idea Whose Time Has Gone." *Daily Telegraph,* 27 August 1985.

Kellner, Douglas. *The Persian Gulf TV War.* Boulder: Westview Press, 1992.

Kennedy, Charles H. "Presidential–Prime Ministerial Relations: The Role of the Courts." Paper presented at the conference "Politics of Social Change in Pakistan," Columbia University, New York, 28 March 1994.

Kennedy, Paul. *Preparing for the Twenty-first Century.* New York: Random House, 1993.

Kepel, Gilles. *Muslim Extremism in Egypt: The Prophet and Pharaoh.* Berkeley: University of California Press, 1985.

———. *Le Prophète et Pharaon: Aux Sources des Mouvements Islamistes.* 2d ed. Paris: Editions du Seuil, 1993.

———. *La Revanche de Dieu.* Paris: Editions du Seuil, 1991.

Kepel, Gilles, and Rémy Leveau, eds. *Exils et Royaumes: Les Appartenances au Monde Arabo-Musulman Aujourd'hui.* Paris: Presses de la Fondation Nationale des Sciences Politiques, 1994.

Kettani, Idris. *Banu Israil Fi Asr al-Intihat al-Arabi.* Rabat: Maktabat Badr, 1992.

Khalidi, Mustafa, and Umar Farrukh. *al-Tabshir wa-al-Istimar fi al-Bilad al-Arabiyya: Arab li-Juhud al-Mubashshirin Allati Tarma Ila Ikhda al-Sharq lil-Istimar al-Gharbi.* Beirut: al-Maktabat al-Asriyah, 1957.

Khalifa, Abd al-Baqi. "al-Tatarruf: Mafahimuh . . . Asbabuh . . . Nataijuh . . . Ilajuh." *al-Mujtama,* 23 November 1993.

Khameini, Ayatollah. Speech given 16 September 1993.

Khan, Riaz Mohammad. *Untying the Afghan Knot: Negotiating Soviet Withdrawal.* Durham: Duke University Press, 1991.

Khashoggi, Jamal. "Arab Mujahedeen in Afghanistan-II: Masada Exemplifies the Unity of Islamic Ummah." *Arab News,* 14 May 1988, 9.

———. "Arab Youths Fight Shoulder to Shoulder with Mujahedeen." *Arab News,* 4 May 1988, 9.

Khawaga, Ahmed. Interview in *al-Alam al-Yawm,* 21 September 1992.

———. Interview in *Sabah al-Kheir,* 5 November 1992.

Kishk, Muhammad Jalal. *al-Ghazu al-Fikri.* Cairo: [n.p.], 1975.

Kramer, Martin. *Islam Assembled: The Advent of the Muslim Congresses.* New York: Columbia University Press, 1986.

———. "Islam vs. Democracy." *Commentary* 95:1 (January 1993): 35–42.

Kramer, Martin, ed. *Shiism, Resistance and Revolution.* Boulder: Westview Press, 1987.

Krasner, Stephen. *Structural Conflict: The Third World Against Global Liberalism.* Berkeley: University of California Press, 1985.

Krimly, Rayed. *The Political Economy of Rentier States: A Case Study of Saudi Arabia in the Oil Era, 1950–1990.* Ph.D. diss., George Washington University, 1993.

Krueger, Anne. "The Political Economy of the Rent-Seeking Society." *American Economic Review* 64:3 (June 1974): 291–303.

Laber, Jeri, and Barnett R. Rubin. *A Nation Is Dying: Afghanistan Under the Soviets.* Evanston: Northwestern University Press, 1988.

Ladd, Valerie J. Hoffman. "Women's Religious Observances." *Oxford Encyclopedia of the Modern Islamic World,* ed. John L. Esposito. Vol. 4. New York: Oxford University Press, 1995, 327.

Landau, Jacob M. *The Politics of Pan-Islam.* Oxford: Clarendon Press, 1990.

Layachi, Azzedine. "The Domestic and International Constraints of Economic Adjustment in Algeria." *North Africa: Development and Reform in a Changing Global Economy,* ed. Dirk Vandewalle. New York: St. Martin's Press, 1996.

Layachi, Azzedine, and Abdel-Kader Haireche. "National Development and Political Protest: Islamists in the Maghreb Countries." *Arab Studies Quarterly,* 14:2–3 (Spring/Summer 1992): 69–92.

Lederman, Jim. *Battle Lines: The American Media and the Intifada.* Boulder: Westview Press, 1992.

Legrain, Jean-François. "Bantoustans Palestiniens et Terrorisme." *Libération,* 26 October 1994.

———. "De la Faiblesse de l'OLP, de la Sincérité d'Israel." *Le Monde,* 10 September 1993.

———. "A Defining Moment: Palestinian Islamic Fundamentalism." In *Islamic Fundamentalists and the Gulf Crisis,* ed. James Piscatori. Chicago: American Academy of Arts and Sciences, 1991.

———. "Les Elections Etudiantes en Cisjordanie (1978–1987)." In *Démocratie et Démocratisations dans le Monde Arabe.* Cairo: CEDEJ, 1992.

———. "Gaza-Jericho, un Accord Contre la Paix." *Libération,* 7 March 1994.

———. "The Islamic Movement and the Intifada." In *Intifada: Palestine at the Crossroads,* ed. Jamal R. Nassar and Roger Heacock. New York: Praeger, 1990.

———. "Le Leadership Palestinien de l'Intérieur." In *Etudes Politiques du Monde Arabe.* Cairo: CEDEJ, 1991.

————. "Palestinian Islamisms: Patriotism as a Condition of Their Expansion." In *Accounting for Fundamentalisms: The Dynamic Character of Movements,* ed. Martin E. Marty and R. Scott Appleby. Chicago: American Academy of Arts and Sciences, 1994.

————. *Les Voix du Soulèvement Palestinien 1987–1988* [The Voices of the Palestinian Uprising 1987–1988]. Cairo: CEDEJ, 1991.

Lewis, Bernard. *The Assassins.* London: Weidenfeld and Nicolson, 1967.

————. "Islam and Liberal Democracy." *Atlantic Monthly* 271:2 (February 1993): 89–98.

————. "The Roots of Muslim Rage." *Atlantic Monthly* 226:3 (September 1990): 47–60.

Little, Ian, Richard Cooper, et al. *Boom, Crisis, and Adjustment: The Macro-economic Experience of Developing Countries.* Oxford: Oxford University Press, 1993.

Luciani, Giacomo. "Allocation vs. Production States: A Theoretical Framework." In *The Rentier State,* ed. Hazem Beblawi and Giacomo Luciani. New York: Croom Helm, 1987.

Mahdavy, Hossein. "The Patterns and Problems of Economic Development in Rentier States: The Case of Iran." In *Studies in the History of the Middle East from the Rise of Islam to the Present Day,* ed. Miriam A. Cook. Oxford: Oxford University Press, 1970.

Mahmud, Abd al-Halim. *al-Ghazu al-Fikri wa-Atharuhu Fi al-Mujtama al-Islami al-Muasir.* Kuwait: Dar al-Buhuth al-Ilmiyah, 1979.

Mahmud, Ali Abd al-Halim. *al-Ghazu al-Fikri wa-al-Tayyarat al-Muadiya Li al-Islam.* Riyadh: Imam Muhammad Bin Saud University, 1984.

"Majd li-l Qassam" [Glory to Qassam]. *al-Sabil* [Organ of the Islamic Action front in Amman]: 5–30 January 1993.

"Makasib Israil Fi Mutamar al-Dar al-Bayda." *al-Mujtama,* 8 November 1994.

Makram-Ebeid, Mona. "Political Opposition in Egypt: Democratic Myth or Reality?" *Middle East Journal* 43:3 (Summer 1989): 423–436.

Malcolm X. *Autobiography of Malcolm X.* New York: Ballantine Books, 1973.

Mansur, Ahmad. "Sarajevo Hiya Akbar Mutaqal li al-Ibada fi al-Alam." *al-Mujtama,* 24 January 1995, 24–26.

Maram-i Hizb-i Islami-yi Afghanistan [Program of the Islamic Party of Afghanistan]. [Peshawar?]: 1986–1987.

Marty, Martin E. *The Modern Schism.* New York: Harper and Row, 1969.

Marty, Martin E., and R. Scott Appleby, eds. *Accounting for Fundamentalisms: The Dynamic Character of Movements.* Chicago: American Academy of Arts and Sciences, 1994.

————. *Fundamentalisms Observed.* Chicago: University of Chicago Press, 1991.

Marzuq, Musa Abu. Speech given for interview, published by *al-Sabil,* 19–25 April 1994.

"Masirat al-Istislam . . . wa-Nuhud al-Umma Min Kabwatiha." *al-Mujtama,* 1 November 1994.

"Matami Israil wa-Iradat al-Shuub al-Muslima." *al-Mujtama,* 8 November 1994.

Mawlana, Hamid, George Gerbner, and Herbert I. Schiller. *Triumph of the Image: The Media's War in the Persian Gulf—A Global Perspective.* Boulder: Westview Press, 1992.

Menashri, David, ed. *The Iranian Revolution and the Muslim World.* Boulder: Westview Press, 1990.

Midani, Abd al-Rahman Habnakat. *Ajnihat al-Makr al-Thalatha wa-Khawafiha: al-Tabshir al-Istishraq al-Istimar.* Damascus: [n.p., 1395H].

Middle East Watch. *A License to Kill: Israeli Undercover Operations Against "Wanted" and Masked Palestinians.* New York: Human Rights Watch, 1993.

Milani, Mohsen. "The Evolution of the Iranian Theocracy." *Iranian Studies* 26:3–4 (Summer/Fall 1994): 359–374.

———. *The Making of Iran's Islamic Revolution.* 2d ed. Boulder: Westview, 1994.

Miller, Judith. "The Challenge of Radical Islam." *Foreign Affairs* 72:2 (Spring 1993): 43–56.

Mitchell, Richard P. *The Society of the Muslim Brothers.* New York: Oxford University Press, 1969.

Moen, Matthew, and Lowell Gustafson, eds. *The Religious Challenge to the State.* Philadelphia: Temple University Press, 1992.

Moore, Clement Henry. *Tunisia Since Independence.* Berkeley: University of California Press, 1965.

Mortimer. Robert. "Islamists, Soldiers, and Democrats: The Second Algerian War." *Middle East Journal* 50 (Winter 1996): 18–39.

Mouffe, Chantal. *The Return of the Political.* London: Verso, 1993.

Movement of the Islamic Jihad. *Masirat al-Jihad al-Islami fi Filastin* [The Development of Islamic Jihad in Palestine]. Beirut: [n.p.], 1989.

"Muftu al-Mamalaka Yuharrim al-Sulh Ma al-Yahid." *al-Sabil,* 29 August 1995, 8.

Mujahid, Sharif. "Pakistan's First General Elections." *Asian Survey* 11:2 (February 1971): 170.

al-Mujtama, 10 January 1995.

Munson, Henry, Jr. *Religion and Power in Morocco.* New Haven: Yale University Press, 1993.

al-Musawwar, 21 August 1992.

al-Muslimun 10:516 (23 December 1994).

———. 10:520 (20 January 1995).

"al-Mutamar al-Iqtisadi lil-Sharq al-Awsat al-Khutwa al-Raisiyya li-Iqamat Israil al-Kubra." *al-Mujtama,* 25 October 1994, 24–26.

al-Nahar, 2 January 1994.

———, 10 January 1994.

"Naiban Kuwaytiyyan Yarfudan al-Tatbi Ma al-Yahud." *al-Mujtama,* 22 November 1994, 8.

Nasr, Seyyed Vali Reza. "Islamic Opposition to the Islamic State: The Jamaat-i Islami 1977–1988." *International Journal of Middle East Studies* 25:2 (May 1993): 261–283.

———. *Mawdudi and the Making of Islamic Revolution.* New York: Oxford University Press, 1996.

———. "Pakistan: Islamic State, Ethnic Polity." *Fletcher Forum of World Affairs* 16:2 (Summer 1992): 81–90.

———. *The Vanguard of the Islamic Revolution: The Jamaat-i Islami of Pakistan.* Berkeley: University of California Press, 1994.

Nassar, Jamal R., and Roger Heacock, eds. *Intifada: Palestine at the Crossroads.* New York: Praeger, 1990.

New York Times, 4 October 1990.

Newburg, Paula. *Judging the State: Courts and Constitutional Politics in Pakistan.* New York: Cambridge University Press, 1995.

Newsline (September 1991): 43.

Niblock, Tim. "Islamic Movements and Sudan's Political Coherence." In *Sudan: History, Identity, Ideology,* ed. Hervé Bleuchot, Christian Delmet, and Derek Hopwood. Reading, England: Ithaca Press, 1991.

Nimr, Abd al-Munim. *al-Islam wa-al-Gharb Wajhan li-Wajh.* Beirut: al-Muassasah al-Jamiiyah lil-Dirasat wa-al-Nashr wa-al-Tawzi, 1982.

Noman, Omar. *Political Economy of Pakistan 1947–85*. London: KPI, 1988.

"Nuarid al-Ittifaqiyya Wala Nataqid Annana Sanastadim Ma al-Sultat al-Urduniyya." *al-Mujtama*, 1 November 1994, 36.

O'Brien, D. C. "Islam and Power in Black Africa." In *Islam and Power,* ed. Alexander S. Cudsi and Ali Hillal Dessouki. London: Croom Helm, 1981.

Oschenwald, William. "Saudi Arabia and the Islamic Revival." *International Journal of Middle East Studies* 13 (1981): 271–286.

Pakistan Times, 16 January 1967.

Pelletreau, Robert H., Jr., Daniel Pipes, and John L. Esposito. "Political Islam Symposium: Resurgent Islam in the Middle East." *Middle East Policy* 3:2 (1994): 1–21.

Peres, Shimon, with Arye Naor. *The New Middle East*. New York: Henry Holt, 1993.

Perlmutter, Amos. "Wishful Thinking About Fundamentalism." *Washington Post,* 19 January 1992.

"The Persian Gulf." In *The Middle East*. Washington, D.C.: Congressional Quarterly, 1994.

Pierre, Andrew J., and William B. Quandt. *The Algerian Crisis: Policy Options for the West*. Washington, D.C.: Carnegie Endowment for International Peace, 1996.

Pipes, Daniel. "Fundamentalist Muslims Between America and Russia." *Foreign Affairs* 64:5 (Summer 1986): 939–959.

Piquard, Patrice. "Pourquoi le Chaos Afghan Peut Faire Exploser l'Asie Centrale." *L'Evènement du Jeudi,* 13 January 1993.

Piscatori, James P. "Ideological Politics in Saudi Arabia." In *Islam in the Political Process,* ed. James P. Piscatori. Cambridge: Cambridge University Press, 1983.

———, ed. *Islam in the Political Process*. Cambridge: Cambridge University Press, 1983.

———, ed. *Islamic Fundamentalism and the Gulf Crisis*. Chicago: American Academy of Arts and Sciences, 1991.

Preliminary Project of the Political Program of the Front of Islamic Salvation. [n.p.]: Front Islamique du Salut, [n.d.].

Przeworski, Adam. *Democracy and the Market*. New York: Cambridge University Press, 1991.

Putnam, Robert D. *The Comparative Study of Political Elites*. Englewood Cliffs, N.J.: Prentice-Hall, 1976.

Quaradawi, Yusuf. *Fiqh al-Zakah: dirasah musaranah li-ahkaniha wa-falsafatiha fi daw al-Quran wa-al-Sunnah*. Beirut: Muassasat al-Risalah, 1977.

Quandt, William B., Fuad Jabber, and Ann Mosely Lesch. *The Politics of Palestinian Nationalism*. Berkeley: University of California Press, 1973.

"al-Quds Lam Taud Qadiyyatukum Ayyuha al-Munhazimun." *al-Mujtama,* 1 November 1994, 4.

Rafii, Mustafa. *al-Islam wa-Mushkilat al-Asr*. Beirut: [n.p.], 1972.

Rahman, Fazlur. "The Controversy over the Muslim Family Laws." In *South Asian Religion and Politics,* ed. Donald E. Smith. Princeton: Princeton University Press, 1966.

Ramonet, Ignacio. "La Révolte d'une Génération Sacrifiée: L'Algérie sous le Choc." *Le Monde Diplomatique,* November 1988.

Rashad, Ahmad. *Hamas: Palestinian Politics with Islamic Hue*. Annandale, Va.: United Association for Studies and Research, 1993.

Rashid, Ali. "al-Ittifaqat Allati Tuwaqqiuha al-Anzima ma al-Sihyuniyya Tuhaqqiq al-Salam li-Israil wa al-Karitha li al-Arab." *al-Mujtama*, 14 February 1995, 36.

Rashid, Muhamma. "Salam ya Salam." *al-Mujtama,* 31 January 1995, 17.

Rastegar, Farshad. "Education and Revolutionary Political Mobilization: Schooling

Versus Uprootedness as Determinants of Islamic Political Activism Among Afghan Refugee Students in Pakistan." Ph.D. diss., University of California, Los Angeles, 1991.

Rekhess, Elie. "The Iranian Impact on the Islamic Jihad Movement in the Gaza Strip." In *The Iranian Revolution and the Muslim World,* ed. David Menashri. Boulder: Westview Press, 1990.

Resurgence 4:3–4 (March-April 1995): 1–2.

Roberts, Hugh. "A Trial of Strength: Algerian Islamism." In *Islamic Fundamentalism and the Gulf Crisis,* ed. James Piscatori. Chicago: American Academy of Arts and Sciences, 1991.

Rodan, Steve. "Peace Upsets Generals' United Front." *Jerusalem Post,* 11 February 1994.

Rodman, Peter W. "Don't Look for Moderates in the Islamist Revolution." *International Herald Tribune,* 4 January 1995.

Rose, G. "Factional Alignment in the Central Committee of the Islamic Republican Party of Iran." In *The Iranian Revolution and the Islamic Republic,* ed. Nikki Keddie and Eric Hooglund. Washington, D.C.: 1982.

Rose al-Yusuf, 29 July 1991.

Rouadjia, Ahmed. "La Violence et l'Histoire du Mouvement National Algérien." *Peuples Méditerranéens* 70–71 (1995).

———. *Les Frères et les Mosquées: Enquête sur le Mouvement Islamiste en Algérie.* Paris: Karthala, 1990.

Roy, Olivier. *The Civil War in Tajikistan: Causes and Implications: A Report of the Study Group on the Prospects for Conflict and Opportunities for Peacemaking in the Southern Tier of Former Soviet Republics.* Washington, D.C.: United States Institute of Peace, December 1993.

———. *L'Echec de l'Islam Politique.* Paris: Editions du Seuil, 1992.

———. *Islam and Resistance in Afghanistan.* Cambridge: Cambridge University Press, 1986.

Rubin, Barnett R. *The Fragmentation of Afghanistan: State Formation and Collapse in the International System.* New Haven: Yale University Press, 1995.

———. "The Fragmentation of Tajikistan." *Survival* 35 (Winter 1993/94): 71–91.

———. "Political Elites in Afghanistan: Rentier State Building, Rentier State Wrecking." *International Journal of Middle East Studies* 24 (1992): 77–99.

———. "Post Cold-War State Disintegration: The Failure of International Conflict Resolution in Afghanistan." *Journal of International Affairs* 46 (Winter 1993): 469–492.

———. *The Search for Peace in Afghanistan: From Buffer State to Failed State.* New Haven: Yale University Press, 1995.

Sadowski, Yahya. "The New Orientalism and the Democracy Debate." *Middle East Report* 23:4, no. 183 (July-August 1993): 14–21.

"al-Sahayina Yushawwihuna Surat al-Amal al-Islami wa-Mashariuna Tashhad Ala Tabiat al-Amal al-Ighathi Alladhi Taqum Bih." *al-Mujtama,* 27 December 1994.

Sahliyeh, Emile. *Religious Resurgence and Politics in the Contemporary World.* Albany: State University Press of New York, c1990.

Said, Edward. "An Instrument of Palestinian Surrender, a Palestinian Versailles." *al-Ahram Weekly,* 7–13 October 1993.

———. "The Morning After." *Inquiry* (Spring 1994): 20.

———. "The Phony Islamic Threat." *New York Times Magazine,* 21 November 1993.

Salahdine, Mohamed, ed. *L'Emploi Invisible au Maghreb: Etudes sur l'Economie Parallèle.* Rabat: Société Marocaine des Editeurs Réunis, [1990?].

———. *Les Petits Métiers Clandestins ou les Business Populaire.* Rabat: EDDIF, 1988.

Salame, Ghassan, ed. *Democracy Without Democrats? The Removal of Politics in the Muslim World.* London: I. B. Tauris, 1994.

Salih, Kamal Osman. "The Sudan, 1985–89: The Fading Democracy." In *Sudan After Nimeiri,* ed. Peter Woodward. London: Routledge, 1991.

Sani, Nasser. "The Kuwaiti Power-Sharing Experience." In *Power-Sharing Islam.* London: Grey Seal, 1993.

Sankari, Farouk A. "Islam and Politics in Saudi Arabia." In *Islamic Resurgence in the Arab World,* ed. Ali E. Hillal Dessouki. New York: Praeger, 1982.

Sartori, Giovanni. "Opposition and Control: Problems and Prospects." *Government and Opposition* 1:1 (Winter 1966): 151.

Sayeed, Khalid B. *Politics in Pakistan: The Nature and Direction of Change.* New York: Praeger, 1980.

Schiff, Zeev and Ehud Yaari. *Intifada: The Palestinian Uprising. Israel's Third Front.* New York: Simon and Schuster, 1990.

Seikaly, May. "Women and Religion in Bahrain: An Emerging Identity." In *Islam, Gender, and Social Change,* ed. Yvonne Y. Haddad and John L. Esposito. New York: Oxford University Press, 1997.

Selbin, Eric. *Modern Latin American Revolutions.* Boulder: Westview Press, 1993.

Shaaeldin, E., and R. Brown. "Towards an Understanding of Islamic Banking in Sudan." In *Sudan: State, Capital and Transformation,* ed. T. Barnett and A. Abdelkarim. London: Croom Helm, 1988.

Shadid, Mohammed K. "The Muslim Brotherhood Movement in the West Bank and Gaza." *Third World Quarterly* 10:2 (April 1988): 658–682.

Shahak, Israel. "HAMAS and Arafat: The Balance of Power." *Middle East International* 468 (4 February 1994): 17–18.

Shami, Mujibul-Rahman. "Jamaat-i Islami awr Peoples Party; Fasilah awr Rabitah, ik Musalsal Kahani" [Jamaat-i Islami and the Peoples Party; Distance and Relations, a Continuous Story]. *Qaumi Digest* 11:2 (July 1988): 24.

Shanti Communication News Agency 63 (19 September 1995).

Shanti Communication News Agency (29 October 1995).

Sharif, Samir Ahmad. "al-Sharq al-Awsat al-Jadid." *al-Insan* 3:12 (October 1994): 7.

Shaykh, Abd Allah. "Sira al-Hadarat . . . wa Dawr al-Islam." *al-Mujtama,* 8 February 1994, 20–24.

"Sheikh Abdullah Azzam Is Martyred." *Mujahideen Monthly* 4 (January 1990): 10–11.

Simon, Reeva, ed. *The Middle East and North Africa: Essays in Honor of J. C. Hurewitz.* New York: Middle East Institute, Columbia University, 1989.

Sisk, Timothy D. *Islam and Democracy: Religion, Politics, and Power in the Middle East.* Washington, D.C.: United States Institute of Peace, 1992.

Skocpol, Theda. *States and Social Revolutions: A Comparative Analysis of France, Russia and China.* Cambridge: Cambridge University Press, 1979.

Smith, Donald E. "The Limits of Religious Resurgence." In *Religious Resurgence and Politics in the Contemporary World,* ed. Emile Sahliyeh. Albany: State University Press of New York, 1990.

———. *South Asian Religion and Politics.* Princeton: Princeton University Press, 1966.

Smith, Hedrick. *The New Russians.* New York: Random House, c1990.

Smith, Perry M. *How CNN Fought the War: A View from the Inside*. Secaucus, N.J.: Birch Lane Press, 1991.

Smith, Wilfred Cantwell. *Islam in Modern History*. New York: New American Library, 1957.

———. *Modern Islam in India*. Lahore: Minerva Book Shop, 1943.

Soto, Hernando de. *The Other Path: The Invisible Revolution in the Third World*. New York: Harper and Row, 1989.

Surat-e Masruh-e Mozakerat-e Majles-e Barresi-ye Nahaie-ye Qanun-e Asassi-ya Jomhuri-ye Islami-ye Iran [The Detailed Deliberations of the Proceeding of the Council on the Final Review of the Constitution of the Islamic Republic of Iran]. Vol. 2. Tehran, 1986.

Swedish Committee for Afghanistan. Cash for Food Program, confidential files, Peshawar.

Syed, Parvez. "Amnesty International Condemns Widespread Human Rights Violations and Calls for Investigations." In *Shanti Communication News Agency*, 28 September 1995.

"Takris Li al-Haymana al-Sihyuniyya Ala Muqadarat al-Alam al-Arabi." *al-Mujtama*, 8 November 1994, 28.

Tal, Abraham. "La Majal li al-Tafawud wa al-Sulh Ma al-Haraka al-Islamiyya Bal Yajib al-Tahaluf Ma al-Duwal al-Mujawira Li-Iqtilaiha Min al-Judhur." *al-Quds al-Arabi*, 19 October 1994.

"Talk of the Town." *New Yorker*, 10 January 1994.

Tamimi, Asad. *Zawal Israil, Hatmiyya Quraniyya* [The Destruction of Israel, Quranic Ineluctability]. al-Qahirah: al-Mukhtar al-Islami, [198-].

Tawana, Sayyed Musa. "Glimpses into the Historical Background of the Islamic Movement in Afghanistan: Memoirs of Dr. Tawana, Part 1." *AFGHANews* 5 (1 April 1989), 6–7.

———. "Glimpses into the Historical Background of the Islamic Movement in Afghanistan: Memoirs of Dr. Tawana, Part 4." *AFGHANews* 5 (15 May 1989), 5ff.

Tessler, Mark. "Anger and Governance in the Arab World: Lessons from the Maghrib and Implications for the West." *Jerusalem Journal of International Relations* 13:3 (September 1991): 7–33.

Thabit, Muhsin. *Nashat al-Jamaa al-Islamiyya fi Sujun al-Ihtilal al-Israili* [Emergence of al-Jamaa al-Islamiyya in Israeli Occupation's Jails]. [n.p.: n.p., n.d.].

"Translation of the Petition Being Submitted in October 1994." [n.p.]

Turabi, Hassan. Address to the Royal Society of Arts (RSA), London, 27 April 1992.

———. *al-Harakah al-Islamiyyah fi al-Sudan*. Cairo: al-Qari al-Arabi, 1991.

———. *The Islamic Movement in Sudan*. Khartoum: IRSS, 1989.

Ubaidi, Zuhair. "al-Ittifaq Ma al-Kiyan al-Sihyawni La Yulzimuna Bi-Ay Hal Min al-Ahwal." *al-Sabil*, 29 August 1994, 25.

United Kingdom High Commissioner, Karachi. Dispatch #INT.48/47/1, 5/25/1959, DO35/8962, Public Records Office, England.

United Kingdom High Commissioner, Karachi. Dispatch #INT.83/6/2, 3/10/1959, DO35/8949, Public Records Office, England.

United States Consulate General, Lahore. Dispatch #189, 5/1/1952, 790D.00/5–152, National Archives, Washington, D.C.

United States Department of State. *Patterns of Global Terrorism 1992*. Department of State Publication No. 10054. Washington, D.C.: Department of State, April 1993.

Usher, Graham. "HAMAS Seeks a Place at the Table." *Middle East International* (13 May 1994): 17–19.

Uways, Abd al-Halim. *al-Muslimun Fi Marakat al-Baqa.* Cairo: Dar al-Itisam, 1979.

Vakili, Vala. "Soroush and the Islamic Republic." Unpublished paper, March 1996.

Vandewalle, Dirk. "Breaking with Socialism: Economic Privatization and Liberalization in Algeria." In *Privatization and Liberalization in the Middle East,* ed. Ilya Harik and Denis Sullivan. Bloomington: Indiana University Press, 1992.

———. "Political Aspects of State Building in Rentier Economies: Algeria and Libya Compared." In *The Rentier State,* ed. Hazem Beblawi and Giacomo Luciani. London: Croom Helm, 1987.

———. "Qadhafi's Failed Economic Reforms: Markets, Institutions and Development in a Rentier State." In *North Africa: Development and Reform in a Changing Global Economy,* ed. Dirk Vandewalle. St. Martin's Press, 1996.

———, ed. *Informal Economies in the Middle East and North Africa.* Forthcoming.

———, ed. *North Africa: Development and Reform in a Changing Global Economy.* New York: St. Martin's Press, 1996.

Vatin, J. C., et al., eds. *Démocratie et Démocratisations dans le Monde Arabe: Actes du Troisième Colloque Franco-Egyptien de Politologie, le Caire 29–30 Septembre–1er Octobre 1990.* Cairo: CEDEJ, 1992.

Vikor, Knut S. *Sufi and Scholar on the Desert Edge: Muhammad B. Ali al-Sanusi (1787–1859).* Ph.D. diss., University of Bergen, Norway, 1991.

Voll, John O. "Hadith Scholars and Tariqahs: An Ulama Group in 18th Century Haramayn and Their Impact in the Islamic World." *Journal of Asian and African Studies* 15:3–4 (July-October 1980): 264–272.

———. *A History of the Khatmia Tariqa in the Sudan.* Ph.D. diss., Harvard University, 1969.

———. *Islam: Continuity and Change in the Modern World.* 2d ed. Syracuse: Syracuse University Press, 1994.

———. "Muhammad Hayyat al-Sindi and Muhammad ibn Abd al-Wahhab: An Analysis of an Intellectual Group in Eighteenth Century Madina." *Bulletin of the School of Oriental and African Studies* 38:1 (1975): 32–39.

Voll, John O., and John L. Esposito. "Islam's Democratic Essence." *Middle East Quarterly* 1:3 (September 1994): 3–11, with ripostes 12–19.

———. "Rejoinder." *Middle East Quarterly* 1:4 (December 1994): 71–72.

Von Laue, Theodor. *The World Revolution of Westernization: The Twentieth Century in Global Perspective.* New York: Oxford University Press, 1987.

Wai, Tawfiq. "al-Kifah al-Haram . . . wa-al-Inhizam al-Mubah." *al-Mujtama,* 15 November 1994, 37.

Waldman, Peter. "Unrest on the Nile: As Egypt Suppresses Muslim Brotherhood, Some Fear Backlash." *Wall Street Journal,* 8 December 1995.

Waltz, Susan. *Human Rights and Reform: Changing the Face of North African Politics.* Berkeley: University of California Press, 1995.

Warburg, Gabriel. *Islam, Nationalism, and Communism in a Traditional Society: The Case of Sudan.* London: Frank Cass, 1978.

al-Wasat, 1 November 1993.

Weinbaum, Marvin G. "Legal Elites in Afghan Society." *International Journal of Middle East Studies* 12 (1980): 39–57.

Weiner, Myron, and Ali Banuazizi, eds. *The Politics of Social Transformation in Afghanistan, Iran and Pakistan.* Syracuse: Syracuse University Press, 1994.

Women in the Middle East: Human Rights Under Attack. New York: Amnesty International, 1995.

Woodward, Peter. *The Horn of Africa: State Politics and International Relations.* London: I. B. Tauris, 1996.

————. "In the Footsteps of Gordon: The Sudan Government and the Rise of Sayyid Sir Abd al-Rahman, 1915–1935." *African Affairs* 84:334 (January 1985): 39–51.

————. *Sudan 1898–1989: The Unstable State.* Boulder: Lynne Rienner; London: Lester Crook Academic, 1990.

————, ed. *Sudan After Nimeiri.* London: Routledge, 1991.

Wright, Robin. "Experts Ask: Did Saudi Crackdown Light Fuse of Bomb? Motives: Critics Complain of Repression. But Anti-American Feelings Have Played a Role." *Los Angeles Times,* 15 November 1995.

————."Islam, Democracy and the West." *Foreign Affairs* 71:3 (Summer 1992): 131–145.

————. *Sacred Rage: The Wrath of Militant Islam.* New York: Simon and Schuster, 1985.

Yemma, John. "Militant Islam Facing Backlash in Middle East." *Christian Science Monitor,* 12 March 1981.

Yousaf, Mohammad, and Mark Adkins. *The Bear Trap: Afghanistan's Untold Story.* London: Mark Cooper, 1992.

Yusuf, Ahmad. "al-Islamiyyun wa-Marhalat Ma Bad al-Ittifaq." *Filastin al-Muslima,* June 1994.

Zahhar, Mahmud. "Al-Haraka al-Islamiyya: Haqaiq wa Arqam, Bayna-l-Haqiqa wa-al-Wahm" [The Islamic Movement: Realities and Figures, Between Truth and Fiction]. *al-Quds,* 10 November 1992.

Zartman, William I., ed. *State and Society in North Africa.* Boulder: Westview Press, 1992.

Zayid, Adil. "La wa-Alf La." *al-Mujtama,* 14 December 1993, 14.

Zubaida, Sami. *Islam, the People and the State.* New York: I. B. Tauris, 1993.

About the Contributors

Lisa Anderson is professor and chair of political science at Columbia University. A specialist on North Africa and former director of Columbia's Middle East Institute, she is currently at work on a study of the impetus and impediments to political liberalization in the Arab world.

Raymond William Baker specializes in the politics of the Arab and Muslim world. His publications include *Sadat and After: Struggles for Egypt's Political Soul,* and he is currently completing a new book, *Islam Without Fear.* Professor Baker is dean of faculty at Trinity College and adjunct professor of political science at the American University in Cairo.

John L. Esposito is professor of religion and international affairs, Georgetown University, and director of the Center for Muslim-Christian Understanding: History and International Affairs at Georgetown University's Edmund A. Walsh School of Foreign Service. Esposito is editor-in-chief of *The Oxford Encyclopedia of the Modern Islamic World.* Among his publications are *The Islamic Threat: Myth or Reality? Islam and Democracy* (with John O. Voll); *Islam: The Straight Path; Islam and Politics; Contemporary Islamic Revival* (with Yvonne Haddad and John O. Voll); *Voices of Resurgent Islam; Islam in Asia; Religion, Politics and Society;* and *Women in Muslim Family Law.*

Yvonne Yazbeck Haddad is professor of the history of Islam and Christian-Muslim relations at the Center for Muslim-Christian Understanding and the Department of History at Georgetown University. Her publications include *Contemporary Islam and the Challenge of History: Islamic Impact; Women, Religion and Social Change; Islamic Understanding of Death and Resurrection; Muslims of America, Islamic Communities in North America; Mission to America; Five Islamic Sectarian Movements in North America; Islamic Values in the United States;* and *Christian-Muslim Encounters.* She is an associate editor of *The Oxford Encyclopedia of Islam in the Modern World* and a past president of the Middle East Studies Association.

Jean-François Legrain is a researcher for the Centre National de Recherches Scientifiques, Groupe de Recherches et d'Etudes sur la Méditerranée et le Moyen Orient in Lyon, France. His publications include *Les Voix du Soulèvement Palestinien 1987–1988* and numerous articles in edited works and publications, such as *Le Monde* and *Libération.* He has also worked for the Centre d'Etudes et de Documentation Economique, Juridique et Sociale (CEDEJ) in Cairo, Egypt.

Mohsen M. Milani is associate professor of politics at the University of Southern Florida, Tampa. Author of *The Making of Iran's Islamic Revolution,* Dr. Milani has written extensively about the politics of revolutionary Iran and the Gulf. He is currently working on a project about Iranian foreign policy under President Ali Akbar Hashemi Rafsanjani.

S. V. R. Nasr is associate professor of political science at the University of San Diego and faculty associate at the von Grunebaum Center for Near East Studies at UCLA. He is the author of *Vanguard of Islamic Revolution: The Jamaat-i Islami of Pakistan* and *Mawdudi and the Making of Islamic Revivalism.*

Barnett R. Rubin is director of the Center for Preventive Action at the Council on Foreign Relations in New York. He was previously associate professor of political science and director of the Center for the Study of Central Asia at Columbia University, assistant professor of political science at Yale University, and a Peace Fellow at the United States Institute of Peace. He is the author of *The Fragmentation of Afghanistan: State Formation and Collapse in the International System* and *The Search for Peace in Afghanistan: From Buffer State to Failed State.* He has also written on human rights, state formation, and conflict in South and Central Asia.

Dirk Vandewalle is assistant professor of government at Dartmouth College. He is editor of *Qadhafi's Libya: 1969–1994* and *North Africa: Reform and Development in a Changing Global Economy.* He has published extensively on issues regarding the political economy of the Middle East and North Africa and is currently studying the impact of commodity booms in Morocco, Yemen, Libya, Indonesia, and Nigeria, with support from the Social Science Research Council, a Fulbright Regional Award, and Rockefeller Center, Whiting Foundation, and American Institute of Maghrebi Studies awards.

John Obert Voll is professor of Islamic history at the Center for Muslim-Christian Understanding and the Department of History at Georgetown University. He is a past president of the Middle East Studies Association. His publications include *Islam: Continuity and Change in the Modern World* and *Islam and Democracy* (co-authored with John L. Esposito).

Peter Woodward is professor of politics at the University of Reading in Britain and formerly taught at the University of Khartoum, Sudan. His publications include *Condominium and Sudanese Nationalism; Sudan 1898–1989: The Unstable State; Nasser;* and *The Horn of Africa: State, Politics and International Relations.* He is editor of *African Affairs,* journal of the Royal African Society, and of *British Documents on Foreign Affairs: Africa.*

Index